W9-BCX-600

Orchestral Performance Practices in the Nineteenth Century

Size, Proportions, and Seating

Studies in Musicology, No. 85

George J. Buelow, Series Editor

Professor of Music
Indiana University

Other Titles in This Series

Orchestral Performance Practices in the Nineteenth Century

Size, Proportions, and Seating

by
Daniel J. Koury

UMI RESEARCH PRESS
Ann Arbor, Michigan

Produced and distributed by
UMI Research Press
an imprint of
University Microfilms Inc.
Ann Arbor, Michigan 48106

Library of Congress Cataloging in Publication Data

Koury, Daniel J., 1926-
Orchestral performance practices in the nineteenth
century.

(Studies in musicology ; no. 85)
Revision in author's thesis (Ph.D.)—
Boston University, 1981.
Bibliography: p.
Includes index.
1. Orchestra—19th century. 2. Music—19th century—
Performance. 3. Orchestral music—19th century—Inter-
pretation (Phrasing, dynamics, etc.) 4. Conducting.
I. Title. II. Series.
ML1200.K68 1986 785'.09'034 85-16345
ISBN 0-8357-1649-X (alk. paper)

Contents

Figures

Tables

Acknowledgments

This study owes much of its present format to two people. First of all, Dr. Murray Lefkowitz, head of the Musicology Department at Boston University, contributed much to the shaping of my original study; it was he who urged me to seek publication. Then Dr. George Buelow suggested the guidelines for the present revision, even finding time to read the final version, offering much insight in his corrections and suggestions. I owe a great debt to both these gentlemen.

Dr. Joel Sheveloff of Boston University first suggested the need for such a study and served as first reader of my original study. He has continued to be a source of sage and friendly advice even at a time when he was hampered by illness. I not only greatly appreciate and value his great knowledge and insight but feel fortunate to call him friend as well as mentor.

I feel a debt of great gratitude to my colleague at Westfield State College, Dr. Peter Demos, who far exceeded the bonds of friendship in proofreading the entire typescript. Then there is Ms. Linda Upper who not only did much proofreading but has been a source of encouragement from the beginning.

I also owe gratitude to many library staffs, principally the Music Department of the Boston Public Library headed by Mrs. Ruth Bleeker, the Music Department of the Library of Congress, Mugar Library at Boston University, the now defunct Boston State College Library and Mr. William Talbot, and the Eda Kuhn Loeb Music Library at Harvard University and especially Head Librarian Michael Ochs who even went to the extent of hand-carrying Gassner's *Dirigent und Ripienist* to a photocopy department in an effort to facilitate adequate reproduction of several seating plans. My thanks also go to Mr. John Morytko, of Media Services at Westfield State College, who expertly printed many of the illustrations for this book.

Last of all but certainly not least, I would like to remember my late parents who were always supportive and who suffered and sacrificed much. To them I would like to dedicate this study.

1

Introduction

Igor Stravinsky's *Rite of Spring* and his *Symphony of Psalms* utilize orchestras which are physically and esthetically worlds apart, sound vehicles for completely different conceptions, despite the fact that these two works are separated by a span of only 17 years. Yet it is not uncommon in the twentieth century to find the same orchestra arranged in the same seating plan, playing the same instruments (save for the omission of winds and/or percussion not called for in the score), whether the work in hand is by Haydn or Mozart, Brahms or Bartók, or any other composer from these various style periods. If the strings overpower the woodwinds, the obvious solution is to double each of the latter instruments in ensemble passages, if not elsewhere. That such practice can be traced at least as far back as Wagner probably imparts some sort of historical blessing on it—the precedent of genius. Yet is it going too far to suggest that to perform Mendelssohn and Schubert with the same orchestra playing the same models of instruments as one uses in Tchaikovsky or Debussy is akin to repainting Ingres or Delacroix in the colors of Monet or Van Gogh? Surely any sensitive person would recoil at such a suggestion; yet the musical equivalent of this has been commonplace.

The aim of this book is to demonstrate that the orchestra has not been a static organization but rather a malleable and fluid one, not only changing from one style period to the next, but even showing differences in makeup and seating from one locale to another within the same time frame. It is also hoped that the reader will keep in mind that the instruments that Beethoven knew before the onset of his deafness sounded quite different from those familiar to Liszt or Wagner in later years. While this book does not lay claim to being the last word on this vast and complex subject, it does offer a contribution toward advancing the cause of authentic orchestral performance practices in nineteenth-century music. We have come a long way in restoring medieval, renaissance, and baroque musics to somewhat of a facsimile of their pristine states. Recent years have seen the growing tendency to accord similar treatment to music of the classic era.[1] But the nineteenth century is still largely ignored in this regard, evidently from the assumption that since it is closer in time, authentic practices have remained a constant tradition. At the very least this book can show the contrary. Even the instruments themselves have constantly undergone change. But more within the scope of this work, the numbers used, especially of the strings, have differed widely, geographically as well as chronologically, and methods of seating (or standing!) have been neither standard nor static and have little or nothing in common with those in current use in many places. The matter of seating alone can affect the sound of a work, and Beethoven may require different treatment in this respect from either Mendelssohn or Wagner.

Though the main body of this work is concerned with the nineteenth century, the eighteenth century will be dealt with briefly in order to set the stage and establish precedents. For one thing seems certain: the flowering of one age provides nutriment for the roots of the next.

Part One

Eighteenth-Century Precedents: From Baroque to Classic

2

Constitution of the Orchestra in the Eighteenth Century

The orchestra had never been in a more fluid state than in the first half of the eighteenth century. The size and makeup of an orchestra seemed to depend more on circumstances than on the demands of the works performed. To a great extent, the players available (usually signifying the economic means available) and the size of the hall seemed to dictate the orchestra's physiognomy. Thus it is probably wise to keep in mind that what one sees in an eighteenth-century score might not necessarily reflect how the work might have been performed in its own time. For example, a work might look on paper as if it were meant for strings only, when in actuality the parts may have been doubled by oboes and bassoons. Often this might not be apparent until one comes across such expressions as *senza oboi* or *senza fagotto* or even *senza violini*. W. S. Rockstro seemed sure of this: "In Handel's time, it was always understood, that, in the *tutti* passages the Violins were to be reinforced by Hautboys, and Violoncellos by Bassoons, in much stronger proportion than that to which we are now accustomed, whether the names of those Instruments were mentioned in the Score or not."[1]

It would seem that if horns, or trumpets, or timpani were available, they would often be added to a performance, even if printed parts for them did not exist. It must be remembered that eighteenth-century orchestral music was sold in sets of parts, full scores being seldom published. The first printed scores of symphonies would appear to be a selection of works by Haydn published by Leduc in Paris in 1801.[2] To keep the cost down, parts for woodwinds, horns, trumpets, and drums—since they were not always utilized—often were not printed. Thurston Dart cites a few sample title pages, with quotations such as: "double-basses, trumpets and timpani will greatly add to the effect of this piece; those who require parts for them should get in touch with M. Lalemand, the copyist of the Opera House" (ca. 1750); or "Six symphonies in four parts, with optional parts for horns, by M. Stamitz. The horn parts are on sale separately" (ca. 1755). Dart points out that "a full score prepared from them will therefore give quite a misleading impression of how the work sounded when performed by the largest orchestras of the time, even though it may adequately represent a small-scale performance."[3]

A similar situation might obtain even for the violas, that is, the lack of a printed part. In such a case, they merely doubled the bass line an octave higher, as long as they did not impinge on the top melodic line, in which case they would drop to unison with the bass part. But the absence of a part does not necessarily mean that violas were not used in a particular piece.

That orchestras might vary greatly in the performance of a work is also suggested by Johann Joachim Quantz's recommendations on the size and makeup of an orchestra.[4] These will be considered more fully later in this study; let it suffice here to indicate that his recommendations range from an orchestra of 4 violins, 1 viola, 1 cello, 1 contrabass, and 1 harpsichord, all the way to one composed of 12 violins, 3 violas, 4 cellos, 2 contrabasses, 3 bassoons, 4 oboes, 4 flutes, 2 harpsichords, and a theorbo, with horns added if suitable to the piece.

Furthermore, Georges Cucuel, writing about the eighteenth-century orchestra, considered it a *"principe essentiel"* to realize that equivalent instruments were freely substituted for each other, according to available resources. He considered the instrumental trio, written for two upper parts and bass, the very basis of the symphony. One could use indifferently a violin, a flute, an oboe, or a clarinet as an upper part, and a cello, bassoon, contrabass, or keyboard instrument as bass.[5] Marie Bobillier makes a similar statement, although she sees the basis as four parts. "The instrumentation remained at the will of the conductor or the performers: composed and published in four parts, these works permitted, without imposing it or making it precise, the use of flutes and oboes joined to the violins, and of the bassoon joined to the cello or to the basso continuo."[6] Sometimes extramusical circumstances might come into play. When at the age of fifteen Louis Spohr became a court musician at Brunswick (in 1799), he found that "according to the custom of the time, cards were played during the music. In order that the card playing should not be disturbed, the Duchess had given orders that the orchestra should always play softly. The *capellmeister,* accordingly, employed neither trumpets nor kettledrums, and saw to it that the sound never reached a proper *forte*."[7]

More will become apparent on this point as this study proceeds. Here we need only remember the almost constant state of flux existing in the eighteenth century. While the late baroque style was reaching its climax in the works of J. S. Bach, the *style galant* had already set in in other quarters, as had the *empfindsamer Stil,* and both of these would culminate in what is now called the classical style. It is obvious that these stylistic changes would be reflected in, perhaps sometimes caused by, concurrent changes in the orchestra. It is only late in the century, in the mature works of Haydn and Mozart, that one finds what is commonly thought of as the classical orchestra, and even here a comparison of Haydn's orchestra at Esterháza with that provided for his London visits will show interesting differences.

The Instruments Used

As the eighteenth century dawned, the string section seemed to be well set as far as parts were concerned, if not numbers. That is, it was divided into the familiar first and second violins, violas, and a bass part doubled by cellos and double basses. The upper instruments appear to have been already "perfected," undergoing only slight changes as time went on; most importantly, near the end of the century, the necks of old violins were slightly lengthened and the fingerboards raised to accommodate a higher bridge.[8] However, cellos seem to have been less standardized. Leopold Mozart, recalling that this instrument formerly had five strings but "now" four, mentioned a variety of sizes but with little difference except in strength of tone, according to the fashion of their stringing.[9] Quantz recognized this variety of sizes, advising that a cellist have two different instruments, one for solo playing and a larger one with thicker strings for ripieno use. He also insisted on a stronger bow for ripieno playing.[10]

There was evidently a variety of instruments used as double bass. Adolphe Adam claims 1700 as the year that the *"contre-basse"* was introduced in the orchestra at the Paris Opéra. He credits "a Monteclair" with the innovation and the instrument caused a veritable revolution in theater music. He describes the instruments replaced as "bass viols, dull and flaccid instruments."[11] F.H.J. Blaze also credited Montéclair (the accent is probably correct) with the innovation but cited the year as 1714. He also called the new instrument the *"violonar"* to distinguish it from its predecessor, the "large bass viol with seven strings, which the Italians called *violone*."[12] He explained his adoption of *"violonar"* as contributing to a "clearer, more logical and more exact language," since instruments like the serpent, trombone, ophicleide, etc., also played *"against the bass,* that is to say, below the bass in several circumstances."[13]

Other string instruments such as the viola da gamba or the viola d'amore seem already to have declined in orchestral use, despite special roles as solo instruments. (One thinks of Bach's *St. John Passion* or Vivaldi's concertos for viola d'amore.) By the end of the century they would be obsolete.

Bows were probably unstandardized until Tourte "perfected" his model in 1785. Even then, some time would pass before a standard model became established in orchestral playing. Meanwhile there were other bows: straight, concave, as well as convex. Galkin feels that the eighteenth-century orchestra was unable to achieve the "vivid" or "pungent" sounds of the modern orchestra because pressure could not be delicately adjusted. He asserts that the modern *sforzando* attack was impossible with the convex bow.[14] However, at least one gamba player has been able to demonstrate the contrary.[15]

Oboes and bassoons were the dominant woodwind instruments early in this period. Although Bach sometimes called for oboe d'amore or oboe da caccia, they seem to have had no stable place in the orchestra and were to become obsolete. One finds occasional references to the English horn, such as in Dittersdorf's description of the Prince's instrumentalists at Vienna, probably in 1751, including "Schmit on the oboe, as well as the English horn."[16] There is also Mozart's question to his father in 1778: "Does Herr Feiner play the cor anglais as well?"[17] And it does make an unusual appearance in Haydn's Symphony No. 22. But the instrument was quite a stranger to the eighteenth-century orchestra.

The contrabassoon remained almost unknown. W. T. Parke described the use of a "newly-invented instrument called a double bassoon" in 1784 at the Handel Commemoration:

> This instrument, which rested on a stand, had a sort of flue affixed to the top of it, similar (with the exception of smoke) to that of a Richmond steam-boat. I am ignorant, however, whether it produced any tone, or whether it was placed in the orchestra to terminate the prospect. The name of this double *bass* and gigantic instrument, which was only fit to be grasped by the monster Polyphemus, did not transpire, and the double bassoon, which had never been *heard,* was never again *seen* after these performances were ended![18]

One suspects that oboe players often doubled on flute, for in many cases one or the other seemed to be used. Notice the following from a title page, for example: "Six Symphonies for two violins, viola and bass, two oboes or flutes, and two hunting horns. The best of the composition of Mr. Stamitz...."[19] Even as late as 1778, Leopold Mozart could write of the orchestra at Milan that it contained "two oboes and two flutes (who, if there are no flutes, always play as four oboes)."[20] Early in the century *flauto* or "flute" meant the recorder; the transverse flute was always clearly distinguished by such terms as *traverso, traversière,* or "German flute." As the century progressed, the recorder dropped out of the orchestra, so that it was no longer necessary to distinguish between the two, "flute" or *flauto* now meaning the transverse variety.

It was mid-century before the clarinet started to make its appearance. Adolphe Adam claimed that it was in 1745 in Rameau's *Temple de la gloire* that it was first employed in the theater.[21] Its use before that time seems to have been sporadic. Cucuel asserted that the words *clarino* and *clarinetto* seemed to have been used imprecisely and that it is often difficult to be sure when the new instrument was indicated rather than the special style of trumpet playing.[22] Indeed, Walther claimed that from a distance it sounded rather like a trumpet, perhaps thus clarifying the choice of name for it.[23] While it was described as "beset with difficulties resulting in the most indescribable coos and squeaks,"[24] those enchanted with it included Mozart, who wrote to his father from Mannheim in 1778: "Ah, if only we had clarinets too! You cannot imagine the glorious effect of a symphony with flutes, oboes and clarinets."[25] As was the case with the flute, the clarinets were used in place of the oboes for years, and again it seems that oboe players were often asked to double on the new instruments.[26] If clarinets were used at Mannheim as early as 1720,[27] it seems that it took them more time to catch on elsewhere. In 1754 a symphony by J. Stamitz was performed in Paris with clarinets.[28] Perhaps this was the stimulus resulting in the presence of two clarinets in the orchestra for the concerts of La Pouplinière in 1762, even though there were only one each of flute, oboe, and bassoon.[29] They appeared in London in the 1760s in operas by Arne and J. C. Bach,[30] and in a "Clarionet Concerto" at Oxford as early as 1772.[31] Parke mentioned French horns and "clarionets" in a performance of the *Beggar's Opera* in London in 1777.[32] If it is true, as Landon asserts, that there were two clarinets at Esterháza from 1776–78,[33] Haydn does not seem to have had them at his disposal again until his second London visit in 1794.[34]

In 1782 two men played in Ludwigslust on entirely "unknown" instruments called basset horns. The reporter described the instrument as having "a range of 4 octaves, a very beautiful and even tone from top to bottom," permitting "such cantabile playing, as to allow the execution of great difficulties."[35] The writer's claim that "they came from Russia" leaves one uncertain as to whether he referred to the players or their instruments. At any rate, despite occasional use, such as in Mozart's *Requiem* or his Serenade for 13 winds, K.361, the basset horn gained no stable footing in the orchestra.

Of the brass family, horns and trumpets were the principal members used. The French *cor de chasse* made its way into German and Austrian orchestras by way of Bohemia, where it seems to have taken hold before the end of the seventeenth century.[36] Horns were added to the opera orchestra at Dresden in 1711 and to that in Vienna in 1712. Carse points out a pair of horn parts in Keiser's *Octavia,* produced in Hamburg in 1705, and uses Mattheson's remarks in *Neu-eröffnete Orchester* (1713) to indicate its spread to North Germany. He tracks its adoption in Italy and England with Scarlatti's *Tigrane* (Naples, 1715), Handel's *Water Music* (1715) and *Radamisto* (London, 1720), and Bononcini's *Astarte* (London, 1720).[37] It seems to have been somewhat tardy in establishing itself in France. Blaze would credit Rameau with the innovation at the Opéra with *cors de chasse* in *Les Sybarites* in 1759; enchanted with the results, Rameau added them (and later clarinets) to his earlier works, *Hippolyte et Aricie* and *Castor et Pollux.* The same source acknowledges horns for fanfares on stage in Campra's *Achille et Déidamie* in 1735, and their use by Coypel in 1718 at the Comédie-Italienne in *Les Amours à la Chasse.*[38] However, Cucuel claimed that the orchestra of La Pouplinière had horns from Germany about 1740.[39] He also pointed out horns in C in a dance in *Fêtes d'Hébé* in 1739 by Rameau, although not *"absolument obligés."*[40]

During the Bach-Handel period, trumpets were more versatile within certain limitations than they were later in the century. Shallow mouthpieces and a narrow bore enabled expert players to use the extremely high harmonics to play brilliant florid passages. Of course, they were limited to the notes available in the key in which the instrument was built or crooked, and these keys were also limited in the baroque to certain longer instruments in D and C.[41] If one interprets Charles Sanford Terry's remarks on this so-called *clarino* technique correctly, three different players with differing mouthpieces would be responsible for different ranges. *Clarino I* was expected to play from the 6th to the 16th harmonic, or, building the series from Great C, from g' up to c'''. *Clarino II* was responsible for the 6th to the 12th harmonic, or from g' to g'', while the lower or *principale* played between the 2nd and 9th, or c to d''.[42] As the century progressed, the *clarino* technique gradually became a lost art, and later in the century only the *principale* range at best seems to have remained.[43] Other attempts at a chromatic trumpet were not successful. The slide trumpet used by Bach did not last; a trumpet with holes and keys similar to those of the woodwinds failed because its tone sounded "like anything on earth but that of a trumpet."[44]

Since trombones were the earliest brass instruments to reach "perfection," that is, the ability to play a fully chromatic scale, it may seem surprising that they did not gain general admittance to the eighteenth-century orchestra. The explanation would seem to lie in the fact that they were for a long time considered church instruments and therefore out of place in the concert salon or the opera house.[45] The trek from church to the opera house and concert platform was long, slow, and arduous. Trombones seem to have been unknown in French music before Gossec, who introduced them in 1762 in his *Messe des morts*—a *"double nouveauté"* along with the gathering of two hundred musicians for the performance. Gossec also claimed the honor of introducing them in the theater with his *Sabinus* in 1773, but he had to get the players from Germany and Transylvania.[46] The inauguration of the Concert of Antient Music in London in 1776 saw one trombone in the orchestra, the player perhaps coming from the King's band.[47] But Cucuel claims they were not used in symphonic music, at least in France, before 1789.[48]

The cornett, an instrument of wood or ivory with six finger holes and a thumb hole but using a cup-shaped mouthpiece, was often used with trombones in church music. It had little or no orchestral importance and was to become obsolete. However, its lower cousin, the serpent, survived longer.[49] It figured among the basses at the Paris Opéra in 1776.[50]

Although a single-action pedal harp already existed in the eighteenth century, it is probably not worth prolonged discussion since its orchestral use was at best sporadic.[51] Handel used a harp in *Julius Caesar,* for example, in 1724.[52] It was heard in the Paris Opéra for the first time in Gluck's *Orphée et Eurydice* in 1774, played by a horn player. In 1780, a harpist was engaged there.[53] In 1789, a Madame Krumpholtz from Paris played a concerto on the pedal harp "for the first time in England."[54]

Timpani were the only percussion in common use. They were smaller than their modern counterparts, however, and could be played *forte* without covering the other instruments.[55] Late in the century the bass drum, cymbals, and triangle began to appear in the opera house (also making an unusual appearance in Haydn's so-called "Military" Symphony).[56] Bass drum and cymbals made their debut at the Paris Opéra in 1779 in Gluck's *Iphigénie en Tauride,* while the tam-tam was used in Steibelt's *Roméo et Juliette* at the Feydeau in 1793.[57] (Another unusual case would seem to be the side drum in Handel's *Royal Fireworks Music.*)

Of course, the continuo was the backbone of the orchestra until well into the latter part of the century. "Thus, no piece can be well performed without some form of keyboard accompaniment. Even in heavily scored works, such as operas performed out of doors, where no one would think that the harpsichord could be heard, its absence can certainly be felt."[58] Thus spoke C. P. E. Bach. (Bass instruments—cellos, double basses, trombones, bassoons—which might play the bass line in conjunction with the instruments capable of harmony have already been mentioned.)[59] The organ was usual in church performances. C. P. E. Bach felt it was "indispensable in church music with its fugues, large choruses, and sustained style. It provides splendor and maintains order."[60] In opera and concert, the harpsichord was essential, starting to give way to the piano only late in the century. In giving his recommendations on orchestral sizes, Quantz assumed "that the *harpsichord* will be included in all ensembles, whether large or small."[61] For example, Landon maintains that the "first 40-odd" symphonies of Haydn "require the presence of a harpsichord as part of the *basso continuo.*"[62] And if the thought of Haydn "presiding" at the piano during the famous London concerts of the 1790s makes one shudder, it is well to remember that the tone of the eighteenth-century fortepiano was closer to that of the harpsichord of that time than to the modern piano.[63] Lute and theorbo continued to be used, at least until mid-century; Quantz gave the theorbo a place in his description of an opera orchestra.[64] Two harpsichords were common in the opera,[65] and it would seem that a concerto grosso would require a continuo player for each group, that is, one for solo and one for ripieno.[66] These points will be given further consideration later in conjunction with the matter of types of conducting in performance practice.

3

Size and Numbers in the Eighteenth-Century Orchestra

Orchestral size was an elastic proposition throughout the eighteenth century. Not only did various orchestras undergo changes in size and makeup as the century progressed, but also there were variances from one locale to another in any given period. How modest J. S. Bach's requirements "for a well-appointed church music" (stated in his famous memorandum to the Council of Leipzig of August 23, 1730)[1] seem to a reader who is used to today's major symphonic aggregations. Perhaps Bach's needs are worth quoting here:

2 or even 3 for the	*Violino 1*
2 or 3 for the	*Violino 2*
2 for the	*Viola 1*
2 for the	*Viola 2*
2 for the	*Violoncello*
1 for the	*Violon[e]*
2, or, if the piece requires, 3, for the	*Hautbois*
1, or even, 2, for the	*Basson*
3 for the	*Trumpets*
1 for the	*Kettledrums*

summa 18 persons at least, for the instrumental music

    N.B. If it happens that the church piece is composed with flutes also (whether they are *à bec* or *Traversieri*), as very often happens for variety's sake, at least 2 more persons are needed. Making altogether 20 instrumentalists.[2]

It would seem that whenever Bach used other instruments, such as oboe da caccia or horn, either some players would have to double on these instruments, or other help would be brought in. From the rest of the memorandum, one can tell that Bach lacked even the numbers he felt were necessary.

That variances in orchestral size and makeup were accepted facts of musical life, and that a work would be performed with the forces at hand as long as certain proportions were observed, is attested to by the recommendations of Quantz:

He who wishes to perform a composition well must see to it that he supplies each instrument in the proper proportion, and does not use too many of one kind, too few of another. I shall propose a ratio which, to my thinking, will satisfy all requirements in this regard. I assume that the *harpsichord* will be included in all ensembles, whether large or small.

With *four violins* use *one viola, one violoncello,* and *one double bass* of medium size.

With *six violins,* the same complement and *one bassoon.*

Eight violins require *two violas, two violoncellos,* an *additional double bass,* larger, however, than the first, *two oboes, two flutes,* and *two bassoons.*

With *ten violins,* the same complement, but with an *additional violoncello.*

With *twelve violins* use *three violas, four violoncellos, two double basses, three bassoons, four oboes, four flutes,* and in a pit *another keyboard* and *one theorbo.*

Hunting horns may be necessary in both small and large ensembles, depending upon the nature of the piece and the inclination of the composer.[3]

This reaffirms not only the inconsistencies in orchestral size, even at mid-century, but the flexibility in performance possibilities hinted at earlier. More will be noted on Quantz's proportions later. At this point, it is interesting to contrast his requirements in conjunction with four or six violins with those of Bach, at the same time keeping in mind that Quantz was theorizing, while Bach probably had to keep a budget in mind. In other words, it is possible that Bach might have preferred eight violins (four and four) if he thought he could have afforded them. (One also notices that Bach liked to divide his violas at that time, resulting in a five-part string section reminiscent of earlier practice.) While he gives no figures, Rousseau also showed concern for the proportions of an orchestra. For example, he warns that the basses must not drown out the higher parts, nor be drowned out. The oboes must not dominate over the violins, nor the seconds over the firsts.[4]

Quite a contrast is evident in the orchestra Haydn had at his disposal at Esterháza in 1783, consisting of 11 violins (including Haydn himself), 2 violas, 2 cellos, 2 basses, 2 oboes, 2 bassoons, and 2 horns.[5] The differences here clearly reflect changing styles as well as the general inconsistencies of the period. But also one must be wary of the accuracy of such lists in the eighteenth century. For example, Pohl recorded the Esterháza-Eisenstadt orchestra in 1762 as consisting of 1 flute, 2 oboes, 2 bassoons, 2 horns, 1 organist, 5 violins (including violas?), 1 cello, and 1 bass. (One bassoon doubled on bass and a singer on violin.)[6] However, Landon claims that it is obvious

from the scoring of Symphonies Nos. 6–8 that Haydn could have at his disposal at least six violins, a viola, two 'cellos and two basses. Undoubtedly the viola part was doubled. Besides these regular members, Haydn could draw upon the orchestra of the Esterházy church choir, which comprised two violins and another bass player; and he also had at his disposal trumpeters and kettledrummers from the Prince's military forces as well as the local "Städtische Thurnermeister" in Eisenstadt. Further players may have been recruited from the Stadtpfarrkirche.[7]

This description gives one some idea of the problem of relying on lists as gospel as far as actual performance forces were concerned. To further complicate matters, Haydn's orchestra was enlarged during "the course of these years" by four horn players, two of whom doubled on lower strings, plus two string players, one of whom was a tenor who doubled.[8]

The records of Esterháza provide further evidence of the dilemma one can face in trying to uncover performance forces. A pay sheet of February 1772[9] included Haydn as Kapellmeister at the head of the list. After six singers, there were three violinists, two listings difficult to decipher (*"Basserelista"* and *"Paritonista"*), six horn players(!), three bassoonists, and two oboists. Could *"Basserelista"* mean bass player? Was *"Paritonista"* a baryton player who could therefore double on cello? Were other players paid in some other capacity as servants or gardeners, etc? This would not be unusual: when Dittersdorf became head of the orchestra of the Bishop of Grosswardein in 1764, he had an orchestra of 34, among whom were "nine servants in livery, a valet, and a confectioner, besides seven musicians, members of the Chapter, who received extra pay from the Bishop...."[10]

There is also the last payroll of the Esterháza opera company of September 1790 before the orchestra disbanded after the death of Prince Nicholas.[11] After Kapellmeister, fourteen singers, seven violinists (one, Polcelli, listed here with no pay as he was paid as a singer above), two cellists, one bass player, four horn players, two oboes, two flutes, three bassoonists, plus *"Garderobba"* and *"Copista"* are listed. Again, one wonders if this represented the full contingent, for, unless the forces had been drastically reduced by then, the list would not agree with the picture purporting to be a performance of *L'Incontro improvviso* in 1775, showing thirteen violins and/or violas,[12] two oboes, Haydn at the keyboard surrounded by a cello and two basses, plus a bit of one kettledrum visible. The other brass needed must have been beyond the confines of the picture.[13] But to confuse things still further, Pohl gave the Esterháza orchestra of 1790 as: one flute, two clarinets (!), three oboes, one bassoon, six horns (!), five violins [violas?], five cellos, and one bass.[14] To be sure, it is sometimes all but impossible to feel that the information is factual in these matters.

Strangely enough, if one compares Bach's needs as cited in 1730 with Haydn's orchestra of 1783, one gets the impression that not much had changed in fifty years. Bach sought 18 or 20 players; Haydn had 23, including himself. The differences lie mainly in Haydn's larger violin section and Bach's violas capable of two parts, at least partly attributable to stylistic differences. However, if one looks around at the forces in other musical centers, it becomes evident that there had been change as well as diversity. In 1783, Berlin had an orchestra of 43, Dresden 42, and Mannheim upwards of 50. Obviously the more important and wealthier courts had larger musical establishments.

Perhaps the best way to gain some perspective on this development is to compare several orchestras and their changing personnel. Table 1 contains some statistics for the orchestra of the King of Prussia in Berlin.

The most dramatic changes seem to have occurred in the listing of 1787 with the addition of seven more violins, more strength in violas and cellos, and the arrival of clarinets and two more horns. But even more striking are the three trombones, missing along with the trumpets in the 1792 list. Another cause for surprise is the presence of a harp after 1772—an instrument so seldom called for in eighteenth-century music and often lacking even in nineteenth-century Germany. At the same time, there are no listings for keyboard instruments in the 1787 and 1792 lists; can this be indicative of the waning of the continuo or was the harp doing this duty (or are the lists merely deficient)? One must also note the continued ripieno strength of the woodwinds in the later listings—a point which will be further considered later.

It is important to keep in mind when studying these lists that trumpets and drums were most often part of the military service rather than the household establishment in this period. However, they could be called on when needed, as long as they were nearby.[15] Furthermore, some of the players listed might be used for other ensembles or double on other instruments.

Table 2, which presents some figures for the Dresden orchestra of the King of Poland, points up the problem of relying on these lists. Note the discrepancies between the two lists for 1756 or between those for 1782 and 1783. Could changes have come about so quickly, or are the sources inaccurate? The early arrival of the horns at Dresden should also be noted. Moreover, where Berlin had 12 violins in 1754, Dresden already had 15. On the other hand, they evidently did not have clarinets until 1787.[16] Surprising is the reappearance of the pantaleon[17] in 1756; one has to wonder how much orchestral use it saw, probably as continuo. It is also unusual to see a gamba so late. And as in Berlin, the woodwinds kept their ripieno strength vis-à-vis the strings in the later listings.

Since the Mannheim Court Orchestra is so often cited as a model of excellence, it might be well to look at its development (table 3). It is interesting to note that Mannheim already had 20 violins in 1756, a figure not reached until 1787 at Berlin. Meanwhile, Dresden reached 18 violins in 1756, but seems to have been back to 15 by 1783. Clarinets arrived early in Mannheim—in 1777—and did not appear in Berlin until 1787. As mentioned before, Dresden also lacked clarinets until 1787. But Mannheim also had four horns in 1756—a number not found at Berlin until 1787. Dresden had three by 1782. Thus, Mannheim certainly merited the label "progressive."

Another problem in dealing with such lists as these is that they do not reveal whether all or some of the forces listed were used in all performances. Were they sometimes split into different performing groups for simultaneous

Table 1. Berlin, Orchestra of the King of Prussia

	1712[a]	1754[b]	1772[c]	1778[d]	1782[e]	1783[f]	1787[g]	1792[h]
flutes		5	4	4	4	4	2	4
oboes	4	3	4	4	3	4	4	5
clarinets							2	2
bassoons	3	4	4	2	4	4	4	5
horns		2	2	2	2	2	4	5
trumpets			x				2	
trombones							3	
timpani			x				1	
keyboard		2 hcd	2 hcd	2 hcd	2	2		
other		1 tho, 1 gba		1 hp, 1 tho	1 hp	1 hp	1 hp	1 hp
violins	6+5	12	12	12	6+7	7+6	20	22
violas	2	3	4	4	4	4	6	7
cellos+basses	5	4+2	5+2	4+3	4+3	6+3	8+4	8+4
Totals	**25**	**39**	**42 (?)**	**39**	**40**	**43**	**61**	**63 (?)**

gba=viola da gamba; hcd=harpsichord; hp=harp; tho=theorbo; x=no number given

a *Kapelletat*, 1712, & L. Schneider, *Geschichte der Kurfürst. Brandenburg und Kgl. preussischen Kapelle*, Berlin, 1852, p. 54, both cited in Carse/18TH, p. 18.

b Marpurg/BEYTRAGE, I, p. 76; there is one player's name without instrument.

c Burney/GERMANY, II, p. 96.

d Anon., *Briefe zur Erinnerung an merkwürdige Zeiten*, Berlin, 1778, I, p. 101, cited in Carse/18TH, p. 19.

e Forkel/ALMANACH, 1782, pp. 146–48.

f Cramer/MAGAZIN, I, pp. 605–8.

g BEMERKUNGEN, p. 56.

h *Mus. Korrespondenz*, Speyer, 1792, p. 10, cited in Schreiber/ORCHESTER, p. 101.

Table 2. Dresden, Orchestra of the King of Poland

	1709[a]	1719[b]	1731[c]	1734[d]	1754[e]	1756[f]	1756[g]	1782[h]	1783[i]
flutes	2	2	3	3	2	3	3	3	3
oboes	4	5	4	3	5	6	5	5	4
bassoons	2	3	3	5	5	6	4	4	4
horns		2	2	2	2	2	2	3	3
timpani					x				
keyboard			2 hcd	2 hcd	2 hcd / 1	1 org		2 org	1 org
other	2 tho, 2 vl	1 pan, 2 tho				1 pan, 1 gba			
violins	4	7	6	12	8+7	18	16	17	8+7
violas	2	5	3	4	4	4	4	4	4
cellos+basses	4+1	5+5	4+2	5+2	3+3	3+2	4+2	3+4	4+3
Totals	**23**	**37**	**29**	**38**	**44 (?)**	**47**	**40**	**46**	**42**

gba=viola da gamba; hcd=harpsichord; lt=lute; org=organ; pan=pantaleon; vl=viol; x=no number given

a Mennicke/HASSE, p. 212, according to whom this is the first appearance of cellos in Dresden. Carse thinks that the *haute-contre* and *taille* in the original list are probably viols, as they are counted here; see Carse/18TH, p. 20.

b Mennicke/HASSE, p. 273.

c Mennicke/HASSE, p. 270.

d Ibid., p. 270.

e Rousseau/DICTIONNAIRE, Plate G, facing p. 224.

f Fürstenau/DRESDEN, II, pp. 294-95. Four are listed as *Novisten*, probably probationers used for ripieno purposes.

g Marpurg/BEYTRÄGE, II, p. 475.

h Forkel/ALMANACH, 1782, pp. 143-45.

i Cramer/MAGAZIN, I, pp. 1235-38.

Table 3. Mannheim, Court Orchestra

	1723[a]	1756[b]	1777[c]	1782[d]
flutes	x (?)	4	2	4
oboes (15 wd)	x	2	2	3
clarinets			2	4
bassoons	x	2	4	4
horns	x (?)	4	2	6
trumpets	x	12	x	
timpani	x	2	x	
violins	12	10+10	10/11+ 10/11	23
violas	2	4	4	3
cellos+basses	2+3	4+2	4+4	4+3
Totals	**37 (?)**	**56 (?)**	**47/49**	**46/54**

wd=winds; x=no number given

a Walter/GESCHICHTE, p. 77.

b Marpurg/BEYTRÄGE, II, p. 567. The trumpets and drums evidently came from a military corps: *Annoch 12 Trampeter und 2 Pauker.* There was also an organ according to Aubert & Landowski/ORCHESTRE, p. 51.

c Mozart/BRIEFE, II, p. 101; trans. Mozart/LETTERS, I, pp. 355–56.

d Forkel/ALMANACH, 1783, pp. 124–26.

e One clarinet, 2 horns, and 5 violins are listed as *Accessisten,* probably probationers.

functions in differing locales? Did the whole string group always take part, or were they reserved for major symphonies? Such questions are not answered by these lists; much remains for conjecture until further information is available. Neal Zaslaw has shown that in many orchestras the higher-paid solo players would perform intricate and/or contrapuntal passages and the lesser paid ripienists would join in the "loud, homophonic tuttis."[18] Mozart's letter describing the Mannheim orchestra in 1777 described the entire group taking part at High Mass; however, it does not necessarily follow that all the available forces indicated in the orchestral lists were always used.

For contrast, the statistics for the orchestra of the Paris Opéra are given in table 4. Of course, none of the above lists is complete, some giving only a total, others giving a total and some of the instruments. The problem of accuracy is again pointed up. Nevertheless, the French orchestra seems to have been larger than its German counterparts, Berlin having only 25 players in 1712, Dresden and Mannheim reaching 37 only in 1719 and 1720 respectively. At mid-century, Dresden matched Paris, and by 1756, Mannheim seems to have exceeded it. But by the 1770s, Paris was ranging from 60 to 72, whereas Berlin did not reach 60 until 1787. So all in all, the Paris orchestra would seem to have been "progressive," at least as far as size is concerned, though it was tardy in admitting the horns. Should one infer from this that French orchestras were necessarily bigger than German ones? One writer reported that in France around 1725, when the *Concert spirituel* was founded, an orchestra of 18 was felt to produce *"un effet admirable."* He credited that organization with a starting size of 60 performers, including orchestra and chorus, a sizeable group for 1725.[19] If one browses through statistics for the *Concert spirituel,* one might at first want to conclude that French orchestras were generally bigger. But further comparisons (rendered somewhat shallow due to the relative paucity of statistics on French as opposed to German orchestras) would seem to reveal a constantly changing situation. The larger German orchestras rivalled the *Concert spirituel* and the Opéra, and some French orchestras appear to have been smaller.

In 1750, for example, the *Concert spirituel* had 36[20] or 39[21] players, depending on which source one consults. But as listed above, Dresden already had 38 players in 1734, and 37 as far back as 1719; Mannheim achieved a similar number a year later. Meanwhile, the Théâtre Pompadour in Paris had only 30 at that time,[22] and in 1754, the Château de Fontainebleau only 29.[23] In 1756, the *Concert spirituel* with an orchestra of 40[24] was more than matched by Dresden and Mannheim. In 1762, the *Concerts de La Pouplinière* at Paris still employed an orchestra of only 15.[25] The *Concert spirituel* had grown to 58 by 1774,[26] but in 1782 the Comédie française at Paris used only 26 men and the Comédie italienne 25.[27] And in 1792, Berlin was rivalling the Opéra with 63, while 1790 saw the *Concert spirituel* with 53 and Paris's Théâtre de

Table 4. Paris, Opéra Orchestra

	1713[a]	1713[b]	1751[c]	1752[d]	1754[e]	1763[f]	1768[g]	1771[h]	1773[i]	1775[j]	1777[k]	1783[l]	1788[m]	1790[n]	1792[o]
flutes	x {8}	x {5}	x {5}	x {10}	x {6}	3			x {5}				2	2	3 "p" (?)
oboes	x	x	x	x	x	3			x				4	4	6
clarinets									1				2	4	
bassoons	x	4	4		3	4			8	8			4	5	
horns								2	2			6	2	4	6
trumpets		1	1	x {2}	1	(2)		2					3	3	
trombones														(3)	
timpani		1	1	x		1		1	1				1	1	
keyboard		1 hcd	1 hcd	1 hcd											
other	5 vl				(2 gba)								1 hp, 2 cyb		
violins	12	16	16	16	16	16		24	22	28	24 (?)	30	28	26	
violas	2	6	6	6	6	6		4	5	5		6	6	6	6
cellos + basses	8	12	12	12	12	8+4		10+4	9+6	12+5		12+4	12+5	12+5	12+4
Totals	**46**	**46**	**46**	**49**	**45**	**45**	**55**	**66**	**60**	**72**	**67**	**?**	**69/72**	**70**	**?**

cyb=cymbals; gba=viola da gamba; hp=harp; hcd=harpsichord; vl=viol; x=no number given; (x)=doubled by other players

a Blaze/ACADÉMIE, II, p. 374.

b Travenol & Durey/OPÉRA, I, p. 121. Violas are listed as *Quintes*.

c *Almanach historique du Théâtre ou Calendrier historique et chronologique de tous les Spectacles*, Paris, 1752, cited by Carse/18TH, p. 25.

d Travenol & Durey/OPÉRA, II, pp. 141–42. This closely approximates the 1751 listing.

e Marpurg/BEYTRÄGE, I, p. 194.

f Blaze/ACADÉMIE, II, p. 354. A total of 45 played at once, since 1 flute and 1 oboe were saved for solos, and the trumpets were played by the horn players. Sometimes 6 or 8 bassoons plus a serpent were used to reinforce the bass *"faiblement tenue par un ou deux violonars!"*

g Blaze/ACADÉMIE, II, p. 374.

h *Ibid.*, II, p. 355.

i *Almanach historique du Théâtre ou Calendrier historique et chronologique de tous les Spectacles*, Paris, 1774, cited by Carse/18TH, p. 25.

j Blaze/ACADÉMIE, II, p. 274.

k *Ibid.* II, p. 374.

l Cramer/MAGAZIN, I, p. 799.

m *Mus. Korrespondenz*, Speyer, 1788, p. 93, cited in Schreiber/ORCHESTER, p. 108.

n *Almanach historique du Théâtre ou Calendrier historique et chronologique de tous les Spectacles*, Paris, 1791, cited by Carse/18TH, p. 26.

o *Mus. Korrespondenz*, Speyer, 1792, p. 10, cited by Schreiber/ORCHESTER, p. 108.

Monsieur with 38.[28] Of course, function and place of performance have not been taken into account here. For example, the concerts of La Pouplinière evidently took place in a salon at his *"hôtel,"*[29] whereas the Opéra orchestra had to fill a large theater. But the Dresden and Berlin orchestras saw service in both concert and opera. Nevertheless, it can be said that there was a general growth in orchestral size during the course of the eighteenth century; Berlin went from 25 in 1712 to 63 in 1792; Dresden from 23 in 1709 to 42 in 1783; Mannheim from possibly 37 in 1720 to perhaps 54 in 1782; and the Paris Opéra from 46 in 1713 to 70 in 1790.

This growth was not always greeted with enthusiasm. A report from around 1740 noted that the Parisian public always complained about an increase in orchestral size. The report quoted the *Mercure* of October 1739, p. 3455:

> Our concerts no longer affect
> If the monstrous assemblage
> Of twenty superfluous instruments
> Does not make a bacchic brawl.[30]

One can find the same sentiment in Germany. A critic writing in 1783 lamented the vogue of some directors who used 30 or 40 players and rejoiced over such an imposing orchestra, while spoiling the sound for the hall and the critic. Commenting on a specific concert, he wrote that the "army" of players was so spread out that the wall acted like a *"Flügel,"* the tones arriving at his ear a quarter to a half second later than from the actual *Flügel*. In short, though the hall and the orchestra were very good, he found the effect unwieldy. He felt that a symphony needed no more than 17 men. To the complaint that such a group was too small for a large audience in a large hall, he responded that "the orchestra is not too small, but the crowd too big."[31]

Before proceeding, it might be worth noting the figures for the Salomon Concerts in London in the 1790s, since the "London" Symphonies of Haydn are so important:

> 2 flutes, 2 oboes, 2 bassoons;
> 2 horns, 2 trumpets;
> 1 drums;
> 12–16 violins, 4 violas, 3 cellos, 4 basses.[32]

The absence of clarinets coincides with their lack in the first six "London" Symphonies, but they must have been added for Haydn's second visit in 1794, as the second six have parts for two clarinets. In fact, a London letter of the *Berliner Musikzeitung* of March 13, 1793 intimated that they were on hand when needed.[33]

Relative Strengths and Proportions

Several observations can be made in light of the above data that are undoubtedly more important than the factor of size alone, which, after all, is dependent on other factors, such as function (concert, church, opera), size of hall, audience, genre of music, and economic means (in turn reflecting prestige; for example, a king versus a prince). These observations have to do with proportions within the orchestra, regardless of size.

First of all, first and second violins seem almost without exception to have been treated as equals, each part usually having the same number of players, whether large or small. Furthermore, the total strength of the lower strings seems to have been generally less than the total violin strength. Dart sums it up this way: "For every fifteen violins, the eighteenth-century orchestra had ten violas, cellos and doublebasses; the modern orchestra has fifteen. The modern orchestra is bottom-heavy, in fact."[34] However, this would seem to be an exaggeration according to the above figures. Dart's ratio is 3:2. Quantz's figures range from 2:1 through 4:3. Esterháza in 1783 was almost 2:1, but many other listings come closer to 1:1. Indeed, Bach's orchestra at Leipzig and those at Dresden and Paris in the first half-century show the lower strings exceeding the violins in strength. And in the second half of the century, Berlin was close to 1:1, Dresden showed Dart's ratio of 3:2, Mannheim stood at 2:1, and the Paris Opéra fluctuated from about 4:3 to 1:1. The Salomon concerts would be in a 1:1 or a 4:3 ratio, depending on whether the violins were closer to 12 or 16 as given in the above figures. On the other hand, Dart's assertion that the modern orchestra is "bottom-heavy" would be upheld by Haydn's letter of 1768 which gave performance instructions for his cantata *Applausus*. Among other things, he stated: "I prefer a band with 3 bass instruments—'cello, bassoon and double bass—to one with 6 double basses and 3 'celli, because certain passages stand out better that way."[35] Charles Rosen would contradict Dart, however. He states that while this letter represents Haydn's taste in the 1760s, he later adapted to "the new sonority"; furthermore, "today's performances of all the later symphonies of Haydn and Mozart suffer from an insufficient reinforcement of the bass line."[36] The figures given above for both Esterháza and the Salomon concerts show a heavier use of basses than just three instruments, seemingly giving support to Rosen's arguments.

What conclusions can one draw from all of this? Probably one might first conclude that no easy formula can cover either the baroque or classical styles as such, and, secondly, that each composer, even each work, should be researched as well as studied intrinsically, if one is to arrive at a fair ratio within a fair overall number for a performing group.

Also worthy of note are the proportions between string and woodwind strength. Carse puts the ratio as approximately 1 woodwind to 3 strings, contrasting this with the nineteenth century's 8 woodwinds to 30 or more strings.[37] Rockstro was a bit more detailed as well as certain on the ratio in Handel's time:

> We have positive proof that the usual proportion was that of one Hautboy to three Violins; with one Bassoon to each Violoncello, and another, to each Double Bass: and until we have given these proportions a fair trial, and doubled, or even tripled our number of Trumpets, at large Festival Performances, it is manifestly illogical to say that the *Messiah* would produce no effect if played as Handel wrote it. No man now living has heard it as Handel wrote it.[38]

If one looks over the figures given above, which, admittedly, are only a selected group and do not represent all orchestras and all eighteenth-century performances, one realizes that one cannot be so blithe about such proportions. Carse's ratio of 1 woodwind to slightly more than 3 strings does not hold up universally. Bach's Leipzig requests of 1730 ranged from about 1:2 to 1:9! Berlin and Dresden showed a 1:2 relationship more often than 1:3 (which Dresden only approached), and Mannheim had 8:30 in 1756, later reverting to approximately 1:3 and 1:2. And if Carse's 8:30+ can be considered roughly 1:4, the Paris Opéra showed this already in 1751, reverting to 1:3 in 1763, but was already back to 1:4 by 1788! Indeed, the 1791 Salomon concerts in London had the 1:4 relationship, too. This is not meant as an indictment of Carse, whose context fully realizes diversity, but only as another realization that hard and fast formulas can be questionable in this area.

As for Rockstro's formula, it did not take into account flutes—already in some orchestras early in the century (in Dresden in 1709, for example)—nor violas, even though they were in a no-man's-land between bass and filler parts in the first half of the century. But the 1759 Foundling Hospital performance of *Messiah* on which Rockstro seems to have based his ratios showed 8 woodwinds to 10 strings—in between 1:2 and 1:3, roughly in keeping with the above conclusions.[39]

Writing in the 1790s, Francesco Galeazzi recommended that if there were more than 16 violins, the winds should be doubled.[40] Neal Zaslaw has come up with a somewhat more sophisticated formula that is perhaps as close as one can come, though as he admits, it also does not fit all the known situations (he measured 125 to arrive at the formula).[41] With S equalling the number of strings and W the rest of the orchestra, the formula is $W = .39S + 5.13$. A bit of work with a calculator shows that this would fit or come close to some groups but not all.

What is obvious, though, is that in the eighteenth century, the woodwinds were used as both solo and ripieno instruments. In solos, naturally, single instruments would play, but in ensemble, the ripieno instruments would join in, giving the woodwinds some measure of equality with the string tone.[42] This is obvious in Quantz's proportions as well as in most of the orchestral lists above. Dart puts it this way: "For every fifteen violins, the eighteenth-century orchestra had six of each woodwind-instrument; the modern orchestra has two."[43] Again, in light of the above figures, this seems to be an exaggeration— between a 1:2 and a 1:3 ratio—but there is no question that the balance was greater for the woodwinds than it later became. Add to this the solo and ripieno alternation even in the strings in some orchestras as mentioned earlier and one realizes that the woodwinds truly had more parity with the strings than was always the case later.

In this regard, it should be noted again that in earlier scores with a common bass part, bassoons (or at least one) were used whenever there were oboes or other woodwinds. During any oboe (or indeed flute or even clarinet) solo, the strings would probably drop from the bass line, leaving it to bassoon and harpsichord.[44]

As the century progressed, quality not quantity of woodwind tone tended to become more valued, as Carse puts it. Each woodwind instrument became one of a pair of soloists, while the ripieno character declined. At the same time, the flute and clarinet became more individual rather than "substitutes or alternates" to the oboes.[45] But if one peruses the above lists as well as those representing many other orchestras, one will notice that the ripieno function continued in many places.

Meanwhile, composers started writing separate parts for bassoons which had previously shared a common bass line. The tenor range of the instrument was discovered and exploited, and it became a solo instrument in its own right. Similarly, the viola started getting treatment other than as a weak violin or, perhaps more often, a higher bass doubling. For example, in the letter on *Applausus* cited earlier, Haydn asked for "two players on the viola part throughout, for the inner parts sometimes need to be heard more than the upper parts, and you will find in all my compositions that the viola rarely doubles the bass."[46]

In sum, by the end of the century, in the late works of Mozart and Haydn, a woodwind section of six to eight members tended to be balanced against a growing string section. Carse puts it as 6 to 8 woodwinds against 18 to 20 strings,[47] but the above figures would suggest more string weight, since Berlin had 38 strings by 1787, Dresden 26 by 1783, Mannheim at least 28 by 1782, and the Salomon concerts 23 to 27 in 1791. Even though some ripieno woodwind strength remained in all of these, save the Salomon concerts, the growth in string strength of the nineteenth century had already begun.

Only two horn parts were common in eighteenth-century music. Therefore, one suspects that where more horns were available, as listed above, they either doubled for more ensemble sound as ripieno instruments, or, as Carse suggests, they were crooked in different keys to make more open notes available.[48]

But lest we become too "purist" in performing eighteenth-century music with a reduced orchestra, it is interesting to keep in mind the obvious delight Mozart took in a performance of one of his symphonies (probably K.338 in C) by what sounds like a twentieth-century orchestra. In a letter to his father from Vienna dated April 11, 1781, he wrote:

> You ask whether I have been to see Bonno? Why, it was at his house that we went through my symphony for the second time. I forgot to tell you the other day that at the concert the symphony went magnifique and had the greatest success. There were forty violins, the wind-instruments were all doubled, there were ten violas, ten double-basses, eight violoncellos and six bassoons.[49]

On the other hand, it seems unwise and misleading to assume, as Rosen does in the following, that

> The orchestra that Mozart preferred is surprisingly large, but he is quite clear about what he wanted. . . . Even remembering that all the instruments of the time were a little softer than those of the present day, this is still a force almost twice that which any conductor dares to use now for a Mozart symphony. Of course Mozart did not often get an orchestra of such size, but there is no reason today to perpetuate those conditions of eighteenth-century performance which obtained only when there was not enough money to do the thing properly.[50]

Though there is enough evidence here to make the inferences plausible, the situation was not so "cut and dried."

"Monster" Performances

The eighteenth century also saw the occasional use of huge orchestral forces, usually for festal occasions. In 1760, for example, two hundred musicians took part in a performance of Gossec's *Messe des morts* at the Church of Saint-Roch in Paris. One hears pre-echoes of Berlioz as one reads that "this master enriched his orchestra with several instruments unknown or until then neglected in France. Four trumpets, four hunting horns, four trombones, four clarinets, eight bassoons thundered in the *Tuba mirum,* in the *Mors stupebit* of his mass for the dead."[51] In 1763, when Padre Martini's *Vespers* were performed at his church in Bologna during a festival *"per la visita della Madonna di San Lucca"* the forces were 160 strong, of which 80 were singers.[52] A benefit performance of Gasmann's *Betulia Liberata* in Vienna in 1771 used an orchestra of 200.[53]

The famous Handel Commemoration of 1784 took place in London in Westminster Abbey and the Pantheon. The concert at the Pantheon was one of secular music with an orchestra and chorus of 200, less than half the number used at the Abbey, but evidently four times more than had ever appeared at the Pantheon.[54] On the other hand, the accounts of the Abbey concerts point up and magnify the problems inherent in controlling accuracy in such lists. But it probably matters little whether there were 251 instruments and 275 voices for a total of 526, as addition of Burney's lists would indicate,[55] or 275 instruments and 246 voices for a total of 521, as Cramer's lists would suggest (he gave 513 as a total);[56] it was a big group! (Carse cites the figures as an orchestra of 244 and a chorus of 262,[57] while Haas gave 250 and 276 respectively.)[58] Since breakdowns are available here, it might be useful to check ratios. Burney gave 26 oboes against 95 violins,[59] while Cramer gave 26 oboes against 102 violins (30–96 in his earlier announcement prior to the actual concerts[60]). In either case, it is closer to 1:4 than to Rockstro's 1:3. And neither Burney's 26 bassoons plus 1 double bassoon to 21 cellos and 15 basses nor Cramer's 25 bassoons and 1 double-bassoon to 30 cellos and 18 basses (28 bassoons to 30 cellos and 20 basses in the announcement) equal Rockstro's 1:1 proportions. But Carse's 1:3 ratio of combined woodwinds to strings is vindicated. Burney's 59:157 and Cramer's 59:182 (58:179 in the announcement) all approximate this. Nor do the 157 strings against the 94 other members in Burney's figures bear out Zaslaw's formula. Parke remembered later London benefit performances: in the Abbey in 1787 where the "band of vocal and instrumental performers" equalled 806 plus 22 principal singers;[61] the Handel performances at the Abbey in 1791 with "the orchestra consisting of a thousand performers" (probably including voices);[62] and the Handel performances at Whitehall Chapel where "the orchestra, ably led by Cramer, comprised five hundred performers."[63]

Enthusiasm for huge festive Handel performances spread to the continent, for in 1786 *Messiah* was done in the Berlin Cathedral with an orchestra of 189 and a chorus of 119.[64] And in Breslau in 1788, the same work was mounted with double chorus and double orchestra, almost suggesting concerto grosso technique. An orchestra of 45 was pitted against one of 84 with 19 brass and one timpanist in the organ loft, while a chorus of 38 joined a larger one of 72—altogether 149 instruments and 110 voices.[65] This seems a clear example of probably using the smaller groups in intricate and/or softer passages, saving the ripienists for thundering strength. And perhaps the performance of Dittersdorf's *Hiob* in the Grand Opera House in Berlin in 1789 is worthy of note, as it was "rendered by an orchestra consisting of some *two hundred and thirty persons*" with a chorus of 80.[66]

However, such "monster" festivals must be regarded as exceptional cases and outside and mainstream of orchestral development, as interesting as they may be. Yet, it would seem as if Berlioz's "dream" orchestra of 465 players with a chorus of 360 had some precedence.

4

Eighteenth-Century Seating Plans

Seating arrangements differed widely in the eighteenth century. Various architectural designs as well as different ideals of sonority were probably responsible for some of the varieties found. Other factors played a part, such as the officiating member and the instrument at which he presided, the visual contact he must have with all his players, and the placement of the basses, who often carried the beat.

That the layout of the orchestra was important to J. S. Bach can be inferred from C. P. E. Bach's letter to Forkel of January 13, 1775, concerning his father:

> As the result of frequent large-scale performances of music in churches, at court, and often in the open air, in strange and inconvenient places, he learned the placing of the orchestra, without any systematic study of acoustics. He knew how to make good use of this experience, together with his native understanding of building design so far as it concerns sound....[1]

Terry's version of the probable layout used by Bach for his forces is shown in figure 1. Note that all the strings were together, except for the continuo players who were strangely divorced from the keyboards—strangely since it seems more usual for them to sit near a keyboard player and even read from his part. One wonders how much of this Terry inferred from the frontispiece of Walther's *Musikalisches Lexicon* of 1732, where, it should be noted, most of the visible players were standing, not seated.[2]

For the performance of a concerto grosso, Dart insists that the two groups, soloists and ripieno, be separated; "this element of space is inherent in the form...."[3] Again, each group should have its own keyboard or other continuo instrument. This strikes one as more sensible and sensitive to the genre than the plan shown in figure 2, drawn according to the ideas of Max Seiffert. It suggests, first of all, a stick-waving conductor, hardly historically accurate, as shall be seen. But more important, it really allows no space between the groups. One might also question the space reserved for woodwind

Figure 1. Terry's Version of Bach's Layout

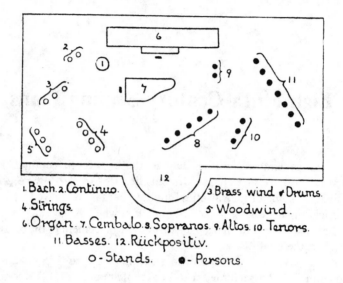

1. Bach. 2. Continuo.   3. Brass wind & Drums.
4. Strings.   5. Woodwind.
6. Organ. 7. Cembalo. 8. Sopranos. 9. Altos. 10. Tenors.
      11. Basses. 12. Rückpositiv.
           O - Stands.   ● - Persons.

Source: Terry/ORCHESTRA, p. 12.

Figure 2. Plan of Baroque Orchestra after Seiffert

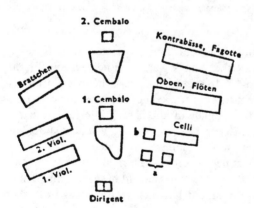

a, b, = Concertino
a: 1. und 2. Solovioline
b: Solocello.

Source: Scholz/DIRIGIERLEHRE, p. 100.

instruments, since one usually thinks of the ripieno in the baroque concerto as consisting of only strings; but in light of earlier remarks on the constitution of the eighteenth-century orchestra, woodwinds might be a possibility.

Opera Seating

Quantz insisted that "the leader must know how to distribute, place, and arrange the instrumentalists in an ensemble."

> Much depends upon the good distribution and placement of the instruments, and upon their combination in the proper ratio. In the orchestra pit of an opera house, the first harpsichord may be placed in the middle, with the broad end facing the parterre and the tip to the stage, so that the singers are visible to the player. The violoncello may be placed on his right, and the double bass on his left. The leader may sit next to the first harpsichord, on the right and slightly forward and elevated. [C. P. E. Bach strongly concurs: "If the first violinist stands near the keyboard as he should, disorder cannot easily spread."[4]] The violinists and violists may form a narrow oval ring, beginning with the leader and continuing so that the violists have their backs to the stage and extend to the tip of the harpsichord, in such fashion that all may see and hear the leader. If, however, the pit is spacious enough to seat four people abreast, the second violins may sit, in two pairs, one behind the other, in the middle between the first violins and the violists sitting with their backs to the stage; for the closer together the instruments are, the better the effect they produce. On the same side, at the end where the violinists stop, there still may be enough room for another violoncello and a double bass. Let the second harpsichord be placed on the left side of the first, parallel to the stage and with the tip turned toward the first, but so that room may still be found behind it for the bassoons, unless you wish to put them on the right side of the second harpsichord, behind the flutes. Another pair of violoncellos may be placed next to the second harpsichord. On this, the left side of the pit, the oboes and hunting horns may sit in a row with their backs to the listeners, like the violins on the right side; the flutes, however, are posted in a diagonal line next to the first harpsichord, so that they turn their eyes toward the harpsichord, and the lower ends of their flutes toward the parterre. In some places, however, where there is an empty space between the pit and the listeners, the flutes are placed with their backs to the parterre, and the oboes are stationed in a diagonal line between them and the second harpsichord. The oboes produce an excellent effect, especially in the tutti, serving as a filler, and their sound justly deserves a free outlet, an outlet which the flutes also enjoy if no one stands close behind them and if the players turn a little to the side, and which they enjoy even more fully, since they are then closer to the listeners. The theorbo may find a comfortable place behind the second harpsichordist and the violoncellists attached to him.[5]

The plan in figure 3 is one drawn by Quantz's translator in the light of this text. Note the two harpsichords, each flanked by continuo instruments. Again the strings are all to one side, with the winds on the opposite side. The players nearest the stage facing out and those nearest the audience facing in show a connection with the picture mentioned earlier of Haydn's forces in a performance of *L'Incontro improviso* [see p. 000]; thus, elements of opera seating from the baroque remained in the classic era, most likely due to the

Figure 3. Quantz's Opera Seating

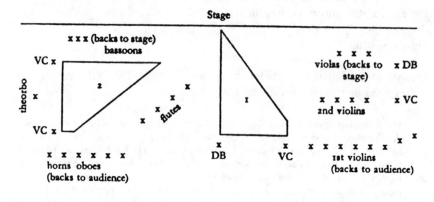

Source: Quantz/ FLUTE, p. 212.

exigencies of the pit. However, Haydn's one harpsichord was to the side, like Quantz's second, rather than in the center. Presumably this first harpsichord would be the one manned by the Kapellmeister.

However, the difficulties arising from verbal descriptions can be seen in the discrepancies between this and the drawn reactions of other writers. The drawing by Arnold Schering,[6] admittedly the basis of the one above, has all the strings in straight lines and the continuo instruments rather separated from the first harpsichord. The flutes are in a line at a right angle to the stage, and the cello and bass on the right are in the corner of the pit and stage. If these differences seem minimal, one should examine the sketch by Georg Schünemann,[7] in which the bassoons are placed at the left behind the cellos, raising the question of what Quantz meant by "behind" the harpsichord. Also, neither Schering nor Schünemann truly showed the "narrow oval" of violins and violas of the text, though the sketch reproduced here suggests it.

While Jean Jacques Rousseau seemed to feel that the "first" orchestra in Europe was that at Naples as far as number and intelligence of its players were concerned, he thought that the best distributed with the best ensemble was that of the Dresden Opera under the direction of Johann Adolphe Hasse.[8] He gives a reproduction of its plan, shown from another source (fig. 4). Note certain similarities to Quantz's plan, for example, the positions of the two harpsichords, the upper strings all on one side, though violas and second violins are reversed in this case. The positions of oboes and bassoons are also reversed, but the general plan is the same. It seems likely that while theorizing, Quantz could well have had the Dresden orchestra in mind.

Rousseau felt that the bass strings should be dispersed around the two

Figure 4. Dresden Opera under Hasse

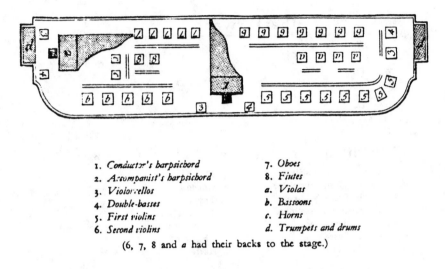

1. *Conductor's harpsichord*
2. *Accompanist's harpsichord*
3. *Violoncellos*
4. *Double-basses*
5. *First violins*
6. *Second violins*

7. *Oboes*
8. *Flutes*
a. *Violas*
b. *Bassoons*
c. *Horns*
d. *Trumpets and drums*

(6, 7, 8 and *a* had their backs to the stage.)

Source: Carse/ORCHESTRA, p. 20; original in Rousseau/DICTIONNAIRE, plate G, facing p. 224.

harpsichords and throughout the orchestra, because they had to *"régler & soutenir"* all the other parts, and all the musicians must hear them equally. The *Maître* at the first harpsichord had to be where he could see and be seen by all; also each violinist had to be seen by the first violinist and in turn be able to see him.[9] This would account for the grouping of both the Dresden and the Quantz plans, and for the positioning of the musicians who had their backs to the stage.[10] But note that Quantz only spoke of the leader of the first violins as *Anführer,* the man in charge, while Rousseau seems to indicate a shared responsibility between him and the *Maître* at the first harpsichord. (This is explored further in chapter 5.)

According to Schünemann, the Berlin Opera orchestra of Frederick the Great, when Karl Heinrich Graun was Kapellmeister (1740-59), was grouped in a semicircle around the first harpsichord and the continuo instruments— probably not different from the plans of Quantz or Dresden. But when Johann Friedrich Reichardt assumed direction in 1776, he gradually reformed the orchestra, even doing away with the keyboard instruments altogether. The layout of this orchestra in 1787 according to a traveler is shown in figure 5. This is a very "modern" plan, evincing features that will be seen in many nineteenth-century orchestras. First of all, notice the separation between first and second violins, although, contrary to what will become general practice in the nineteenth century, the firsts are to the right, the seconds to the left. The

Figure 5.   Berlin Opera under Reichardt

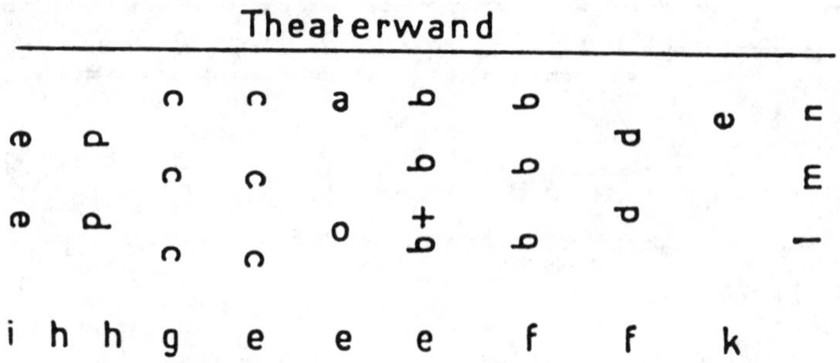

Theaterwand

a. Kapellmeister.
b.† Konzertmeister.
b. Erste Violinen.
c. Zweite Violinen.
d. Bratschen.
e. Bässe.
f. Hörner.

g. Flöten.
h. Oboen.
i. Fagotte.
k. Klarinetten.
l. m. n. Posaunen, Trompeten und
        Pauken.
o. Harfe.

Source: BEMERKUNGEN, p. 57, here reproduced from Schünemann/DIRIGIERENS, p. 202. In BEMERKUNGEN, however, the line from conductor to harp is more centered, and the basses on the right ("e") are more in a line from "m" to between the two "d"s.

Kapellmeister seems to be facing the stage with his back to the players as he stands right at its edge—another feature that will often be seen in later plans or pictures. Unusual from a later standpoint is the split of the violas, perhaps a remnant of their being considered as usually doubling the bass, and the basses here are still scattered around the edges of the orchestra. (Those in the middle would seem to have obstructed the audience's view, but this too will be seen in some nineteenth-century plans.) The grouping of the horns closer to the woodwinds than to the brass perhaps reflects their being considered more mellow and melodic instruments, whereas the trumpets and drums were used to punch out emphasis when needed. Trombones are present, as well as a harp, which may have replaced the keyboard for recitative. Schünemann thought that the clarinets were placed near the brass because they replaced the sound of the *clarino* at this time.[11] Add to this the fact that Reichardt beat time in the modern way,[12] and one must conclude that both Reichardt and his patron Frederick the Great were really forward-looking.

A plan[13] for the San Carlo Opera in Naples in 1786, the orchestra earlier so admired by Rousseau, also shows the violins split but in a more modern fashion, as the firsts are at the left. However, a remnant of earlier practice is apparent in the placing of half of each section with their backs to the stage, the others closer to the audience with their backs to them. The conductor's harpsichord is way to the side, reminding one of the position of Haydn's in the picture referred to earlier; there is a second harpsichord directly to the right. This way of facing the strings, observable also in the Quantz and Dresden Opera plans as well as the Haydn picture, relates to the manner of conducting, to be discussed later. All players had to see the Kapellmeister at the first harpsichord and the leader of the first violins. There was no baton conductor in the modern position, a situation which was a long way off, although the concertmaster in the San Carlo plan was centrally placed with his back to the audience—the conducting position of a modern opera orchestra. One notes also in this plan the scattering of the basses and comparatively few cellos which was characteristic of eighteenth-century Italian orchestras. There is also a strange spatial division of the woodwinds in that oboes and flutes are to the right with clarinets and horns to the left, separated by a couple of cellos, while the bassoons are backed up to the first keyboard, two violas in a similar position near the second keyboard at the right.

Galeazzi preferred the strings and winds to be distributed across the orchestra rather than in the Dresden or Quantz manner, because a "proper blend" could thus be heard from any place in the house.[14] His plan of the Turin Opera in the 1790s is shown in figure 6. This was also a sizeable orchestra, as can be seen from the figures given. Notice that the direction seems to have switched from the conductor at position "A" to a first violinist at position "q" for the ballets. One wonders if the first conductor led in the modern manner with a baton.

Concert Seating

Quantz recommended the following as ideal concert seating:

> In a composition for a large ensemble, performed either in a hall or in some other large place where there is no stage, the tip of the harpsichord may be directed towards the listeners. So that none of the musicians turns his back to the listeners, the first violins may stand in a row next to the harpsichord, with the leader on the right of the keyboard player, who has the two bass instruments playing on either side of him. The second violins may come behind the first, and behind them the violas. Next to the violas, on the right, place the oboes in the same row, and behind this row the hunting horns and the other basses. The flutes, if they have solo parts to play, are best placed at the tip of the harpsichord, in front of the first violins, or on the left side of the harpsichord. Because of the weakness of their tone, they would not be heard if they were to stand back. Singers also may take the same place; if they were to stand behind the keyboard player and read from the score, they would not only hamper the violoncellists and double-bass players, but would obstruct their own breathing and stifle their own voices if poor sight forced them to bend over [to see the music clearly].[15]

A drawing of this plan by Quantz's translator is given in figure 7. Again, the continuo instruments are together, and there is no gap between the two violin

Figure 6. Turin Opera Orchestra

A	Sito del Direttore dell'orchestra più elevato degli altri .... Num. 1.	L	Controbassi primi 2
b	Violini Primi....... 20.	m	in Bassi ; cioè Violoncelli, e Controbassi .... 9.
c	Violini Secondi..... 16.		
d	Oboe .... 4.	n	Altri Corni da Caccia................. 2.
e	Clarinetti........... 2.		
f	Corni da Caccia ..... 2.	o	Timpano .... 1.
g	Viole .... 6.	p	Trombe .... 2.
h	Fagotti............. 3.	q	Primo Violino de' Balli .... 1.
l	Violoncelli primi-.... 2.	r	Cembali .... 2.
			Totale .... 75.

Source: Galeazzi/ELEMENTI, vol. 1, Tavola IV, reproduced from the copy in the Music Library at Cornell University with gratitude to Ms. Lenore Coral, Music Librarian.

Figure 7. Quantz's Concert Seating

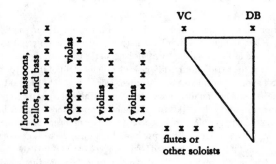

Source: Quantz/FLUTE, p. 213.

sections, an arrangement seemingly typical of baroque seating and not evidently restricted to the exigencies of the opera pit. Quantz did not clearly explain what he meant by the "left side of the harpsichord"; did he mean the player's or the audience's left? Schünemann drew a similar plan but with the flutes or other soloists on the opposite side of the keyboard from the above.[16] But are not other realizations of Quantz's description possible? The problems of verbal descriptions of concert seating are such that the plan in figure 8 could easily be deduced.

Quantz was not without his critics, however. His idea that the singers be placed with the flutes provoked the response that with a large instrumental ensemble in a large hall, neither oboes nor flutes should be so near the singers. "No musical instruments swallow up the tone and the words of high voices as much as flutes and oboes, if they are too near to the singers, although no instruments are more useful for strengthening and supporting them than the oboes, and none provide greater amenity than the flutes." Since the words are so important, nothing should be allowed to interfere with them.[17]

Figure 9 is the plan for the years 1746 through 1748 of the orchestra that was predecessor of that made famous in the Leipzig Gewandhaus Concerts from Alfred Dörffel's history of that institution. He attributed it to Herr Riemer, the first horn player, who evidently also doubled on viola and timpani and in addition chronicled some of the orchestra's history. Several things about this plan strike one as strange. If one wonders which way it should face,[18] later versions in books by Hans-Joachim Nösselt[19] and Schünemann,[20] undoubtedly based on this one, would seem to remove any doubt: both have the keyboard player with his back to the audience. Yet it is quite contrary to Quantz's plan and contrary to eighteenth-century etiquette to have any player's back to the audience in a concert situation. It would also seem unusual to have the first violins farther from the audience than the seconds and the singers behind them. Still, if one wanted to argue that such a placement would be backwards, that the point of the harpsichord should face the audience, then on the other side, the bassoons and double basses would be in front of the oboes and flutes. A baroque-type seating, on the other hand, continues in the placing of the violins all on one side.

This seems a fitting place to interject that "seating" must be understood in a generic sense here. While seating is a suitable word for opera performances, it seems highly probable that in concert situations, the performers stood to play, except for cellists, bassoonists, and keyboard players. In some places this custom lasted even into the twentieth century. One observer of the *Liebhaberconcert* in Berlin in 1787 noticed that horns, oboes, and violas sat,

Figure 8.   Another Possible Realization of Quantz's Plan

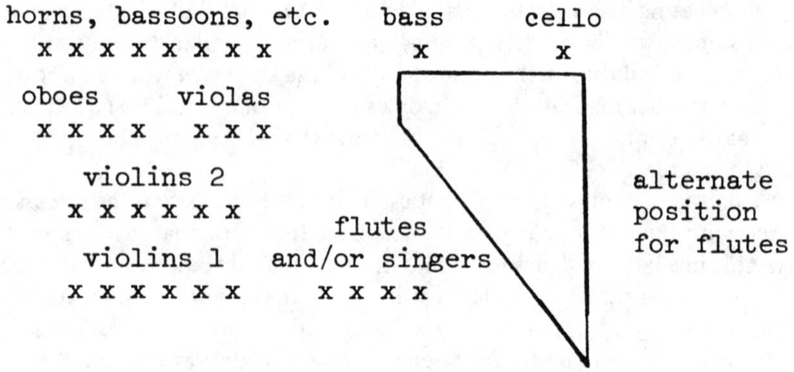

```
horns, bassoons, etc.   bass      cello
  x x x x x x x           x          x

   oboes      violas
   x x x x    x x x

      violins 2                              alternate
      x x x x x x        flutes              position
      violins 1      and/or singers          for flutes
      x x x x x x      x x x x
```

Author's suggestion of a possible deduction.

but the other players stood.[21] And there are a number of extant illustrations that attest to such a practice.[22] However, standing was not a universal practice and musicians possibly sat to play in Vienna, as suggested by the experience of Dittersdorf when he became head of the orchestra of the Bishop of Grosswardein in 1764. He ordered long benches and desks to be made and introduced the "Viennese plan" of having the players sit to play, arranging the benches so that "every player fronted his audience."[23] If the players did not "front" the audience before this, one wonders if they were perhaps in some sort of semicircular arrangement so that the players on each side faced sideways. There is documentation of such arrangements extant from the eighteenth century. Only in opera was a player seated with his back actually to the audience, and there it was for reasons of coherence and visibility of the leader.

Referring back to the Leipzig plan (see fig. 9), one can see how much could be obtained from 27 performers. The two horn players doubled on viola and second violin respectively. If trumpets and drums were needed, a first violinist and the second oboist played trumpet, and the first horn switched to timpani. Both oboists doubled on flute, and if both oboes and flutes were needed, one of the bassoons would help on flute. A slight reading knowledge of German will show other doublings, including two of the singers on viola.

In a tract on the duties of a conductor published in 1782,[24] Carl Junker considered among other things the proper placement of an orchestra. His

Figure 9. Leipzig, Concert Society, 1746–48

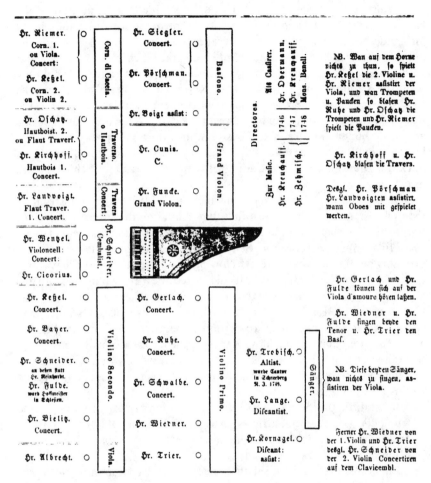

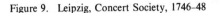

Source: Dörffel/GEWANDHAUS, p. 6.

description leaves much unsaid and is not easy to visualize. Schünemann succeeded perhaps as well as can be expected (fig. 10).

Junker echoed Quantz and Rousseau in stating that the position of the keyboard instrument determined the distribution of the other parts (admitting difficulties in the case of the organ because of space problems). However, he did not state which way the keyboard should face. Schünemann's placing it with the player's back to the audience does seem questionable, even if only from the standpoint of etiquette. Like Rousseau, Junker also felt that the basses belonged around the keyboard instrument in order to transmit the tempo, with one player standing directly near the keyboard player. If one accepts Schünemann's keyboard position, then the above positioning of the basses would seem to follow. But the keyboard player could be facing outward; then only the one leading bass would change in Schünemann's drawing.

Junker did not actually state on which side of the keyboard instrument the violas should be placed, just that they should border on the basses. The horns should be behind the basses and the trumpets and timpani behind them, according to his description. Schünemann had ignored this somewhat, probably because of what a literal following of Junker's plan would have done to the horn players' visibility. He did place the first violins next to the keyboard instrument, opposite the violas, but again they could just as easily have been on the right and fit his description. One wonders if Schünemann chose this arrangement to portray Junker because it became traditional. Junker allowed that one might want to place the second violins directly across from the firsts, but then the violas might come sidewards towards the basses, perhaps more to the left than in Schünemann's drawing (if one accepts second violins on the right).

It is difficult to interpret Junker's positioning of "the other wind instruments, such as oboes, flutes, clarinets." They should "stand farthest from the basses, below the string instruments." Perhaps Schünemann's position is as viable as one can get.[25]

But Junker acknowledged that there were also orchestras for which special stages were erected; in such cases he found the above described distribution not useful. He fully approved of such stages, not only because of improved musical effect, but because they afforded greater freedom and ease to the orchestra in general and the solo player in particular, since no noble who could "scrape or pipe" a bit would be behind him, looking at his music and embarrassing him. In a footnote he added tellingly that there must be absolutely no one except the players on these stages.

To Junker these stages yield another smaller advantage: one could see the whole orchestra, all the players were in sight, and the sounds united in a better harmonic whole. Such stages rose gradually, as did the *parterre*. The keyboard instrument should stand so that "it butts on the beginning of the

Figure 10.   Seating Plan Drawn after Junker

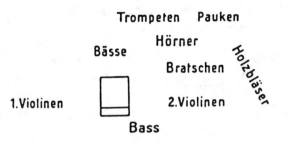

Source: Schünemann/DIRIGIERENS, p. 191.

stage." These stages had to be deep enough for each player to hear the keyboard, thus facilitating true definition of the tempo.

Singers belonged at the keyboard, reading from one part with the keyboard player. This allowed for greatest security of pitch and rhythm for the singer, since it was the keyboard player whose duty it was to give the pitch to the singer and otherwise help or even restrain him. Obviously the singers could not be dispersed around the keyboard in such a situation, but could only stand sidewards to the keyboard, next to one another. Note that Junker's ideas on the singer reading from the score behind the keyboard differ starkly from those of Quantz, who found difficulties with such a practice.

Junker would place the row of first violins on the right and the row of seconds opposite on the left. Unless one wants to interpret this as stage right and left, his scheme is the exact opposite of Schünemann's drawing and also of what later became traditional. Junker placed the oboes behind the first violins, the flutes behind the seconds, with the basses in the middle behind the keyboard. The violas could border on the oboes and the cellos on the flutes. But it is strange that neither in this nor the foregoing descriptions did he mention bassoons! Perhaps one can attempt to diagram this description (fig. 11).

With organs, each situation would have to be treated as special. But the Kapellmeister would have to be in the foreground, visible to each player. Interestingly, Junker dubbed the Kapellmeister as "not player but time-beater." This will be discussed in greater detail later.[26]

Junker next gave a description of the Mannheim Hofkapelle up to his time. Schünemann's drawing seems to reproduce the Hofkapelle quite accurately (fig. 12).

Again, the Kapellmeister seems to have been a time-beater; his position is quite modern. Also striking is the positioning of the two violin sections—the firsts "to the right of the Kapellmeister" and "on his left even so, the second

Figure 11. Junker's Orchestra on Stage

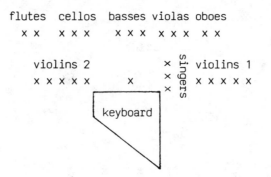

Drawing by author.

Figure 12. Mannheim Hofkapelle, Drawn after Junker

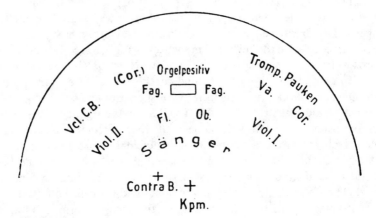

Source: Schünemann/DIRIGIERENS, p. 198.

violins,"[27] unless he were still facing the audience. This drawing may answer the previously raised possibility of stage right. The split between the two sections is confirmed in Mozart's letter to his father from Mannheim in 1777: "Now I was at High Mass in the Kapelle. The orchestra is excellent and very strong. On either side there are ten or eleven violins, four violas, two oboes, two flutes and two clarinets, two horns, four violoncellos, four bassoons and four double basses, also trumpets and drums."[28]

One wonders if by "to the sides"[29] in relation to the positive organ, Junker really meant that the bassoons were split, as Schünemann has them. Also unclear is the position of the horns to the left of the positive organ, in parentheses in the drawing. Junker wrote: "Over the second violins, were even so, the cellos, and contrabasses, also indeed sometimes a double-choir of horns brought in."[30] Does this mean that the second pair of horns was split from those behind the first violins, or were four horns near the cellos and basses, vacating the former position? Junker was not clear on this point.

The organ loft had rising steps, necessary, noted Junker, if the effect of the rear instruments was not to be lost in the church. But he found faults in the foregoing distribution. "First, if the organ links all the harmonizations of the individual instruments, so does it stand too distant...."[31] He would place it where the higher wind instruments are in the drawing. Junker further complained that the Kapellmeister was not visible to all. He found the singers and violins "too deep" under the Kapellmeister and those in the farthest part of the curve too far from him. He would cut the horns from the half-moon or "fill them out" ("*sie ausfüllen*") and move the director forward; "that, it seems to me, would be my cure."[32]

An anonymous traveler to Berlin in 1787 gave a plan for the *Liebhaberconcert* there under the direction of Karl Ludwig Bachmann. It is redrawn in figure 13. The text actually indicated three desks of first violins, including the leader's space, and two desks of seconds. The writer found the plan unsatisfactory because the leader had his back turned to "all the principal people" of the orchestra and they in turn could not see him very well. Note that the first and second violins were both on the same side of the orchestra except for the leader's desk, one row behind the other. It is strange that the oboes were with the horns, separated from the flutes and bassoons which were to the front and side, facing center. The orchestra was raised about a foot and a half.[33]

The same anonymous traveler also presented a plan for the *Concert für Kenner und Liebhaber* in Berlin in 1787. It appears in figure 14, also redrawn from the original. First, note the risers. The writer found this arrangement better in that the concertmaster or *Anführer,* as he called him, stood near the keyboard director ("for in this Concert direction happens with the keyboard") and could easily be seen by the players. It is also noteworthy that the keyboard instrument here was the fortepiano, rather than the harpsichord. That inconsistencies from one group to another existed contemporaneously is illustrated by the fact that here the violins were split—with the firsts again to the right. Both here and in the *Liebhaberconcert* the habit of having bass instruments near the keyboard instrument lingered. "Basses" in both plans undoubtedly included cellos as well as double basses. Here, flutes and oboes were together, split from the bassoons, which in turn were separated from the horns.

One other plan reproduced by Schünemann is worth looking at because of some strange features (fig. 15). He attributed it to J. S. Petri. First of all, this

Figure 13.   Berliner *Liebhaberconcert*

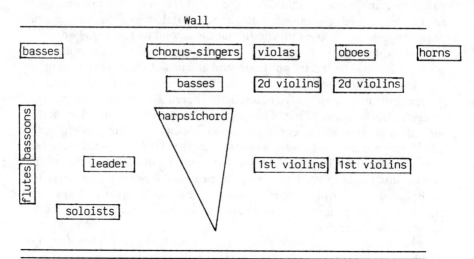

Redrawn from BEMERKUNGEN, pp. 12–13.

Figure 14.   *Concert für Kenner und Liebhaber,* Berlin

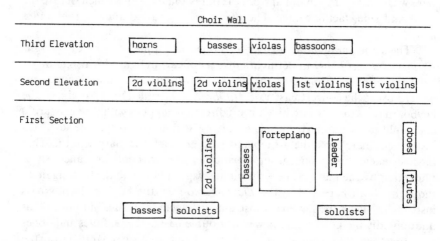

Redrawn from BEMERKUNGEN, pp. 25–26.

Figure 15. Petri's Seating Plan

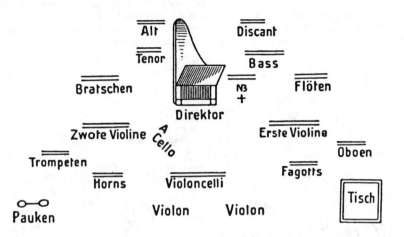

Source: Originally, from J.S. Petri, *Anleitung zur praktischen Musik,* Leipzig, 1782, here from Schünemann/ DIRIGIERENS, p. 192.

plan seems to face the opposite way to most of the others. It would be difficult to accept the timpani and basses as nearest the audience, the singers furthest away, and the keyboard director with his back to the listeners. Taking that for granted, then the split violin sections were like the later tradition, firsts to the left from the audience's viewpoint. Note that the woodwinds were separated from each other and from the horns which were further back than the trumpets! And the violas were in front of the second violins. Petri also thought it important that the violin leader be at the side of the keyboard director and be able to see him well and thus lead his forces well. The first cellist ("A Cello" in the plan) was also near the keyboard and read from the same score or figured bass as the director. Sitting sidewards, he could lead the other basses well ("NB" and "+" denote the places of the solo singers.)[34]

Neal Zaslaw credits Haydn with introducing an amphitheater arrangement for the London concerts of 1791–93. He has hypothetically reconstructed the placement according to contemporary descriptions, a plan worthy of reproduction here considering the importance of these concerts (fig. 16). Here the two violin sections are separated in the later manner, firsts to the left. Again one is left wondering whether this was stipulated in the descriptions or conjectured because they were divided. The basses and cellos on both wings would become a common feature of many nineteenth-century arrangements. Note that in the plan that Haydn is facing the audience with Salomon in proximity to him and visible to all the players. Also interesting is the way the

Figure 16.   Haydn-Salomon Concerts, London, 1791–93
Hypothetical reconstruction (by Neal Zaslaw, after contemporary sources) of the amphitheatre arrangement of the orchestra introduced to London by Haydn for the Salomon concerts of 1791–93: positions are indicated for the organ, chorus and soloists (although oratorios were not given at these concerts).

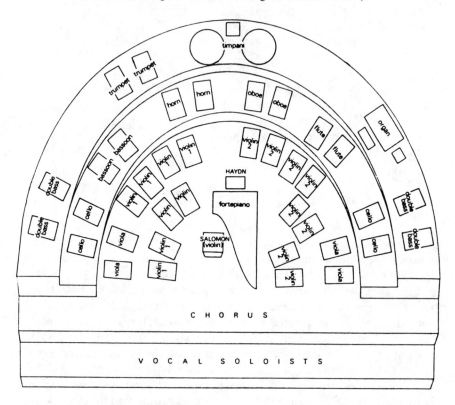

Source: Westrup, Zaslaw & Selfridge-Field/ORCHESTRA, p. 829, with the kind permission of Dr. Neal Zaslaw, Stanley Sadie, and the Royal Musical Association. This plan corrects the diagram appearing in Zaslaw/REVIVAL, p. 165, and in Westrup & Zaslaw/ORCHESTRA, p. 684, which has Haydyn with his back to the audience and Salomon in the curve of the piano and thus on the second-violin side of that instruments.

woodwinds and horns were in a ring around the higher strings with the bassoons near other bass instruments.

Although "monster" performances are really out of the mainstream and subject to special exigencies, it is perhaps interesting to peruse two available plans briefly. Burney provided the plan of the Handel Commemoration of 1784 in Westminster Abbey (fig. 17), numbers for which have already been discussed.[35] Probably the most immediately striking aspect of this plan is the

Figure 17. Plan for 1784 Handel Commemoration

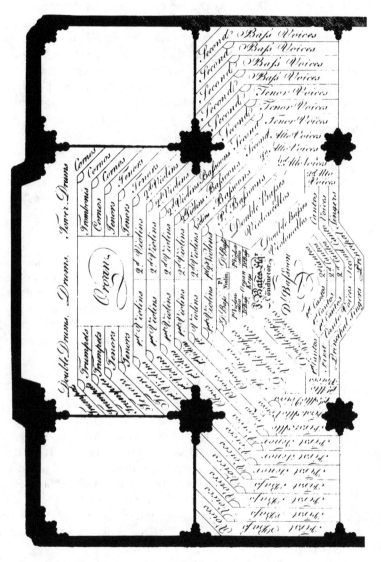

Source: Burney/HANDEL, facing p. 26 (after 56).

position of the double bassoon—indeed the fact that a double bassoon should appear in a work of Handel at all! But further study discloses that trombones and extra drums have also been added to the orchestra.

Further perusal reveals that the violins were bunched together in the middle, with no real separation between the two sections. Cellos, basses, and bassoons were toward the front around the organ console, much as might be expected in a baroque orchestra, given the loss of intimacy here. On the other hand, the violas were split on both sides of the organ, though not possibly for any antiphonal effect—they had so little to do polyphonically. But the choir was also divided, doubtless to accommodate works on the program with double choruses. Missing are places for the flutes which were mentioned in the lists of both Burney and Cramer.[36]

The performance of *Messiah* in Berlin two years later had the plan illustrated in figure 18. Here the orchestra numbered 189 against 119 voices. Note that the position of the director suggests a time-beating conductor—perhaps not unusual for such forces. The violin leader was closer to him than to his cohorts. But here the first and second violins were divided—the firsts to the left in the more modern manner—with basses and cellos between them. But again the violas were split on both sides, seemingly with no rationale evident. Handel did not divide the violas in *Messiah* as J. S. Bach might have done. The orchestra was evidently on risers with the timpani in the organ loft, while trumpets, trombones, and the choir were on raised platforms level with the organ loft, each group separated by pillars. Note also that flutes and bassoons were together, while oboes and horns were on the opposite side— strange bedfellows to modern ears, though there are some baroque scores that might suggest such positions.

Some Conclusions on Eighteenth-Century Seating

Perhaps some generalizations can be drawn at this point. First of all, the keyboard instrument was the focal point in most seating plans. Its place was almost without exception such that its player could be seen by all the others. It was lacking in only a few of these groups (e.g., the Berlin Opera and Mannheim), and these were late in the century, suggesting the later classical style. Other continuo instruments were clustered around the keyboard. Exceptions to this would seem to be really modern and possibly questionable from a historical standpoint (e.g., Terry's Bach layout and the plan drawn after Max Seiffert).

First and second violins were generally grouped in proximity early in the century. Even where there was space or other instruments between them (as in Rousseau's depiction of Dresden, where violas were between firsts and seconds), they were on the same side of the orchestra; there seems to be no

Figure 18. Handel's *Messiah* in Domkirchen, Berlin, 1786

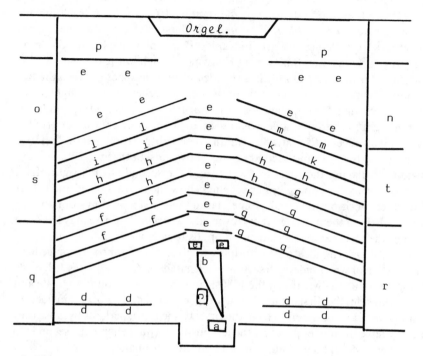

a) *Director.*

b) *Flügel, mit einem Violon-*
   cell u. Violon zur Seite.

c) *Anführer der Violinen.*

d) *Principal Sänger.*

e) *Violoncelle und Violone.*

f) *Erste Violinen.*

g) *Zweyte Violinen.*

h) *Bratschen.*

i) *Flöten.*

k) *Oboen.*

l) *Fagotte.*

m) *Waldhörner.*

n) *Trompeten.*

o) *Posaunen.*

p) *Pauken.*

q) *Discantstimmen.*

r) *Altstimmen.*

s) *Tenorstimmen.*

t) *Bassstimmen.*

Nota p p ist das Orgelchor, wo in der Mitte ein Stück der Brustlehne heraus-
genommen ist; diesem wagrecht laufende Tribunen auf beyden Seiten der Kirche
sind o, n, s, t, q, r, die durch Pfeiler von einander abgesondert werden.

Reconstructed after Hiller/NACHRICHT, p. 28.

attempt at an antiphonal effect. Later in the century, however, seemingly with the advent of the classical style, the two violin sections were more often separated. Often the firsts were to the right, contrary to later developments (Berlin Opera, *Concert für Kenner und Liebhaber,* Junker, Mannheim), but sometimes to the left (San Carlo in Naples, Petri's plan, the Haydn-Salomon concerts, the 1784 London Handel Festival—though not really separated— and the 1786 Berlin *Messiah*). But the idea of putting space between the two sections seems to be characteristic of the classic orchestra. This might strike one as surprising, for if the purpose is to clarify two voices contrapuntally, at first thought the baroque style would seem to be the more contrapuntal of the two. This also seems to contradict Adam Carse's observation that the "relative positions of the first and second violins show no sign that the 19th-century custom of placing the firsts to the left and the seconds to the right of the conductor was developing. Some schemes show them so arranged and others show their positions reversed. Some placed their first violins in front and the seconds behind them, while others reversed that order."[37] Carse may have lost sight of the fact that the placement on opposite sides was a later development, and that it was the idea of the antiphonal effect that formed the precedent, irrespective of which side each section is relegated to. Zaslaw quotes J. J. O. de Meude-Monpas as writing in the 1780s: "put the second violins opposite and not alongside the firsts," not stipulating either side.[38] Some nineteenth-century plans will be seen to have the firsts to the right, perhaps because they usually have the higher part and the left position would enable the seconds to have their f-holes facing out, giving them more brilliance.

On the other hand, aside from the fact that trumpets and timpani were set logically either to the rear or to one side, it is difficult to argue with Carse's appraisal that "the disposal of the woodwind players is as varied as that of the strings. There seems to have been no generally accepted plan, except in so much that they are not usually placed together in a compact group, nor are they strung out in a straight line or in a semi-circle."[39] In Quantz's opera plan, horns and oboes were together, while in his concert plan, horns were with bassoons. In the Dresden Opera plan, horns and woodwinds were on the same side of the orchestra but quite spread out, while in the Berlin Opera, horns were with clarinets and on the opposite side from the other woodwinds, which were grouped together. And if all these instruments were quite compactly together in the Leipzig plan, horns and oboes were together and rather distant from flutes and bassoons, which were neighbors in the *Berliner Liebhaberconcert.* But in the plan for the Berlin *Concert für Kenner und Liebhaber,* flutes and oboes were off to the side and bassoons and horns were at opposite rear corners. Apparently only Mannheim anticipated later usage.

5

Conducting in the Eighteenth Century

In the eighteenth century, a time-beating conductor, wielding some implement other than an instrument which he played at least part of the time, was more the exception than the rule, at least as far as orchestral performance was concerned. In Germany and Italy, such a time beater might be employed in church or some other situation where the performing forces were quite spread out.

The frontispiece of Walther's *Musikalisches Lexicon* already referred to above shows such a time beater with a roll of paper in each hand, standing near the organist. This or some other such picture perhaps inspired Bach's position in Terry's layout (see fig. 1). He explained that "Since Bach occasionally used the harpsichord and organ, displacing the regular player of the latter, he would adopt a position as conductor which would give him quick access to both keyboards, and at the same time enable him to control his singers and players."[1] Yet in 1738 Johann Matthias Gesner described Bach as conducting from the keyboard. After an enraptured description of Bach's clavier and organ playing, he continued:

> If you could see him, I say, doing what many of your citharoedists and six hundred of your tibia players together could not do, not only, like a citharoedist, singing with one voice and playing his own parts, but watching over everything and bringing back to the rhythm and the beat, out of thirty or even forty musicians, the one with a nod, another by tapping with his foot, the third with a warning finger, giving the right note to one from the top of his voice, to another from the bottom, and to a third from the middle of it—all alone, in the midst of the greatest din made by all the participants, and, although he is executing the most difficult parts himself, noticing at once whenever and wherever a mistake occurs, holding everyone together, taking precautions everywhere, and repairing any unsteadiness, full of rhythm in every part of his body—this one man taking in all these harmonies with his keen ear and emitting with his voice alone the tone of all the voices.[2]

Perhaps it should be pointed out that Gesner was addressing his remarks to Marcus Fabius Quintilianus.

On the other hand, C. P. E. Bach, in a letter to Forkel in 1774, had his father leading as a violinist.

He heard the slightest wrong note even in the largest combinations. As the greatest expert and judge of harmony, he liked best to play the viola, with appropriate loudness and softness. In his youth, and until the approach of old age, he played the violin clearly and penetratingly, and thus kept the orchestra in better order than he could have done with the harpsichord.[3]

There seems to be great discrepancy here. Could C. P. E. have been referring to chamber or orchestral performance, perhaps in Cöthen, while Gesner was describing church or choral performance?

What is clear is that, for the most part, orchestral direction in the eighteenth century was under the dual control of the keyboard-playing *Kapellmeister* and the leader of the violins or the *Konzertmeister*. The primary figure in this partnership was probably determined according to whether the arena was the opera house, the concert platform, or the church, or even one locale or another.

As theorists, Quantz and C. P. E. Bach differed as to who should be leader. Quantz favored violin leadership. "Whether a leader plays this instrument or that may be of no importance. Since, however, the violin is absolutely indispensable in the accompanying body, and is also more penetrating than any of the other instruments used for accompanying, it is better if he does play the violin."[4] He then continued at length concerning the qualities necessary for leadership.

However, C. P. E. Bach held the conviction "that the keyboard is and must always remain the guardian of the beat."[5] He elaborated on this belief:

The keyboard, entrusted by our fathers with full command, is in the best position to assist not only the other bass instruments but the entire ensemble in maintaining a uniform pace. . . . time is beaten today only in larger compositions. The tone of the keyboard which, correctly placed, stands in the center of the ensemble, can be clearly heard by all. And I know that even diffuse, elaborate compositions played by impromptu, average performers can be held together simply by its tone. If the first violinist stands near the keyboard as he should, disorder cannot easily spread. . . . Should someone hasten or drag, he can be most readily corrected by the keyboardist, for the others will be too much concerned with their own figures and syncopations to be of any assistance. Especially those parts that employ the tempo rubato will find herein a welcome, emphatic beat. Finally, it is easy (and often necessary) to make minor changes of tempo by this means because exact perception will not be hindered by the keyboard's excessive noise, and, in addition, those performers located in front of or beside the keyboard will find in the simultaneous motion of both hands an inescapable, visual portrayal of the beat.[6]

This is quite a convincing and eloquent defense of keyboard direction, though it is in contradiction with his later evaluation of his father's violin leadership quoted above.

Carse surmised that in these statements, C. P. E. Bach was thinking in terms of the opera and vocal music while Quantz probably had instrumental music in mind.[7] But there seems to be nothing in either context to indicate that such is the case. However, Forkel also considered the keyboard player better fitted to lead, with the first violinist as his adjutant, but for some different reasons. Among the leader's important duties he included insight and taste in choosing pieces for performance. One who played keyboard could weigh the full harmony and gain an insight into the whole field of music with greater facility than one who read only one part. He also mentioned the greater ease with which the keyboard player could control tempo through the basses, and pointed out that if helping erring players was a leader's duty, only the keyboard player could have the whole score before him.[8]

In actual practice, in the opera, the Kapellmeister at the first harpsichord was in charge of the performance as a whole, the voices in particular. He controlled tempo by playing chords, giving cues or notes to singers, playing any part which might go astray. He might move his head or use his feet if necessary to keep the beat, but he evidently did not conduct with his hands. The rest of the group, that is, the orchestra, was under the subordinate control of the Konzertmeister. This accounts for the positions of both of these men in the layouts presented above, where the keyboard leader could be seen by all, and the leader of the violins was stationed in proximity to him. It was at the keyboard that composers would appear for the first performances of their operas, only later relinquishing this position to another for remaining performances. (Remember that Haydn was at the keyboard in the picture of a performance of *L'Incontro improvviso* mentioned earlier—if indeed this picture is authentically Haydn.) And it was to the keyboard that Mozart went when he wanted to resume control of an opera. In reference to *Die Entführung aus dem Serail*, he wrote to his father from Vienna on October 19, 1782:

> The Russian Royalties left Vienna today. My opera was performed for them the other day, and on this occasion I thought it advisable to resume my place at the clavier and conduct it. I did so partly in order to rouse the orchestra who had gone to sleep a little, partly (since I happen to be in Vienna) in order to appear before the royal guests as the father of my child.[9]

However, Neal Zaslaw has pointed out that "Galeazzi makes it quite clear that, leaving aside the first three performances of the opera, which the composer led from the first harpsichord, by 1791 the *primo violino* had full control of the performance, and that both instrumentalists and singers followed his signals."[10] Whether this held for countries outside of Italy is not clear.

In concert performances (symphonies, concertos, etc.), the keyboard director might sometimes be primary, but more often the violin leader took control with the keyboard player as his subordinate. One would draw such an inference from Mozart's letter to his father from Paris, July 3, 1778, concerning his Symphony K.297 [300a].

I have had to compose a symphony for the opening of the Concert Spirituel.... I was very nervous at the rehearsal, for never in my life have I heard a worse performance.... I decided next morning not to go to the concert at all; but in the evening, the weather being fine, I at last made up my mind to go, determined that if my symphony went as badly as it did at the rehearsal, I would certainly make my way into the orchestra, snatch the fiddle out of the hands of Lahoussaye, the first violin, and conduct myself.[11]

At Esterháza, Haydn reportedly conducted from the position of first violin. Forkel's list of this orchestra for 1783, for example, showed Haydn as *"Direktor und Capellmeister,"* adding "Also plays first violin."[12] On the other hand, in the previously cited letter on the cantata *Applausus,* Haydn gave instructions on when the orchestra should enter in accompanied recitatives (after the singer has "quite finished his text, even though the score often shows the contrary"). But he finished with "But I leave this to the harpsichord player, and all the others must follow him."[13] Of course, since voices were involved, perhaps primacy shifted.

In discussing the situation at Leipzig's *Grossen Concerts* in the 1740s, Creuzburg stated that in choral works, ensemble pieces, and concertos, the Musikdirektor sat at the harpsichord and "'directed' from here." But orchestral works were "directed" more often by the Konzertmeister who played with them himself, giving the sign for the beginning and occasional cues. He added that the practice of the Konzertmeister leading purely orchestral works lasted there through the beginning of the nineteenth century, the first true *"Dirigent"* in the Gewandhaus being Mendelssohn.[14] In fact, such practice would suggest the origin of the word Konzertmeister: he who was "master" in purely orchestral "concerts."

Looking back earlier, Dart mentioned a performance of *Il Trionfo di Tempo* with Corelli leading the overture and Handel playing continuo. He claimed that Handel took the violin to show how it should be played.[15] And about 1751, Dittersdorf described Gluck rehearsing for concerts in Vienna.

A rehearsal was always held on the evening before the concert, so as to ensure a perfect and accurate rendering of all the music, and particularly of the new things; and on these occasions Gluck, violin in hand, appeared *à la tête* of the orchestra, which had been strengthened as usual by a large number of the choicest players. No wonder that our Academies were acknowledged to be the best in all Vienna![16]

In England also, double direction seems to have been the rule, and one gets the impression that the violin leader had primacy there over the keyboard "conductor." And if the famous Salomon concerts of 1791 with Haydn "presiding" at a piano would seem to contradict this, Haydn's presence was probably more honorary, and one suspects that Salomon had real control from his desk as concertmaster.

Parke's observations point to the primacy of the violinist leader in the England of the 1780s and 1790s. He described the leader of a concert at Vauxhall Gardens in 1787 as being in an elevated seat.[17] He spoke of Haydn's presence at the Salomon concerts of 1791, saying that he was there "to preside during the performance of his symphonies, but calling Salomon the leader.[18] On the other hand, he mentioned Pleyel coming to England the same year to write 12 pieces and "to direct them at the piano-forte."[19] But his description of a Handel concert in 1796 with an orchestra of five hundred "ably led by Cramer" would again seem to give credit and, therefore, primacy, to the violin leader.[20] Even in the grandiose Handel concerts of 1791 with a thousand performers, "Cramer led the band, and Mr. Bates presided at the organ."[21]

France was seemingly unique, for time beating was evidently the rule, and often audible time beating at that, using a large wooden stick.[22] Rousseau complained bitterly of the *"bruit insupportable"* at the Opéra in Paris which covered and deadened the effect of the orchestra.[23] The practice went back at least to the seventeenth century; the story of Lulli and his self-inflicted, fatal foot wound is well known.[24] The practice was not restricted to the Opéra either; Bobillier wrote, for example, of a *batteur de mesure* at the *Concert spirituel* who, armed first with a cane, later with a short stick or roll of paper, helped himself noisily with his heel on the floor. In 1762, the *"mode d'Italie"* was tried there with Gaviniés at the head of the first violins, setting off controversy between partisans of the Italian and French styles. The attempt did not last, evidently abandoned when Gaviniés left the orchestra in 1764.[25] However, one has to wonder if the manner had again changed by 1778 when Mozart reacted by swearing to grab the violin to take over the orchestra.

Carse maintained that the *batteur de mesure* at the Opéra *"was in no sense the conductor of the orchestra,* but was there solely in order to make the time-beat audible to the scattered chorus singers and dancers on the large stage."[26] And Zaslaw makes clear that he was there "to set the tempo and keep the forces together—not to 'interpret' the music."[27] He incidentally also claims that it was only in large-scale choral and dance pieces that he "beat his stick on his music desk" in order to maintain the tempo and that he made patterns in the air in solo and other smaller ensembles.[28] But Bobillier, in discussing the situation at the *Concert spirituel* in 1762, included in the table of personnel "two conductors designated thus: 'M. Dauvergne beats the time; M. Aubert is his assistant'," using the term *chef d'orchestre* for conductor.[29] And, according to Blaze, around 1774 the Académie (or Opéra) proposed to Beck, *"chef d'orchestre* at the Bordeaux theater," that he come there to "take up the *bâton de mesure.*"[30] These examples challenge the idea that the *batteur* was no more than a time beater with no other authority. Other examples could be found.

The "French" style must have spilled over to other places. Burney reported that in 1772 a theater orchestra in Brussels was under the direction of a *"maestro di capella,* who beats the time" and a M. Vanmaldere who "plays the principal violin, though the violoncello is his instrument."[31] And Parke reported a humorous incident at Drury Lane in 1786, where at rehearsals for a performance of a "popular French piece," the leader "impatiently exclaimed, 'Mr. Kemble, that won't do at all!—you *murder* time abominably!" (Kemble having the leading role). "'Well, Mr. Shaw,' replied Kemble, 'it is better to *murder* it, than to be continually *beating* it as you are.'"[32] Parke seemed to share with Burney an aversion to time beating. He also reported a benefit concert of The New Musical Fund in 1787 "under the direction of Dr. Hayes and Dr. Miller, who, with a large roll of parchment, beat time most unmercifully."[33] In another place, Parke discussed the Handel Commemoration of 1784 in Westminster Abbey and the fact that Dr. Hayes and Dr. Miller had offered to split the duties of conducting by beating time:

> When the time of performance had arrived, and Mr. Cramer, the leader, had just tapt his bow (the signal for being ready), and looked round to catch the eyes of the performers, he saw, to his astonishment, a tall gigantic figure, with an immense powdered toupee, full dressed, with a bag and sword, and a huge roll of parchment in his hand.... "Who is that gentleman?" said Mr. Cramer.—"Dr. Hayes," was the reply.—"What is he going to do?"— "To beat time"—"Be so kind," said Mr. Cramer, "to tell the gentleman that when he has sat down I will begin." The Doctor, who never anticipated such a *set down* as this, took his seat, and Mr. Cramer did begin, and his Majesty and all present bore witness to his masterly style of leading the band.[34]

Indeed, Burney, in discussing the Commemoration, wrote that "Foreigners, particularly the French, must be astonished at so numerous a band moving in such exact measure, without the assistance of a *Coryphaeus* to beat the time, either with a roll of paper, or a noisy *baton* or truncheon. Rousseau says, that 'the more time is beaten, the less it is kept.'"[35] Even in the 1786 *Messiah* in Berlin, which also had large numbers of performers involved, time was only beaten in some of the choral movements.[36]

However, one gets the impression that the lack of a time beater did not always mean silent conducting. Not untypical is a complaint that at the Italian opera, the violin leader, stamping his foot "like one possessed," could be heard to the end of the hall, while the keyboard player struck chords so roughly he would have done well to have worn leather gloves in order not to break his fingers.[37] And even Mozart in a concert of his works at the Gewandhaus in Leipzig in 1789, stamped so energetically in an effort to keep the tempo from flagging that the buckle flew off one of his shoes. (There are discrepancies in the reports as to whether this occurred at the rehearsal or at the concert, but considering who it was, one would like to hope it was at the former.)[38] And probably significant in this regard is the compliment paid Dittersdorf after he conducted his *Der Apotheker* at Charlottenburg in 1789. Of course, "there was only room for an orchestra of thirty-six players," but after the first rehearsal, Vachon, first violinist and leader of the King's band, praised Dittersdorf's conducting without "lots of noise and useless grimaces."[39] It is entirely possible that Dittersdorf was already conducting with a silent baton in the later manner; no indication is given. But as time went on, the violin leader took over more and more control, using his bow as a baton, playing only when necessary. Already in the 1780s, Johann Friedrich Reichardt, Kapellmeister at Berlin, had discarded both keyboard and violin, using "silent implements to mark time, control the *ensemble,* and guide the interpretation."[40] Indeed, the anonymous traveler to Berlin in 1787 reported that while the *Liebhaber-concert* was directed by Herr Bachmann, "a wretched violin player, and an extremely miserable leader," and at the *Concert für Kenner und Liebhaber* "the direction took place with the keyboard," at the opera "Mr. Reichardt beat the time, for the very reason that the singers, especially if they were somewhat distant from the orchestra, pulled away wholly in character."[41] His successor, Anselm Weber, was said to have used a leather baton stuffed with hair.

Perhaps because of the audible time beating in France, using a stick, the new method of orchestral conducting with a silent baton, was considered to have been French in origin, at least in Germany. Thus, a report of the French opera at Hamburg in 1799 described the conducting of a Guillaume Alexis Paris "as is quite the general custom in France, by means of a small foot-long stick, mostly through signs," commenting that he was only heard when there was some serious error. The writer seemed surprised that, although the orchestra consisted mostly of local Germans—and Paris spoke no German— Paris made himself quickly intelligible "through the precision and steady equality of his signs."[42] But the full development of this style of conducting belongs to the nineteenth century.

Adam Carse summed up the general practice of orchestral conducting in the eighteenth century as: (a) aural control—the keyboard and violin leaders; (b) visual control—the physical movement of head, arms, or body; and (c) audible control—foot stamping, hammering with an implement, tapping with the bow. He claimed that they were "invoked in that order" with (c) "as a last resort." While the "present system is based on (b), yet it derives from (a)."[43]

Part Two

The Emerging Conductor and His Changing Forces

6

Conducting as a Métier

Although divided leadership, or at least some semblance of it, persisted in some quarters well into the nineteenth century, the métier of conductor is already evident in the words of J. Arnold. How modern sounding, for example, is his dictum that the "fusion of the individual members to the reproduction of a single feeling is the work of the leader, concertmaster, music director, or conductor."[1] This seems quite distant from the eighteenth-century double direction still in vogue in many areas. While Arnold did not recommend a conductor who only beat time, the recognition that such activity existed in 1806 seems implicit in his assertion that "a music director must understand something more than to beat time with a rolled-up sheet of music, or to impel his way raging at the keyboard, and to scrape on the violin and stamp with his feet."[2]

Arnold deplored the fact that musicians and composers were trained in *Kapellen* and conservatories but the art of directing was treated with neglect, beyond the mechanics of time beating and "glancing over a score," evidently in the belief that such art was learned from practice itself.[3] Nor did he accept the notion that one could be a good *Musikdirektor* without "even being able to handle an instrument as a virtuoso."[4] Indeed, Arnold still may have envisioned the conductor as leading primarily with his instrument, rather than always beating time. But what instrument should he play? Acknowledging that many, especially from earlier times, employed a keyboard instrument, he gave preference to the violin. He found that if a piano were used, it was ineffective in full orchestra, and may not even be heard through the ensemble. On the other hand, the Flügel "beats through, to be sure," but its "ringing sounds" spoil the effect of the other instruments without rendering any real service to the director as he is kept so busy with his Flügel-playing that he can concern himself with nothing else.[5]

Arnold added to his considerations the uncertainty of tuning that was as inevitable in winter with the changing room temperature as it was in summer with its greater heat; nor could it be so easily remedied on a keyboard instrument as it could with the violin. Besides, the violin joins the orchestra so well, both in respect to its mechanical handling and its tone. Its tone is penetrating without obscuring other instruments, and its bow is at the same time a natural baton, so that the beat can be marked with it during the playing. Also the violin can help each instrument and replace any which might miss an entrance.[6] "The Flügel cannot do this, for its strumming gives only a disgusting, ineffective disturbance against the tone of the orchestra, and the orchestra is in truth to be pitied, whose unskilled director can play no violin and must make shift only by strumming at the Flügel."[7] Arnold went so far as to postulate that no musician should be accepted as a director unless he were a skilled orchestral violinist, able to execute a violin concerto. A *Flügeldirektor* was a stranger in the orchestra, "who is equally innocent in a succeeding or failing performance," contributing as little to the direction of the whole "as the organist riding backwards in church music."[8]

After further embroidery on these arguments, Arnold summed up by acknowledging that a good *Musikdirektor* must be an accomplished keyboard player, able to play each score at the piano. "Just as indispensable as keyboard playing is for private study, so, on the other side, is violin playing necessary in the orchestra, where he [the director] should not perform but only lead the performance."[9]

F. S. Gassner, writing in the early 1840s, stated that a director should play violin or piano, if possible both, well enough to supply any part which was deficient.[10] A director should not fall short of those in his charge as far as virtuosity was concerned; where words could not suffice, he should be able to demonstrate his will through his instrument.[11]

In addition to choosing works to be performed and having the right conception of these pieces, he should also value the setting of the parts.[12] The conductor should be careful to consider the appropriate setting of all the parts, especially solo parts. "Here let *art* lead him, not however *favor!* On the setting depends the main effect of a work; many a piece has made a bad impression solely on account of an unsuccessful setting, while another less worthwhile composition only through the setting has been able to enjoy general approval."[13]

Gassner never stated that he considered either the bow or the baton as conducting implements, yet this seems implicit in one of his remarks: he deplored the bad effect ensuing when the conductor's presence was not noticed and he had to tap with his bow or baton or even with his snuff box for attention.[14]

On the other hand, at the turn of the century, Friedrich Rochlitz took issue with the disappearance of the keyboard and the growing use of the violin for conducting purposes. He observed that since tempered tuning had become all-pervasive, the surest help in maintaining good intonation was thereby lost, the strings tuning to pure fifths instead. He found the keyboard a most excellent means to hold together "the fullness of the harmony," so necessary in the newest works with their "excess of harmonies and chopped up distribution of single ideas to several instruments" (a development that he blamed on "blind imitators of Mozart"). And finally he noted the keyboard's irreplaceable loss in accompanying recitative. "Have you enough against violin direction? I think, yes!"[15]

The Persistence of Double Direction

The way in which double direction worked in London's Philharmonic Society from its founding in 1813 has been described by George Hogarth, Hon. Secretary of the Society from 1850–64:

> The duty of the leader was not only to execute his own part with exemplary accuracy and firmness, but to attend to all the other performers, who were to look to him for the time of the movements, and to be governed by his beat. His coadjutor, at the pianoforte, and with the full score before him, was to watch the performance and to be ready to correct any mistake. This method, borrowed from the usages (far from uniform) of foreign theatrical and other orchestras, was liable to obvious objections. Neither of these functionaries could efficiently perform his duties separately, and they could not perform them jointly without interfering and clashing with each other. The leader could not execute his own part properly, and at the same time attend to, and beat time to, the whole band; while the person at the pianoforte could scarcely exercise any influence on the "going" of the performance without coming into collision with the leader.[16]

The Society by-laws encouraged a great sharing of authority, particularly in the following article: "There shall not be any distinction of rank in the orchestra, and therefore the station of every performer shall be absolutely determined by the leader of the night."[17] The absence of one permanent leader must have contributed to loose authority and affected the quality of performance.[18]

The person presiding at the piano evidently was not even considered as conducting in any way, despite holding such a title. In discussing two concerts at Hanover Square in 1820, Parke named the leader before the conductor in both cases (one concert was of "antient music," the other a vocal concert). He then continued:

> The leader of an orchestra was formerly considered the conductor (leader and conductor being synonymous terms), but latterly the fashion crept in of having a leader and a conductor also, and the practice has at length become so familiar, that no apparent jealousy exists between them, though the conductor evidently considers himself the best man of the two, feeling perhaps that degree of superiority over the leader which the physician does over the apothecary. This innovation, however, at first gave considerable uneasiness to the leader; but I suppose he was appeased by the conductor in the same way as Trinculo appeases Stephano in the "Tempest," by saying to him, "You shall be king, and I'll be viceroy over you."[19]

This passage indicates two things about so-called double direction in England: (1) that the leader (or concertmaster) was supreme, and (2) that the person presiding at the piano tended to oversee the performance as a helper and corrector (or coach) rather than time giver and interpreter.

In 1823 Moscheles was astonished at the English custom of placing a famous musician in front of the orchestra, seated at a piano. Speaking of a Philharmonic concert, he commented: "What do they mean by the term 'Conductor,' Mr. Clementi? He sits there and turns over the leaves of the score, but after all he cannot, without his marshall's staff, the baton, lead on his musical army. The leader does this, and the conductor remains a nullity."[20] Even in 1831, Moscheles observed that the "conductor" at the Philharmonic concerts was still at the piano, without a baton.[21]

Even large festivals kept this custom. For example, a festival at Wakefield in 1824 with a chorus of 95 and an orchestra of 85 was reported as having Dr. Camidge at the organ, Mr. Knapton at the piano, with Mori and White as leaders.[22] And one at Newcastle in 1824 with a chorus of 64 and an orchestra of 44 had Mr. Thompson at the organ, and listed Sir G. Smart as conductor and Mr. Mori as leader.[23] Although Smart later used a baton, there is no indication that such was the case here. And in the Edinburgh Musical Festival of 1824, with 137 performers, "Mr. Yaniewicz led the band, occasionally assisted by Mr. Loder; and Sir G. Smart conducted."[24] There does not seem to be much doubt who was primary there. Similarly, the Yorkshire Amateur Meeting in 1825 had a "band" of 47, "ably led" by Mr. White, "assisted" by Dr. Camidge.[25]

The primacy of the leader did not die easily in Britain. In 1865 at the Gloucester festival, when Samuel Sebastian Wesley conducted Mendelssohn's Piano Concerto in G Minor with Arabella Goddard as soloist, the music was reported as having gone "well enough" in the "accustomed hands" of the pianist and the leader, a Mr. Blagrove, with the "Doctor's" beat being little regarded. But it did not seem to trouble him.

> Gradually Wesley's face lightened and beamed. The music having hold of him, presently took entire possession. He swayed from side to side; he put down the baton, treated himself to a pinch of snuff with an air of exquisite enjoyment, and then sat motionless, listening. Meanwhile Blagrove conducted with his violin-bow.[26]

François Joseph Fétis made interesting comments on the situation at London's Philharmonic Society in 1829. He could not approve placing the *chef d'orchestre* (leader to the English, but the real conductor to the French) in a position facing the public in the middle of the other violins. "Placed in that way, the *chef* cannot see the players, and cannot direct them with eye and gesture, as M. Habeneck does so well in the concerts of the Paris Conservatory." He wrote that Cramer and Loder who alternated as leaders (*chefs d'orchestre* in his eyes) had to confine themselves to indicating the tempo and to playing all the time as "simple violinists." To see the other players and to truly direct them, they would have had to continually turn "as on a pivot, and to be occupied ceaselessly in raising and lowering the head: that which is impossible." Nor was Fétis entirely pleased with the retention of the *"conducteur au piano"* at these concerts. He understood that in vocal pieces its use could be good because "it helps the singer, especially for recitative"; but in a symphony or a "noisy overture, like the majority of modern compositions," its effect was "null, and must be, so as not to become detrimental"; for if its sound could be heard, its sonority, unforeseen by the composer, would "spoil his thought."[27] In other words, he found the sound of the piano offensive, but did not remark on the pianist's efficacy as a conductor, since, like Parke, he considered the leader to occupy that position. One also notes a certain discrepancy here from the complaint of Moscheles, who did not seem to imply much playing on the part of the "conductor."

Probably quite naturally the situation in the United States reflected English usage early in the century. In a concert program in Philadelphia in 1820, the "Leader" is named before the principal members of the orchestra. Then one finds: "The CONDUCTORS of the VOCAL Music will alternately preside at the ORGAN." The program included 100 performers.[28] And as late as 1841, at a festival performance of Mozart's *Magic Flute* with an orchestra of 64, "Mr. B. C. Cross 'presided at the piano,' probably from force of habit. There could be no other reason in the full orchestra, which included basset-horn and ophicleide."[29] The writer's remarks more than imply that "presiding at the piano" no longer had any effect on the conducting of the music.

There is evidence that in the field of opera the custom of having the composer at the piano for the debut of a new work still lingered on, at least in some situations. In 1824 Rossini became director and composer to the King's Theatre in London. The season began with his new *Zelmira,* and Rossini "was to preside at the piano-forte the first three nights."[30] And in Rome in 1831, Mendelssohn attended the performance of a new opera by Pacini who "appeared at the piano, and was kindly welcomed."[31]

So a "conductor" seated at the piano did not quickly become a thing of the past. Some sat there, turning the pages of the score. Others who adopted the stick still sat at a keyboard, as if unwilling to give up a means of tangibly correcting some errant performer. For example, at the opera in Munich in 1825, the conductor "beat time at a small pianoforte which he touched but once or twice."[32] And in Vienna the same year at the theater in "der Leopoldstadt" the "conductor sat at a queer-toned long pianoforte and beat time with a roll."[33] Also, in England the same year, at the Second Yorkshire Festival, "Dr. Camidge...presided at the organ."[34] At the Italian Opera House in Paris in 1825, Smart found a M. Hérold at the piano. "The leader was Mr. Cassé, who occasionally directed with his bow when necessary."[35]

The Violin Conductor

As has been seen, even in England where double direction seems to have survived the longest, the violin leader proved to be the most hardy survivor. The "conductor" who "presided at the piano" was mostly an anachronistic fixture with little if any effectiveness. So when Parke discussed oratorios given at the Theatre-Royal, Haymarket, he mentioned that "Mr. Salomon led the band."[36] Also typical was the reaction of Sir George Smart in France in 1802. At an open-air concert at the Tuileries Gardens with Napoleon in attendance, "Rode, the great violinist, and solo violinist to the First Consul, led. I could hear the conductor but I could not see him or learn his name."[37] One must assume that some "conductor" was dutifully playing chords at the keyboard; at any rate Smart was evidently not struck with his importance.

In France orchestral playing had been entirely in control of the leading violinist, who sometimes had to beat time with his bow in order to steady the ensemble. As the nineteenth century progressed, this leader developed into a time-beating conductor who now used his bow as a baton. François-Antoine Habeneck (1781–1849) was perhaps the best known of these. He was chief conductor at the famous Paris Conservatory concerts as well as at the Opéra for almost two decades, his career spanning the transition from violin leader to time-beating *chef d'orchestre*.[38] Even Wagner was amazed in 1839 at the precision and understanding with which the Conservatory Orchestra under Habeneck performed the Beethoven Symphonies.[39] Wagner's report had precedence in Henry F. Chorley's observations on a visit to Paris in the 1830s:

> Nothing can exceed his perfect sway over his forces. Though he directs with his violin bow, I have never seen him use it; and by the exquisite neatness and precision of the least important or most unmanageable instruments (the *piccoli*, for example), as they enter, not *scramble*, into their parts when the composition demands them, it may be seen that his presence is everywhere—that his method and meaning have pervaded the whole hundred he commands ere they are paraded before the public.[40]

High praise indeed for the old style, echoed by A. Elwart: "Habeneck, at the Conservatory, has all his world under his hand; thus he obtains an ensemble unknown here."[41] "Here" meant Bonn, Germany, in 1845, at the Beethoven celebrations. One has to wonder, though, if Habeneck had tried the stick and found it unsatisfactory, for Elwart earlier stated that Habeneck replaced Kreutzer at the head of the Opéra orchestra (ca. 1824?). "It was at the first performance of *Comte Ory* that Habeneck put aside the baton to conduct with the bow. The shadow of J. J. Rousseau, who had so ridiculed the woodcutter of French opera, must have leaped for joy."[42]

However, one will remember that it was principally the noise to which Rousseau objected, and evidently even Habeneck could be reduced to noisy moments. In one of his entertaining tales, Berlioz claimed that

Habeneck noticed some twenty years ago that the people on the stage paid little attention to his gestures, hardly ever looked at him, and consequently often missed their cues. Since he could not speak to their eyes, he conceived the idea of warning their ears, by rapping with the end of the bow he uses to conduct, thus: *tack!*—a smart rap of wood on wood, which can be heard through all the more or less harmonious emissions of the other instruments. This beat preceding the beat that opens the phrase has today become the one necessity of all performers at the Opéra.[43]

This and the amusing story of the prompter on whose box Habeneck was supposed to have tapped may have been embroidered by exaggeration, knowing Berlioz's grudge against Habeneck, but there is probably at least a basis of truth in the whole story. The root of the grudge: Habeneck, according to Berlioz, "laid down his baton and, calmly producing his snuff-box, proceeded to take a pinch of snuff"[44]—right at a tenuous moment of the *Tuba mirum* of Berlioz's *Requiem,* one of the forces moving Berlioz to a conducting career himself. This incident has been corroborated in some places,[45] but has also been refuted.[46] (Incidentally, did Berlioz really mean "baton" here or was it the "bow"?)

Louis Spohr found violin conducting at La Scala in Milan when he was there in 1816:

The performance surpassed my expectations. It was clean, strong, and secure. Rolla, an artist already known beyond the borders of Italy as a composer, conducted from his post as leader of the violins. There was no further direction, either from piano or time beater, except for a prompter who occasionally beat time for the chorus.[47]

However, in Paris in 1820–21, he was not so pleased at the Italian Opera.

The orchestra, rated by Parisians the best in the world, had some bad moments. The winds failed conspicuously on two occasions, and several times things got so out of hand that the director had to resort to beating time. I am more convinced than ever that a theater orchestra, be it ever so good, can only be directed by continuous time-beating, if only because the outer extremities of the orchestra are too far apart. Certainly it is not sufficient to attempt to mark time as Grasset did, by movements of his body and his violin.[48]

Of the Court Chapel at Paris during the same trip, Spohr noted that the "directors do not themselves conduct the music, but rather preside in court dress at the head of the choir, without actually taking part in the performance. The actual musical director is Plantade. Kreutzer is leader of the first violins, and Baillot, of the second violins."[49]

Sir George Smart noted in Vienna in 1825, "There was no director of the orchestra";[50] does this suggest direction from the first violin? At the Italian Opera in Paris the same year, Smart found: "At the pianoforte, placed as at our opera-house, was M. Hérold. The leader was M. Cassé, who occasionally directed with his bow when necessary."[51] But in a theater at Stuttgart, also the same year, "the conductor stood in the centre facing the stage beating time with his violin bow and occasionally playing the violin."[52] All of this suggests a varying practice. And in Cologne in 1825 at the opera, "Weber, an elder brother of Weber at Dresden, is the director. He beat time at the usual place in the centre with his violin bow, only using his violin once."[53]

Although in England a "conductor" still overlooked the score while seated at the piano or organ, we note with interest whom Parke mentioned in reporting a music festival at York in September of 1828. "The band, led by F. Cramer, consisted of six hundred, two hundred and fifty of whom were instrumental, and three hundred and fifty vocal performers!"[54] Note that "band" here included the singers as well as the players and that there was no doubt as to whom was in control.

In reading Berlioz's *Mémoires,* one has to wonder whether Meyerbeer was a violin conductor. On a trip to Germany that began in 1841, Berlioz wrote to Habeneck concerning the Berlin Opera:

> Chorus and orchestra were at full strength—120 voices, 28 violins, double wind—and Meyerbeer in command at the first desk. I was eager to see him conduct, especially to see him conduct his own work. He does it as a man would a job he has been doing for twenty years; he holds the orchestra in the hollow of his hand and does with it as he pleases.[55]

These quotations more and more noted the growing sense of the concept of a conductor in control, whether he held bow or baton.

Violin leading was also common in the United States early in the century. One observer talks of a performance in the new Howard Atheneum in Boston. "It had, for those days, quite a sizable orchestra. The leader sat facing the stage, and was for a long time the only first violin."[56] Sizable, indeed! The same writer discussed an opera "troupe" in Boston

> with Arditi (afterwards so well known) as *maestro,* or conductor, and first violin,—it being the custom in those days for the leader to beat time with his bow, playing on his violin when he desired to assist or to animate his men. This fashion still prevails in many parts of the world. Johann Strauss, the famous waltz composer, played the violin when conducting his compositions in the second Gilmore Jubilee. His brother Eduard, who more recently visited this country with his own orchestra, conducted in the same way.[57]

On Johann Strauss's appearance at the Second Peace Jubilee in 1872, he wrote:

> Strauss, violin in hand, conducted the orchestra daily.... His manner of conducting was very animating. He led off with the violin bow to give the *tempo,* but when the right swing was obtained and the melody was singing out from the orchestra, he joined in with his fiddle as if he *must* take part in the intoxication of the waltz. While playing or conducting he commonly kept his body in motion, rising and falling on his toes in a really graceful manner.[58]

The same writer observed that when the Steyermark Orchestra came to the United States in 1846, "they numbered about twenty men, good players, with Francis Riha as first violin and director...."[59] And in 1848, the Lombardi Orchestra visited "with August Fries as leader and first violin."[60]

In Europe, when Jules Pasdeloup founded the Société des Jeunes Artistes du Conservatoire in 1851, he conducted with a violin bow.[61] And a visitor to Italy in 1856, commenting on two Verdi operas at Trieste, observed:

> You know in Italy the director only *rehearses* the opera; in the performances there is no conductor; the *first violin* leads, as used to be the case before Costa's time in London. The result is sometimes a want of precision, very different from German clockwork playing; however they accompanied at Trieste the delicate parts beautifully.[62]

It is conceivable that Paganini conducted his legendary performances as he played violin. The following language would certainly suggest as much.

> For a few moments he stood before his breathless audience, as if thinking of what he should play; then he slowly placed the violin under his chin, as deliberately raised his bow and let it rest on the strings, as if meditating how to proceed. Having apparently made up his mind, he turned to the orchestra, and, with a gentle inclination of his head, gave the signal to commence.[63]

In the Leipzig theater the concertmaster seems to have controlled the performance at least as much as the conductor well into the 1840s. In Nösselt's description, "The *Musikdirektor* sits directly in front of the stage, in order to lead the vocal ensemble; the *Konzertmeister* remains responsible for the orchestral part and unity with the stage."[64] And Berlioz gave a rounded picture of the situation as a whole in Germany in the early 1840s:

> Almost everywhere I went in Germany I found discipline and alertness combined with a genuine respect for the maestro. I should say, "maestros," for there are several: the composer, who nearly always directs both rehearsals and performance of his work, without the conductor's pride being in the least offended; the kapellmeister, generally a competent composer, who is in charge of the large operas in the repertoire—all the important works of composers who are dead or elsewhere; and the leader, who looks after the smaller operas and the ballets and, when not conducting, plays the first violin part and in his capacity as leader conveys the kapellmeister's instructions and comments to the back desks of the orchestra, keeps an eye on all the material side of the orchestra's work, sees that nothing is missing with regard to instruments or music, and sometimes demonstrates the bowing or the correct way of phrasing a passage—which the kapellmeister cannot do, as he always conducts with a baton.[65]

So even with a baton conductor, the concertmaster continued to have directing responsibilities. One writer gave the following summation:

The violin-conductor continued to survive in the opera house where the orchestra traditionally faced the stage with their backs to the audience, and where the independent conductor was indeed at a severe disadvantage—for he was constantly compelled to turn his back on the orchestra in order to concentrate on stage ensemble, and at those very moments when the attention of the orchestra was most needed. It fell to Carl Maria von Weber in 1818, as director of the Dresden Court Theater, to change this arrangement.[65]

But evidently the situation persisted beyond 1818.

Bow or Baton?

A news note in a British journal in 1825 reported the situation in Paris:

The ancient quarrel between the *bâton* and the violin is not yet settled at the royal academy of music. After certain observations, launched forth in some of the journals, like pilot-balloons to discover which way the wind blows, it appears that, in the orchestra, the violin is to be reinvested with the government. It seems however to us, that the leader of a numerous musical army, will encounter great difficulties, if at the same time he must attend to the singers; to his own particular troops; to the score, and at the same time, draw those pure sounds from an instrument which ought alone to claim all his attention. But MM. Habanek [*sic*] and Valentino, whose talents are so well known, are the most proper persons to decide to which the sceptre belongs. We only wish to observe, that a general should direct his army, and rarely fight himself.[67]

One has to wonder if this report reflected a British point of view, since the "leader" still prevailed in England at this time, with a figurehead at the piano.

That such a dispute was not short-lived is indicated by Edouard Deldevez's treatise on conducting which appeared in 1878, and which seems dedicated to the idea that the violinist was the most natural conductor, and that the bow was a more practical and expressive utensil for him than was the baton. For example:

It is incontestable that, among the players of an orchestra, the instrumentalist whose right arm is most disposed to managing time is that of the violinist. Besides let one point out, it is easy to perceive in it, an aptitude more or less real, more or less particular, in the manner of holding the bow, of positioning the arm and marking the time. Always the arm movements of a conductor-violinist are different from those of a conductor not a violinist. The first has, in effect, a directive action more communicative, more intimately tied to performance, for he seems to perform himself.... The piano is particularly the instrument of the composer; the violin is the natural instrument of the conductor.[68]

Just as the ideas of the Florentine Camerata find resurrection in the theories of Gluck, and again in Wagner, these words echoed those of Quantz and C.P.E. Bach, if with a different set of inflections.[69] Deldevez continued:

The bow...alone knows how "to play the orchestra," but on condition of being held by the hand of a violinist. The hand, exercised in the performance of the instrument, will feel better than any other when it must mark the time without the help of the arm, when the time must be outlined in large strokes, that is to say with breadth, or if it is suitable to beat it shortly and simply from the wrist....[70]

And after discussing the main beat patterns, he claimed:

The distances which the bow covers, with the aid of a simple movement of the wrist, can only be, on the contrary, leaped over by the baton with an incessant displacing of the arm. The beats of the measure, and especially the subdivisions, being necessarily brought from high to low, from left to right, by each necessary movement of the arm, there results, in seeing it, a trouble which can occasion on the part of the players and the listeners a false interpretation of the general indication of the measure. In effect, the subdivided beats of a large measure, as, for example, that in 12/8, appear to be so many small measures indicated in a particular way.[71]

It would seem that wrist motion could be used with a baton just as easily as with a bow. Certainly there is a danger that subdivisions might appear to be little measures—or even big measures—but this failing would not seem necessarily to be tied to the baton alone. The argument over subdividing is still alive today. Perhaps Deldevez's discussion becomes more clear if one realizes that he was taking issue with a tract appended to Berlioz's treatise on instrumentation (1856) in which baton conducting was examined in great detail.

Finally, Edouard Blitz, writing in 1887, had his say. Acknowledging that conducting could be accomplished with stick or violin bow, he found that the "heavy *bâton de mesure* ornamented with ivory and silver is excellent... to receive as a gift and will make its effect, richly framed; but it has the disadvantage of being worth nothing for the use to which it is destined: it is too short and too heavy." He described a short ebony baton as being in general use in German theaters, but also mentioned one of 16 to 18 inches covered with white hide, "the instrument recommended by Berlioz" and used by many. Blitz felt that the bow was the best implement for the novice because "by reason of its fragility, it prevents the latter against the detestable madness of exaggerating the movements of the arm and body." Also "the bow would not be able to resist for a quarter of an hour the disordered movements one would inflict on it." But ultimately Blitz would recommend the stick, after experience with the bow.[72]

One should also not forget the role of the bass instruments in maintaining tempo, a role acknowledged in the eighteenth century. For example, speaking of the great Dragonetti, one writer claimed: "So powerful was the tone he could produce from his instrument, that I have frequently heard him pull a whole orchestra back with one accent if they wavered in the least."[73] And in Leipzig in 1816, certainly before the days of a baton conductor, since Mendelssohn was acknowledged as the first real *Dirigent* there,[74] Moscheles credited the bass player Wach with keeping the whole orchestra together "with his force and energy."[75]

The Baton

What was the status of the art of conducting in the 1840s? One writer opined: "As a profession of independent dignity, conducting was still in a primitive state, for Berlioz was still to write his chapter (1856) and Wagner his brochure (1869) on this métier."[76] But there were partisans of the modern baton (as opposed to the *bâton de mesure*) early in the century. Here is an opinion from 1807: "I know no bottomless dispute as over the instrument which is most fit for directing in performance of full-voiced musical works?—None, but the baton! is my avowal." The writer went on to define the powers of the conductor, giving him far more authority and responsibility than was probably usual during the eighteenth century: "Directing means the ordering and leading of the whole and concern for maintenance of unity during performance—consequently the leading of all individuals in one and the same direction, and taking over the decision for the moment over uncertainty arising by chance." He saw the director as representing the common will, "even like the regent in his state," and since consultation is impossible during performance where there is no time for hesitation, there remains only "the monarchic or despotic condition (at least during performance)." In sum: "Now if all follow this one, the whole chorus and orchestra can come asunder even as little as the two hands or the ten fingers of the keyboard player. . . ." And as for the most fit instrument for the conductor, if one wants audible direction, "let one choose timpani or contrabass, or reintroduce the Roman *Pedicularius!*" If one wants an audible beat, with foot-stamping or bow-tapping on the desk, then "confer both direction and first violin on the so-called *Vorgeiger.*" However, if one wants to see all this disorder banished, "place a man at the head, who, busy with no instrumental part, can dedicate himself undividedly to concern for the whole; who merely beats time—well marked, never audible through hammering of downbeats on the desk, but always only visible."[77]

The performance of *The Creation* in March 1809, at which Haydn made his last public appearance, seems to have been led by a time-beating conductor. A letter to a journal indicated that "the signal was given by Salieri, who directed the orchestra. At the piano was Kreutzer, Clementi was first violin, . . ."[78] This would not have left room for Salieri at either of the traditional directing places. Of course, one could counter that a time beater for large choral works was not unknown in the eighteenth century.

There is evidence that in Germany baton conducting was considered to be French in origin. From a description of the royal orchestra at Kassel in 1810 we learn that the conductor was a Hr. Legaye, who directed the opera, "and to be sure, according to the French style, with the baton."[79] Beethoven is described in many places as a baton conductor, if not always an effective one, especially after the onset of his deafness.

In 1820, Louis Spohr made orchestral history in England by conducting with a baton, claiming to have displaced the old system of dual control. But as has been seen, the old system persevered there.[80] Spohr had previously gone from bow to roll of paper and then to the baton as conducting implements. And Carl Maria von Weber evidently came to the baton early in his career. In 1826, he was "at the conductor's desk" to direct his *Oberon* in London's Covent Garden.[81] Later that year Weber conducted the overture to *Ruler of the Spirits* in concert; yet when Moscheles appeared as soloist, he "sat down to my piano on the stage, and gave a sign to the band beneath me to begin my 'Recollections of Ireland.'"[82] Moscheles's further description of the incident clearly showed that in a piece with solo, the leading violinist took charge of the orchestra, with no conductor at the helm. Similarly at Leipzig, during Mendelssohn's tenure as conductor, it was David, the concertmaster, who was supposed to conduct solos with the orchestra.[83] Of course, Mendelssohn was a baton conductor and from most accounts an effective one. His first appearance at the Gewandhaus in October of 1835 produced a "brilliant performance" with a "precision until now unheard in Leipzig." A "truly substantial innovation" was the fact that he conducted himself and did not leave instrumental works to the concertmaster as had been the case previously.[84]

Meanwhile, in London Sir George Smart had adopted the baton by 1834, for he conducted at the Handel Festival in Westminster Abbey in that fashion, though seated at the piano, as if clinging to some remnant of the old.[85] But in 1842 when the Philharmonic Society was contemplating breaking with tradition by naming a single director, the *Morning Post* opposed such "a dictatorship," insisting that "if we are to have a *chef,* he must at all events be a violinist and not a pianist. We have no notion of the latter placing himself solely at the head of a Philharmonic orchestra, and if there be any individual who has made this calculation, the sooner he divests himself of an absurd preposterous notion the better."[86] However, in 1846 when Michael Costa, active as an opera conductor in London since 1833, was appointed conductor of the Philharmonic Society, he stipulated that the leader be suppressed and that he, Costa, be in sole control.[87] Robert Elkin, who named the year as 1848, claimed that the leader's "time-beatings with the bow, so far from producing precision, had by now become merely distracting and confusing."[88] According to Sir George Grove, Costa was a "splendid drill-sergeant" who "brought the London orchestras to an order unknown before."[89] Meanwhile, Jullien, the indefatigable if flashy conductor of the Promenade Concerts, was described by Mrs. Moscheles as directing a "good orchestra, sometimes with a bâton, sometimes playing a 'flauto piccolo,' which with its shrill tones marks the rhythm."[90]

In 1845 Moscheles gave an eloquent description of the growing concept of conductor as he prepared to lead the London Philharmonic Society in rehearsal.

> Gentlemen, as we are here assembled together, I should like to compare your performance with the fingers of an admirably trained pianoforte-player's hand. Now, will you allow me to be the hand which sets these fingers in motion, and imparts life to them? May I try to convey to you all the inspirations I feel when I hear the works of the great masters? Thus may we achieve excellence.[91]

This sounds like an echo of words quoted earlier in this chapter! Indeed, perhaps Moscheles did embody the idea of conductor-interpreter, for according to the London *Times* of May 4, 1841, the public was indebted to him for the recognition that Beethoven's Ninth Symphony was a work of majesty and grandeur as well as simplicity. "As a conductor he surpasses almost all our musicians, for whenever he swings his bâton he leads the orchestra, whereas others are led by it." And "he is one who inspires the orchestra with a respect due to him...."[92]

At the same time the baton had made progress on the continent. At the opera in Darmstadt in 1825, Wilhelm Mancolt "sat sideways with his little stick."[93] At Dresden in addition to Weber, Heinrich Marschner "directed at the square pianoforte."[94] The same year in Leipzig, "Mr. Schulz directed—the vocal pieces only—at a desk, there was no pianoforte in the orchestra."[95] And in Ghent at the theater, "the conductor beat time in the centre, close to the lamps, but he and the leader did not seem very good friends."[96] And at the Josephstadt-Theater in Vienna, still in 1825, "the conductor beat time at a desk in the centre even with the violins."[97] Heinrich Dorn mentioned a Heinl conducting at the Paris Opéra using a baton at least the length of a violin bow.[98] And William Knyvett seems to have utilized a baton when he took over London's Antient Concerts in 1835.[99] But at Leipzig's Gewandhaus even in 1831–32, Wagner found that only vocal works had a baton conductor. And when it came to Beethoven's Ninth Symphony, the first three movements were conductorless, "played straight through like a Haydn symphony, as well as the orchestra could manage it." For the fourth movement, the conductor Pohlenz "took his place at the desk" but was overwhelmed by the difficulties of the piece, especially in the double bass recitative, until a veteran of the orchestra prevailed upon him to "put down the baton, and in this way the recitative really proceeded properly."[100] Is it any wonder that the progress of the baton was fought in so many quarters!

To be sure, Hector Berlioz was an important figure in the progress of the baton. His tract on the subject has already been mentioned. And very modern sounding was his claim to Franz Liszt that "the composer-conductor lives on a plane of existence unknown to the virtuoso. With what ecstasy he abandons himself to the delight of 'playing' the orchestra! How he hugs and clasps and sways this immense and fiery instrument!"[101] That he considered conducting a craft to be learned and not just a mechanical act of time beating is further attested to by his great joy and satisfaction in a performance of his *Roméo et Juliette* in St. Petersburg in 1847: "I remember it as one of the great pleasures of my life. And I was in such good form that I had the luck to conduct without a mistake, which at that time did not often happen to me."[102] And, as previously pointed out, he believed in the baton. "The bow is somewhat flexible; this lack of rigidity and the greater resistance it offers to the air because of the hair make its movements less precise."[103] Other baton conductors important during the course of the nineteenth century were Gasparo Spontini, Johannes Brahms, and Wagner himself.

In a letter to Wagner from Munich dated June 21, 1869, and referring to *Tristan und Isolde,* Hans von Bülow claimed to have conducted better because of practice with the baton.[104] David Wooldridge considers this the first reference to baton technique as something more than beating time clearly.[105] Yet myriad descriptions of Beethoven's gestures suggest that he certainly did more than just beat time. Indeed, one wonders if he did beat time at all.

Late in the century Felix Weingartner evidently took baton practice even further. "His conducting was unostentatious and precise, and his elegant gestures were a household word.... Weingartner was the first conductor who was said to practice his gestures in front of a mirror."[106] Sir Henry Wood was said to have told his players that he put in a half hour of practice with the baton every morning.[107] And Hermann Zopff, writing in 1881, suggested that one practice before a mirror and carefully mark the beat and parts of the beat while holding the body quiet. He allowed expedient tapping on the desk for attention before beginning, but the first beat must be "only in the air."[108]

An unusual implement was used by Theodore Thomas to conduct large forces at the Columbian Exposition in Chicago in 1892. The large forces[109] were so spread out that Thomas feared that a baton would not be seen well from all viewpoints. So he used a white handkerchief instead. One would think that a wavy handkerchief would cause rhythmic uncertainties, but evidently the way he held it, "gathering in the ends so that they could not flutter," worked so that "the attack of these thousands was as sharp and steady as in an ordinary concert."[110] Wrote one reporter, "His peculiar skill or gift or whatever it was that enabled him to cause great conceptions to move smoothly to a perfect execution was never better seen."[111]

In a way, full circle was reached by the Vienna Philharmonic Orchestra. In Strauss programs, now a New Year's tradition, the orchestra plays without a conductor, the concertmaster taking over as *Stehgeiger*—a reversion not only to the habits of the Strausses but to the earlier type of violin conductor.[112] But by the end of the century, conducting was taken for granted as an art and a craft. According to Maurice Kufferath, Brussels had had symphonic concerts since 1865, with famous composers such as Rubenstein, Tchaikovsky, Rimski-Korsakov, Cui, and Saint-Saëns as guest conductors. When Hans Richter appeared there in 1890 he created an extraordinary impression. Within a few rehearsals he transformed the playing, phrasing, nuances, and expression so completely that works, even the well-known classics, appeared almost new, even though they may have been heard 20 times before, played by the same players. Other great conductors followed there: Hermann Levi, Felix Mottl, Richard Strauss.[113] Much the same experience could undoubtedly be reported in every great city.

Noisy Conducting

Unless one misunderstands Castil-Blaze, the *baton de mesure* persisted at the Paris Opéra at least until 1810.[114] Nor was this the only noisy "conducting" going on. An article from 1803 on conducting opera acknowledged that "through foot-stamping or audible raps with the baton or bow" errors "against the beat" could be stopped. "This quite usual way of keeping opera personnel in time is, however, not the best, and to the public it is often as annoying as the error itself."[115] Another observer of the German theater commented on one particular "Director" who after entering the pit with showy hustle and bustle, continued the noise by taking out his violin and loudly tuning it, showing what a "Herculean task" he was about to begin. He moved stands and lights, called to one player that he was tuning too high, to another that he was too low, etc., until he was interrupted by the signal to begin. Then he hastened back to his place before the prompter's box, tapped with his bow on it the first sign of attack, then with his head and eyes spinning gave the second signal "with his mighty bow." Then setting his violin under his chin, he and his instrument rose on tiptoes, and he swept the bow "as if he wanted to cut through all the strings." Not only did he shake the floor with all this, but then "he rapped the beat very audibly, now with the bow, now with his foot, now with his head, now with all three together...."[116]

In 1831 Berlioz found the orchestra at San Carlo in Naples to be "excellent," "compared with those I had encountered until then...." Yet he found some faults. "The highly disagreeable noise made by the conductor tapping with his bow on the desk was another point I was disposed to criticize; but I was told that without it his musicians would sometimes have been hard put to it to play in time."[117] Mendelssohn also found a similar situation in Naples in the same year. "The first violinist, all through the opera, beats the four quarters of each bar on a tin candle-stick, which is often more distinctly heard than the voices (it sounds somewhat like *obbligati* castanets, only louder); and yet in spite of this the voices are never together."[118]

No, the quiet stick did not yet reign everywhere. Wagner wrote of having his Symphony rehearsed in Prague in 1832 under the "dry and terribly noisy baton" of Dionys Weber.[119] And in reviewing a performance of an oratorio by the Handel and Haydn Society in Boston in 1839, the observer bemoaned "the want of unity in the conducting." He found no unity where the "Conductor" governed the choir and the leader the orchestra. "Besides, we have too few violins to permit us to spare the leader from his instrument; and he must therefore mark time by stamping with his foot, which is a most unpleasant accompaniment."[120]

The Importance of the Conductor

Much has already been either stated or inferred on the growing sense that a conductor could influence, and even mold, a performance and the concept of a work. Perhaps a few more statements will suffice. Blaze, writing in 1820, was convinced of the importance of the *chef d'orchestre* and his influence on performance. While each musician should be capable of perfectly rendering his individual part, "in large ensembles, it is necessary that the will be one, and that the most able submit himself to the common law. Depository of the secrets of the composer, the conductor has the score under his eyes...." Notice that he wrote "score," not first violin part. "The first violin conducts, it is true, but he sees only his part, and all that he can do is to regulate the beat, to command forte, piano, crescendo, according to what is prescribed."[121] One also has to wonder how the first violin could handle scores in which dynamics were not simultaneous in all parts, or where articulation was similarly varied. Referring to the noisy French *baton de mesure* of earlier times, source of Rousseau's complaints, Blaze wrote: "this baton still exists, but with lesser dimensions, and he who holds it in his hand contents himself with leading it in space to mark the first beats of the measure." But later he admitted that the orchestras of the Opéra-Comique and most of the provincial theaters were still directed with the bow.[122]

One can find opinions on the importance of the conductor in the United States also. An anonymous article "On Concerts" published in Boston in 1839 calls for "the greatest care" on the part of the "director" in the "selection and arrangement" of works to be performed. After this the director must turn his attention to a "*careful rehearsal,* as well of the single parts, as of the whole." The importance of this is underlined by the assertion that "it is mainly by his activity, skill and exactness in the rehearsals, that unity in the performance is to be effected." In the concert "he must preserve a dignified calmness; beating the time with the full score before him, so as to be able to detect, and quietly to point out to the individual performer, any mistake or inaccuracy." The duties of the "leader" are also spelled out. He must "coöperate with the director, following his directions, and communicating them to the Orchestra; and especially by his own playing he must move the whole Orchestra to energy or softness, as may be required." But later the writer adds: "The Director has a great responsibility resting on him ... it is to him that the composer looks, for guiding those over whom he holds his sceptre, to keep the right degree and measure."[123]

Perhaps musical influence in such matters in the United States came to a great degree from Germany, for another article on the "Uses and Duties of the *Conductor* and the *Leader*" in the same periodical is acknowledged as being translated from the German. (The usage of capital letters for common nouns and the punctuation would make one suspect that the article discussed above was also translated from German.) The article first described the difficulties of interpretation when a number of performers were involved.

> An Orchestra, therefore, has one or two individuals, who may represent, as it were, the composer and his work. These are the *Conductor* and the *Leader.*
>
> The *Conductor*'s duty is the most important. He must study the spirit of the whole composition: he must fully *understand* the composer, and enter into his conceptions. The rehearsals are his proper field of action, where he must labor with the greatest patience and perseverance.... His duty extends over the manner of performance of each Solo or Chorus or *ripieno* part.... During the performance, the Conductor must first give the time by his beating, with the full score before him; thus keeping the instruments and singers together, and giving life to the whole.

This is already a modern philosophy of conducting.

> The *Leader* must follow the hints of the Conductor in the rehearsals, with close attention; and take from them the true conception of the spirit of the whole, as well as of the single parts; and then, at the performance, he must communicate this spirit, by his playing, or by hints if necessary, or by winks of his eye, to the full Orchestra.... He must have his eye constantly on the Conductor, who looks primarily to him for any *particular effect* which he wants brought out.[124]

Standing or Seated?

Should the conductor stand or sit? Berlioz admitted that it would be "rather difficult ... to endure the fatigue caused by standing the entire evening" when conducting in the theater. "On the other hand, it is obvious that the conductor loses part of his power by being seated, and that he cannot give free course to his temperament (if he has any)."[125] But Deldevez did not share Berlioz's opinion that the conductor lost any power by being seated. Stating that one generally conducted standing in concert but seated in the theater, he found that in concert "the *chef d'orchestre* is actor; one sees him forcibly, which is a constraint for those who do not understand it." But in the theater, "he is seen only when one looks at him." In concert, gestures are more reserved, arm movements held within limits by an easily exercised discipline. The standing *chef* can place himself at an advantageous point and turn so that his bow can be seen by all, calling attention from any point which needs special care. "But what moderation must he not observe in his movements, precisely because of the freedom of action of which he disposes! what considerations to watch for!"

Acknowledging that theater direction was governed by scenic execution, Deldevez also mentioned that the seated position offered repose to the fatigue caused by the length of performances. But the conducting arm "finds itself naturally carried to the right of the orchestra" and "masked obliquely, to the left, by the body." So a revolving seat is necessary "to be able to instantly lead the bow to the middle of the orchestra by a movement of rotation." Further, the seat should be elevated. The ability a seated conductor had of helping the seen beat to be heard by use of his foot was only too often exercized. Deldevez found reasons for this—influence of the stage, divided attention between choral masses and orchestra—yet the modern reader feels somewhat scandalized. Deldevez concluded: "One should not then consider the two positions, seated or standing, as presenting for the *chef d'orchestre* more advantages one than the other; they characterize simply two different natures of direction...."[126]

Weber sat to conduct in the theater early in the century,[127] and this position seems to have remained common for a long time at the opera. Angelo Neumann's recollections of a performance of *Lohengrin* in Leipzig in 1876 with Josef Sucher making his first appearance there as conductor have been translated thus: "With breathless attention, then, they watched the young conductor as he entered and took his chair."[128] Bruno Walter left no doubt that Gustav Mahler always sat to conduct, "yet in his first Vienna years, as in Hamburg, his mobility was astounding. But his movements were not excessive or superfluous—they seemed rather like some kind of fanatical conjuration."[129] Blaze had also depicted the conductor at the Opéra as seated "on his throne."[130]

Which Way Should the Conductor Face?

While in the theater the conductor might be at the foot of the stage with his back to the audience, in concert such was not the case until much later. Habeneck conducted mostly "with his face to the public."[131] In 1829 when

Mendelssohn, then 20, conducted for the first time (the occasion being the famous *St. Matthew Passion* in Berlin), he faced diagonally across the stage.[132] "His movements were short and decided, and generally hardly visible, for he turned his right side to the orchestra."[133] The famous conductor of the London Promenade Concerts, Louis Antoine Jullien, conducted facing the audience, standing in the midst of his players (fig. 19). But when "various soli obligati were forthcoming, he would turn to the players thereof; and the audience then saw him conduct that little or big phrase, give emphasis and expression to it, and coax it out with his baton—his wizard baton—in such a way that seeing and hearing were simply one fact. Jullien did it all."[134] Mendelssohn's sideways position seems to have prevailed at the concerts in honor of the unveiling of Beethoven's statue in Bonn in 1845. Liszt and Spohr both were directors in these concerts. "They both conducted from a tall closed-up pulpit, the conductor's back to the secondo side, a bad plan this."[135] And even in the 1870s in Berlin, a Benjamin Bilse conducted "still in the olden style, standing before his orchestra, his stern face turned to the public."[136]

But in 1881, Hermann Zopff recommended that the conductor place himself so that he could see all the players and they could all see his facial expressions which can exert great influence; this suggests his back to the audience.[137] And writing in 1889, Carl Schroeder not only recommended a similar position but found "entirely to be discountenanced ... the practice, prevailing amongst many concert conductors, of turning the back to the orchestra, and conducting with the face towards the audience, coquetting with them when possible, as many Band conductors and Promenade Concert conductors are in the habit of doing."[138] However, the "Mendelssohn" sideways position seems to have survived even into the last decade of the century.

> In Germany the conductor does not stand quite in the centre of the orchestra, but a little to the right, with his left side turned slightly towards the room. At restaurant concerts the curious spectacle is presented of the conductor (presumably from ideas of politeness) turning his back upon the musicians, and facing the audience, generally reversing the position, however, for important classical works.[139]

Score or Part?

According to Castil-Blaze, the *chef* did not use a full score, but "an epitome of the score, of which the braces combine only five lines," including the first violin, the woodwind instruments, the brass group, the dominating vocal part, and the orchestral bass. He called the full score an "almost useless impediment"; the *chef* has other things to occupy him than "turning pages without having time to read them." In fact, Castil-Blaze himself had made editions and "suppressed that enormous volume and replaced it by a score reduced for the keyboard, where figure all the vocal parts, where I have taken

Figure 19. A Promenade, 1849, the Conductor Probably Jullien

Source: Nettel/ENGLAND, p. 137.

care to indicate the entries of all the instruments.... Several publishers have adopted this system, with which I acquainted them in 1828."[140]

Indeed, using a full score was not at all common, at least early in the century. One writer reports that Habeneck's conducting parts had all the important entrances inserted in red "so that he could help musicians in case of need."[141] But Berlioz considered the ability to read a score essential, a skill today taken for granted as an essential part of a conductor's equipment.

> The man who makes use of a simplified score or of a mere first violin part, as is often done, especially in France, cannot detect half the mistakes that are made; and when he does point out an error, he is open to counterattack by the player in question, who may riposte, "What do you know about it? You haven't got my part there." And that is the least disadvantage of this deplorable system.

And he added tellingly: "Habeneck used to direct the Conservatoire concerts from a violin part. His successors have, in this respect, faithfully followed him."[142]

Deldevez included a chapter "On Which Part Should the *Chef d'Orchestre* Conduct?"[143] He called a reduction of the score for conducting purposes a *"conducteur."* He felt, though, that for study of a new work of any importance, the chef needed the full score. And at performance, in certain cases, it must be the same. However, in the theater not long before, Deldevez wrote, things had been different. A simple first violin part had the voice dialogue added in the recitatives; "such was the *violon conducteur* of *Comte Ory* at the Opéra."

Deldevez also described a *violon principal* which consisted of: (1) an upper staff with a textual transcription of the first violin; (2) a lower staff with the textual bass; (3) two lines between these devoted to an orchestral reduction; (4) a third line with the principal vocal entrances. This sounds much like Blaze's "epitome." Perhaps the fact that the full score would be a copy of the author's manuscript, voluminous and often "in an abominable disorder" with incessantly quick page turns could explain the use of a part for performance. But, Deldevez asks, how can the *chef* "play the orchestra" without a full score? "The score is the living author, announcing his thought, performing it himself!"

Like Berlioz before him, Deldevez did not believe in conducting from memory, for fear one would supplant the feelings and intentions of the composer with one's own. Perhaps some contemporary conductors might consider this a proper subject for meditation! He also felt one might be distracted, looking at the players or the audience. He felt that the conductor with the score before him would always mirror the composer's intentions to the player glancing at him. Likewise he would have greater control over unforeseen difficulties.

Remote Control

Castil-Blaze claimed that in 1854 a M. Verbrugel invented an electric "metronome" in Brussels. Wires could be disseminated from the conductor's desk to any part of the theater. Thus, by pressure of the director's left index finger, isolated groups could be kept in time without the "least divergence," even though some could neither hear the other groups nor see the conductor's baton.[144] Berlioz not only used this device at the Exhibition in the Palace of Industrial Products in 1855 where he had 1200 performers, but even took credit for its invention.

> I had called in an inventor of my acquaintance, and he had come to Paris and set up an electric metronome with five separate arms. By simply moving one finger of my left hand, while holding the baton in my right, I could indicate the time to five different and widely spaced points in the huge area which the performers occupied; the electric wires transmitted

my tempo to five sub-conductors who straightway gave it to the forces under their direction. The ensemble was marvellous. Since then, most opera houses have adopted the electric metronome for use with offstage choruses in cases where the chorus-master can neither see the beat nor hear the orchestra. The Opéra alone rejected it; but when I was directing the rehearsals of *Alceste* I managed to get this valuable device introduced there too.[145]

In August of 1852 at the Teatro Argentina in Rome, *Potifar, Giuseppe,* and *Giacobbe*—three oratorios by Pietro Raimondi which could be performed simultaneously—were given on a tripartite stage by three different groups and orchestras. One has to wonder how this was managed and if the electric metronome had any part in that monster performance.[146]

7

New Sonorities:
The Romantic Orchestral Palette

The fact that the orchestra changed in size during the course of the nineteenth century needs little documentation. Changes in sound were due not only to the larger numbers of players but also to the addition of instruments rarely if ever used in the eighteenth century, e.g., the English horn or contrabassoon. More difficult to measure, however, are the subtle changes wrought by "improvements" in the instruments themselves, and where and when these "advances" were incorporated. Indeed, one has to wonder whether such subtleties can be accurately traced at all, whether current performance practices in this regard can ever be refined to the point of absolute certainty. In the 1940s Sir Henry Wood reminisced:

> The tone quality in all departments of the modern orchestra has changed even within my living memory. I can still hear the Crystal Palace Orchestra under August Manns, and the Richter Orchestra at St. James's, so hard blasting, so different from the B.B.C. Symphony Orchestra and our other fine permanent orchestras of to-day.[1]

This quotation suggests other even more elusive problems: How much are variances or differences in sound due to conceptions from one conductor to another, to technical variances from one player to another, to differences resulting from differing methods between makers, and, of course, shades of tonal quality which changed due to innovations such as the Boehm system in several woodwind instruments and the incorporation of valves on most brass instruments. The quest for accurate performance practices can certainly be confounded by such considerations, but the drive to come as close as possible is not to be easily stilled.

The problem is particularly acute in nineteenth-century music, since tone color became such an important ingredient in Romantic musical language, often amounting to the most salient component of many a passage. In the 1880s Blitz wrote that "modern" music demanded the introduction of new sonorities to attenuate the uniformity of sound into which most of the wind instruments had fallen. He felt the use of instruments with timbres which stand out, like the English horn, saxophone, bass clarinet, harp, sarrusophone, etc., had become a necessity.[2] And indeed, it was not only the color of the orchestra which had changed but even its power, the result not only of larger numbers, but also of changes in individual instruments. In an interesting article at the turn of the present century, John Borland pointed out that the orchestra had acquired many instruments louder than Handel's orchestra had possessed and that with perhaps the exception of the oboes, even the instruments used by Handel had increased in power. If "this were not the case, it would be impossible to understand how the old composers wrote obbligato parts so freely for instruments like the trumpet, against a single voice."[3] While playing on the upper partials probably tended to thin out the sonority, a fact which Borland may have overlooked, his statement nevertheless does emphasize the problem.

The Woodwinds

In addition to the flutes, oboes, tardy clarinets, and bassoons which could be considered as staples in the woodwind section by 1800, voices were added which had been seldom heard or were truly newcomers. These included the piccolo, English horn, the small E♭ clarinet, the bass clarinet, and the contrabassoon. Other instruments of promise, such as those of the saxophone family, did not reach true fulfillment during this period.

Though a flute with eight keys might be considered as the "up-to-date" instrument of the early nineteenth century, those in use during the time of Beethoven, Weber, and Schubert had anywhere from one to eight keys. They were made of boxwood, ebony, cocuswood, or ivory. The first real Boehm flute, still with a conical bore, was produced in 1832.[4] By 1847, Boehm had produced a flute with a cylindrical bore. And by mid-century, cocuswood (grenadilla), silver, and German silver had become the favorite materials for this instrument.[5]

In 1842, Ferdinand Gassner gave the flute a range of d' to a''' [the a'''' of his text has to be a printer's error]. He admitted the range could be forced up to c''''. He also knew of instruments with extra feet going down even to small g, but since these were rare, c' was the safest low note to use.[6] In 1844, Berlioz concurred, giving the range as then c' to c'''', the last note being "very shrill." He also felt the low c' and c♯' were better not used for orchestral music.[7] But by 1904, Richard Strauss found the restriction on the lower notes "no longer valid." While cautioning against c'''' played piano, he claimed that even c♯'''' and d'''' could be played forte. Strauss also felt that wooden flutes had a finer tone than those of metal, though the latter responded more easily.[8]

Berlioz felt that by mid-century the flute had achieved "such perfection and evenness of tone that no further improvement remains to be desired." He predicted that all the woodwinds would soon follow suit with "rational division of the sound-tube" instead of holes made where they could be reached by the "natural distance of the fingers." He was sure that instruments "built according to Gordon's and Boehm's system" would "displace the old woodwind instruments within a few years."[9] However, on his German tour in the 1840s, he was not happy with German flute playing; "nowhere do you hear the flute played as it is in Paris."[10] But not everyone considered the Boehm flute an unqualified success. In the 1880s Edouard Blitz felt the older model possessed "a quality of sound much sweeter and softer," though the Boehm model had the two extra low notes and made all trills playable.[11] Hermann Zopff in the same period found the character of the flute nondescript, though effective for such expressions as "lassitude, resignation" in the low register and "harmless-gay, light and fragrant" in the high.[12] But to Berlioz's prophecy that the Boehm would soon replace all others, Richard Strauss retorted in 1904 that "unfortunately, this is still not so in Germany."[13]

If the piccolo has "added sparkle and brightness to many a score" since Rossini's time,[14] its entry into the symphony orchestra is usually associated with the last movement of Beethoven's Fifth Symphony. While Gassner restricted its sounding range from d″ to a♯″″, both Berlioz and later Zopff allowed it up to c″″″, though Berlioz declared the highest note "difficult to produce" and "almost intolerably harsh" and to be avoided. However, Berlioz allowed it the c″ and c♯″, but cautioned against the lowest octave as "scarcely audible."[15]

While Gassner warned that it should only be employed "in big sound-dimensions" or for a "piercing, biting, striking effect,"[16] Berlioz felt it was frequently misused and recommended the second octave for "joyful character" and the higher tones "in fortissimo for violent and incisive effects—for example, in a thunderstorm or in a scene of fierce or infernal character."[17] Later Zopff complained that it had become "insufferably a shriek-instrument," remembering more delicate treatment by Mozart and Weber. "As shrill as it is on the one hand, so charming is its tone on the other hand in piano owing to its sensuous prickling."[18]

During the first quarter of the nineteenth century, oboes with between 2 to 13 keys were in use, the most advanced being a model made according to the ideas of Josef Sellner, whose design has remained typical of German and Austrian oboes even to the present. Around 1840 some of the mechanics of the Boehm flute were adopted for the oboe, and boxwood started to give way to cocuswood, pearwood, and ebony as materials. Designs by Charles Louis Triébert, Apollon Marie-Rose Barret, Louis Auguste Buffet, and others led to instruments with up to 17 keys by the 1870s and 1880s. While Germany still valued an oboe with good blending qualities, England, Belgium, and Italy favored the French type with just the opposite virtues.[19]

While Gassner gave the oboe's range as c' to f''', Berlioz and later Zopff allowed small b, Berlioz mentioning small b♭ as existing but not generally available.[20] But Berlioz warns against the two highest notes as being "risky." As for the lowest tones, Mendelssohn wrote to his sister in 1831: "Do you not know that you ought to take out a license to sanction your writing the low B for oboes, and that it is only permitted on particular occasions, such as witches, or some great grief?"[21] But by Strauss's time, the upper restriction was no longer necessary and he allowed a range up to g''' on "modern" French oboes, and even to a''' "but only legato."[22] While the oboe is capable of many effects, Berlioz warned against increasing excitement "to the cry of passion, the stormy outburst of fury, menace or heroism."[23] Zopff agreed with Berlioz and others that its tone is "on the one side pastoral" but found it "on the other side penetrating and painful," with the higher tones "thin, biting, nasal, old-maidish."[24] Strangely, Edouard Blitz found no appreciable difference in tone quality between older and more modern oboes.[25] As for instruments in the United States, it seems incredible that in 1893 an orchestra of 35 in Los Angeles performed Wagner, Rossini, Mendelssohn, and other music while lacking both oboe and bassoon![26]

Though the English horn appeared at the *Concert Spirituel* in Paris as early as 1782,[27] its entry into the orchestra on anything like a permanent basis is a nineteenth-century phenomenon. French composers seem to have spearheaded the way for this instrument, introducing solo parts for it in Paris early in the century.[28] Blaze, crediting Italian operas with having used it for a long time, claimed that it appeared first in France at the Opéra in a ballet by Catel named *Alexandre chez Apelles* in December 1808. Pleased with its "brilliant success," Catel used it in the opera *Les Bayadères* in August, 1810. Halévy used two in *La Juive* which appeared in 1835.[29] But evidently the instrument took longer to catch on elsewhere. In Munich in 1831 for an orchestra of 80, Mendelssohn had to engage regimental musicians for English horns as well as trumpets.[30] And during his German tour of 1843 Berlioz found it almost nonexistent or deficient. Commenting on German orchestral problems in general in a letter to Liszt, he wrote that one had to transpose English horn solos for oboe; "the orchestra does not possess the instrument in question and the oboist is inclined to be nervous about transposing it himself."[31] He found the Weimar orchestra good but with no English horn; he transposed its part for clarinet.[32] From Leipzig he wrote to Stephen Heller of trying "in vain" to procure three additional instruments, English horn, ophicleide, and harp, which were called for "in several of my scores (another crime!)," the English horn turning out to be "of such poor quality and in such bad condition and, in consequence, so remarkably out of tune" that it had to be abandoned and its solo entrusted to the first clarinet player.[33] And though he found a good English horn in the Dresden orchestra,[34] he complained to Heinrich Heine from Brunswick that there was no English horn and he had to arrange its solos for oboe.[35] At Hamburg he had to "dispense with the services" of the English horn player,[36] and at Hanover the first oboe player "can play the cor anglais, but his instrument is badly out of tune."[37] As for the United States, Theodore Thomas claimed to have introduced both the English horn and the harp here in 1862.[38] But even in 1918 when the Cleveland Orchestra was founded, local recruitment could not provide the "scarce" oboe or English horn, although 57 men took part in the benefit concert of December 11, 1918.[39]

Gassner, Berlioz, and later Zopff gave its written range as c' to f''', though Berlioz allowed that there were instruments with the low written b♭. Gassner found its tone "rounder, fuller, not so piercing, as that of the oboe" and Berlioz characterized it as "melancholy, dreamy, noble, somewhat veiled—as if played in the distance." Zopff added the adjective plaintive.[40]

Of course, as the nineteenth century progressed, the clarinet became more and more entrenched as a permanent member of the orchestra. If 6-keyed clarinets were fairly common around 1800, by 1825 there were instruments with from 11 to 13 keys. Originating in Paris, Iwan Müller's 13-keyed system, stemming from 1812, was very influential, providing "the means of playing in all the keys and of rendering every kind of idea with an equal facility."[41] The modern big mouthpiece dates from the 1840s, and after the middle of the century, boxwood began to lose ground to cocuswood as material for the clarinet. There were two streams of development: the simple, or 13-keyed, perhaps reaching its greatest influence in the work of Eugène Albert of Brussels from 1860 on, and that known as the Boehm clarinet, devised by Hyacinthe Klosé working with Buffet, patented in 1844. From the 1870s the latter became more and more accepted everywhere but in Germany.[42]

Gassner gave the clarinet a written range of from small e to g''', "even—however already contrary to the nature of the instrument—up to c'''' through all semitones." Berlioz extended this up to d'''', however, marking a''' and b♭''' as difficult and the highest three semitones *"très dangereux."* Zopff, though writing later, was more restrained, limiting the upper register to f''' and g'''.[43]

Berlioz divided the range into four registers: the low, from e to e'; the chalumeau as f' to b♭', ("These tones are generally dull"); the medium, b' to c''', and the high, d''' to d''''.[44] But Gassner considered e to e' as "chalumeau or schawm-tones."[45] Zopff was even less precise, but gave descriptions for several registers, from the lowest "very full, almost lowing" to the highest "more piercing, for erotic moods irreplaceable, but also near to the bounds of the materially vulgar."[46]

The presence of clarinets in different keys is of course due to the difficulties the pre-Boehm instrument encountered. As a remedy, Blaze claimed there once were "as many clarinets as there are tones and even semitones in the scale.... Thus, starting with the clarinet in G, which is the longest of all, up to that in F, which is the shortest, the instrument gradually loses about half of its length and diameter." But only those in A, B♭, and C were admitted into the orchestra, with the B♭ considered to have "the most gratifying sounds."[47] Berlioz acknowledged four clarinets in general use at the time, adding the small E♭ instrument to the above-mentioned three, and giving the small instrument a written range of e to g‴. But he lamented the fact that the clarinet in D was so infrequently used. "Its tone is pure and possesses considerable power of penetration." Strauss concurred, adding that it was "even today" replaced by the clarinet in E♭." He incidentally added a‴ and b♭‴ to the range of the small clarinet, but "to be used only with caution, or ff in a tutti!"[48]

Discussing the characteristics of the various clarinets at length and their various tone colors, Berlioz condemned the practice of "certain virtuosos" of transposing everything on the B♭ instrument as "an act of disloyalty toward the composer in most instances."[49] Edouard Blitz concurred in this,[50] as did F. L. Schubert in the 1860s. Schubert put the blame for such practice on the conductor.[51] But as far as sound in general is concerned, Blitz found the difference between the older clarinet and the Boehm instrument "less marked" than was the case with the flute.[52]

The bass clarinet was probably used in France earlier than in most other countries.[53] It appeared at the Paris Opéra in Meyerbeer's *Les Huguenots* in 1836.[54] But apparently it was not too common in Germany. For the performance of *Lohengrin* at Weimar in 1850, Liszt had to purchase one. He was faced with a similar problem for the Leipzig performance of the same work in 1853: "the bass clarinet ordered from Erfurt has not arrived; and when it does arrive at Leipzig, it is not certain whether the clarinet-player there will be able to play it."[55] And it was not until 1886 that a bass clarinet chair with responsibility for second clarinet was established in the Gewandhaus Orchestra at Leipzig.[56]

While acknowledging a bass clarinet in C, Berlioz described that in B♭ as "much more common." He gave its written range as e through g‴, sounding great D to f″. "The bass clarinet is not intended to replace the high clarinets with its upper notes, but to extend their range downward. Yet the effect of doubling the high tones of the clarinet in B♭ in the lower octave by the bass clarinet is very beautiful."[57] Zopff later agreed with this range, finding "its considerably fuller tone" to be "of darker color and for the portrayal of uncomfortably furtive intrigue very suitable."[58]

Berlioz gave brief space to the alto clarinet in F or E♭, respectively a fifth below the clarinets in C and B♭, lamenting that it is "a very beautiful instrument, but unfortunately is not to be found in all well-constituted orchestras."[59] And though the basset horn does not seem to have figured in nineteenth-century composition to any appreciable degree, it was quite frequently discussed, probably to encourage its use in appropriate works of Mozart. Berlioz gave it some space,[60] but Gassner seemed to consider it as the bass clarinet, giving as alternate names: *"Bassethorn, Krummhorn, Bassclarinette,"* with *"Corno di Bassetto"* in parentheses. There is no mistaking the instrument, as his range agrees with that of Berlioz, sounding F to c‴.[61] Perhaps in Germany it was thought of as the bass of the family before general acquaintance with the real bass in that country; its lowest note is only a third above that of the bass clarinet in B♭, and others have pointed out a similarity in sound between the two instruments.[62] Zopff lamented that it was so seldom found, finding it incredible that at a time when composers were giving such prominence to the "improvement and expansion of the orchestra," two "such marvellously beautiful instruments" as the basset horn and the English horn should have been so neglected.[63]

Evidently the bass clarinet was often used as a substitute for this uncommon instrument. Berlioz, always interesting to read, observed:

> The omission of the basset horn from the syllabus of students of clarinet was until recently a serious error, for it meant that a great deal of Mozart's music could not be performed properly in France—an absurd state of affairs. But now that Adolphe Sax has perfected the bass clarinet to the point where it can perform everything that lies within the range of the basset horn and more (it can play a minor third lower), and since its timbre is similar to the basset horn's but even more beautiful, the bass clarinet should be studied in conservatories alongside the soprano clarinet and the smaller clarinets in E flat, F and high A flat.[64]

This was written during Berlioz's second German tour of 1846, not long after the publication of his treatise. Sir George Smart heard a basset horn, "well played" and "very effective" in a concert featuring a scena, *Al desio,* by Mozart at the Gewandhaus in Leipzig in 1825.[65] A bass clarinet in A became common in the second half of the century, often used by Dvořák, for example. Strauss also mentioned a double bass clarinet. "Its range is that of the double bassoon, with the timbre of the clarinet."[66] One has to wonder how much use it saw.

An 8-keyed bassoon was standard during the period in which most of Beethoven's symphonies were composed. As the century progressed, two distinct lines of development emerged in matters of tone quality and mechanism, one in France, the other in Germany. The French strove for lightness and ease of articulation, while the Germans aimed for evenness and blending qualities of tone. In the first half of the century the French bore began narrower and flared at a greater rate; its 17 keys influenced most other countries. In the third quarter of the century the number of keys went from 17 to 19 and 22, while attempts to adapt the Boehm system to the instrument were not very successful.

Meanwhile in Germany, Karl Almenräder had bassoons with 15 and 16 keys by 1828. His followers the Heckels, father and son, continued his line of work, and by about 1880 the "Heckel-Almenräder" or German bassoon was a "finished product." If it was not easier to finger, it was "immensely easier to blow, and it solves most of the problems of intonation, rapid *Legato,* and response to an average reed," having also a "smooth, buzz-free tone."[67]

Gassner gave the range of the bassoon as B_{b1} to b', even c'', though the latter notes are very difficult to produce.[68] Berlioz gave it a slightly bigger range, B_{b1} to e_b'', but he labeled c'', d'', and e_b'' as *"dangereux,"* calling it inadvisable to go above b_b'.[69] Somehow in the Strauss revision the range became extended to e'', with e_b'' and e'' labeled "dangerous."[70] In 1881 Zopff was far less daring, allowing only up to b',[71] while Carl Schroeder added c'' and confirmed that the latest instruments had A_1 at the bottom.[72] Pointing out that Wagner had taken the bassoon to c'' in *Die Meistersinger,* "where he depicts the pitiable condition of Beckmesser after his thrashing," Strauss claimed that e_b'' "can now be quite easily produced, but its production is harmful to the embouchure of the player."[73] This should find a ring of agreement with bassoonists who have struggled with the d''s in the opening solos of *Le sacre du printemps.*

Though the middle and higher tones "come very near to a beautiful tenor voice," Gassner felt the bassoon had limitations as a solo instrument because of "too little variety" and in places "too much raspy and nasal quality."[74] Berlioz mentioned its "tendency toward the grotesque. This should always be kept in mind when the instrument is used prominently."[75]

The contrabassoon also came to the fore during the nineteenth century, although Haydn as well as Beethoven had used it to reinforce the bass.[76] And it had found good use in Vienna in Mozart's *Requiem* as well as Haydn's *Creation.*[77] At the other extreme, it must have been a rarity in the United States, even late in the century, for Theodore Thomas had not heard one until his European trip of 1867. In May at the Paris Opéra he reported: "For the first time I heard a contrabassoon, the effect was wonderful."[78]

Berlioz gave it a written range of B_{b1} to f', sounding, of course, an octave lower, with the warning that the two lowest diatronic notes "are produced with difficulty and can hardly be distinguished on account of their extreme depth." Because of its "extreme ponderousness," it can be "only suitable for grand harmonic effects and for bass movements of moderate speed."[79] In the 1880s Zopff gave the same range as Berlioz, but complained that it had "almost wholly disappeared, and only seldom is there a capable player for it."[80] By 1904, Strauss noted that it had been "much improved" by Wilhelm Heckel, and "its use is urgently recommended."[81]

There were evidently some other bassoon derivatives which saw little lasting action. For example, Berlioz mentioned a "tenoroon" or *"Basson quinte"* sounding a fifth higher than the normal instrument.[82] And Gassner in a chapter on "Woodwind Instruments Useful in Military Music" called *"Contrafagott"* or *"Quartfagott"* an instrument a fourth lower than the normal bassoon, acknowledging in a footnote, however, "another, though very seldom existing contrabassoon-type...exactly a whole octave lower than the usual bassoon."[83] Things must have changed very quickly after 1842.

Perhaps the saxophone deserves brief mention here, since Berlioz had high hopes for it, giving it a prominent place in a discussion of his ideas on a conservatory curriculum. He felt it would prove very useful "when players have learnt to exploit its qualities," and "before long every composer will want to use it."[84] Of course his prophecy remained unfulfilled, even by Berlioz himself. He included six in his treatise: high, soprano, alto, tenor, baritone, and bass. Interestingly, the alto was then available pitched in either F or E♭. And he announced that Sax was about to produce a seventh, a double bass saxophone.[85] Produce it he did, for Jullien was using one in his orchestra in the 1850s.[86]

The Brass

Of course, the most far-reaching innovation concerning the brass instruments was the development of valve systems. Robert Haas considered the orchestra to have been "substantially transformed" by the melodic versatility" which resulted.[87] A valve mechanism was invented in 1813 by a Silesian named Fredrich Blühmel, but he sold it in 1816 to Heinrich Stölzel of Berlin who patented the idea in 1818.[88] In some quarters there were complaints that the effects on timbre were not advantageous. Even in the last quarter of the century, for example, Blitz found the resulting "great homogeneity of sound" to be "disastrous...for coloring, diversity of timbres, for instrumental richness, in a word." He claimed that since the composer used winds "principally with the intention of taking advantage of their special sonority," it had become impossible to distinguish "the sound of the low horn from that of the trombone, the valve trumpet comes close to the cornet, the trombone to the tuba, etc." In sum, while the brass section had become "excellent for augmenting the instrumental intensity and completing the sonority of the orchestra," it had "sacrificed its most precious quality, namely: diversity of timbres."[89] This argument will be further explored in discussions of individual instruments.

But Berlioz had another complaint, which he attributed to a rise in pitch, asserting that horn, trumpet, and cornet players were no longer able to be sure of high notes that had formerly been in general use. Citing particular cases, he goes on: "At every moment, frayed and broken notes, vulgarly called *couacs*, appear to the detriment of an instrumental ensemble, sometimes composed even of the most excellent artists." He put the blame ultimately on wind-instrument makers, who raised the pitch of woodwinds to gain more brilliance, in turn forcing brass players to have their instruments shortened in order to conform.[90] Mendelssohn corroborated the same complaint, at least in part: "What the deuce made you think of setting your G horns so high? Did you ever hear a G horn take the high G without a squeak?"[91]

Nor was the brass situation uniform everywhere. Though Berlioz found much to grumble about in Germany, he had general praise for the brass, citing "how far superior the Germans are to us in brass instruments, especially trumpets."[92] And it was not just a matter of instruments. In Berlin he found players who were "all good readers, masters of their instruments, playing in tune, and blessed by nature with lips of leather and indefatigable lungs; hence the ease with which the trumpets, horns and cornets produce high notes that our players cannot reach at all."[93] Yet his praise was not all unqualified; earlier in Frankfurt he had found the horn sound "brassy," a result of forcing high notes and "a fault very common in Germany."[94] And Fétis had found a mixed situation in London: an inferior first horn but an excellent first trumpet "whom the orchestras of Paris could envy of England."[95]

The valved horn did not immediately supplant the natural instrument, but rather the two coexisted until the last quarter of the century. Halévy is usually given credit for introducing the valved horn into the orchestra. In *La Juive,* produced in 1835, he used two *cors à pistons* and two *cors ordinaires.*[96] But Beethoven had already written a part for it in the Adagio of the Ninth Symphony—played by the fourth horn, evidently meant for a valve horn in E$\flat$. The explanation is that the fourth horn player at the Vienna Theater was the only one with a valved instrument at his disposal, a fact known to Beethoven.[97]

In 1828 a horn solo for *cor à pistons* figured at a concert at the Paris Conservatory.[98] In the 1840s Berlioz found a preference in Germany for the rotary valve over the piston type, crediting Adolphe Sax for the "superiority" of the *"cor à cylindres."*[99] He found that nearly all orchestras in northern Germany had adopted it with the virtual exception of Leipzig.[100] Even more interesting and worth quoting at length is his comparison of the natural and valved horns. The passage occurred in a letter to Louise Berton discussing the Berlin Opera.

The horns are splendid, and all of the rotary-valve variety—much to the regret of Meyerbeer, who thinks as I did until recently about the new mechanism. A number of composers object to the rotary-valve horn because, they maintain, its timbre is inferior to that of the natural horn. I have several times experimented by listening to the open notes of the natural horn and of the chromatic or rotary-valve horn one after the other, and I must confess I could not detect the slightest difference in timbre or volume. There is at first sight more substance in another objection that has been raised against the new horns, but it can be easily disposed of. Since this instrument (now perfected, in my opinion) was introduced into orchestras, certain cornists who play natural-horn parts on rotary-valve horns find it less trouble to produce the stopped notes indicated by the composer, as open notes. This is certainly a serious abuse, but the fault lies in the player and not in the instrument. Far from it, indeed, for in the hands of a skillful artist the rotary-valve horn not merely produces all the stopped notes which the natural horn produces but can actually play the entire compass without resorting to a single open note. The conclusion is simply that horn players should know the technique of hand-stopping as if the rotary-valve mechanism did not exist, and that composers should henceforth indicate by some special sign the notes that are to be played stopped, the player producing as open sounds only those notes which carry no such indication.[101]

One has to wonder how many players today follow this advice. It would seem simple enough to play a natural horn part with one valve setting. For example, if the part were for horn in E, the player on an F horn could just simply depress the second valve and play the whole part that way. But though some agreed with Berlioz to some extent,[102] there were also dissenting voices.[103] And Berlioz himself in his treatise had found the piston valved horn less satisfactory, to be "treated almost as a separate instrument."[104]

Gassner would seem to have been rather out of date on the horn if Berlioz was correct about the prevalence of the valved horn in Germany. Gassner relegated it to brief mention in a chapter on "Brass Instruments Common in Military Music,"[105] devoting more space to the natural horn. But he did state the basis for the existence of high and low horn players—the fact that high notes on the horn require not only a different embouchure from low, but normally a narrower mouthpiece, too. Of course, he discussed the various crooks and tonalities, ranges and difficulties.[106] However, Berlioz was much clearer, probably more correct, and certainly more detailed. Stating that it "is impossible to indicate its precise range without also naming the particular key of the horn in question," he included a rather thorough discussion of the various horns and the peculiarities of each. Where Gassner inferred one horn in many keys by means of crooks, Berlioz suggested a plenitude of actually different instruments, including ranges in terms of open notes for eleven horns, with subranges for first and second horns.[107] Not as detailed but worth checking are Zopff,[108] Schroeder,[109] and Blitz.[110]

Several statements by Berlioz indicate that in the 1840s he found Germany also ahead of France as far as trumpets were concerned, with a widespread adoption of the rotary-valve trumpet.[111] As with the horn, he felt that there was no loss of brilliance with this instrument and lamented that in France "the incredible popularity of the cornet has stood in their way—quite wrongly in my view, for the cornet has nothing like the trumpet's nobility and splendour of timbre."[112] But things must have changed considerably since Sir George Smart had been in Germany in 1825, for he had expressed quite different opinions on the quality of German brass. In Munich he had observed "but I have not yet heard a good sounding trumpet."[113] Again in the same city, the "tromboni were good but I have not yet heard a trumpet equal to Harper," an active London player.[114] Even in 1845 in Bonn Smart felt that the "trumpets are not so well toned as ours."[115]

In the 1880s Blitz also showed concern for tone quality and disdain for the "vulgar" cornet with its "pasty sonority," urging that the conductor constrain his players to use the instrument indicated by the score.[116] With the natural trumpet abandoned, the conductor must not let the "sonority of the trumpets be...muffled by the abandonment of crooks." He felt that the facility of performance offered by the piston cornet had had deleterious effects on the other brass, that trumpet players and trombonists were pushed to have their tubes constructed too wide, thereby losing the "fresh, clean, precipitate attack, *de rigueur* for the trumpet."[117]

The valve trumpet had not, however, rendered other types obsolete by 1875. In France, most composers compromised by using both natural and valved instruments.[118] And in his treatise, Berlioz had reported that at the time, most of "our" orchestras [meaning French?] provided two trumpets and two cornets,[119] a section still typical of the early works Stravinsky later wrote for Paris. Incidentally, the *cornet à pistons* had made an appearance at the Paris Opéra in 1829 in Rossini's *Guillaume Tell.*[120]

Gassner provides the range and natural series for the trumpet, [121] but again Berlioz is more complete, showing how ranges are affected by crooks.[122] Schroeder also provided similar information, lamenting that in the 1880s many players performed everything on A and B♭ trumpets, a practice which should not be allowed, "since the effect is often much impaired."[123] Zopff also provided the range, and felt that the trouble with using valved instruments to replace the natural was that with the former the lower tones had an "unnoble frog-sound."[124] But Strauss reported: "To the best of my knowledge, trumpet players now prefer the following keys: first trumpets—high A, B♭, C; second trumpets—F, E, E♭.[125] This is hardly the case today. Incidentally, Gassner still mentioned the keyed trumpet,[126] and Berlioz claimed that they were still being used in some Italian orchestras at the time of his treatise.[127]

Menke pointed out that one consequence of valves was a gradual return to one instrument in one tuning, usually B♭, a parallel to early baroque practice, whereas the eighteenth century had seen a proliferation of tunings in consequence of the trumpet's "deficiencies." He felt it unfortunate that in South Germany the C trumpet had become more and more common. At any rate, the more recent instruments are shorter by half than the old natural instruments. The advantage of easier handling went hand in hand with a more acute and penetrating tone quality in the high register.[128]

Widor clarified the problem or deficiency of using the high B♭ trumpet to play older parts. He provided a theme which on the older instrument would have been played between harmonics 4 and 12, but on the modern instrument would be played between harmonics 2 and 6. The result has to be quite different.[129] And speaking of the older trumpet, Forsyth claimed: "No one who has heard two of these instruments enter *pp* at the 346th bar of Beethoven's *Violin Concerto* can have any doubt" that "in actual breadth of tone-colour, especially in its lower notes and in the *p*, it is without a rival. . . . Magical passages like this lose half their intention when played on the small-bore instrument."[130]

Berlioz also provided a thorough discussion of the cornet with either pistons or cylinders.[131] Schroeder mentioned the bass trumpet "often used by Wagner," sounding an octave lower than the "usual" trumpet and in different tunings.[132] Another writer gave these as E♭, D, and C tunings, adding that they were seldom used alone but in combination with the other brass.[133] Widor clarified this, saying that although Wagner wrote for it as a transposing instrument, it was always played in C—the player transposing when necessary—and that bass trumpets in E♭ and D were not being made.[134] Forsyth clarified this even further when he remarked that the instrument Wagner imagined would have been "poor in quality" at the lower end and "unplayable by human lips" at the higher end, and therefore it was modified to a valve instrument which Forsyth considered as really a valve trombone "halfway in pitch between the Tenor- and the obsolete Alto-Trombone."[135]

By the 1820s, three trombones were fixtures in most large orchestras.[136] Smart found them in Munich—"the tromboni were good"—in 1825.[137] Costa had them with the Sacred Harmonic Society, founded in the 1830s. Costa, according to one description, "remained to the end a noisy musician, and trombones were more dear to him than any other instruments in the orchestra. They were but three, but he valued them, I am sure, above the 'sixteen double-basses' so persistently advertised by the Society's managers."[138] But in 1810 they still seemed unusual enough to be singled out in a list of works conducted by Spohr at Frankenhausen in a musical festival: "a big new overture for the whole orchestra (also with trombones) by Mr. Spohr."[139] And they probably remained scarce for a time in the United States. For a performance of *The Creation* in Philadelphia in 1822, "it was found that the trombone parts could not be filled by the musicians of the city. Again the aid of the music-loving Moravians was invoked."[140]

The trombones are generally considered to be the instruments that have undergone the least change in their history,[141] but their characterization as "noisy" instruments would suggest at least a change in mouthpiece construction from the narrow bore and shallow bowl of eighteenth-century vintage, when they seem to have been considered more mellow instruments.[142] One usually looks for them in threes. Thus it seems strange to read Blaze's recommendations that in "ordinary" orchestras, one (the bass trombone) was enough, and three—alto, tenor, and bass—were needed only when the number of strings was multiplied "in the necessary proportions."[143]

Gassner discussed the alto, tenor, and bass trombones, giving ranges. He also alluded to a "totally out of use" soprano which was "truly nothing other" than a "trumpet with slide," a *"Quartposaune,"* a *"Quintposaune,"* and even "Gottfried Webers *Doppelposaunen,"* but these latter seem not to have had orchestral use.[144] Berlioz knew of the soprano trombone, though "it is unknown in France," but he saw no reason why it should not be used since "it is by no means certain as yet whether it can be successfully replaced by the valve trumpets." This seems like a discrepancy since elsewhere he had expressed so much faith in valve trumpets. He also stated that "the alto trombone is not found in all French orchestras and that the bass trombone is almost unknown there." Berlioz found the tenor "undoubtedly the best of all." He gave information on a bass instrument in E♭, but also acknowledged one in F.[145] Schroeder kept to narrower ranges than Berlioz, noting that in many orchestras only tenor trombones were used, but insisting on alto or bass where prescribed by the composer.[146] Zopff's remarks are also interesting; he insisted that the "power of a trombone passage in part lies precisely in its three-partedness, in the might of the simple three sounds. A fourth trombone obscures the brassy penetrating quality . . . through overloading."[147]

Although Berlioz had spoken highly of German brass in general, at Mannheim he had to suppress the finale of *Harold in Italy* "because the trombones were manifestly unequal to it."[148] And in Berlin the fanfare in the *Tuba mirum* of his *Requiem* gave the trombones the same trouble it had given Paris players!

> Impossible! Quite impossible! We have to give up the attempt. Can you imagine it? It's enough to make one batter one's head against the wall. Yet when I asked the Paris and the Berlin trombonists why they didn't play in the fatal bar, they could not answer. Those two notes hypnotized them.[149]

On the other hand, Mendelssohn found that good trombone playing stood out from an otherwise inferior orchestra at Düsseldorf in 1835; "but that is just the misery in Germany—the bass trombones and the drum and the double bass excellent, and everything else quite abominable."[150]

Besides the bass trombone, a variety of instruments acted as contrabass to the brass section at one time or another. In France and England "the choice fell on the old wooden serpent, an instrument which had for long been at home in French church music, and was now becoming the strongest bass voice in military bands."[151] Indeed, Adolphe Adam complained of Gregorian chant being performed in a Paris church with the accompaniment of one, even two serpents.[152] And in 1831, Mendelssohn lamented that "not a single Mass is to be heard on Sundays in all Paris, unless accompanied by serpents."[153] In England, Joseph Bennett had vivid recollections of the serpents Costa used with the Sacred Harmonic Society:

> The trombones were well supported by an ophicleide, long in the hands of Phasey, most stalwart and large-lunged of Costa's men, and there were always, high up among the men-singers, two "serpents," which led the attack in that exalted region. For old acquaintance sake I was much interested in those serpents, although I knew that Handel had remarked of their kind: "They are not the serpents which seduced Eve." The reason is, that when, as a boy, I played the violin in the gallery of a village church, a serpent had place next to me, and emitted the most appalling sounds that ever pretended to be music. Wherefore I wondered when I saw a pair in Exeter Hall, where, rightly, sounds infernal had no place.[154]

Of course, the serpent, made of wood but with a mouthpiece instead of a reed is really a hybrid instrument. Gassner grouped it not with the orchestral instruments but with the woodwind instruments customary in military music, stating that in military music a serpent in E_b was usual, while in the orchestra one in D was more customary.[155] Berlioz discussed it as a wooden instrument "covered with leather" with the "same range as the bass ophicleide, but less agility, purity and sonority." He called it a transposing instrument in B_b with a "truly barbaric tone . . . better suited for the bloody cult of the Druids than for that of the Catholic Church, where it is still in use." He found only one suitable use for it in church: in masses for the dead "where the serpent serves to double the dreadful choir of the Dies Irae. Here its cold and awful blaring is doubtless appropriate."[156]

The ophicleide appeared in Paris in 1817. Though it was "eventually driven out by the superior claims of the valved tuba," it "lingered long" in England, and "was not wholly extinct in 1880, when it still figured in the list of the Crystal Palace orchestra."[157] It made its first appearance at the Paris Opéra in 1822 in *La Lampe merveilleuse* by Nicolo Isouard and Benincori.[158] But if it flourished in France and England, it was rather scarce in Germany. Berlioz complained of its lack in Mannheim, Weimar, Leipzig, Dresden, Berlin, and Hanover,[159] and was surprised to find the instrument in Hamburg and Darmstadt.[160] Blitz still listed the ophicleide with the brass in the 1880s, omitting the tuba, though admitting in a later chapter that the ophicleide was always replaced by the tuba. He approved the substitution "unless the author wished to make use of the grotesque sonority of that instrument, like Mendelssohn, in the overture of the *Midsummer Night's Dream,* where its presence is indispensable to wholly render the comic intention of the composer."[161]

The instrument probably saw little use in the United States. Ryan recalled a "little orchestra" made up of a violin, a clarinet, a contrabass, and an ophicleide to make up for the lack of an organ in a Boston church![162] And Theodore Thomas remembered an ophicleide coming to the United States with Jullien in 1853, remarking that he also now "missed" it in works like the *Midsummer Night's Dream*.[163] Yet in England, "Hallé kept an ophicleide in his orchestra until the day of his death." Indeed, it seems to have been 1896 before it was replaced by a bass tuba in that orchestra.[164]

Perhaps the reputation the ophicleide suffered as being of a course and rough tone is not entirely justified. Prospère's performance with Jullien in London in 1842 was described thus:

> And last, but not least, M. Prospère on the giant instrument the Ophicleide, which is as gentle and as docile in his hands as *Hamlet* would have the recorder to be. Truly this gentleman's execution and power of subduing this usually obstreperous instrument passes all understanding, amongst those who have heard them; how vain would it be then to attempt a description to those who have not.[165]

This was echoed in an appreciation of the performance of *Elijah* which Mendelssohn conducted in London.

> The sensation produced by the last chorus of the first part of the "Elijah," "Thanks be to God," was truly wonderful. One felt as if the Divine Presence had been evoked, so impressive, so awe-inspiring was its effect upon the listeners. The marvellous effect of the rain and rushing of waters given by the violins, and the stupendous bass *F* fortissimo, was beyond human conception. I think Prospère with his monstrous ophicleide added materially to this splendid tone effect.[166]

That Gassner discussed the ophicleide in conjunction with military music seems in keeping with Berlioz's findings of the situation in Germany.[167] Berlioz called them the "altos and basses of the bugle," the bass being "excellent for sustaining the lowest part of massed harmonies." Bass ophicleides were common in C and B♭, though there was also a seldom used A♭ version. Though the bass "under a mass of brass instruments...works miracles...nothing is more clumsy—I could almost say, more monstrous—nothing less appropriate...than those more or less rapid passages played as solos in the medium range of the ophicleide in certain modern operas. They are like an escaped bull jumping around in a drawing-room."[168] But much later a German observer found them "rough and uneven," only a "passing phenomenon," and "wholly vanishing since the invention of the tuba (about 1848)."[169]

Berlioz had already mentioned the tuba in 1843, reporting that it had "completely dislodged the ophicleide in Prussia, if indeed the latter was ever prevalent there, which I doubt." He understood it as "derived from the bombardon and fitted with a mechanism of five rotary valves which gives it an enormous range in the lower register." He found its tone "full and vibrant and well matched with the timbre of trombones and trumpets, to which it serves as a true bass, blending perfectly with them."[170] However, its blend and effectiveness have been challenged by others.[171] And if this seems contradictory, so is the general situation concerning instruments which might be called tubas.[172]

Then, to confuse things further, there were the Wagner tubas, "really a misnomer.... It is possible that the mistake originated when the German conductor—presumably Richter—pronounced the word 'tube' in the German manner... when *The Ring* was first produced in London." Wagner tubas came in two sizes, equivalent to B♭ and F horns, but in bore they were "midway between the horn and the saxhorn," and meant to be played by horn players with their own mouthpieces.[173] They never found widespread use. The Russian bassoon was also mentioned in the literature of that time for those interested in curiosities.[174]

Percussion

As far as percussion instruments are concerned, the timpani were no newcomers. "Symphonies, overtures, choruses, finales, could not do without timpani. Famous composers have always put them in their noble, grand or brilliant arias" where they can be "of a magical effect."[175] But where the classical orchestra was usually satisfied with two kettledrums, the romantic orchestra increased this to three, four, and more. It is difficult to know where this practice began. In a book published in 1820, Castil-Blaze complained of the practice of tuning the timpani in tonic and dominant, and then after a modulation not having them on the dominant of the new key, which was usually the climax of a crescendo. He suggested that composers write for three drums, the third to be placed opposite the player and a bit forward, making "the apex of a triangle, of which the two others would form the base."[176] Indeed, in 1831—a first at the Paris Opéra—Meyerbeer used four kettledrums in *Robert le Diable*. And guess who complained about it! "To add two timpani is to wish to create a jam and nothing more; this childish addition has no other result than that of congesting the orchestra." Then Blaze pointed out that it was not an innovation, since two pairs of kettledrums had been used in 1665 in a march by Philidor (L'Aîné).[177]

Fétis found that in London timpani were played with thicker and more trimmed [*garnis*] sticks than in France, producing "felicitous effects, particularly in the storm of the pastoral symphony of Beethoven." He proposed to take a pair to Paris. But in the Germany of 1843, Berlioz found fault with the timpanists as well as with their utensils. The following amusing anecdote appeared in a letter to Liszt.

"Timpani, why are you making such a frightful din over there?"
"I have a fortissimo, sir."

"You haven't, it's mezzo forte—*mf,* not *ff.* In any case you're playing with wooden sticks when you should be using sponge-headed ones. It's the difference between black and white."

"We don't know them," the kapellmeister interposes. "What do you mean by sponge-headed sticks? We only know the one kind."

"I suspected as much, so I brought some with me from Paris. Take the pair on the table there."[178]

In Berlin he found similar problems as well as drums that were too small.[179] In this as in many other cases, Berlioz placed most of the blame on the conservatories for lacking classes in many areas.[180] These deficiencies probably were indicative of the growing demands on orchestral members. Perhaps it should not be surprising that in a list of *"Schulen für Instrumente"* provided by Gassner, there are none for any percussion, although there are for harp and guitar.[181]

Gassner described the timpani as made of brass, copper, or silver, the opening covered with parchment or donkey hide, with a "recent invention" facilitating tuning by means of an inner mechanism, the skin being "tightened or slackened" by twisting. He also showed by examples how more than two drums could be used.[182] But Berlioz suggested not only more than two drums but more than one player.

> For many years composers complained about the impossibility of using kettledrums in chords in which neither of their two tones appeared, because of the lack of a third tone. They had never asked themselves whether one kettledrummer might be able to manipulate three kettledrums. At last, one fine day they ventured to introduce this bold innovation after the kettledrummer of the Paris Opera had shown that this was not difficult at all. Since then composers writing for the Opera have three kettledrum notes at their disposal. It took seventy years to reach this point! It would obviously be still better to have two pairs of kettledrums and two drummers: this is indeed the scoring used in several modern symphonies. But in theaters progress is not so rapid, and there it will probably take another score of years.[183]

Of course, one of the "modern symphonies" was the *Symphonie fantastique* which asked for even three and four drummers! Strauss pointed out that the young Verdi let the timpani play notes of different harmony with "indifference" in "strong tutti chords," citing the first finale of *Un Ballo in Maschera* as an example, and explaining it as based on "the practical experience that the sound of kettledrums is too indefinite to stand out disturbingly from a compact mass of harmonic tones. Nevertheless, this is not entirely to my taste."[184] Zopff called the timpani the only percussion instrument "of artistic merit."[185]

As for the pedal timpani, Hanslick in a review in 1884 credited Hans von Bülow with introducing them with the Meiningen Orchestra.[186] While the invention is attributed to Ernst Pfundt (1806–71) who had been Mendelssohn's timpanist with the Gewandhaus Orchestra, Schroeder would credit Bülow with the invention itself.[187] Strauss claimed that Bülow even had them double the first theme of the first movement of Beethoven's Eighth Symphony, presumably in the recapitulation "to reinforce the insufficiently audible bass."[188]

Other percussion instruments had played but a small part in eighteenth-century music. The "Turkish" or "Janissary" music had a growing fascination for European composers, and little by little drums, cymbals, and triangle began to be needed as composers included more and more parts for them. Their growing use was evidently spurred on by their presence in military bands.[189] They seem to have made an appearance in the Leipzig Gewandhaus as early as 1802.[190] Yet in 1825, Sir George Smart must have thought them still unusual enough to point out "some bars of Turkish instruments" in the overture to Winter's Italian opera *Maometto* at Dresden.[191] And an English periodical that same year deemed it noteworthy enough in reporting on one of the concerts at the Yorkshire Amateur Meeting that the finale was "Rossini's striking overture—*La Gazza ladra,* in which the military drums and fife are prominently introduced."[192]

In his remarks on the performance needs of *Wellingtons Sieg,* Beethoven specified that the largest size bass drums were needed for the cannon shots; he had used some "five Vienna shoes square" [a *Wiener Schuh* = 1.037 U.S. feet]. He also prescribed rattles used in the theater for thunder or platoon volleys to represent the musketry.[193] In his book on the opera published in 1820, Blaze commented on cymbals, side drums, triangle, bells *("clochettes"), le sistre* (some type of rattle), the tamtam (which he also referred to as the *beffroi* [!]) and their uses.[194] But by 1842, Gassner had a separate chapter on *Schlaginstrumente* which included besides timpani the bass drum, side drum, a *Roullirtrommel* (which "has a muffled tone and is more suitable for rolls in piano, where the usual drum would have too harsh an effect, covering the other instruments too much"), tambourine, cymbals, triangle, the *Schellenbaum* or Turkish crescent (a shaken instrument containing bells and other sounding materials), the Glockenspiel, the tamtam, and castanets.[195] It is especially interesting that these instruments were not relegated to a chapter on military music. In his treatise published two years later, Berlioz included bells, sets of small bells *("Les Jeux de Timbres"),* Glockenspiel, glass harmonica, ancient cymbals, bass drum, cymbals, gong (or tamtam), tambourine *("Le Tambour basque"),* side drum, tenor drum, triangle, and crescent (which he calls *"le Pavillon chinois").*[196] One would think that most of these instruments were quite settled in the orchestra by mid-century, yet Berlioz again found much to complain about in Germany concerning either lack or quality.[197] Instruments must have been lacking in Russia also, for in 1847 in St. Petersburg, the funeral knell in the last movement of the Fantastic Symphony saw a piano act as a substitute for the bells.[198] And as late as 1863 at Loewenberg, one would wonder if percussion players were lacking, for the husband of the harpist—herself brought from Weimar—played cymbals in *Harold in Italy*.[199] Again Berlioz castigated the conservatories as having an obligation to improve this situation.[200]

As late as 1881 one can get the feeling of reading about something still exotic in a book on conducting that spends less than half a page on *"türkische Janitscharenmusik,"* singling out cymbals, tamtam, triangle, side drum, tambourine, Glockenspiel, and *"Papagenopfeife"*.[201] And even in 1889 only brief mention is given in a similar book to side drum, bass drum, cymbals, tambourine, tamtam, and triangle, almost as if they can be taken for granted. The same work does, however, devote more space to Glockenspiel.[202] Evidently the celeste was new to the orchestra when Tchaikovsky introduced it in *The Nutcracker*.[203]

Other Instruments

As far as the keyboard is concerned, it has already been seen that though the piano lingered on, especially in England, its presence became more and more a physical rather than a sounding one, and eventually it disappeared. As far as the harpsichord is concerned, even at the turn of the nineteenth century, Rochlitz, who still believed in the keyboard conductor, felt the piano to be a better instrument for his use with its milder tone quality, its dynamic control, its better stability of intonation, and the ability to blend in better.[204] On the other hand, in England Fétis felt that the piano, if and when it could be heard, spoiled the effect; he wanted it suppressed.[205] And Gassner seemed to suggest that its value was for composers and arrangers as well as for accompanying singers in place of the orchestra.[206] Although Berlioz provided a concerto example in his discussion of the piano, he also included an excerpt from *Lélio,* where he used two pianos as part of the orhcestra in "a chorus of airy spirits."[207] But such use was unusual, and though at least one writer suggested utilizing the piano as an orchestral instrument,[208] such use was only to return in the twentieth century, remaining rare in the nineteenth.

Although the harp had figured at the *Concert spirituel* in Paris as early as 1761,[209] it was in the nineteenth century that this instrument made its gradual way into the orchestra as a quasi-permanent member, first by way of opera.[210] In fact, twelve harps played at the Paris Opéra in *Les Bardes,* an opera by Le Sueur in 1804![211] It would almost seem that harpists early on were thought of as successors to the keyboard players (they were used for recitative in some places); else why the complaint that "there are very few harpists who read from score, and I do not know of any who can follow exactly the motions of a condensed harmony and a motive treated fugally"?[212] And in Brüggen in 1825,

Smart wrote of having breakfast at a post-house "while a most excellent violin and tolerable harp played in the Hall," a seeming substitute role as accompanist.[213]

Gassner treated the harp in a chapter on "Concert, Chamber Music," which would seem to indicate his thinking in terms other than the orchestra. But he knew the harp with six or seven pedals, "so complete, that one, with few exceptions, can compose almost the same for the harp as for the piano."[214] This is another parallel with the keyboard. But Berlioz knew the double-action harp whose range he gave as $C\flat_1$ to f''''. And contrary to Gassner, he stated concerning the fingering that "many composers confound it with that of the piano, which it does not resemble at all."[215] Richard Strauss warned that: "The harp must always be treated as a solo instrument, also in the orchestra, lest one write unnecessarily notes which are inaudible."[216]

The harp seems to have been another instrument which made headway in France much more rapidly than it did in Germany. From Stuttgart Berlioz wrote in 1842:

> There is also an excellent harpist (Krüger)—a great rarity in Germany. The practice of this splendid instrument is absurdly, not to say barbarously, neglected, and for no discoverable reason. I am inclined to think this must always have been so, for none of the composers of the German school have made use of it. There is no harp anywhere in Mozart's works.... Weber never wrote for it, Haydn and Beethoven likewise. Gluck went so far as to compose a very simple part for one in *Orphée,* an opera which in any case was written and performed in Italy. There is something in this that I find both irritating and extraordinary. It is a blot on the orchestras of Germany, every one of which should have at least two harps, especially now that they perform French and Italian operas, in which harps are so often used.[217]

Berlioz obviously was not aware of Mozart's Concerto for flute and harp, K.299, but then this really does not detract from the truth of his assertions, especially since this unusual work was commissioned and composed in Paris. In Germany in 1843 Berlioz had to put up with substituting the piano for the harp parts in the "Ball" movement of the *Symphonie fantastique* at Hechingen,[218] Weimar,[219] and Leipzig,[220] with Mendelssohn himself doing the honors at the last city. And if he was pleased at Hamburg[221] and Hanover,[222] the harpists at Brunswick[223] and Darmstadt[224] were less than adequate. However, he was quite impressed with the English harpist Parish-Alvars whom he met at Dresden and called "the Liszt of the harp."[225]

Even in 1845 a harpist was lacking for the performance of Liszt's cantata at Bonn during the festivities in honor of the unveiling of Beethoven's statue,[226] yet in 1846 at Prague Berlioz found "a charming artist whose talent, all too unusual in Germany, was of great service to me personally: Mlle Claudius, excellent harpist, capital musician, and Parish-Alvar's best pupil."[227] By 1863, Weimar had a harpist who went to Loewenberg to play at Berlioz's concert,[228] and by 1862 Theodore Thomas had introduced the harp as well as the English horn into an orchestra in the United States.[229] In 1881, Zopff could still give a narrow range, F_1 to d'''', for a harp with seven pedals with no mention of double action,[230] but by 1889, Schroeder gave the pedal harp a range of C_1 to f'''' with all chromatic notes. He even admitted that usually there was "only" one harp in the orchestra, but in big orchestras two.[231] Yes, Berlioz and the French do seem to have been progressive in most aspects of orchestral sound.

The Strings

The strings may have changed less than the wind sections of the orchestra during the course of the nineteenth century; nevertheless there were some innovations that must have had an effect on sound. Until about 1820 and even later, for example, violins and violas were played without a chin rest, the invention of which is credited to Spohr.[232] It seems probable that this as well as the spike used by cellists made possible a much wider vibrato than had previously been used.[233] Strings were made by hand until the development of a mechanical procedure in the middle of the century.[234] The nineteenth century also saw the "perfecting" of the screw mechanism for tightening the bow hairs.[235] Nor were there universal standards for style and technique. Comparing Germany with France, Berlioz wrote: "Their double basses are more powerful, but their cellos, violas and violins, though splendid, are not seriously to be ranked with our younger school of string players; the violins, violas and cellos of the Paris Conservatoire Orchestra have no rivals."[236]

The violin had some "improvements": a longer neck, presumably to stretch its range, and a higher, rounder bridge.[237] In fact, commenting on a performance of a violin concerto at a program of *Ancient Music* in 1828, Parke was struck with the precision of intonation of the player "almost up to the bridge," and wondered what the reaction of "the eccentric" Tom Collet would have been. Collet had led the orchestra of Vauxhall Gardens in 1745 and "had such an aversion to playing high, that he dismissed one of his violin performers for flourishing on the half shift; viz. one note above the confined compass of that time."[238]

Gassner still described the violin as being strung with four gut strings, but then described its range as from the silver string g' through a'''', obviously meaning small g to a'''.[239] Berlioz extended this a bit up to c'''', in "view of the high degree of skill attained nowadays by our young violinists." Strauss added that this "has been frequently extended in the orchestra" to g''''.[240] With regard to such improvements Berlioz found more cause for complaint in matters of conservatory teaching. He thought that study was incomplete without instruction in pizzicato and harmonics among other things, stating that the "little that our young violinists have learnt about it they have acquired for themselves since Paganini's appearance."[241] One gets the impression that Berlioz was anxious to bring into the orchestra techniques then considered the sole domain of the virtuoso.

Fétis claimed for Rossini the innovation of dividing the violins into four parts.[242] As for unanimity of bowing, it was not practiced everywhere. Reviewing the Drury Lane orchestra in 1838–39, one writer found the group "lamentably deficient in this nicety of musical execution, without which the highest clearness and the most decided expression are quite unattainable." On the other hand he cited Habeneck and the Paris orchestra for "a greater correspondence in the *coups d'archet.*"[243]

The viola generally retained its subordinate position even at mid-century, often being played by violinists of lesser calibre or past their prime. Early in the century at least one writer had complained that it was incomprehensible to him that even in otherwise good orchestras, the viola "is the worst and weakest part." It was bad enough that "the gentle, often nasal tone" of the viola was "stifled" by the "gritty, cutting tone" of the violin. Add to that the fact that it was in the hands of players who "think little or even not at all to its maintenance and improvement."[244]

Very telling are the comments of Ernest Reyer on working with the orchestra of the Théâtre-Lyrique in the 1850s.

> I was rehearsing a work of mine in which the viola part, without being duly complicated, is of genuine importance. As I could hear nothing, I went over to the section of the orchestra normally occupied by the violas and found a solitary old man, his coat collar turned up to his ears (for it was very cold), timidly drawing a bow innocent of rosin across the silent strings of his instrument. I politely suggested that as he was the only one, he might give a little more. He replied that there was no point in his doing so; and when I showed surprise, added: "I'm the rehearsal viola; there will be a different one at the performance: he will play with more tone than I."[245]

And if this also throws light on the problem of rehearsal players as opposed to performance players, a subject which will unfortunately have to remain beyond the scope of this study, it corroborates the generally low level of viola players and viola playing. Wagner claimed that the viola was "commonly (with rare exceptions indeed) played by infirm violinists, or by decrepit players of wind instruments who happen to have been acquainted with a string instrument once upon a time...." He went on to say that at best one might find a competent player at the first desk, able to handle an occasional solo passage, but he had seen this function performed by the leader of the first violins. In fact, he cited a case of a large orchestra with eight violas, only one of whom could deal with rather difficult passages in his own later scores.[246]

It is not surprising, then, that Berlioz also castigated conservatories for neglecting this instrument in a passage which sounds like an up-date of Haydn's pronouncements on the subject. Berlioz found it "lamentable" that there were no classes for viola and labeled "obsolete" the "usual reaction" to a mediocre violinist—"He'll make a good viola player"—where "modern" music was concerned. "The leading composers at any rate do not write fill-in parts in orchestral music any more; they give every part an interest relative to the effect to be produced and refuse to regard some as inherently less important than others."[247] But the situation as described by both Berlioz and Wagner was well illustrated in Berlioz's concert in Loewenberg in 1863: "The Kapellmeister played the viola solo in *Harold* impeccably, with a beauty of tone and a rhythmic poise that absolutely delighted me (in the other pieces he resumed his violin)."[248] Can one assume that there was no leader of the violas who could have done the job well enough?

If one wonders about the presence of the viola in some earlier French scores, it was also called *taille, tenor, quinte, alto-viola,* and *violette.*[249] Gassner described it as having four gut strings of which the lowest two were covered with silver wire. Typically he felt that a violin player could in a short time learn to play viola, experiencing only the difficulties due to its greater size. Seldom should one have to play above e″ or f″. He still described it as going along often in unison or octaves with the bass.[250] On the other hand, Berlioz gave its "ordinary range" as "at least three octaves," that is, up to c‴. But he found fault with most of the violas "currently used in our French orchestras" as not being of "requisite proportions." As a result "neither in size nor in tonal volume are they real violas. They are more like violins strung with viola strings."[251]

Strauss mentioned a "Viola alta" constructed by a Professor Hermann Ritter which had a fifth string tuned to e″. Its larger size gave it greater volume, and of course it had a higher range, "very advantageous for modern orchestral works." Its requirement of "greater physical power" from the player is credited with its limited use.[252] Evidently it was used in the Meiningen Orchestra in 1884, and Bülow received credit for the innovation. Hanslick found that "of stronger construction than the common viola, [the viola alta] surpasses it in fullness of tone and reduces the all-too-great distance normally separating violas and violoncellos."[253] One would think that the fifth string would rather reduce the distance between viola and violin. Hanslick also claimed that it was adopted by Wagner for Bayreuth.

There is not much to say about the cello in the nineteenth century. Gassner described it as having four gut strings, the lowest two covered with silver wire. He recognized it as "extremely effective as a solo instrument," but "its true character is noble song rather than brilliant passages." He was also aware that in "recent" works, the cello appeared often as other than a foundation with the contrabass, acting sometimes as a middle or melody-carrying part. Gassner stated that because the cello often must accompany recitative with chords, the cellist must not only be an accomplished master of his instrument but also possess a knowledge of harmony.[254] This practice of playing harmony under secco recitative was evidently done in a masterly way by the eminent English cellist Robert Lindley, who spent many years as first cellist with the Philharmonic Society. One writer described an ability he had, not to be found in "any other violoncellist, viz. that when accompanying a recitative, he gave the full chord, and frequently the note on which the singers were to commence. Some one or two tried to imitate his mode, but all failed."[255]

Berlioz gave the cello's range as from C to g″, but "great virtuosos go still higher." By the way, he warned about the usage of the g-clef—the "double meaning"—often met with in older scores; that is, a g-clef at the beginning of a piece or directly after a bass clef is to be read an octave above actual sound. Only after having gone through the tenor clef will the g-clef denote actual pitch. "There is nothing to justify this practice; it frequently leads to errors."[256]

The contrabass remained somewhat problematic. "The contrabass is to music what the supporting pillars are to a building; and yet more concern is shown over the good maintenance and improvement of all other string instruments than over the bass's." Thus begins an article from 1803–4 concerned with its lot. In the first place the writer claimed that most basses were mass-produced from the worst wood and finished with the most common lacquer, that some calling themselves instrument-makers ordered them by the dozen from small towns at a pittance, blackened in their own names, added a strong peg and whatever else, and distributed them as their own work at enormous profit. Wondering why, unlike violins, new basses sounded better than old ones, the writer had taken an old one apart and discovered that the base [*Boden*] and even more the sounding board [*Decke*] had been planed much too thin, obviously to facilitate a stronger and fuller tone. But this would last only until the heterogeneous [*fremdartigen*] particles became dried up and evaporated, after which the older it became and the more it was used, the worse it got. Realizing that the usual makers will not "deviate a hair" from their tradition, the writer directed his article towards players, proposing a means of strengthening and improving the tone of "their badly worked instrument" with slight care. Claiming that every string player knows from experience that if a string breaks and he is forced to play on three strings, the instrument will have a stronger and fuller tone, he cited as the reason for this the fact that the instrument, particularly the sounding board, is thus less strained and compressed and consequently can vibrate more quickly and freely. He therefore proposed stringing the instrument with only three strings, tuning the highest A, the middle one D, and the lowest G. All one would lose is a minor third in the low register. Since bass players were used to not always playing everything as written and to octave-transpositions, they would not be embarrassed by the notes thus lacking. Besides, in the type of bass described above, the weak base and sounding board made the contra E through F♯ "faint, dull, untrue," and a good musician avoided them when he could. As to advantages, the instrument could be less expensively strung, and the player could tax his instrument more without risking touching a neighboring string, since they could be placed farther apart. The few players who possessed a truly well-made instrument did not need this provision, but since they were so few "my proposal, it seems to me, deserves consideration."[257] Of course, a three-stringed bass had been used in the eighteenth century, but the argument is none the less interesting.

Blaze indicated the use of a three-string bass around 1820. He described it as "deprived of the fourth string"; "abridged sometimes by the tuning of the three others, its range has little scope."[258] Evidently tuning was not standardized early in the century. The article just cited pointed out that it was tuned opposite to the violin—thus its designation of *Kontraviolon* [!]. More likely its tuning is a legacy of the bass viol da gamba, but to continue, the same writer also allowed that other players tuned the three highest strings like the cello—A, D, G—but an octave lower, and the lowest string F or E.[259] In 1825 in Cassel, Sir George Smart considered it worth writing down that Spohr had told him "that the double basses with four strings are tuned the reverse of the violins, that is, the lowest string is E, then A, D and G. At Vienna they formerly had five strings."[260]

Calling the good contrabassist "the soul of the orchestra," Gassner stated that the instrument was "rarely with five, frequently with three, most commonly and best strung with four gut strings" tuned "g, d, A, E," obviously sounding an octave lower, while the five-string variety would be tuned "a, f♯, d, A, F." He went on to say that the tuning differed according to the "school" from which the player came. "One rarely writes up to g for this instrument, since its efficacy in the high notes declines."[261] Berlioz also acknowledged two "kinds" of basses—those with three and those with four strings, again showing a difference in ambience between France and Germany within a couple of years. He also gave the three-string tuning as A, D, G₁; the four-string as G, D, A₁, E₁. Yet their ranges were close: E₁ to a for the four-string variety, G₁ to a for the three-string (of course, written an octave higher). Berlioz preferred the four-stringed bass and had some interesting ideas:

> Tuning in fourths makes for greater facility of execution because the player is not compelled to shift on the finger-board when playing scales. Furthermore, the three low notes E, F and F♯ . . . are extremely useful; their absence frequently spoils the form of the best-designed bass part by requiring unpleasant and difficult transposition to the higher octave. This deficiency is still more apparent in the English double-basses, which, although tuned in

fourths, have only three strings [G, D, A_1]... A Good orchestra should have several four-string double-basses, some of them tuned in fifths and thirds [A, G_1, E_1].... Together with the other double-basses tuned in fourths, a combination of open strings would be available which would greatly increase the sonority of the orchestra.[262]

Zopff, writing in 1881, gave the modern tuning in fourths, G, D, A_1, E_1. He gave its range also as up to sounding small a. Reminiscent of the earlier writer quoted above, he also called it "the supporting pillar of the whole orchestra."[263] But there were individual players who exceeded the norm. Early in the century, a Viennese player, Johann Hindle, with a "peculiar way" of tuning his instrument, was reputed to have a range of five and one half octaves.[264] Strauss added that a fifth string tuned C_1 had been in use "for many years." He found the additional low range "doubtless a gain in sonority" but "counter-balanced by the increased difficulty in pressing down the strings, since with five strings the middle ones are placed very high above the fingerboard." Therefore, he found a four-stringed bass with a "lever device" to change E_1 to C_1 "definitely preferable." He cited a device invented by a Max Poike. He also noted two types of bows in use "to this day": those with "a curved stick, which are not good in cantilena and produce a harsh and brittle tone, and the "enlarged violoncello bow, which permits all the styles of bowing possible on the other stringed instruments."[265] Bülow was credited by Hanslick with introducing the five-stringed bass with the Meiningen Orchestra in 1884.[266]

The great Dragonetti was probably as responsible for a general advance in bass playing as any one man could be. He was described as "perfection" on his instrument. "The power and tones he produced from his unwieldy instrument were wonderful, and to this he added great and rapid execution." And he was a "supporting pillar.... So powerful was the tone he could produce from his instrument, that I have frequently heard him pull a whole orchestra back with one accent if they wavered in the least."[267] Smart noted in Vienna in 1825 that "the double bass here had four strings and Mittag said some had five, but with three Dragonetti does more than I have yet heard."[268] In addition to being an encomium, it would seem to indicate a difference in national usage between at least England and Austria at the time. But perhaps generalities are dangerous here, for Bottesini who led the basses in the New Philharmonic Society in the 1850s "used a small instrument of the type called a chamber bass, strung with harp-strings, but Dragonetti used an exceptionally large bass."[269] So there were variants within England, too. And it is worth noting that in contrasting German with French orchestras, Berlioz considered the basses of the former to be "more powerful."[270]

One finds discussions of other instruments, for example: viola d'amore[271] (first appearing at the Paris Opéra in Meyerbeer's *Les Huguenots* in 1836),[272] viola da gamba,[273] guitar,[274] a *Terzguitarre* ("new," smaller, and a third higher than the usual one),[275] mandolin,[276] lute,[277] and theorbo.[278] But one suspects that they were included for the sake of being thorough and only saw occasional use, often in older works. as, for example, works of J. S. Bach which employed viola da gamba. Actually, Gassner did not include them with orchestral instruments.

Late in the century Blitz thought it curious that composers had not thought of using the human voice as an orchestral instrument, making it "execute only sounds with closed mouth" or even others, but without words. "The voice is a very sonorous instrument which could dominate the whole orchestra; a double quartet of men's or children's voices would suffice for an orchestra of eighty musicians."[279] While this strikes one as a very modern idea waiting for twentieth-century fulfillment, it could easily have been suggested by the wordless chorus with closed mouths behind the scenes in the storm music in Act IV of Verdi's *Rigoletto*.

The same author, though not in favor of substituting other instruments for those specified by the composer, realized that such was often necessary since many were not always available. Therefore, the conductor must use "talent and tact" in making choices which would not "bring harm to the character of the piece." He stated that the instruments most often lacking were the harp, English horn, bass clarinet, contrabassoon, trumpet, bass trombone, ophicleide, viola d'amore, and basset horn. Harps were generally replaced by the piano. Though several instruments called *"piano-harpe, harpe à clavier,* etc." had been built to replace it, "nothing, up to now, has come along to imitate the ideal sonority of these magnificent instruments." He advised replacing the English horn with the oboe or the clarinet, according to the character of the piece, the bass clarinet by the E♭ baritone saxophone or the bassoon, the contrabassoon by *"la contrebasse à anche"* [?] or better still by the contrabass sarrusophone, the trumpet by the valve cornet, bass trombone and ophicleide by bass tuba, the viola d'amore by the viola, the basset horn by the clarinet when the part is not too low, otherwise, as a last resort, by the alto saxophone. Citing high horn and trumpet parts by Handel, Bach, and Haydn that had been declared unplayable by "modern" virtuosos, Blitz recommended the horns take such passages an octave lower, the trumpets play such parts on the little trumpet in D, "production of Mahillon at Brussels."[280]

Referring to an article by Saint-Saëns concerning an innovation which would have all the instruments in C, Blitz pointed out that as desirable as that might be, the clarinet in C, the horn in C, and the cornet in C are much inferior to the B♭ clarinet, the F horn, and the B♭ cornet. And even if the invention should be perfect, prejudice would probably prevent universal application.[281]

Finally, it seems significant that Berlioz commented on women singing at a mass at Bonn in 1845.

The clergy of Bonn were fortunately less strict than the French clergy, and had seen their way to allowing women to sing at this service. I am aware that otherwise the performance of Beethoven's Mass would have been impossible; but this reason might have seemed of little weight, despite the unusualness of the occasion. In Paris, I know, it would have been unavailing. There women may make themselves heard in church only on condition that they are neither singers nor musicians.[282]

It is surprising that such restrictions lasted so late into the century!

Part Three

Size, Numbers, and Proportions in the Nineteenth-Century Orchestra

8

Expansion—Ideas and Reactions

It goes without saying that the general increase in orchestral size seen in the course of the eighteenth century continued unabated in the nineteenth. However, it will also be seen that lack of uniformity continued as well. The commitment to hugeness was not universal. For example, one writer in 1802, in order to discuss the proper placing of an orchestra, chose as an example a "small" orchestra of 25, including only 2 flutes, 2 oboes (or clarinets), 2 bassoons, 2 horns, 2 trumpets, timpani, 1 keyboard [*Flügel*], 5 first and 4 second violins, 2 violas, 1 cello, and 1 bass, for a room about 70 feet [*Schuh*] long and 40 feet wide.[1] Now this reads more like a mid-eighteenth-century attitude rather than one on the edge of the romantic era. On the other hand, another writer in 1807, in discussing ways of reinforcing dynamic levels, chose as an example a "strongly set" orchestra with 15 to 20 violins.[2]

It is still surprising to many musicians, so accustomed to the modern contingents generally heard in performances of Beethoven's orchestral music, to discover that he only requested a string section of *"4 Violinen, 4 Secund, 4 Prim, 2 Contrabässe, 2 Violonschell"* to perform his middle symphonies (probably numbers 4 to 6) and two overtures: *The Ruins of Athens* and *King Stephen.*[3] Now it is not exactly clear what he meant by this, unless possibly he meant to write *"Violen"* and a slip of the pen produced *"Violinen"* instead.[4] This would read, realigned, as: 4 first violins, 4 seconds, 4 violas, 2 cellos, and 2 basses—a total of 16—certainly small by contemporary standards. Haas has pointed out the "plastic" effects possible with the winds against so weak a contingent of strings.[5] However, Beethoven eventually also fell subject to the "fever" for expansion, for in 1814 at a concert in Vienna, his Seventh and Eighth Symphonies were performed by an orchestra including 18 first violins, 18 second violins, 14 violas, 12 cellos, 7 basses, and 2 contrabassoons.[6] Even more surprising, as pointed out by Asher Zlotnik, is the fact that the above works do not call for even one contrabassoon, but for some reason Beethoven must have felt that weak basses had to be reinforced.[7] [This reminds this writer of a radio discussion of Beethoven's orchestration in which the recapitulation of the Eighth Symphony was singled out (measure 190 of the first movement) as a place where Beethoven had miscalculated. The speakers wondered how much obligation the conductor had to "correct" such a problem.] In the passage in question the cellos, basses, and bassoons have the melody *fff*—an unusual way to recapitulate, to be sure—while the rest of the orchestra is also playing *fff* above them. It should be remembered that the number of winds and upper strings Beethoven had experienced previously had in all probability always been considerably fewer than were involved in this Vienna performance, and much less than in a present-day situation, where woodwinds are often doubled. Is it possible that Beethoven wanted the contrabassoons to compensate for the increased forces in such passages as the above? Even at that stage of his hearing problem he certainly would have been aware of the imbalance. (Of course, the question can even be raised: why is it so certain that the "main" theme is meant to stand out in this place?) And even for his later symphonies it was more usual in Vienna to find only 16 strings pitted against the usual winds.[8] In 1815, Beethoven had demanded that against the two wind bands in *Wellingtons Sieg,* the "rest of the orchestra must, of course, with proper balance, be as well manned as possible: the larger the hall, the more players."[9] But in 1817 in a letter to Ferdinand Ries concerning possible performances of his music by the Philharmonic Society in London, Beethoven seemed to be greatly interested in the size of the performing group, with such questions as: "How powerful is the Society's orchestra, how many violins and so forth; and are there *one or two of each wind-instrument?* Is the hall large and resonant?"[10] This would suggest a growing awareness of the dynamic impact his music must have. Schindler writes that Beethoven desired an orchestra of at most "about 60 good musicians."[11] But in 1824 when the Ninth Symphony and portions of the *Missa solemnis* were to be performed, Beethoven wrote to Tobias Haslinger: "Piringer has been instructed to select the eight best violinists, the two best viola-players, the two best cellists.... That is the number who are to augment the orchestra."[12] One source reports: "Drawing from the amateur forces of the *Gesellschaft der Musikfreunde,* the orchestra was to be augmented to twenty-four violins, ten violas, and twelve cellos and basses, and wind instruments were to be doubled."[13] Such statements, which occur with some frequency, cause one to hesitate and ponder whether "double" means, for example, two flutes, or two first flutes and two seconds; the ambiguity can be a very important one. But it is, perhaps, fantasizing by Siegfried Borris to assert that "Beethoven thought in future dimensions of the orchestra, and he seized upon these sound-visions in his scores."[14] However, Schindler does explain that some of Beethoven's problems in obtaining performances on the "so-called *Norma-Tagen*"—about four days a year when long works could be performed in Vienna—were due to the need for larger forces and the necessity to augment the orchestra and chorus.[15]

Some of Ludwig Spohr's experiences are revealing in this regard. In 1799, at the age of fifteen, he became a court musician at Brunswick, where the court orchestra was small and the trumpets and timpani were suppressed in order to prevent "a proper forte."[16] What a contrast he must have felt just a few years later in St. Petersburg in 1802, when at a Lenten concert the court orchestra included 36 violins, 20 basses, and "doubled winds," besides "as reinforcement for the chorus," the 40 horn players of the Imperial Band.[17] Even more impressive must have been the performance of Haydn's *The Seasons* in which Spohr took part with an orchestra which was "the largest I had ever heard," with 70 violins, 30 basses, and doubled winds. "The effect was magnificent."[18] And in Hamburg at a festival "staged by English residents" there "in honor of their King," Spohr heard an outdoor rehearsal for which "a kind of canvas shell" had been set up. The orchestra, "some hundred strong, was placed in tiers." Dussek rehearsed a cantata composed for the occasion. It "gained much" by means of a large organ behind the orchestra. The result "sounding through the stillness of the night, had such an effect of solemnity that I was entirely carried away."[19]

Back in Germany in 1810, Spohr himself conducted the Thuringian music festival at Frankenhausen. The orchestra for that occasion, which included Haydn's *Creation,* consisted of 4 flutes, 4 oboes, 4 clarinets, 4 bassoons, 4 horns, 3 trumpets, 3 trombones, 1 *"Basshorn,"* 2 timpanists, 2 organists, *"Flügel,"* 42 violins, 12 violas, 11 cellos, and 9 contrabasses, with solo voices and a chorus of 28 sopranos, 20 altos, 20 tenors, and 30 basses. The totals were an orchestra of 106 and a chorus of 98.[20] This does not appear to be as hefty a group as in the St. Petersburg *Seasons,* but quite full for so early in Germany. In 1815 he commented on a celebration for the "liberation of Germany on the anniversary of the Battle of Leipzig." While he did not enumerate the forces on this occasion, he did make some interesting observations, such as the impression that in large auditoriums and with large orchestra and chorus, the simplest pieces have the "greatest effect, assuming a noble and dignified style of composition, whereas a richly figured scoring and rapid harmonic progressions are out of place." Yet oddly, on the following day he found the "Jupiter" Symphony of Mozart "precisely and spiritedly played and irresistibly effective!" The performance convinced him that "in this setting and with adequate orchestral forces, the four themes of the concluding fugue, where they come together at the end, can be followed easily by a practiced ear. Whereas this passage had formerly impressed me as simply a technical tour de force, I recognized this impression today as an error."[21] Surely there is some contradiction here. Later that year in Munich he heard the Royal Orchestra in the first of its winter concerts. He reported 12 first and 12 second violins, 8–10 violas, 10 cellos, and 6 basses in that aggregation. This orchestra evidently had the reputation of being "one of the best in the world," so Spohr's "expectations were high." But he found that in Beethoven's C minor Symphony "they were unsurpassed." He felt it "hardly possible" that this work could be performed "with more fire and more strength and, at the same time, with more tenderness and with more precise attention to every nuance." He found then that it had a "greater effect" than he could have "thought possible" even though he had heard it "frequently in Vienna and under the composer's direction."[22]

Spohr also made some acute observations following the Swiss Music Festival in Fribourg in 1816. For *The Creation*, the hall was "satisfactory" and the orchestra "well placed," except for the fact that the organ was at the opposite end of the hall and could not be used. But where former festivals had at least 300 performers, this occasion had "hardly" 200, and with more than half in the chorus, the orchestra, "particularly in the big choral episodes, was much too weak. Indeed, it was at times inaudible." Another festival concert, intended for a smaller hall, had to be moved to the larger one. Spohr thought that therefore a larger orchestra was needed, but since there were no extra parts available, the "result was an orchestra considerably weaker than that which had supported *The Creation*, and its deficiencies were even more painfully apparent."[23]

At La Scala in Milan in 1816, Spohr again connected room size with orchestral size. He described the orchestra as "very large" with 24 violins, 8 cellos and 8 basses, "plus all the familiar wind instruments, trombones, bass horn, and Turkish music." All the same, it was "none too large for the auditorium."[24] Elsewhere he noticed another Italian propensity: many basses.

> The Italians generally stick too much to the old patterns and devices. Violas and bassoons double the basses, while clarinets and oboes play in unison. Since, in most Italian orchestras there are six to eight basses to a single cello, and usually not a very good cello at that, the use of the cello for a middle voice, customary with us since Mozart's time, and so effective where appropriately introduced, is practically unknown.[25]

Particularly noticeable is Spohr's tendency to judge orchestral size by the numbers of violins and basses included. Sir George Smart seemed inclined to use basses as a yardstick. In Paris in 1802, he reported that in the theater in the Rue Feydeau, there was "a most excellent band, about forty, the basses were in the last row next to the pit. There were eight violins and four double basses, one of them in the centre."[26] But on his tour of the continent in 1825, he noted at Stuttgart: "There were only four double basses."[27] At Munich for *Der Freischütz*, he found "the orchestra no great things [*sic*] and contained only three double basses."[28] And in Berlin for Spontini's *Fernando Cortez:* "The band was excellent and larger than I have ever yet heard here, though there were only four double basses; however, there were two other Royal theatres open this evening which were also supplied from the Royal band."[29] Smart's remarks shed light on another problem, usually not discussed. In judging orchestras and orchestral size, allowance should most probably be made for the fact that more than one event on a given day would be manned by members of a court or, in the case of Leipzig, city orchestra. Here are some further comments on Berlin:

> Spontini is the general music director, Seidel the Kapellmeister and Schneider, Music Director. There are twelve first violins, as when they use a full orchestra two out of the following three players are included, namely, Möser, the Kapellmeister, Seidler, who always leads when his wife sings, and Bohrer, senior, who they suppose will soon leave for Munich. There were twelve second violins, ten 'celli, and seven bassi, four flutes, five oboes, five clarinets, five fagotti, five corni, three trumpets, three tromboni and two drums. There are also as supernumeraries two first violins, two second violins, two 'celli and three corni. This is the full orchestra but it seldom plays as such except in Spontini's operas. The players take duty in different weeks but sometimes there are performers at both the Royal Theatres on the same night and sometimes also there is a performance at the Royal Theatre at Charlottenburg, a little way out of Berlin, in which case all are employed.[30]

Thus, one must be cautious in relying on orchestral lists since they often only state the number of musicians generally available but nothing about particular performances. Fewer musicians might be used, or more might be added for particular occasions. This caution should be kept in mind when considering numbers of players mentioned throughout this study. The question of conducting should also be raised again in this connection. Spontini was a baton conductor, but when Seidler "leads when his wife sings," is this meant in the old sense of "taking command" or in the later sense of what is now expected of a concertmaster? Smart is not clear on this point.

Other observations recorded by Smart during his trip in 1825 include a review of a small theater in Mödling where the music was "wretched" with only about eight players in the orchestra.[31] On the other hand, he was quite impressed at the theater in Prague. "The power of this band is extraordinary, considering that it consists of but eight violins, two viole, two 'celli and four-stringed bassi [sic], with the usual wind instruments, but Pixis lamented that the band was so small for the size of the theatre."[32] If indeed the orchestra was small for the theater, then one has to wonder what made it so impressive to Smart, especially from the standpoint of power: the ensemble, the calibre of the players, or something about the acoustics of the building? Would a group of lesser ensemble ability have sounded inadequate there though equal in size, or would the same group have made a less dynamic impression in a theater of different acoustical properties? At Dresden, Smart heard *Der Freischütz,* "directed by Weber, who consequently was not dead." Smart had heard rumors at several of his stops to that effect. His comments: "The band, particularly the oboe, was good, but not strong. More strength of string is required, the exact strength as yet I know not." He later enumerated the theater orchestra as: "five first violins, five second violins, two viole, two 'cellos, two basses, two of each wind instrument—the flutes taking the piccolo—four horns and three tromboni."[33]

At Kassel Smart was informed "that the full Royal band consisted of sixteen violins, four viole, four 'celli and four bassi, though I only counted three, together with a double set of wind instruments, therefore they had always two good ones of each."[34] Again there is ambiguity here, but the passage seems to suggest that a "double set" was not always used, even though available. It also seems to imply that "doubled winds" when used by Smart and others meant four flutes—that is, two firsts and two seconds. At Cologne, Smart seemed unimpressed, or perhaps rather badly impressed. "There was a bad orchestra consisting of eight violins, two viole, two 'celli and two bassi, with the usual number of wind instruments. Weber, an elder brother of Weber at Dresden, is the director.... The theatre is rather small, dark, and dingy...."[35]

Perhaps some idea of Spontini's views is not out of place here. He was in Leipzig in 1829, and Heinrich Dorn remembered his reactions:

> The ins and outs of our Leipzig theater, and especially of the music room situated within, Spontini found horrible, and at the sight of the orchestra space intended for only 6 first violins and 2 contrabasses he altogether downright shuddered. *"Grandioso"* was to him no decorative epithet—it was the element of his existence.[36]

And it seems that even at Berlin the available forces might have been less than Spontini really wanted, for when Wagner was preparing the *Vestalin* for him at Dresden in 1844, Spontini expected much. Wagner reported that as far as chorus and ballet were concerned, Spontini "took it for granted" that there would be nothing lacking "to the dignity of the performance," and as for the orchestra, he expected to be pleased, presuming the "necessary complement of excellent instruments," the whole "garnished with twelve good contrabasses." Wagner continued: "This phrase bowled me over, for the proportion thus bluntly stated in figures gave me so logical a conception of his exalted expectations, that I hurried away at once to the director to warn him that the enterprise on which we had embarked would not, after all, prove as easy as we thought."[37] One gets the impression of a grand *poseur*. In 1844 Dresden seemed to have had only 4 basses.[38] Some idea of the forces actually supplied Spontini for the performance can be gained by Wagner's description of his outburst "Are the violas dying?" and the frightened reaction of the "two pale and incurably melancholy old men who held on tenaciously to their posts in the orchestra, notwithstanding their right to a pension."[39] If they occupied the first desk, one wonders what could have been the quality of the possible second desk, as a seating plan shows four violas in the Dresden orchestra at this time.[40] (The size of the Berlin orchestra including those years when Spontini reigned as music director will be taken up at a later point in this study.)

As in so many areas of music, Berlioz had much to say about orchestral size, and it is always worthwhile to pay attention to him. In his scores he often gave indications of the numbers of strings needed for what he considered proper balance. One can only lament that more composers did not do likewise, giving some idea of their conception of sound in planning a piece. Here are a few examples. For the Fantastic Symphony (ca. 1830) Berlioz asked for 2 flutes, the second doubling on piccolo, 2 oboes, the second doubling on English horn, 2 clarinets, the second doubling on E♭ clarinet, and four bassoons; for brass he asked for 4 horns, 2 trumpets, 2 cornets, 3 trombones, and 2 ophicleides; percussion included 4 timpanists and about 3 other players; there are two harp parts with "at least 2" players on each; then come "at least" 15 first violins, "at least" 15 second violins, "at least" 10 violas, "at least" 11 cellos, and "at least" 9 basses.[41] Altogether, then, he demanded at least 94 players.[42] At first sight, this strikes one as a large orchestra, and one is tempted to label Berlioz a trail-blazer. Indeed, he has carried that reputation for a long time—"madman"—"dreamer." But Beethoven's orchestra in 1814 was heavier in string strength, and though fewer winds were called for, it must have come near this number. Remember the two contrabassoons?

Berlioz's *Requiem* demands 4 flutes, 2 oboes, 2 English horns, 4 clarinets, 8 bassoons, 12 horns, 10 timpanists, 16 percussion, 25 first violins, 25 second violins, 20 violas, 29 cellos, and 18 contrabasses, in addition to a chorus of 80 sopranos and altos (presumably 40 of each), 60 tenors (divided I and II), and 70 basses (likewise divided). But added to this the four satellite orchestras combine for another 12 trumpets, 4 cornets, 16 trombones, and 6 tubas.[43] If this seems already grandiose, a footnote adds that the numbers given are only relative. Space permitting, the chorus could be doubled or tripled and the orchestra increased in proportion. But with an "exceptionally large chorus— say 700 to 800 voices—," the whole group was to be used only for the *Dies irae, Tuba mirum,* and *Lacrymosa,* the remainder being restricted to 400 voices.[44] One should remember that the work was envisioned for a large church, not an ordinary concert hall; Berlioz always tried to keep all factors in mind. One should also take note of the necessity of increasing the orchestra "proportionately," should the chorus be enlarged. More will be noted on choral versus orchestral balance later, but notice that here it is 210 versus 140, and 210 versus 202 when the satellite groups come in—not overwhelming odds for the chorus.

The *Roman Carnival Overture* (1844) shows a return to more restraint, with the concert hall obviously again in mind: 2 flutes, 2 oboes, English horn, 2 clarinets, 4 bassoons, 4 horns, 2 trumpets, 2 cornets, 3 trombones, timpani and

3 other percussion, at least 15 first violins, at least 15 second violins, at least 10 violas, at least 12 cellos, and at least 9 basses—a total of at least 87.[45] Thinking in terms of the concert hall and the "Fantastic," this does not show a great increase in demand. But one must note in all these figures the ripieno strength in the bassoons. This seems to have been typical for Paris. Almost every available list of the orchestras of both the Paris Opéra and the Conservatory shows four bassoons, and if there is any doubt of their ripieno use, two lists of players for benefit concerts of the Conservatory Orchestra show "*1.ᵉʳ Pup. des Bassons*" followed by two names and "*2.ᵉ Pup. des Bassons*" followed by two more names.[46]

Lest one remain convinced that Berlioz always demanded unreasonably large forces, it is well to take note of his correspondence with Prosper Sainton in London on behalf of a Miss Dolby, a singer who was to offer a concert in Paris in 1856. In a letter of January 16 Berlioz stated that he was going to book *"la salle de Herz"* for the date in question and in estimating costs suggested an orchestra of 54 musicians.[47] In a following letter he stated that the number of strings could be reduced a little for the *"Salle Herz,"* indicating that 8 first violins, 8 seconds, 4 violas, 4 cellos, and 4 basses "would seem to me enough, unless you mean to perform some large-scale symphony."[48] In other words, unless a major orchestral work were to be performed, this string strength would suffice for a hall this size.

On the other hand, there was the grandiose side to Berlioz, especially where his own works were concerned. In 1824 he hoped for "an orchestra of a hundred picked musicians, and an even larger choir which would rehearse for a month"; the intent was a performance of an early Mass of his. But when the "huge forces" came together for the full rehearsal, they consisted of only 15 tenors, 5 basses, a dozen choirboys, 9 violins, 1 viola, 1 oboe, 1 horn, and 1 bassoon. "My shame and despair at offering the celebrated conductor [Henri Valentino] of one of the world's leading orchestras [the Opéra] such a rabble of musicians may be imagined."[49]

In 1840 Berlioz organized and conducted a festival with a combined chorus and orchestra of 600. The program included music by Gluck, Handel, Palestrina, as well as some of his own music, the *Dies irae* and *Lacrymosa* from the *Requiem* among them. The rehearsal was enlightening as to problems that can arise with such a huge group.

Everything went reasonably well except the Queen Mab Scherzo, which I had rashly included in the programme. The piece is too swift and delicate to be performed by an orchestra of this size, nor should it be. With so short a bar, it is virtually impossible to keep the extremities of such a huge body of players together. Those farthest from the conductor soon get behind because they cannot quite keep up with the very rapid beat. I was in such a state of agitation that it never occurred to me to form a small picked orchestra which, concentrated near me in the middle of the stage, could have carried out my intentions without difficulty. After the most fearful struggles we had to abandon the scherzo, and it was removed from the programme.[50]

In 1844 Berlioz conducted a festival concert for the close of the Exhibition of Industrial Products. He engaged "virtually every orchestral player and chorister of any ability" in Paris and assembled "a body of a thousand and twenty-two performers."[51] He got amazing results by holding nine sectional rehearsals and only one general rehearsal, each performer then being only engaged for two rehearsals. He claimed "marvelous results" from the nine sectional rehearsals in which no player was involved in more than one, results which in his mind could not have been obtained from even five full rehearsals. He singled out the session with 36 double basses as "particularly interesting." At first the scherzo of Beethoven's Fifth Symphony sounded like "the grunting of a herd of stampeding pigs, the playing was so ragged and out of tune." But slowly improvement came, "ensemble was achieved, and the passage emerged clearly in all its rough-hewn energy."[52] At the performance, Berlioz was assisted by two assistant conductors: one for winds, the other for percussion. There were also five chorus masters dispersed at different points. Imagine the *Andante* of the Overture to *Der Freischütz* played by 24 horns, or the prayer from Rossini's *Moses* where 25 harps "sounded like a hundred, because they played the arpeggios in four-part chords instead of in single notes, thus quadrupling the number of strings in vibration."[53] Yes, Berlioz did have an ear for the gigantic! Of course, it must be remembered that the performance took place in the huge "hall of Machinery" in the exhibition building, and the results were not as staggering as one might think. His "March to the Scaffold" which "sounds so vigorous and powerfully scored in a normal concert hall, appeared muted and feeble." He found the same result with the scherzo and finale from the Fifth Symphony of Beethoven. "Mendelssohn's Hymn [from *Antigone*] seemed heavy and uninteresting; one paper remarked a few days afterwards that the priests of this Bacchus must have drunk beer instead of Cyprus wine."[54]

For a concert in Lyons in 1845, Berlioz wrote to George Hainl that he desired 2 flutes, 2 oboes, the second doubling English horn, 2 clarinets, 4 bassoons, 4 horns, 2 natural trumpets, 2 cornets, 3 trombones, an ophicleide, 2 timpanists, 4 other percussion, plus at least 34 violins, 10 violas, 11 cellos, and 9 basses. This is of the same order as the orchestras called for by the scores of the *Symphonie fantastique* and the *Carnaval romaine*. However, for the last movement for two orchestras of the *Symphonie funèbre et triomphale* he would need beyond the above: a flute "tierce" (in E♭), a D♭ piccolo, 2 oboes, 9 clarinets, including one in E♭, 2 horns, 2 trumpets, 3 trombones, 2 ophicleides, and 4 drummers. Finally, he also would need a chorus of 70–80 men and 20–30 women.[55] So Berlioz still seemed to adhere to a basic orchestra which was enlarged for specific works.

In 1851 he wrote that his *Te Deum* could be done with 300 performers, if the hall were not too huge. But that would be skimpy; 400 would be passable.[56] Here, obviously, is a specific work in which he thought beyond the normal, indeed, again in terms of the large spaces of the church. In 1853, he wrote that for the Covent Garden performance of *Benvenuto Cellini,* he would compensate in the parts for their lack of such instruments as third and fourth bassoons, third and fourth harps, and a third kettledrum. Again, this description shows a ripieno use (or desired use) in these parts. But Berlioz said they would have to hire two first-rate cornets, one good timpanist, a cymbal player who could not be the same man as the bass-drum player, and a second harp. This requirement infers that Covent Garden then possessed only trumpets, one timpanist, one other percussion player, and one harpist, normal for that time outside of Paris. Berlioz also wanted on stage two guitars, two tambourines, and a small anvil.[57] Yet in 1855 he wrote to J.W. Davison that for two concerts at St. Martin's Hall in London which would include *L'Enfance du Christ* and the *Te Deum,* he would like 100 choristers and an orchestra of 68 or 70—seemingly modest forces, especially for the latter work. Of course, it is rather obvious from the letter that cost is a consideration, and he stated that they could use the little chorus from Covent Garden for the first work "which does not require powerful masses," reinforcing it with a "little army of Hullah's" for the second work at a second concert.[58] More and more one realizes that Berlioz related mass and size of performing group to work and place of performance. And in this case, some consideration of expense entered in—inevitable even in the world of art. But compare the London *L'Enfance* with a Strasbourg festival performance in 1863, presumably in a huge setting, where there were 800 in the audience and 500 performers. "The effect was stupendous."[59]

What about Berlioz the theorist, and even further, Berlioz the dreamer? One can again turn to the treatise. There one finds the complaint that whereas in the past the number of strings in opera orchestras was "always in correct proportion" to the number of other instruments, this was no longer the case. A comic-opera orchestra with 2 flutes, 2 oboes, 2 clarinets, 2 horns, 2 bassoons, "rarely" 2 trumpets, and "hardly ever" any timpani, was "well balanced" with 9 first violins, 8 seconds, 6 violas, 7 cellos, and 6 basses. "Nowadays," however, with 4 horns, 3 trombones, 2 trumpets, bass drum, and timpani, but the same number of strings as above, the balance is "completely destroyed." The violins "are scarcely audible, and the total effect is extremely unsatisfactory." He found the orchestra for grand opera with 2 cornets and an ophicleide in addition to the winds named above, various percussion instruments, and even 6–8 harps, to be "equally unbalanced" with 12 first violins, 11 seconds, 8 violas, 10 cellos, and 8 basses. He felt there should be at least 15 first violins, 14 seconds, 10 violas, and 12 cellos, "although not all of them need be used in works with very soft accompaniments."[60] Most commentators accept the reference to the grand opera orchestra as referring specifically to the Opéra in Paris. Can it be coincidence that Berlioz's recommended string strength here closely approximates the Conservatory orchestra in these years which in 1840 was 15-15-10-12-9,[61] and in 1841 was 15-15-10-13-11?[62] It also approximates that called for in the "Fantastic" and the *Carnaval romaine*. Berlioz seems to have been too practical a musician not to have been influenced by aural experience as well as purely theoretical considerations.

For the symphonies of Haydn and Mozart, Berlioz felt that what he called a "comic-opera" orchestra would suffice. "A greater number of stringed instruments might even be too strong in some instances for the tender effects which these masters frequently assign to flutes, oboes and bassoons." But the symphonies of Beethoven, Weber's overtures, and more recent compositions in "the monumental or passionate style" required the number of strings "just indicated for grand opera."[63] One has to be impressed with his flexibility, with his insistence that the orchestra must not only be internally balanced but also set for specific works and the manner in which works make use of the forces.

Berlioz the theorist-dreamer, however, waxing musically philosophic, proposed as the "finest concert orchestra"—meant for a hall "scarcely larger" than that of the Paris Conservatory—"the most complete, the richest in shadings and tone colors, the most majestic, the most powerful and at the same time the most mellow," the following:

21 first violins, 20 second violins, 18 violas, 8 first violoncellos, 7 second violoncellos, 10 double basses, 4 harps, 2 piccolos, 2 flutes, 2 oboes, 1 English horn, 2 clarinets, 1 basset horn or bass clarinet, 4 bassoons, 4 valve horns, 2 valve trumpets, 2 cornets with pistons or cylinders, 3 trombones (1 alto and 2 tenor or 3 tenor), 1 bass trombone, 1 ophicleide in B♭ (or 1 bass tuba), 2 pairs of timpani with 4 drummers, 1 bass drum, 1 pair of cymbals.

For a choral work, Berlioz would add to this orchestra: "46 sopranos (first and second), 40 tenors (first and second), 40 basses (first and second)." He added that doubling or tripling these numbers would "doubtless" provide a "magnificent" orchestra for a festival. However, he felt that it would be an "error" to assume that all orchestras "must be composed according to this system" based on the "preponderance of the strings." He felt an "opposite plan" could bring forth "beautiful results" also. "In this case the string instruments, too weak to dominate the mass of clarinets and brass instruments, serve as a harmonious link between the brilliant tones of the brass, sometimes softening their sharp sound, sometimes stimulating their movement with a tremolo which even transforms drumrolls into music by blending with them."[64] Notice again that the chorus tallies only 126 against the 119 total of the orchestra. There are 84 strings against 14 woodwinds and 13 brass, with probable ripieno strength only in the bassoons. Even if one combines the winds it is 84 against 27, and that is without counting the harps. More will be said about proportions and balance later, but string strength is considerable here. However, one notes that Berlioz was not locked into this plan but allowed for other proportions, producing different effects. Also important to remember is his dictum that enlargements must be proportionate. But let him go on: "Common sense tells us that the composer— unless he is forced to employ a particular kind of orchestra—must adapt the number of performers to the character and style of his work and to the principal effects demanded by its ideas." He described as an example the orchestra and "four small bands" he used in his *Requiem:* "It is certain that the peculiar effects achieved by this new kind of orchestra would be impossible with any other combination."[65] Adaptability, flexibility, the character of the work—these are points worth remembering.

But what is really usually considered as Berlioz's dream orchestra is somewhat larger yet. He wrote of how interesting it would be to combine all the available musical forces in Paris to perform a work "especially composed for the occasion." The latter phrase is an extremely important point. "If this combination were put at the disposal of a master, in a hall built for this purpose by an architect with a good knowledge of acoustics and music, the composer would have to determine the exact plan and arrangement of this gigantic orchestra first and then design his work accordingly." Berlioz's point is that at past music festivals, only "ordinary" orchestras and choruses had been heard, "quadrupled or quintupled according to the number of performers available." But his proposal would be "entirely different."[66] Berlioz was not wildly dreaming here or re-orchestrating any work for an ordinary "monster" festival; he was thinking in terms of a specific work, composed for a specific group, arranged in a specific way, in a hall specifically built for the occasion. And here are the forces he proposed:

120 violins, divided into two, three or four groups
40 violas, divided into first and second, if necessary; at least 10 of the
    players able to play the viola d'amore
45 violoncellos, divided into firsts and seconds, if necessary
18 double-basses with three strings, tuned in fifths (G, D, A)
15 other double-basses with four strings, tuned in fourths (E, A, D, G)
 4 octobasses
 6 large flutes
 4 flutes in E♭
 2 octave piccolo flutes
 2 piccolo flutes in D♭
 6 oboes
 6 English horns
 5 saxophones

4 tenoroons
12 bassoons
4 small clarinets (in E♭)
8 clarinets (in C or B♭ or A)
3 bass clarinets in B♭
16 French horns (6 with valves)
8 trumpets
6 cornets
4 alto trombones
6 tenor trombones
2 bass trombones
1 ophicleide in C
2 ophicleides in B♭
2 bass tubas
30 harps
30 pianofortes
1 very low positive organ with at least a 16′ stop
8 pairs of kettledrums (10 drummers)
6 drums
3 bass drums
4 pairs of cymbals
6 triangles
6 sets of small bells
12 pairs of ancient cymbals (in different keys)
2 large, very low bells
4 gongs
4 crescents

———
465 instrumentalists
40 children sopranos (first and second)
100 women sopranos (first and second)
100 tenors (first and second)
120 basses (first and second)

———
360 chorus singers

And Berlioz continued with myriad ways in which such forces could be subdivided and used for various effects.[67] Note that here the orchestra outweighs the chorus. He included both ophicleides and bass tubas, presumably for their differentiated tone colors. The pianos would obviously be used as members of the orchestra, an effect seldom heard in nineteenth-century music. He even outlined methods for sectional rehearsals for such a strong group. The dream evidently lingered, for in 1851 after hearing a chorus of 6,500 children in St. Paul's in London, Berlioz mused:

> Suppose next that instead of 6,500 ignorant children, we had in the amphitheater 1,500 young *musicians,* 500 musical women with real voices, and 2,000 men singers sufficiently equipped by nature and training. Suppose further that instead of allotting the central space of the hexagon under the dome to the public, we placed there a little orchestra of three or four hundred instrumentalists, and entrusted to that well-trained mass of 4,300 musicians the performance of a fine work, written in a style suited to such a means, on a subject in which grandeur blends with nobility, and in which one is stirred by the expression of all the elevated thoughts that can move the heart of man: I believe that such a manifestation of the most powerful of the arts, aided by the magic of poetry and architecture, would be truly worthy of a nation like ours and would leave far behind the vaunted festivals of antiquity.[68]

It should be added that he had the Pantheon in mind as the proposed locale. Incidently, he was not unimpressed with what he heard, even if the excerpt might have suggested that he was.

Elsewhere Berlioz ruminated on the differences between playing large masterworks with such forces and writing especially for them. He felt that works with the "breadth of style" of the oratorios of Handel, Bach, Haydn, and Beethoven "no doubt have much to gain" from performances by large forces. Here it was only a question of "reinforcing the parts to a greater or lesser degree." However, composing specifically for a large or huge group, a composer "understanding the immense possibilities of such an agglomeration of forces, could not fail to produce something as novel in detail as it would be imposing in general effect." Berlioz felt that when "so-called monumental" works were performed under such circumstances the "form and texture remain uninfluenced." Though they are performed "with pomp" in huge halls, they would not lose much in "more modest surroundings" with a small group of performers. "They do not absolutely demand an exceptional concentration of voices and instruments; and when they get it, nothing extraordinary or unforeseen results, only a greater emphasis."[69]

One should not conclude that Berlioz liked a lot of noise. He did not see it that way.

> General prejudice charges large orchestras with being *noisy.* However, if they are well balanced, well rehearsed and well conducted, and if they perform truly good music, they should rather be called *powerful.* In fact, nothing is as different in meaning as these two expressions. A shabby, little vaudeville band may appear noisy, whereas a large orchestra, skillfully employed, will be extremely soft and of the greatest beauty of sound even in passionate outbursts. Three trombones, if clumsily employed, may appear noisy and unbearable; and the very next moment, in the same hall, twelve trombones will delight the listeners with their powerful and yet noble tone.[70]

And Berlioz could also see excellence in miniature. In Vienna in 1846, he was able to describe the orchestra of the Imperial Guard as "small but superb."[71]

Perhaps the festival at Bonn in 1845 for the unveiling of Beethoven's statue highlights some of the problems of gatherings of this type. Spohr and Liszt shared the conducting responsibilities. In a letter to Habeneck,[72] Elwart wrote that there were 400 in the chorus (at least for the Mass in D) and nearly 400 in the orchestra, but he felt that though the violins, violas, and basses (probably meaning, or at least including, cellos) were numerous, they still were not strong enough.[73] Sir George Smart concurred: "The band was not strong enough for the voices. I suppose there was not room for a larger band."[74] Berlioz wondered why excellent players in the audience had not been invited to take part, for example, to help "the eight or nine cellists that tried to struggle against the dozen double-basses." He felt that "without being bad, the orchestra did not come up in either size or quality to what the character of the festival, the name of Beethoven, and the instrumental riches of Europe gave us the right to expect."[75] Indeed, Haas has remarked: "The most striking disproportions as to the combination of vocal and instrumental parts are found in the large dilettante concerts, the so-called music festivals, where as large an army as possible without practical distribution of strengths are brought together."[76] But perhaps one could have expected better at such a festival as this. Berlioz also felt that the chorus was unbalanced, the men being weak both in "quantity and quality," though as far as the 130 sopranos were concerned, "one had to admit that outside Germany no one has any notion of such a women's chorus, its ensemble, its rich sonority, its fervor."[77] The problem of augmenting a group for such occasions (as opposed to writing works specifically for a special group as advocated by Berlioz) is indicated in the following remark of Sir George Smart: "The concert went well but Spohr took the last movement of the chorus in *The Mount of Olives* slow, perhaps he was afraid to push so large an orchestra."[78] And Elwart considered the Fifth Symphony to have been mutilated by the huge mass:

> The C minor Symphony was done by a formidable mass of performers, but not rendered! O Habeneck! O my friends of the Concert Society! How I congratulate you for not having taken part in that brilliant and pompous mutilation of the gigantic thought of your idol, of the incomparable artist to whom, by your fine combined talents, by your religious and poetic interpretation, you raise a monument more durable than that which, since yesterday, dominates the great square of Bonn![79]

Actually Fétis had quite a bit earlier presaged the idea of specific works for a particular setting by inveighing against formula in scoring. He claimed that while variety is the "grand desideratum in the arts," it was "the rarest to be met with." He complained that since the invention of musical drama, accompaniments have used the "same system." Though instrumental resources had been "progressively augmented," yet the "forms" of instrumentation have "always remained the same." He lamented the monotony of "this obstinate adherence to the constant reproduction of the same sounds, the same accents, the same associations!" He recommended imitating the "happy idea" of Monteverdi by "imparting to each piece a particular character, by employing the variety of sound afforded by different instruments. . . . This variety of effect which I propose, might be adopted not only in different pieces, but even in the course of the same scene."[80]

In England in the 1820s, Fétis quite naturally made comparisons with Paris. He found the violins "always weak" in English orchestras and the basses usually good.[81] According to him there were never enough instruments in English theaters.[82] And he complained that in English theaters the sonority of the strings was always stifled (*"étouffée"*) under that of the winds and percussion.[83] But was there a growing "ear" for stronger string tone regardless of wind strength? Around 1816 in Dresden, Moscheles had found "grand" the effect of a Mass performed with 20 violins, 6 violas, 4 basses and cellos, but only one of each wind instrument, with the exception of four bassoons.[84]

In Munich in 1831, Mendelssohn had more than 80 performers in the orchestra for his concert. They included about 36 violins, 6 basses, and "double sets" (*"doppelte"*) of wind instruments.[85] Once again one sees a return to ripieno winds, reminiscent of the baroque orchestra. In 1835, before assuming the position of conductor at the Leipzig Gewandhaus, Mendelssohn had to direct the Seventeenth Lower Rhenish Music Festival in Cologne. For a "demanding program" he assembled a large orchestra of 91 violins, 33 violas, 26 cellos, 17 basses, 19 woodwinds, 16 brass, bass drum, and timpani. Added to that was a "massive" chorus of 118 sopranos, 101 altos, 120 tenors, and 137 basses.[86] This amounts to a chorus of 476 versus an orchestra of 204— over twice as large, quite different from what had been the norm. While discussion of such ratios belongs to a later chapter, it is perhaps worth noting here that Haas dates the beginning of huge choruses from Mendelssohn's Berlin revival of the *St. Matthew Passion* with a chorus of 400.[87]

In 1839 Mendelssohn wrote to his friend Carl Klingemann that a music festival with one thousand performers was being planned for Vienna in November of that year. *St. Paul* was to be given "which I shall probably go to conduct."[88] But Mendelssohn was not always used to such large forces; he conducted the Gewandhaus Orchestra in Leipzig from 1835 to 1843, and in 1838–39, besides the "usual winds," there were only 9 first violins, 8 seconds, 5 violas, 5 cellos, and 4 basses.[89] Schumann also knew this orchestra during this period, and Zlotnik has pointed out that it numbered less than 60 during the time in which he was acquainted with it.[90] The figures just given would suggest no more than 50. Zlotnik also noted that the Düsseldorf Orchestra, which Schumann had conducted, numbered only 34 in 1864.[91] That was small indeed for so late in the century.

If the drive towards ever larger forces was not aided and abetted by Louis Jullien at mid-century, he at least was symptomatic of this romantic fever. "Jullien was the first, as I remember, who played with a large orchestra—I think he had, in Castle Garden, twenty first violinists," wrote Theodore Thomas.[92] While that statement may not be entirely accurate, it fits Jullien's reputation. In 1845 he was conducting an orchestra of 300 at the Surrey Zoological Garden, playing Rossini, Haydn, and Beethoven—at least isolated movements—as well as polkas, waltzes, and quadrilles.[93] In 1849 he was at Exeter Hall for two concerts of a *Congrès musical* which was to embrace "six grand musical fêtes, with 400 instrumentalists, 3 distinct choruses, and 3 distinct military bands." After a third concert at the Surrey Gardens, "the rest of the scheme seems to have been abandoned."[94] In 1853 he came to the United States, bringing 45 to 50 men with him.[95] He augmented them with Americans to bring the total up to one hundred. In New York in June 1854, he instituted the first of America's "jumbo" concerts which would later be called festivals. The "Grand Musical Congress" which included 1,500 instrumentalists and 16 choral societies performed oratorio and symphonic movements.[96] Back in England in 1856, Jullien inaugurated a new "gigantic music hall" at the Surrey Zoological Gardens with an orchestra and chorus combined equalling one thousand for a performance of *Messiah*.[97] A second season commenced in May 1857 with *Elijah* performed by close to one thousand.[98]

In one sense, a balanced fulfillment of certain romantic aspirations would seem to have been achieved in the music of Wagner. It is useful, then, to scrutinize the orchestra as he knew it and viewed it. When he was conducting opera at Riga from 1837 to 1839, Wagner is said to have had an orchestra of 24 which he described as "one calculated for a string quartet," with only two first violins, two seconds, two violas, and one cello.[99] Indeed, a sketch of the performance of *Rienzi* at Dresden in 1842 suggests an orchestra of about 29.[100] So Wagner had his experiences with small orchestras, too. And in 1859 he could still write: "I am not aware that the number of permanent members of an orchestra has, in any German town, been rectified according to the requirements of modern instrumentation."[101] He further complained that older Kapellmeisters did not see the need to increase the number of strings in order to balance the augmented winds and the more complicated use made of them in romantic music. He felt that celebrated German orchestras were far behind France in the power and capacity of their violins and particularly of cellos.[102] Does it not seem somewhat contradictory then that on conducting Beethoven's Ninth Symphony at Dresden in 1846 Wagner should use doubled winds, which would seem to further exacerbate such an imbalance? "In particular I took careful advantage of the local custom of doubling the 'wind' at grand musical performances, which formerly had been used in the clumsy style of giving the 'piano' phrases to one set of instruments, the forte-passages to both."[103] As an example, he cited a passage in the second movement where he felt that the woodwind melody was completely lost in a string accompaniment.

> As no letter-piety in the world could induce me to sacrifice the master's true intention to his erroneous marks, I here allowed the strings to give a mere suggestion of strength, instead of actual fortissimo, until they take up the extension of the new theme in alternation with the wind: on the other hand I made the doubled wind exert the utmost force, with the result that their motive was heard distinctly for the first time—as I believe—since the creation of this symphony. I proceeded in a similar way throughout, to ensure the greatest definition in the dynamics of the orchestra.[104]

If the tradition of tampering with Beethoven's orchestration had been at least started by Habeneck, Wagner's performance must have given it new impetus. He used "an exceptionally strong chorus" of 300 voices in this performance, and while he gave no overall size, he felt the orchestra was "finely-balanced."[105]

In 1849 Wagner drew up a plan for a national theater in Saxony. Naturally taking into account the "size of the space in which the orchestra has to perform, and the teachings of experience as to the necessary proportions of its several groups," he proposed an orchestra of 62: 3 flutes, 3 oboes (including English horn), 3 clarinets (including bass clarinet), 3 bassoons, 4 horns, 3 trumpets, 3 trombones, 1 drummer, 20 violins (besides 2 *Konzertmeister*), 6 violas, 6 cellos, and 5 basses.[106] This plan reflects Wagner's thoughts at the time and will be compared with his later ideas in a subsequent chapter on ratios.

In terms of later performances, it is difficult for us to believe the small forces with which Liszt performed *Lohengrin* at Weimar in 1850. In 1843 Berlioz wrote to Liszt that the Weimar orchestra was "a good one" and they had "hunted up" all the extra string players they could find to bring its strength up to 22 violins, 7 violas, 7 cellos, and 7 double basses. There was a "full muster" of wind players, but no English horn, no harp, and no ophicleide, "a tolerably powerful bombardon being substituted."[107] Now this was, even augmented, a far smaller group than Berlioz had indicated as desirable for his works, and indeed it seems not to have grown at all when Liszt took it over. Its strength in 1851 has been given as 37: 2 flutes, 2 oboes, 2 clarinets, 2 bassoons, 4 horns, 2 trumpets, 1 trombone, 1 timpanist, 5 first violins, 6 seconds, 3 violas, 4 cellos, and 3 basses.[108] Indeed, one can see how much augmenting had been done for Berlioz. While one writer claims that

Liszt gave this world premiere of *Lohengrin* with an orchestra of 38, adding only a tuba,[109] one gets a more liberal impression from Liszt himself. He wrote to Wagner that the number of violins would be "slightly increased (from sixteen to eighteen)" and that a bass clarinet had been purchased. "Nothing essential will be wanting in the musical material or design. . . . It is *understood that we shall not cut a note, not an iota,* of your work, and that we shall give it in its *absolute beauty,* as far as is in our power."[110] Note the discrepancy with the 1851 list, which shows violin strength as 11! In a later note Liszt wrote: "'We float in the full ether of your *Lohengrin.* I flatter myself that we shall succeed in giving it according to your intentions." He added that they had ordered a bass clarinet which would be "excellently played by Herr Wahlbrül" and that the cellos would be strengthened by the "arrival from Paris of Gossmann." He felt this "an excellent acquisition, which will, I hope, be followed by some others of the same sort, etc., etc."[111] But these do not necessarily constitute additions; Wahlbrül could easily have been one of the existing two players, and Gossmann could have filled a vacancy. But in view of the fact that the score calls for an English horn—declared missing by Berlioz in 1843—in addition to the principal woodwinds in threes at some points, plus three trombones, tuba, and several percussion instruments, it would appear that, given Liszt's avowed intentions, either the 1851 list is inaccurate, or the orchestra shrank after *Lohengrin,* or Liszt must have added more than a tuba, a couple of violins, and a bass clarinet.

Meanwhile Wagner, exiled at Zürich, evinced more indications of his orchestral bent, particularly with respect to Beethoven's music. He wrote to Liszt in December 1849 that the "local concert society" had asked him to "study with their orchestra" a symphony by Beethoven and one of his own works. In return they would arrange a benefit concert for him. "The necessary increase of the strings, which I had to demand as a point of honour, has delayed the matter up till now."[112] Apparently this came to fruition by 1851, for he recorded in his autobiography that he had been asked to "appear again" at the society's winter concerts. "However, I only did so occasionally, to conduct a Beethoven symphony, making it a condition that the orchestra, and more especially the string instruments, should be reinforced by capable musicians from other towns."[113] Schonberg states that Wagner's proposed revision of the orchestra at Zürich suggested "a minimum of thirty-two players for the opera and forty-six for the concerts."[114] But in letters to Liszt, Wagner indicated a desire for a much larger orchestra for a concert of excerpts from his own works in May 1853: "It was a mad undertaking to find an orchestra of seventy men when there were only fourteen competent musicians in the place. I have plundered all Switzerland, and all the neighboring states as far as Nassau."[115] A later letter offered some breakdown of the group, claiming that he had "almost nothing but concertmasters and musical directors," including 20 "most excellent" violins, 8 violas, 8 "splendid" cellos, and 5 double basses. "All had brought their best instruments; and in the acoustical orchestra, constructed according to my indications, the tone of the instruments was most bright and beautiful."[116] One can only wish that he had given some description of the construction of the acoustic shell he had devised. The string section here closely approximates his figures for the Saxon national theater; there he had proposed only 6 violas and 6 cellos to complement 20 (or 22) violins and 5 basses.

Meanwhile, Liszt still performed the offices of good friend at Weimar. There was an occasion in 1852 in which a grand Romantic urged smaller rather than larger forces. Wagner had heard that his *Liebesmahl der Apostel* was to be performed at Weimar. He wrote to Liszt:

> I call your attention to the fact that the orchestration of this work was designed for vast space (the Frauenkirche of Dresden) and for a chorus of a thousand men. For a smaller room and a less numerous chorus the brass orchestra should be reduced to the usual limits, and especially the four trumpets should be reduced to two.[117]

Here again the relationship between strength and space is seen to be important to Wagner. This also recalls Berlioz's entreaty for works designed for a particular group and place. In 1853 Liszt was to conduct a festival at Karlsruhe and would include excerpts from *Tannhäuser* and *Lohengrin*. He considered that since the theater did not hold more than 1,400 or 1,500 people, a "trebling of the parts" would be "quite sufficient" and an orchestra of 190 and a chorus of about 160 would "have a good effect."[118] Here again the chorus was smaller than the orchestra it complemented. And Wagner must have taken for granted a ripieno use of woodwinds, at least at times, for in 1853 he pointed out a passage in the "Bridal Procession" in *Lohengrin* where woodwinds should be doubled.[119]

Liszt reported to Wagner on a performance of *Tannhäuser* in Berlin in January, 1856. Though the chorus had "studied its part well," it was "much too weak for Berlin, and in proportion to the vastness of the opera house, scarcely more efficient than ours, which always gives me great dissatisfaction." He felt that the strings were "not sufficiently numerous" and should "like the chorus, be increased by a good third." He opined that 8-10 basses and 15-20 first violins, "etc., would certainly not be too many at important performances" in a "large place like this."[120] Now this would be a larger string group than even Wagner had proposed up to this time. And again, size and space were considered to be related. But a performance of the same work in Munich in December of that year elicited a different reaction from Liszt. He found the winds, especially flutes, clarinets, and bassoons, "excellent, but the violins and 6 double basses were "a little hazy" and lacking "the necessary energy, both in bowing, which is short and easy-going, and in rhythm. The *pianos* and *crescendos* are insufficient, and for the same reason there is no fullness in the fortes."[121]

Bülow is said to have complained to Wagner in 1859 that he found only 12 violins—6 + 6—in Berlin, not enough to perform the Prelude to Act I of *Lohengrin*.[122] In 1861 Wagner himself had similar complaints in Paris, trying to mount *Tannhäuser*. "For instance, it was impossible in the whole of Paris to find the twelve French horns which in Dresden had so bravely sounded the hunting call in the first act."[123] Now this does sound more like a luxury than was the subject of Bülow's complaint. But Wagner seemed well treated and supplied in Russia in 1863. At St. Petersburg, he was "eminently satisfied" with the orchestra of 120 in the "large and handsome hall of the Society of Nobles."[124] In Moscow he had an orchestra of 100, "on the whole, far inferior to that of St. Petersburg," though containing some excellent players.[125]

For the performance of the Beethoven Ninth Symphony in 1872, celebrating the laying of the "foundation stone" at Bayreuth, Wagner wrote to Richter that he wanted "an 'elite-orchestra' of 100 players."[126] Indeed, the orchestra, coming from all over Germany, was described as "composed of one hundred master musicians."[127] He again used a chorus of three hundred in this performance, a group three times as big as the orchestra.[128] But not everyone was pleased with Wagner's version of the Ninth, which included many emendations to Beethoven's orchestration. Wagner published his ideas on this, and they appeared in several periodicals, even in London.[129] Gounod's reaction may have been typical of those opposed:

> I do not know the Choral Symphony of Beethoven "according to Wagner"; I only know it according to Beethoven, and I confess that that is enough for me. I have heard and read this gigantic work many times, and I have never felt, either on hearing it or reading it, the need of a correction.... I do not admit that one assumes the right to correct the masters.[130]

Gounod admitted certain difficulties in the work, but felt that they were superable:

> It is true that the vocal part of the Ninth Symphony is difficult to perform, and that the way in which the voices are treated requires qualities and a knowledge of music which are way above the average singers and choristers. However, I must say that, contrary to the assertions advanced by the critic whom I oppose, I heard in 1842 at Vienna, Austria, under the direction of Otto Nicolai, the Choral Symphony performed by 1,200 musicians (around 450 instrumentalists and 750 voices), and that that performance was admirable from all points: ensemble, steadiness, precision in attacks and in rhythm, accuracy of perfect intonation and observance of nuances, even in the highest notes and the roughest passages.[131]

Certainly such a performance as Nicolai's would have warmed Berlioz's heart, though one has to wonder what Beethoven would have made of it!

The orchestra at Bayreuth can probably best be seen as the fruition of Wagner's thoughts and ideas on the orchestra, at least for his own works. And it is important to keep in mind that the renderings at Bayreuth have always been considered in the nature of a festival, and festivals have always had about them the air of being beyond the ordinary. In 1876 the orchestra included 4 flutes, 4 oboes, 1 English horn, 4 clarinets, 1 bass clarinet, 4 bassoons, 1 contrabassoon, 7 horns, 4 trumpets, 1 bass trumpet, 4 trombones, 1 contrabass (?) trombone, 2 tenor tubas, 2 bass tubas, 1 contrabass tuba, 3 timpanists, 8 harps, 32 violins (16 + 16), 12 violas, 12 cellos, and 8 basses.[132] Albert Lavignac, the source of these figures, has pointed out that the composition of the orchestra is "almost fixed and invariable" because of the impossibility of adding any more space for it, though "certain works necessitate the presence of a greater or smaller number of instrumentalists on the stage."[133] Indeed the size of the orchestra varied only slightly, at least during the nineteenth century. For example, the number of violins has remained 32, except for 31 in 1888, and 33 in 1896. The winds have shown more variety, probably reflecting the works that were performed. For instance, there were 9 horns in 1886, 11 in 1891 and 1892. The number of harps used shows the most drastic changes. After 8 in 1876, 4 became the usual number, not reverting to 8 until 1896. According to Lavignac, the largest orchestra was that of 1896 with 125 musicians which was 9 more than in 1876.[134] Of course, the orchestra is somewhat muted by its recessed position under the stage. Hanslick reported that "from this muffled sound hardly anyone would have guessed the numerical strength of the orchestra, whose eight harps sound like two or three."[135] But Wagner had evidently long been conscious that such an orchestra of variegated colors but enormous size could far overbalance voices. The theater manager Angelo Neumann, who handled the Berlin production of the *Ring* cycle, related an anecdote bearing on this:

> His little admonition to the musicians was most characteristic and worthy to be noted by many an orchestra of this day. "Gentlemen," he said,—"I *beg* of you not to take my 'fortissimo' too seriously! Where you see 'ff,' make a 'fp' of it, and for 'piano' play 'pianissimo.' Remember how many of you there are down there, against the one poor single human throat up here alone on the stage!"[136]

At Bayreuth it is possible that Wagner overemphasized such a plea for the first performances. J. W. Davison claimed that during the first series of performances the orchestra played in a "subdued tone" and though "faultless" in execution played with a "sense of dullness," but during the second series they resumed their ordinary or "bolder" tone, which "successfully dissipated" any such sense.[137] This was not meant really as adverse criticism, as the same critic had characterized the orchestra's "playing from first to last" as "little short of marvelous—as marvelous, indeed, as the task set before them by the uncompromising master."[138] Incidently, one has to wonder what kind of effect the *Ring* made in Cologne in 1882, where the performances were staged in the old theater whose pit had space for hardly 50 players. As Siegfried Borris wrote, "the manner of the setting and the sound remains for us a mystery."[139]

Still, it is nice to realize that all was not colossal with every Romantic, that Wagner retained a sense of balance and proportion, and that music could be intimate as well as imposing. Zlotnik has pointed out that in order to verify the *Siegfried Idyll* before publishing it, Wagner assembled an orchestra of 1 flute, 1 oboe, 2 clarinets, 1 bassoon, 2 horns, 1 trumpet, 6-8 first violins, 7 or 8 seconds, 4 violas, 4 cellos, and 2 or 3 basses.[140] Such a group would tend to give almost a chamber character to the work. However, Zlotnik also referred to Ernest Newman's viewpoint on this:

> The conductors of today who regard it as a pious duty towards what they call "the composer's intentions" to give the *Idyll* with some half-dozen strings are therefore labouring under a delusion: Wagner had contented himself with the bare minimum of string players at Triebschen for two excellent reasons,—the stairs would not hold more, and he could not afford more.[141]

As Zlotnik also has pointed out, Sir Adrian Boult concurred with this view, citing the practice of Hans Richter, one of Wagner's closest associates and himself a participant in that memorable gift to Cosima. Sir Adrian noted that Richter himself had participated in that first performance of the work and always used all the strings "he could get hold of" when performing it himself. "Not for him the seventeen-player stunts, which no doubt have their place on certain occasions, and throw into relief the solo woodwind parts in one or two of the tuttis."[142]

Galkin brought forth an interesting way of looking at Wagner's work, seeing in it a recapitulation of the history of orchestration. His thesis: the early works, such as *Der fliegende Holländer* (1843), used a "classical concert-hall" orchestra with strings, woodwinds in pairs, and 4 horns; the middle period extended the importance of the winds and increased their number; late works, such as *Siegfried* (1871), were scored for "complete harmonic sections" of brass, woodwinds, and strings, "such as Berlioz had used in the *Symphonie fantastique*.... Since then, with the exception of those works not founded on permanent practice, the orchestra has remained basically the same instrument as it was in the middle of the nineteenth century."[143] Indeed, Strauss's *Ein Heldenleben* (1898) seems almost made for the Bayreuth orchestra, calling for a piccolo, 3 flutes, 3 oboes, English horn (doubling 4th oboe), E♭ clarinet, 2 B♭ clarinets, bass clarinet, 3 bassoons, contrabassoon, 8 horns, 5 trumpets, 3 trombones, tenor tuba, bass tuba, timpani, 4 other percussion, 2 harps, 16 first violins, 16 seconds, 12 violas, 12 cellos, and 8 basses.[144] *Till Eulenspiegel* calls for an identical string section of 16/ 16/ 12/ 12/ 8.[145]

One side of the late romantic attitude is perhaps well summed up in their view of the past. A capsule view is presented by the orchestras used by Theodore Thomas for the Cincinnati Music Festival of 1902. Mrs. Thomas recalled:

> In only one particular did Thomas depart from the originals of the classic scores, and that was in the number of musicians used in the performances. In a hall of the size of the Cincinnati Music Hall, it was, of course, impossible to use the small orchestra of the classic writers. But to offset this Thomas balanced the various choirs of the orchestra in such a way as to give the same relative tone quality, using in the "Mass" [Bach's] an unheard-of number of wood-winds in proportion to the strings.[146]

Here is Thomas's "Bach" orchestra for the *Mass in B minor:* 6 first flutes, 6 second flutes, 6 first oboes, 6 second oboes, 2 third oboes, 2 oboes d'amour, 2 D clarinets, 4 A clarinets, 8 bassoons, 2 horns, 6 cornets, 4 timpani, 1 organ, 21 first violins, 19 second violins, 12 violas, 12 cellos, and 12 basses.[147] If this seems overgrown and stalking to our tastes, at least there was some semblance of the ripieno use of woodwinds so typical of the baroque. Perhaps this was a result of his having "read everything about Bach that had been printed in English, French, German."[148] But why clarinets and cornets—instruments unknown in Bach's time? Perhaps Thomas should be allowed to speak for himself:

> For the last few years I have given works of Bach which allow massing—both instrumental and choral—with an orchestra, which not only balanced the chorus, but in which, also, the same proportion between the woodwind and string choirs was observed as in the orchestra for which he wrote. By thus massing all the choirs, I used the method of the modern orchestra pallette for the three so-called trumpet parts, and by a discreet rewriting of these parts for four D cornets for the first and second, and two trumpets in A for the third, and duplicating these with four D and two A clarinets—according to compass—I obtained a charactristic color of the trumpet parts, and at the same time made them powerful enough to blend with sixteen first violins, twelve flutes, twelve oboes, etc.[149]

One notes the discrepancy with the figures from the *Memoirs* given above; but Upton's "Reminiscences and Appreciation," which follows the Auto-biography quoted here, while agreeing with the *Memoirs* as to clarinets and cornets, names only 4 first and 4 second flutes.[150] But whichever figures are correct, the idea is clear. The presence of an organ for continuo is possibly another result of Thomas's "reading." At the same festival, Thomas used as a "Beethoven" orchestra for the Third Symphony: 2 flutes, 2 oboes, 2 clarinets, 2 bassoons, 3 horns, 2 trumpets, 2 timpani [2 drums or 2 players!?], 21 first violins, 19 seconds, 12 violas, 12 cellos, and 12 basses.[151] This setting would seem to have drowned the woodwind in string tone and it contrasts sharply with Wagner's use of double woodwinds with a substantially smaller string group.

Thomas's "Berlioz" orchestra for the *Requiem* corresponded with that called for in the score as far as strings and woodwinds are concerned. But in the "south" orchestra he used 4 ophicleides instead of the tubas. (Can one assume that the "4 tenor trumpets" is a misprint for "trombones" or might they have been Flügelhorns?)[152] Outside of omitting the 4 tamtams, which might be a printer's oversight, and using 16 timpanists—2 players per pair—throughout the eight pairs, instead of only for two pairs, Thomas has stuck religiously to the demands of the score; and after all, Berlioz himself might well have used ophicleides instead of tubas.

His "Wagner" orchestra for the Prelude to *Die Meistersinger* had 2 piccolos, 2 flutes, 2 oboes, 2 clarinets, 2 bassoons, 4 horns, 3 trumpets, 3 trombones, 1 tuba, 2 timpani [?], 1 cymbal player, 21 first violins, 19 seconds, 12 violas, 12 cellos, and 12 basses.[153] It seems strange that he should have doubled only the piccolo part and have left the other woodwind parts single-handed against a string section much larger than Wagner used at Bayreuth. If the larger number were needed for the big hall, as in the Bach *Mass,* then here and in Beethoven's music, should the woodwinds not have been doubled to compensate? One wonders if "2 Timpani" meant one player but two drums. Again, perhaps oversight omitted the triangle and harp called for by the score.[154]

But not all orchestras could afford to be huge, nor were all composers in favor of large forces. Hans von Bülow wrote to Richard Strauss in 1886 that Brahms was against augmenting the strings for his Fourth Symphony (Bülow referred to it as "No. XIII," obviously adding Brahms's four to Beethoven's nine).[155] In 1885 Bülow referred to the Meiningen Orchestra which he was conducting at the time as consisting of only 49 men, yet good for Strauss.[156] And Strauss could write to Bülow in 1888 concerning a Meiningen concert: "The orchestral balance, moreover, despite the 8 first violins, was quite excellent."[157] Hanslick heard this orchestra under Bülow in 1884 and wrote:

> Where the Meiningen Orchestra does not measure up to the Vienna Philharmonic is in sensuous beauty of tone, fullness of sound, warmth and temperament of interpretation, and, finally, in brilliance of total effect. One should not forget, of course, that it has only forty-eight men, as compared with the Vienna Philharmonic's ninety.[158]

These are two extremes compared. However, size is not always conducive to good ensemble, and Hanslick went on: "The most admirable discipline has transformed it into an instrument upon which he [Bülow] plays with utter freedom and from which he produces nuances possible only with a discipline to which larger orchestras would not ordinarily submit."[159]

9

Some Particular Nineteenth-Century Orchestras

One way of getting some idea of orchestral growth in the nineteenth century is to trace several particular orchestras as was done for the eighteenth century in Part One. Once again it is well to recall problems of accuracy, as well as the fact that some orchestras did double duty between opera and concert, often using a different make-up for each genre. Another problem is the uncertainty whether different citations for the same city refer to the same or different orchestras. With these cautions in mind, some figures for Berlin are presented in table 5.

The late eighteenth-century figures still show possible ripieno strength in flutes, oboes, and bassoons, and greater strength than Beethoven had in Vienna for his early symphonies. In 1811, clarinets joined the other woodwinds in ripieno strength. The large number of horns probably reflected the practice of using different players for different keys in order to alleviate crook-changing, in addition to ripieno strength. One must keep in mind that horns were often thought of more in conjunction with woodwinds at that time rather than with trumpets and timpani which were so much more limited as well as bolder in color. In 1811 the trombones have joined the brass section. Perhaps surprising is the drop in the number of violas in line with a gain in the other strings—surprising because, remembering Haydn's statements, one would have thought the violas would have gained in appreciation. (On the other hand, recalling the complaints of Reyer and Wagner, such a drop may not be viewed as surprising.)

While wind strength is not given in the 1820 figures, the strings seem better balanced within the section. Certainly the violas are in a more advantageous relationship. In 1823, the winds seem to have even more potential ripieno strength. The keyed Flügelhorns are an interesting addition, probably another experiment on the way to valves. The four concertmasters raise the question whether one only played a specific performance, or whether they all played, rotating the leadership role, making 26 violins in all—13 + 13.

Table 5. Berlin Orchestras

	1792[a]	1811[b]	1820[c]	1823[d]	1825[e]	1830[f]	1843[g]	1844[h]	1849[i]	1890[j]
flutes	4	4		5	4	4	4	2	5	2
piccolo				1				1		2
oboes	5	4/5		5	5	4	4	2	4	2
clarinets	2	4		5	5	4	4	2/4	5	2
bassoons	5	4		5	5	4	4	2/4	5	2
horns	5	7/8		8	5/8	4	4	4	9	4
trumpets		2		3	3	6	4	2/4	3	2
trombones		3		2	3	3	4	3	3	2
tubas, etc.				2 k fh				1+1 oph		1
timpani		1		1	2		1	1	2	1
other	1 hp			1 hp, 1 pno			2 prc, 2 hp	2(?)prc	(2 hp)	1 hp, 1 kbd
violins	22	22/25	12+12	11+11, 4 cm	12/14+ 12/14	24	14+14	8+8	27	12+10
violas	7	5	8	7	?	12	8	6	8	8
cellos + basses	8+4	10/11+5	9+7	10+7	10/12+7	6+6	10+8	8/10+4/5	11+7	8+8
Totals	**63**	**71/77**		**89**	**73/89(?)**	**ca.70 (/100)**	**87**	**55/65**	**89/91**	**65**

cm=concertmaster; hp=harp; kbd=keyboard; k fh=keyed Flügelhorn; oph=ophicleide; prc=percussion; pno=piano

a "Kgl. Kapelle"; listed in *Mus. Korrespondenz*, Speyer, 1792, p. 10, cited in Schreiber/ORCHESTER, p. 101.

b "Königl. Orchester," listed in AMZ, XIII (1811), col. 607.

c "Court Opera, Spontini, director," listed by Dorn/LEBEN, II, p. 126.

d "Königlich-Preussische Kapelle, Spontini, first conductor," in AMZ, XXV (1823), col. 237-38.

e "Opera, Spontini, conductor," in Smart/JOURNALS, pp. 167-68.

f "Court Opera," in HARMONICON, VIII (1830), p. 5.

g "Opera," in Berlioz/MEMOIRES, II, p. 119; or Berlioz/MEMOIRS, p. 318.

h "Opera," Gassner/DIRIGENT, Beilage 9.

i "Kgl. Kapelle" (or Court Opera?), OSVD 1849, S. 6f, cited in Schreiber/ORCHESTER, p. 101; *Das Orchester*, 1849, p. 6, cited in Carse/BEETHOVEN, p. 46, which lacks the 2 harps.

j "Opera," from seating plan in Kling/VOLLKOMMENE, p. 272.

But notice the 1825 entry. Sir George Smart has noted: "There are also as supernumeraries two first violins, two second violins, two 'celli and three corni. This is the full orchestra but it seldom plays as such except in Spontini's operas."[1] This explains the variances in the figures as given in table 5, but is also important in judging all these lists, because such information is not too often, in fact, seldom specifically stated. The keyed Flügelhorns evidently did not survive very long. But otherwise the size is basically the same as in 1823; one would guess about seven or eight violas.

It is unfortunate that the woodwinds are not listed in the figures for 1830. The trumpets seem unusually numerous, as do the violas, equalling each of the violin sections in strength. Meanwhile, the cellos have taken quite a loss! One would be inclined to put more faith than usual in the 1843 listing, and it seems truly well balanced as well as coming from the observations of Berlioz. The reappearance of the harp, in twos no less, after a long absence seems most welcome. One notes that the woodwinds still retain the potential for ripieno fullness. It is also important to note that Berlioz said that this was the orchestra for important performances (*"ainsi composée aux jours des grandes représentations"*).[2] The 1844 list again points up the problems inherent in this type of research. Could the orchestra have changed this drastically in roughly a year? The drop in violins and violas seems especially severe. But realistic are the differences allowed for between smaller and larger works, the larger figures reflecting the size for larger works (*"bei grossen Opern"*).[3]

The 1849 list would seem more reflective of the size one would have anticipated after the 1843 list of Berlioz. In this case the woodwind strength would seem to allow doubling two parts plus extras such as piccolo, bass clarinet, or contrabassoon. The number of horns is quite impressive. But the 1890 list is telling. Now ripieno winds seem to have disappeared. Very striking is the fact that woodwinds and brass here are close to the size popularly associated with the orchestra at the end of the eighteenth and beginning of the nineteenth century! The string strength had diminished, too. Perhaps this reflects some economic realities and the loss of royal patronage. Also for the first time in the century, the second violins are weaker than the firsts. Strangely enough, this total is only two players more than in 1792; if one saw only these two listings, one would not realize the fluctuation of these one hundred years.

Dresden offers another opportunity to trace an orchestra in the nineteenth as well as the eighteenth century. Again, one cannot be sure that all the listings, opera and church, are for the same orchestra, including concert purposes. The 1801 listing already seems much weaker in numbers than does the Berlin. [One wonders why three flutes and oboes—to double only the first part?] It seems a bit early to be providing piccolo and English horn. Violas and cellos seem weak compared to the violin strength. The 1805 list adds an important bit of information, seen before in eighteenth-century lists: trumpets and timpani are *"mit den Hoftrompetern und Paukern besetzt,"*[4] a reminder that when these instruments are lacking in the list, they were in all probability available from the military. The similarity of this list with that of 1801 would seem to reinforce one's trust in the accuracy of each. The obsolete lute is gone in 1805, as are three of the violins.

By 1817, whereas one would have expected a decline in ripieno woodwind strength, in table 6 one sees the opposite; yet Carse encouraged the idea that such was an eighteenth-century phenomenon, that at this point in time the ideal woodwind section was 2/2/2/2. One wonders at the lack of timpani— probably an omission, since trumpets are listed. Violas and cellos still appear comparatively weak. The 1819 list provides another case where one listing gains validity from the support of another; little seems changed in the two years from 1817-19. Even the timpani are still lacking, despite the presence of the trumpets. By 1823, little has changed, except that timpani have finally arrived. The use of so-called *"Accessisten"* was rather widespread, evidently an effort to get more for less money. Wagner inveighed against the practice: "The make-shift institution of 'accessists' cannot be justified, especially in view of their rate of wages: exactly the same duties are demanded of them as of a fully-appointed bandsman, yet they are paid but half the wage of the lowest Kammermusikus."[5] While Wagner was writing specifically of the situation in Saxony, probably much the same practice obtained elsewhere.

In view of earlier lists, the 1825 list leaves one astonished that Weber had such a small group for German opera at this time, unless the theater afforded but little space. Yet Smart was an eyewitness who meticulously recorded his impressions, estimating when not sure. The size of the orchestra elicits sympathy for Weber's complaints that German opera was not treated with the same respect and support in Germany as was Italian opera. One positive note: trombones had arrived. The 1832 list is substantially larger. Of course, Weber was dead by this time, but in light of the controversy between him and Morlacchi over the favor shown the Italian opera at Dresden, this could be the orchestra for the Italian opera. But note the absence of trombones again. The 1835 listing is for church music, possibly accounting for the smaller wind contingent and larger string group. Interestingly enough, the total size is the same as that for the opera in 1832.

One is struck by the absence of trombones in 1839; it certainly would suggest a chronicler's error. The lower strings seem comparatively weak, but have remained much the same since 1832, allowing that the 1835 listing was for church music. As in Berlin, the woodwinds retained ripieno strength. In 1842 the trombones are back, but the strings remain much the same. One is surprised by the three bassoons in the wake of the other woodwinds in fours. The bassoons are the very instruments the French kept as four against the

Table 6. Dresden Orchestras

	1801[a]	1805[b]	1817[c]	1819[d]	1823[e]	1825[f]	1832[g]	1835[h]	1839[i]	1842[j]	1844[k]	1850[l]
flutes	3	3	5	5	5	2	5	3	4	4	2	4
oboes	3	3	5	5	5	2	4	3	4	4	2	4
clarinets	2	2	5	5	5	2	4	3	4	4	2	4
bassoons	4	4	5	4	5	2	5	4	4	3	2	4
horns	4	4	6	6	6	4	5	2	4	5	4	5
trumpets			2	2	2		3	2	3	4	4	4
trombones						3		3		3	3	3
tubas											1	1
timpani					1		2	1	1	1	1	1
other	1 lt, 2 org	2 org	2 org	3 org	2 org				4 org	1 hp	1 prc, 1 hp	1 hp
violins	20	17	21	19+ 2 cm	18+ 3 Acc	5+5	16	10+10	16	17	8+8	18
violas	4	4	5	5	4+ 2 Acc	2	4	6	4	4	4	5
cellos + basses	4+4	4+4	5+5	5+5	5+5+ 1 Acc	2+2	6+4	5+1 Acc+ 5	3+4	4+4	4+4	5+5
Totals	**51**	**47**	**66**	**66**	**69**	**ca.34 (?)**	**58**	**58**	**55**	**58**	**51**	**63**

Acc=Accessisten; cm=concertmaster; hp=harp; lt=lute; org=organ; prc=percussion

a "Königl. Capelle," NZFM. XIII (1840), p. 153.

b "Kurfürstlich-Sächsische Kapelle," AMZ, VIII (1805/6), col. 137–39.

c "K. musikal Capelle," Weber/WEBER I, II, pp. 37–39. Meusels Mus. f.K.u.K., cited in Schreiber/ORCHESTER, p. 103, has 20 violins (lacking concertmaster) and lacks organists.

d "Königl. Capelle," NZFM. XIII (1840), pp. 157–58.

e "Königlich-Sächsische Kapelle," AMZ, XXV (1823), cols. 317–18.

f "Hoftheater, Weber," Smart/JOURNALS, p. 140.

g "Court Opera," Prölss, Geschichte des Hoftheaters zu Dresden, p. 423, cited in Carse/BEETHOVEN, p. 48.

h "Kirchenmusik," AMZ, XXXVII, col. 69, cited in Schreiber/ORCHESTER, p. 103, & in Carse/BEETHOVEN, p. 49.

i "Königl. Capelle," NZFM. XIII (1840), p. 158.

j "Court Opera," Prölss, Geschichte des Hoftheaters zu Dresden, p. 489, cited in Carse/BEETHOVEN, pp. 48, 488.

k "Opera," from seating plan in Gassner/DIRIGENT, Beilage 2.

l "Court Opera," Prölss, Geschichte des Hoftheaters zu Dresden, p. 557, cited in Carse/BEETHOVEN, p. 48.

other woodwinds in pairs. One possible answer is that a vacancy existed when the list was made. Notable as a first in these lists is the harp, cited by Berlioz as so rare in Germany. The total of 58 equals 1832 and 1835, though internal changes have occurred.

The 1844 list brings up a possible problem in taking numbers from a seating plan. One usually has to infer numbers by drawings of desks, space indications, etc. But it does not seem reasonable that the woodwinds were halved in two years, only to resume previous strength in 1850. Of course, there is always the other possibility that all four players of each instrument were not always or not normally used in every performance. But the strings have not really changed, and one notes the presence of a tuba. In 1850, as stated before, the woodwinds again show double strength. Each string part has been slightly strengthened by the addition of one player. But the tuba seems to have disappeared. Impressive is the fact that while Berlin had 89 to 91 players in 1849, Dresden showed only 63 in 1850. Thus, one should not take for granted any unanimity in the romantic orchestra as far as size is concerned.

It will be profitable to scrutinize one more German orchestra in this way: that of the Gewandhaus in Leipzig, perhaps the longest existing orchestra still active today that dates back to the eighteenth century. The fact that Mendelssohn was its conductor from 1835 to 1843 gives it added glamor. Table 7 has listings for it.

Although the winds are not given in 1798, the 13 over the string total would have allowed for 8 woodwinds, 4 brass, and timpani. Certainly this orchestra would have more than satisfied Beethoven even ten or fifteen years later. Since the strings show little change in 1802 (one additional cello, violas not mentioned), one would guess not much else had changed either. Here is another example of one list more or less confirming another (unless both had the same original source). While the listing of ca. 1808 confirms the projection of wind strength advanced above, the string section has slightly shrunk. It is less than half the size of Berlin at this time, and makes even Dresden seem huge. In 1825 little change is evident again, except that the horns are doubled, and the violins are back to their 1802 strength.

In the list marked as "before 1830" and "in the old theater," it is interesting that the problem of a need for harp and piccolo has been solved by having one man double on these two instruments. This probably reflects a reasoning that two flutes would more often be called for with either harp or piccolo than would harp and piccolo together. But even then, one would presume that a flutist could take up the slack. In the 1830 list, also *"im alten Theater,"* though only one more has been added to the total, three trombones have been introduced. To accomplish this, the harpist evinced even more versatility by adding side drum to his accomplishments. The 1831 *"Konzert"* orchestra is quite different from the theater orchestra of 1830, showing

Table 7. Leipzig, Gewandhausorchester

	1798[a]	1802[b]	ca.1808[c]	1825[d]	ca.1828[e]	1830[f]	1831[g]	1833[h]	1838-39[i]	ca.1844[j]	1848-60[k]	ca.1875[l]	1881[m]	1890[n]	1896[o]
flutes	2		2		2	2	2	2		2			2	3	2
piccolo					(1)	(1)							1		1
oboes	2		2		2	2	2	2		2			3	3	2
English horn													1		1
clarinets	4		4		2	2	2	2		2(+1)			3	3	2
bass clarinet													1		1
bassoons	2		2		2	2	2	2					3	3	2
contrabassoon													1		1
horns	2		2		4	4	2	2		4			5	5	4
trumpets	2		2		2	2	2	2		2			3	3	3
trombones						3	3	3		3			3	3	3
tuba														1	1
timpani	1		1		1	1	1	1		1			1	1	1
other					2 prc, 1 hp, (dbl pc)	2 prc, 1 hp, (dbl pc),(dr)				1 prc			1 hp	1 prc	1 prc, 1 hp
violins	6+6	6+6	8	12	6+6	6+6	8+8	5+5	9+8	6+6			12+10	20+20	18+14
violas	3	?	2	2	2	2	4	4	5				8	13	10
cellos + basses	2+3	3+3	2+2	2+2	3+2	2+2	3+3	2+2	5+4	3+3			8+6	10+10	10+8
TOTALS	33	?	27	ca.33	37	38	39/40	34	ca.47	ca.40/41	35(?)	60	72	98	86

prc=percussion; hp=harp; dr=drum

a "Gewandhausorchester," chr. G. Thomas, *Unpartheische Kritik...*, Leipzig, 1798, p. 18, cited by Schreiber/ORCHESTER, p. 106.

b "Gewandhausorchester," AMZ, IV (1801/2), cols. 783-84, note.

c "Theater," Nösselt/GEWANDHAUS, p. 96.

d "Theatre," Smart/JOURNALS, p. 159.

e "Im alten Theater," Nösselt/GEWANDHAUS, p. 269.

f "Im alten Theater," ibid. p. 269.

g "Konzert," Dörffel/GEWANDHAUS, p. 78.

h "Gewandhaus," Nösselt/GEWANDHAUS, pp. 118-19.

i Creuzberg/GEWANDHAUS, pp. 85-86.

j "Konzert u. Opernorchester," BMZM3, p. 30; MKRp. 1844, p. 418; OSVD, 1849, p. 42; Eckardt, a.a.o., p. 218; all cited in Schreiber/ORCHESTER, p. 106.

k Nösselt/GEWANDHAUS, p. 167.

l Ibid. p. 173.

m Dörffel/GEWANDHAUS, p. 181.

n Seating plan in Kling/VOLLKOMMENE, p. 276.

o Seating plan in Nösselt/GEWANDHAUS, p. 271.

somewhat greater string strength. The 48 total reflects a statement that 9 more musicians could be added for *"Extra'Instrumente"*; these 9 must have included trombones and harp. Carse claimed that the players for the theater were drawn from the concert orchestra,[6] so one could have expected to find such instruments as basic to the list.

In 1833 the trombones are listed, but the harp is gone and the strings have shrunk. This seems a rather small group for two years before Mendelssohn was to assume command. Also still notable is the lack of ripieno winds so much in evidence in Berlin and Dresden. In 1838–39, the violins are back to their previous strength and the lower strings are stronger than they have been. This growth, while not huge, has to be attributed to the presence of Mendelssoh. But the list from around 1844 and marked as *"Konzert u. Opernorchester"* seems like a regression, coming just after the end of Mendelssohn's tenure. The strings seem to have weakened perceptibly. The lack of a harp is still consistent with Berlioz's report on Leipzig, when Mendelssohn had to play the harp parts for the *Symphonie fantastique* on the piano.[7]

The fact that from 1848–60 the orchestra had "no less than 35 players" constitutes a real reversal of the popular view of what happened to the romantic orchestra. But if the orchestra did increase from "42 to 60" around 1875, this was indeed quite a jump! If Leipzig was laggard, she was suddenly catching up. The 1881 listing presents much more the romantic orchestra which one would expect. However, the strings seem weak if compared with Berlioz's demands or the Bayreuth orchestra. And one might have expected a tuba to be included in a group otherwise so full. The 1890 contingent is really a "modern" orchestra as far as strings are concerned, yet lacking tuba and harp. One would assume that the woodwinds in threes took care of piccolo, English horn, bass clarinet, and contrabassoon which are present in its two neighboring lists. And if the 1896 list clarifies the woodwind situation, it also restores the harp and adds the tuba. The string section even looks "modern" in the smaller number of second violins as compared to the firsts.

Perhaps a quick review of orchestras in one more German city of some size might be profitable. Some statistics for Munich are given in table 8. The two 1803 listings are obviously two different orchestras, illustrative of the research problem mentioned above—that of not being sure from year to year, from list to list, that one is dealing with the same group. The first, marked *"Churbayerschen Kapelle"* and led by Cannibich, is small but not unusually so for its time. But its delinquency in clarinets and timpani is not as surprising as the lack of bassoons in the other group, named as *"Kurfürstl. Hofmusik,"* where trumpets and timpani probably came from the military. Surely there is an error here. The great difference in size is evidence, however, that one cannot really speak of the "classic orchestra" or the "romantic orchestra" in

Table 8. Munich Orchestras

	1803[a]	1803[b]	1806[c]	1815[d]	1820[e]	1827[f]	1831[g]	1844[h]	1844[i]	1844[j]	1844[k]
flutes	1	7	4		6	7		2 (?)	2	2	4
piccolo									1	1	
oboes	2	6	4		5	7		2 (?)	2	2	4
clarinets		4	3		7	7		2 (?)	2	2	4
bassoons	2		3		5	6		2 (?)	2	2	4
horns	2 (4?)	7	6		7	8		2	4	4	4
trumpets	4		12			x		4	6	4	4
trombones			3		1	1			3	3	3
tuba										1	
timpani	1		4		1	1		1	1	1	1
other	1 kbd		4 org		1 hp	1 hp		1 org	1 b dr, 1 hp	3 prc, 1 hp	1 b dr
violins	10	28 (+2)	27	12+12	24 (+1)	24	ca.32	6+6	10+10	10+10	20+20
violas	2	6	4	8	6	6		2	8	8	10
cellos + basses	3+2	5+7	6+5	10+6	5+5	6+5	?+6	2+2	6+6	6+6	10+10
Totals	**30/32**	**70/72**	**85**	**?**	**72/73+**	**79+**	**80+**	**34 (?)**	**65**	**66**	**99**

b dr=bass drum; hp=harp; kbd=keyboard; org=organ; prc=percussion; x=no number given

a AMZ, V (1802/3), cols. 277-79.

b MMGL, p. 33, cited in Schreiber/ORCHESTER, p. 107.

c AMZ, VIII (1805/6), cols. 313-15.

d Spohr/LEBENSERINNERUNGEN, I, p. 203; or Spohr/JOURNEYS, p. 125.

e AMZ, XXII (1820), col. 550.

f AMZ, XXIX, col. 437, cited in Schreiber/ORCHESTER, p. 108.

g Letter to his father, Mendelssohn/BRIEFE, I, pp. 296-97; or Mendelssohn/ITALY, pp. 300-301.

h Seating plan in Gassner/DIRIGENT, Beilage 15.

i Ibid., Beilage 14.

j Seating plan, Becker/ORCHESTER, col. 182.

k Seating plan in Gassner/DIRIGENT, Beilage 13.

anywhere near static terms. The 1806 orchestra, labeled "königlich Bayerischen Kapelle" and still led by Cannibich, is certainly the same as that of 1803. It has grown greatly in three years, gaining ripieno strength in the woodwinds, as well as in the strings, especially the violins. The trumpets and timpani are certainly from the military in such numbers. Trombones are here early. The "königliche Kapelle" of 1815 would seem to be the same group, but the strings seem to be better distributed, the lower strings gaining with slightly less violin strength. The only indication as to wind strength is the "einfachen Harmonie"; whether this means only one each of the woodwinds or no ripieno strength is not clear. One would suspect the latter. But 1820 finds this same group back to ripieno strength in the winds, though one trombone is difficult to understand. The harp stands out as unusual for Germany. The woodwinds continued to grow in 1827, but still only one trombone remains. The 1831 listing was a special occasion for a concert of Mendelssohn. The "double sets of wind instruments, etc." ["doppelte Blaseinstrumente"] show that ripieno woodwinds were at least sometimes used and not just available in case the orchestra had to do double duty. If this was the same orchestra as most of the above listings, the violins seem to have been augmented for the occasion. The 1844 lists are interesting in that one can speculate whether these are basically the same orchestra adjusted in size and make-up to suit purpose and locale, or whether one is here dealing with two or more different orchestras. The first one is the "Hof-Kapelle," presumably a concert and/or church orchestra. The list again points up the difficulty in being sure of numbers from a seating plan, especially for the winds. But if this is still the same orchestra, either it has shrunk, or the plan indicates that all the players were not always used for all occasions. It is probable that the second list, the "Hof-Theater" orchestra, was the same in nucleus as above though somewhat larger for this arena. If so, it once again shows the fluidity that reflected the locale, occasion, and the works being performed. The third listing for 1844 is the "Hof- und National-theater," yet the seating plans make it clear that these are both the same orchestra in the same theater, though they provide slightly different statistics. Once again the complete accuracy of the statistics is questionable. The last list is for the "Odeon Concert Saal," and two principal ideas would seem to be reaffirmed here. This large group is situated in a large concert hall—this will be evident when the seating plan is reproduced in a later chapter. Secondly, the plan makes it apparent that the woodwinds are there in ripieno strength against this large, "modern" body of strings. But as in Berlin and Dresden, there was also a steady growth towards mid-century.

A brief look at one of the foremost Italian orchestras is in order. Table 9 contains some listings for La Scala at Milan. The lack of bassoons in the 1814 list must be an oversight. The violins are already quite numerous. The basses' overpowering the cellos in number is an Italian orchestral trait; indeed Burney

Table 9. Milan, La Scala

	1814[a]	1816[b]	1825[c]	1890[d]
flutes	2	x	2	2
piccolos				2
oboes	2	x	2	2
clarinets	2	x	2	2
English horn				1
bassoons		x	2	4
bass clarinet				1
horns	4	x	4	4
trumpets	2	x	2	2
trombones	1	x	3	3
other brass		1 b hn	1 spt	1 tuba, 1 cnt
timpani	1		1	1
other	prc	prc	prc, kbd	4 prc, 2 hp
violins	25	24	13+13	16+14
violas	6	?	6	10
cellos + basses	4+8	8+8	6+8	11+11
Totals	**56/58**	**?**	**67**	**95**

b hn=basshorn; hp=harp; kbd=keyboard; prc=percussion
  spt=serpent; cnt=cornet; x=no number given

a AMZ, XVI (1814), col. 252.

b Spohr/LEBENSERINNERUNGEN, I, p. 245; or Spohr/JOURNEYS, p. 145.

c Seating plan in HARMONICON, III (1825), p. 140; also AMZ, XXVIII (1825), cols. 131-32.

d Seating plan in Kling/VOLLKOMMENE, p. 277.

had found this a fault in Italian orchestras,[8] and it seems to have persisted. Remember, in 1816 Spohr would also comment on this characteristic.[9] In 1816, the trombones earlier lacking are present, but what can be meant by *"Basshorn"*? Can it have been some type of tuba, or what was later to be called *"cimbasso"*? Or could it have been the bass trombone of the previous list? The equal number of cellos and basses does not correspond with Spohr's claim that "in most Italian orchestras there are six to eight basses to a single cello, and usually not a very good cello at that,"[10] but perhaps when he had visited La Scala the situation had been different.

Ripieno strength in woodwinds seems not to have been typical of Italy, as it had been in the larger German orchestras. Note the cello-bass ratio in 1825: 6 to 8, again showing the Italian trait. But the 1890 orchestra is quite "modern" in many ways. It reflects demands that later romantic operas made on the woodwind section. French influence would seem to be there in the presence of cornets mixed with trumpets. The greater strength of first over second violins—often seen in present-day orchestras—is "modern" in that earlier, if there was any discrepancy between them, the seconds would usually be favored. Basses and cellos are now equal in numbers, but still show greater bass strength than common elsewhere. Of course, harps and several percussion players would be taken for granted in a major opera house at this time.

An English orchestra should also be included here: table 10 provides some statistics for the Philharmonic Society of London which was established in 1813. Not much can be inferred from the 1813 "Foundation" list which is first, but from the second list which is from the fourth concert, it looks as if all 30 strings did not always participate in performances. One also wonders what was performed without trumpets or kettledrums. And there is the ever-present piano, still so much a part of the English orchestral scene. While the 1833 entry is only an approximate total, it does show great growth from humble origins, making London more than competitive with great German cities.

The 1837 list seems to give a breakdown of the total of 1833, and shows this orchestra to be as rounded as any on the continent. But again, as in Italy, one notes the thinner woodwind strength. Perhaps the idea that the classic-romantic orchestra had basically eight woodwinds or four pairs is a notion from England rather than Germany. The gain of five in 1839 is in the three upper strings, losing the bass support of the ophicleide. The strings are stronger vis-à-vis the woodwinds than in the larger German orchestras of the time. In 1842 the only change is an additional doublebass. With Dragonetti still alive and playing, one has to wonder at the need.

One is struck in the 1846 list not so much by the arrival of the harp and the return of the ophicleide, as by the growth of the basses and cellos at the expense of the violins. In 1858 the two violin sections are even again, though

Table 10. London, Philharmonic Society

	1813[a]	1813[b]	1833[c]	1837[d]	1839[e]	1842[f]	1846[g]	1858[h]	1860[i]
flutes		1		2	2	3	2	2	2
piccolo				1	1				
oboes		2		2	2	2	2	2	2
clarinets		3		2	2	2	2	2	2
bassoons		2		2	2	2	2	2	2
horns		2		4	4	4	4	4	4
trumpets				2	2	2	2	2	2
trombones				3	3	3	3	3	3
other brass				1 oph			1 oph		
timpani				1	1	1	1	1	1
other		1 pno					1 hp		
violins	x	4		14+14	16+16	16+16	15+14	14+14	12+12
violas (30)	x	3		8	10	10	10	8	8
cellos + basses	x	3+1		8+6	8+6	8+7	9+9	9+8	8+8
Totals	?	22	ca.70	70	75	76	77	71	66

hp=harp; oph=ophicleide; pno=piano

a Nettel/ENGLAND, p. 90.

b Ibid., p. 93-94.

c Elkin/LONDON, p. 100.

d *Musical World*, March 3, 1837, p. 175, cited in Carse/BEETHOVEN, pp. 52, 490.

e Ibid., March 7, 1839, p. 149, cited in Carse/BEETHOVEN, p. 52.

f Announcement, reproduced in Carse/ORCHESTRA, p. 29.

g *Illustrated London News*, March 21, 1846, cited in Carse/BEETHOVEN, p. 52; Nettel/ENGLAND, p. 145, has the same group but minus the harp.

h Printed announcement, cited in Carse/BEETHOVEN, p. 53.

i Nettel/ENGLAND, p. 94.

somewhat smaller than they had been. It seems incredible that harp and ophicleide have disappeared when they would be needed more than before. Perhaps they were hired as needed. If the 1860 figures are accurate, it seems that this orchestra was shrinking in the only place it could, given that the winds were already at a bare minimum for the repertoire. But the popular notion is that string strength greatly increased everywhere in the romantic era, especially late in the century. It seems that all generalities are just that: generalities.

The orchestra of the Opéra at Paris is another that was traced through the eighteenth century. Let us pick it up from there in table 11. In 1790 ripieno strength was manifest in oboes as well as bassoons. Just as flutes and clarinets were given access to the orchestra earlier via doubling oboists, here trumpet players apparently doubled on trombones. If this orchestra already seemed large in 1790, it showed growth very early in the 78 total of 1803, probably rivalled only by Munich.

Paris was progressive in the eighteenth century; signs of this continued in the arrival of contrabassoon and trombones by 1810. One would have expected that the harp too would already be here, but by 1820 there were already four! Yet one has to question the validity of the 1820 list in view of the two before and after it; it would not seem probable that the orchestra had grown and then reverted to size in so few years. Surprise at the appearance of four harps is also mitigated when one remembers that Castil-Blaze had cited the appearance of twelve in an opera *Les bardes* by Le Sueur in 1804.[11] While the 1825 list seems to be close to that of 1810, the cornets are surprisingly early, showing the desire for brass mobility. But 1826 shows how naive it can be to expect a steady progression towards "the" romantic orchestra. If this list is accurate, the cornets did not last long, unless they were available as *"externes"* since an addendum to the list shows four clarinets, more trumpets, bass drum, etc. to be available as such. Fluctuations in woodwind strength are also notable in this list. The list for 1827 sort of confirms the 1826 list; not much has changed. But one has to suspect the availability of more percussion and at least another harp.

By 1830 the woodwinds seem to be back to simple strength except for the bassoons, but the brass have what came to be a typical French setting, still to be seen in Stravinsky's *Petrushka,* except for a tuba in place of the ophicleide. Again, one suspects that harps were available. The 1839 list brings to one's attention the fact that the string section has remained quite stable since 1825. The English horn had made a timely appearance, but keyed bugle? The side-paths that music history has explored! It is generally assumed that Berlioz was referring to the Paris Opéra in the 1844 list which comes from his *Traité,* but in counting the "wind instruments already named," he might have by oversight forgotten their general use of four bassoons. Again the number of harps has swelled, but the strings still retain their stability.

Table 11. Paris, Opéra

	1790[a]	1803[b]	1810[c]	1820[d]	1825[e]	1826[f]	1827[g]	1830[h]	1839[i]	1844[j]	1845[k]	1847[l]	1855[m]	1890[n]
flutes	2		2	4	2(?)	3	3	2	3	2	3		3	4(?)
oboes	4		4	4	2(?)	3	3	2	2	2	3		3	2
English horn									1					
clarinets	2		2	4	2(?)	3	3	2	2	2	3		3	2
bassoons	5		4	4	4	4	3	4	4	2(?)	4		4	4(?)
contrabassoon			1											
horns	4		4	6	x	4	4	4	4	4	6		5	6(?)
trumpets	3		4	3		2	2	2	2	2	4		4	2
cornets					4			2	2	2	2			2
trombones	(3)		3	3		3	3		3	3	3		4	3
other brass				1 spt				1 oph	k-bg, 1 oph	1 oph				tuba
timpani	1		1	1		1	1	2	1	1	1		1	1
other			prc, pno	4 hp		1 hp	1 hp	4 prc	prc, 2 hp	prc, 6/8 hp	prc, 2 hp		4 prc, 2 hp	prc, 1 hp
violins	26		12+12	20+20	24	12+12	24(+2)	12+11	12+12	12+11	12+12		11+11	12+11
violas	6		8	14	8	8	8	8	8	8	8		8	8
cellos + basses	12+5	2+6	12+6	13+9	12+6	10+8	10+8	10+8	10+8	10+8	10+8		10+8	10+8
TOTALS	**70**	**78**	**77**	**110**	**(?)**	**ca.74**	**75**	**74**	**79**	**77/79**	**82**	**85**	**81**	**77**

hp=harp; k-bg=keyed bugle; oph=ophicleide; pno=piano; prc=percussion; spt=serpent

a Almanach historique du Théâtre ou Calendrier historique et chronologique de tous les Spectacles, Paris, 1791, cited by Carse/18TH, p. 26.

b Blaze/ACADEMIE, II, p. 374.

c AMZ, XII (1809/10), cols. 729-31.

d AMZW, 1820, p. 716, cited in Schreiber/ORCHESTER, p. 108.

e Smart/JOURNALS, p. 237.

f AMZ, XVIII (1826), col. 342.

g MMZW, 1827, p. 64, cited in Schreiber/ORCHESTER, p. 109.

h Deldevez/CHEF, p. 106.

i Kastner, Cours d'instrumentation, Paris, 1837, p. 4, cited in Carse/BEETHOVEN, p. 56.

j Berlioz/TRAITE, p. 294; or Berlioz-Strauss/INSTRUMENTATION, p. 406.

k Kastner, Cours d'instrumentation, Suppl., p. 2, cited in Carse/BEETHOVEN, p. 56.

l Blaze/ACADEMIE, II, p. 374.

m Ibid., II, p. 446.

n Seating plan in Kling/VOLLKOMMENE, p. 273.

Around 1845 the woodwind fluctuations make one wonder if the third players were to provide piccolo, English horn, bass or E♭ clarinet, and double bassoon. One also noticed changes in horns and trumpets, with a reversion to two harps. The year 1847 saw a slight increase in the total number of musicians, nothing else being revealed there. In 1855 the third woodwind players are still listed. But can two of the trumpets be cornets, even though Berlioz preferred the valve trumpet? And one misses ophicleide or tuba. Perhaps the fourth trombone was of the bass variety.

The 1890 numbers come from a seating plan, and once again it is difficult to be certain of reading correctly, although in this case the strings are given as definite numbers. The strings have remained stable almost throughout the century, but of course an already full pit without room for expansion might account for this. Tuba has replaced ophicleide, and more percussion must have been available. But an orchestra that was 70 in 1790 has only gained 7 players in 100 years, though it did swell to slightly over 80 at times.

At the risk of inordinate length, one more orchestra is offered, since it played an important role in the development of concert life in the nineteenth century: that of the Paris Conservatory or the *Société des Concerts,* as it was more properly called (table 12). The 1825 list is for a benefit concert. It is about the same as the orchestra at the Opéra at that time, and probably included much the same players. One wonders about the program, with trumpets lacking. These lists seem to show players available for specific concerts, the 1826 list also being for a benefit, so the orchestra was probably potentially larger. While piccolo and trumpets are here, the string section is somewhat smaller.

The year 1828 was the year of the actual founding of the *Société,* so that one might expect a more stable membership. The strings are noticeably stronger in violins and cellos than was the Opéra at the same time. The greater strength of the second violins over the firsts is worth noting too, especially since the 15 include Habeneck, who cannot have done much actual playing. As in other cases, this situation could well have been to compensate for the seating at the right of the seconds, whose f–holes faced away from the audience. Not really surprising, the ophicleide is here early. The 1835 list was for a benefit concert at the Odéon. Whether it was purely voluntary to take part and many could not, or whether space was limited at the Odéon is unknown. But this seems more like what is popularly considered a classic orchestra than a romantic one. It is interesting to guess what types of pieces were performed by this group: certainly an early Beethoven symphony would have been possible.

The 1840 string section continued to be larger than at the Opéra. Here again, bassoons retained their ripieno strength, even when the other woodwinds were at the minimum. The 1841 list suggests that the slight

Table 12. Paris, Conservatory Orchestra

	1825[a]	1826[b]	1828[c]	1835[d]	1840[e]	1841[f]	1844[g]	1855[h]	1859[i]	1878(?)[j]
flutes	2	2	4	2	2	4			4	
piccolo		1								
oboes	2	2	3	2	2	3			2	
clarinets	2	2	4	2	2	2			2	
bassoons	4	4	4	2	4	4			4	
horns	4	4	4	2	4	4			4	
trumpets		2	2	1	2	4			2	
cornets									1	
trombones			3		3	3			3	rarely
other brass			1 oph						1 oph	
timpani	1	1	1	1	1	1			1	
other			1 hp			1 pno			1 hp	rarely
violins	12+12	10+10	15+16	5+5	15+15	15+15			15+14	15+14
violas	8	6	8	2	10	10			10	10
cellos + basses	11+8	9+8	12+8	2+4	12+9	13+11			12+9	15+10
Totals	**66**	**61**	**86**	**30**	**81**	**90**	**63**	**64**	**85**	**?**

oph=ophicleide; hp=harp; pno=piano

a List in Paris Conservatory/ARCHIVES, Box 4.
b Ibid., Box 4.
c Elwart/SOCIETE, pp. 98–103.
d List in Paris Conservatory/ARCHIVES, Box 4.
e Seating plan in *Musical World*, 3/26/1840, p. 194, reproduced in Carse/BEETHOVEN, p. 476.
f Schindler/PARIS, pp. 10–18.
g Elwart/SOCIETE, p. 95, note 1.
h Ibid., p. 95.
i Ibid., pp. 103–8.
j Deldevez/CHEF, p. 107.

fluctuations from year to year could have depended to a great extent on when the observer was present, what concert he attended, etc., though many lists, such as Elwart's in 1844, might have been based on basic membership lists, another reminder that allowances must be made for some flexibility in perusing these lists. The 1844 list does suggest a rather large drop in membership though, just when one might have expected the opposite. Indeed, the Opéra remained larger at this time. The trimmer size continued in 1855. It is too bad particulars were not given, so that the instruments actually cut could be ascertained. But since a certain minimum of winds is indispensable—let us say roughly 17—most of the reductions must have been in strings. Yet, the orchestra was back to previous size in 1859. One has to wonder whether the intervening reductions were for reasons of economy, or whether the forces were actually augmented for concerts. The reappearance of ophicleide and harp suggest a more "progressive" repertoire.

The last list is undated, but since it comes from Deldevez's book, it seems safe to assume that the figures are for the orchestra in his own time. Certainly the lower strings were fuller than previously. His statement that trombones were rarely used is startling, considering the nineteenth-century repertoire, added to the fact that they had appeared in previous lists. Yet Deldevez had to have been an eyewitness. At any rate, as with the other orchestras surveyed, there does not seem to have been any steady pattern of growth, but rather periods of growth interspersed with regressions in size. Admittedly, perception is influenced in all cases by uncertainty as to whether each list represents only a certain concert or basic forces to which instruments could be added or subtracted. Also, one must remember the probability that economic factors, the size of locale of performance, as well as the style of the work being performed, were among circumstances affecting the overall size.

Cross Sections

While following individual orchestras has some value, it would be probably just as enlightening to survey particular periods in order to see whether a general pattern was developing. For example, in 1823, while Berlin numbered 89 and Dresden totalled 66, the Royal Academy of Music in London gave their first "exhibition" in the Hanover Square Rooms with an orchestra of one oboe, two pianos, four violins, one viola, one cello, and one double bass for a grand total of ten![12] What sort of program with what extent of "doctoring" could have been given?!

To enlarge on this picture, the following totals are given for five orchestras at the dawn of the century:

1800—Ludwigslust, Kapelle: 17;[13]
1801—Dresden, Königl. Capelle: 51;[14]
1802—Paris, théâtre in rue Feydeau: ca. 40;[15]
1803—Munich, Churbayerschen Kapelle: 30-32;[16]
1803—Paris, Opéra: 78[17]

This certainly presents quite a large spread: 17 to 78. Of course, Ludwigslust was a rather small court; it is even probable that tastes there adhered to classic principles and classic works. At the other extreme, Paris was a large artistic center, mounting new dramatic works in spacious quarters. The following are some orchestras around the quarter-century mark:

1823—Berlin, Königlich-Preussische Kapelle, Spontini: 89;[18]
1823—Dresden, Königlich-Sächsische Kapelle: 69;[19]
1825—Darmstadt, Court Opera: 66;[20]
1825—Milan, La Scala: 66-67;[21]
1825—Paris, Conservatoire, benefit: 66;[22]
1826—Paris, Opéra: 74, with extras available.[23]

This group shows less of a spread: 66 to 89 or a difference of 23. Certainly one would conclude that a general growth had taken place, a guarded conclusion though, keeping in mind that these represent only certain groups, figures for which happen to be available.

Here is a group at mid-century:

1847—Paris, Opéra: 85;[24]
1848—Leipzig, Gewandhaus: ca. 35;[25]
1850—Manchester, Gentlemen's Concerts, Hallé: 40;[26]
1852—London, New Philharmonic Society, Berlioz: 90;[27]
1855—Paris, Société des Concerts: 64;[28]
1856—Paris, Opéra-Italien: 54.[29]

While the spread seems to have grown again—35 to 90 or a difference of 55—it must be kept in mind that some different groups are again represented here, playing for different purposes in auditoriums of different size with varying financial supports available. It does strike one, though, that the largest group is the New Philharmonic Society which was conducted by Berlioz that year.

Here is a cross section later in the century:

1876—Bayreuth: 107;[30]
1881—Boston Symphony Orchestra: 72;[31]
1881—Leipzig, Stadtorchester: 72;[32]
1885—Manchester, Hallé Orchestra: upwards of 100;[33]
1890—Berlin, Opera: 65;[34]
1890—Milan, La Scala: 95;[35]
1891—Chicago Symphony Orchestra: 85.[36]

These figures confirm the popular impression that tremendous growth took place in the romantic orchestra. Especially telling are the newly founded groups—Bayreuth, Boston, Chicago—which felt compelled to have a minimum size to meet the demands of the contemporary repertoire. But one should not overlook the tremendous variations found from one locale to another all during the century, variations which make difficult if not impossible any handy generalities about the nineteenth-century orchestra and its size and make-up.

10

Relative Strengths and Proportions

Undoubtedly more important than mere overall size is the inner balance between sections. After all, the reason usually advanced for the growth of the string section is the effort to keep pace with the burgeoning winds. And as stated before, size in itself can be influenced by several factors: size of hall and financial support would be leading considerations. At least one writer early in the century (1803-4) recognized the "proportionate setting" [*"verhält- nismässige Besetzung"*] of the parts as being of great importance to the director. As an example, he mentioned that he noticed the bad effect of 16 violins against one cello and two basses, and the ensuing result of a scarcely audible, untrue bass, and too incisive and conspicuous violins. He also complained of the weak setting of the violas he found common—often two violas against eight violins—when given few good instruments and players in the viola section, it was no wonder that one violinist had more effect than two violas. He proposed making the viola section as strong as one of the two violin sections.[1]

But what is a right balance? And, while one would expect to find a "romantic" proportion, different from classic or baroque, what was it? Nettel pointed out that at its foundation in 1813, the London Philharmonic Society orchestra "was more up to date in construction and of finer quality than that of its great rival the Concert of Antient Music." The latter group was composed of 4 oboes, 4 bassoons, 4 horns, 2 trumpets, a trombone, and timpani, in addition to the string section. "From this we may assume that their ideas of tone-balance remained much as they were in Handel's time."[2] Since the string numbers are not given, one can only assume that Nettel was referring to the lack of flutes and clarinets as well as to the ripieno strength in oboes and bassoons. But then the business of this group was "antient" music. As noted above the Philharmonic Society at its fourth concert had 1 flute, 2 oboes, 3 clarinets, 2 bassoons, 2 horns, 1 piano, 4 violins, 3 violas, 3 cellos, and 1 bass,[3] which hardly seems "up to date" in string or brass strength.

More in line with "romantic" expectations was the situation at the Leipzig Gewandhaus pointed out by Borris: in fifty years, presumably from

1781 to 1831, the strings gradually grew from 19 to 30, while the wind strength scarcely changed.[4] But how this contrasts with the condition of the Handel and Haydn Society in Boston in 1839! According to a Boston periodical of the time, neither the choir nor the orchestra was ever "rightly balanced." In the chorus, the male voices "predominated" over the female, and the altos were "always deficient" in numbers. In the orchestra the strings were "altogether smothered" by the winds. "In well regulated Orchestras in Europe, the former amount in number to at least four times that of the latter, and for such proportions the composers write their orchestral music." The writer complained that "here" one seldom heard more strings than winds. "In the Handel and Haydn Society, for instance, there are eleven stringed instruments to fourteen wind instruments, of which latter seven are brass—a most outrageous disproportion, and in itself enough to spoil the true effect of a piece."[5] Certainly such a balance (or lack thereof) would be inappropriate to music of any period!

Another article in the same periodical offered some advice on this subject. The writer postulated that the number of instruments and voices "must depend of course on the size of the saloon, and on the character of the piece." But he felt it far more important that the different instruments and voices be "in the right proportion to each other." He gave as a "general rule" that "all the parts should be kept in even proportion; that is, so that no one is covered by the too great preponderance of another." He complained that in "our" orchestras a "deficiency in this respect" was often to be found in second violins and violas which were "sacrificed" to first violins; and the strings were "constantly drowned" by the winds. For him right proportions would be about six first violins, five seconds, three violas, four cellos, and two double basses, and all the wind instrument parts should be "single." The winds "ought not to be doubled, even though the stringed instruments should be double the above quantity."[6] Interesting in this light is the fact that most European orchestras at this time treated first and second violins as equals; when there was a discrepancy, it was more often than not in favor of the second violins. By keeping the winds "single" one assumes that the writer meant no ripieno or filling-in instruments, rather than one flute, for instance, where there are two separate flute parts. A brief look at the lists above, however, will show that this would be contrary to much European—especially German—practice, where ripieno strength in the woodwinds rivalled string sections similar in size.[7] And a German bias in this periodical has previously been pointed out.

Indeed, Theodore Thomas claimed that proper proportions did not obtain in the U.S. until much later. "In 1857, for the first time in America, the proportions of grand opera were properly balanced. There were first-rank singers, an increased chorus, and an enlarged orchestra, which had reached the efficiency of European grand orchestras."[8] He was speaking of Bernard

Ullmann's opera company at New York's Academy of Music. Over thirty years later, on assuming the conductorship of the new Chicago Symphony Orchestra, Thomas would assert that "modern" repertoire required an orchestra of about ninety.[9]

Writing in 1873, F. L. Schubert noted that both setting and placement must be considered so that one section or instrument does not drown out another. He admitted that one could not lay down a general norm since "to some extent" the locale of performance must come into account, taking into consideration the space for both performers and listeners. "A strong setting is not proper for small rooms and a weak one not for large locales." Musical works themselves also "imply to some extent" a larger or smaller locale. In large performances the space must be considered so that placing of the performers does not encounter impediments. The stronger brass section, with four instead of two horns, four trumpets, three trombones, ophicleide or tuba besides the "recently added" English horn and bass clarinet "among others" require a stronger contingent of strings. He wondered about a performance of *Tannhäuser* in Elbing bei Danzig with single setting of the strings(!), not knowing what to say about such a disproportion, since Wagner desired 18 to 20 first violins and the remaining strings in proportion. "This is a mockery of art and a boast: 'we have also performed *Tannhäuser*', but the 'how' comes not thereby into consideration."[10] Schubert's remarks remain general and set no really concrete guidelines.

In 1887, Eduard Blitz was more definite: "In an orchestra, the diverse elements are distributed in these proportions, which must be kept, despite the large number of musicians one might have at one's disposal." He listed 2 flutes, 2 oboes, 2 clarinets, 2 or 4 bassoons, 4 horns, 4 trumpets or 2 trumpets and 2 cornets, 3 trombones, 1 ophicleide, 1 pair of timpani and 1 other percussion player (bass drum and cymbals), 10 first violins, 10 seconds, 8 violas, 8 cellos, and 6 basses.[11] A formula can be deduced from this. Woodwinds to brass to strings can be reduced to about 10:12:42 or about 1:1:4. Or combined winds to strings is about 22:42 or roughly 1:2. And within the string section itself one finds 10:10:8:8:6 or 5:5:4:4:3. In the previous consideration of the eighteenth-century orchestra above, the ratio of violins to the lower strings was perused; here that would be 20:22 or almost 1:1. These figures can be a starting point in delving into proportions in the nineteenth-century orchestra. Meanwhile, it brings to mind Dart's complaint that the modern orchestra is "bottom-heavy," citing what amounted to a 1:1 ratio of violins versus the lower strings, compared to what he considered the eighteenth-century's 3:2.[12]

But first one more reminder on the relationships between size, hall, and works to be performed might be worthwhile. This time it comes from Hermann Zopff who wrote in 1881. Reiterating that the "nature and strength of the distribution are determined essentially by the room," he averred that a "strong setting and roaring brass" were not suitable for small rooms just as weak strings would not fill large ones or open-air performances. He also pointed out that some works "reach true effect" in larger but others in smaller locales. He counseled further care for "correct as possible part-relationship, so that no individual parts be stifled by the others." He found "critical in this respect" the very "dissimilar sound-power" of the individual instruments. For "medium-sized" theaters and halls, counting on "a single setting" of the winds, he recommended 8 first violins, 6–8 seconds, 3–4 violas, 2–3 cellos and 2–3 basses. For larger orchestras, he increased the numbers up to 24 first and 20 second violins, 12 violas, 12 cellos, and 12 basses. For large music festivals or "so-called monster-concerts" where the strings are even stronger, he advocated doubled winds. However, the "augmenting or so-called ripieno-instruments" join in only in "tuttis and forte-passages and pause in all solo and piano-passages" and some of the strings should do likewise.[13]

If one is seeking a working ratio for the nineteenth-century orchestra, Zopff's figures can be even more confounding. His smaller group would yield 21 to 26 strings against about 8 woodwinds and probably 9 to 11 brass, or roughly 2:1:1. But his larger group amounts to 80:8:11 or 10:1:1—vastly different ratios and in conflict with Blitz's 4:1:1. Zopff's combined winds versus strings would be about 19:26 in the smaller group or roughly 2:3, and 19:80 in the larger or 1:4. Blitz's was 1:2. Zopff's string section varies from 8:8:4:3:3 or almost 3:3:1:1:1 to 24:20:12:12:12 or 2:2:1:1:1. Blitz's was 5:5:4:4:3. And violins versus lower strings come out for Zopff 16:10 or 3:2 and 44:36 or 5:4, against Blitz's 1:1. Certainly there is little basic agreement here.

It might be interesting, even if more confounding, to compare these ratios with those of some actual orchestras. First, a review of woodwinds versus brass versus strings has Blitz as about 1:1:4, Zopff at roughly 1:1:2 and 1:1:10. Carse's ratio of 1:4 for woodwinds versus strings[14] would be close to Blitz's. And if Dart's "modern" orchestra can be taken to include any of the nineteenth century (his comparison was with the eighteenth), he gave two of each woodwind for every 15 violins.[15] Since his "typical" modern orchestra has 22 violins or a total string strength of 44, and 8 woodwinds, adding clarinets to his chart, one comes out with 8:44 or roughly 1:6. How do these correspond to some actual figures?

Berlin showed about 1:1:3 or 1:1:4 in 1811, 1:1:3 in 1823, 2:1:5 in 1843, 1:1:3 in 1844, 1:1:3 or 1:1:4 in 1849, 1:1:6 in 1890. Dresden showed 3:1:8 in 1801, 3:1:7 in 1805, near 3:1:5 in 1817 and 1819, 3:1:5 in 1823 and 1832, 1:1:3 in 1835, 2:1:4 in 1839, 1:1:2 in 1842, almost 1:1:4 in 1844, and 1:1:2 in 1850. Milan had 1:1:7 in 1814, 1:1:6 in 1825, and 1:1:4 in 1890. The London Philharmonic Society had 4:1:6 in 1813, 1:1:5 in 1837, 1:1:6 in 1839, 1842, 1846, and 1858, and 1:1:5 again in 1860. The Opéra at Paris reduces to 1:1:4 in 1810, roughly

1:1:6 in 1820, closer to 1:1:4 in 1826 and 1827, 1:1:5 in 1830, 1:1:4 in 1839, 1:1:6 in 1844, 1:1:4 in 1845 and 1855, and 1:1:4 in 1890. Meanwhile the Paris Conservatory Orchestra went from 2:1:10 in 1825 to 2:1:8 in 1826, 1:1:6 in 1828, 3:1:6 in 1835, 1:1:6 in 1840, 1:1:5 in 1841, and 1:1:5 in 1859. While these ratios are not exact reductions and some could arguably be interpreted slightly differently, they are still diverse enough to beg any attempt at a pat formula which would distinguish "romantic" from baroque, classic, or any other label. In other words, one cannot take any proportion as basic, multiply it by a convenient figure (convenient to purse and hall) and come up with a "typical" romantic orchestra.

If one looked for a simpler proportion between combined winds and strings, there would still be widespread disagreement. Blitz's figures would reduce to 1:2, Zopff's to 2:3 in his small orchestra, 1:4 in the large one. Nor do the statistics for actual orchestras show any more agreement. At Berlin, for example, one finds 2:3 in 1811, 3:4 in 1823, 2:3 in 1825, 1:2 in 1843, 2:3 in 1844, 3:5 in 1849, and 1:3 in 1890. Nor would a list of other orchestras clarify the situation. Ratios vary as much as from 4:5 in Dresden in 1817 to 8:9 there in 1839 and 9:10 in 1842. Leipzig shows 6:7 in 1808 and 5:6 in 1833. Munich provides 9:11 in 1827, and Milan 2:7 in 1814. So it seems fruitless to pursue this further; these ratios are no closer than the woodwind: brass: strings were, and there is no agreement.

Neither is there any standard running within the string section. The two violin sections are most often equal; when they are not, the seconds are more often the stronger, contrary to much twentieth-century practice. This was undoubtedly due to the fact that in most nineteenth-century orchestras, the second violins were at the listeners' right facing the center, so that their f-holes were not "speaking" out at the audience. This situation is rare in the twentieth century, even when eighteenth- and nineteenth-century music is on the program.

Blitz's numbers for strings reduce to 5:5:4:4:3. Zopff's vary from about 3:3:1:1:1 in his small orchestra to 2:2:1:1:1. Remembering Dart's complaint against bottom-heaviness, Zopff has more violins than lower strings, Blitz the reverse. But going back to actual orchestras, Berlin had roughly 3:3:1:3:1 in 1811, 3:3:3:2:2 in 1830, and 4:3+:3:3:3 in 1890. The majority of the Dresden lists reduce to about 2:2:1:1:1, though 1801 is more like 5:5:2:2:2. The Paris Opéra runs at 2:2:1:2:1 in almost all lists. Again there is no underlying proportion fitting the orchestra even in one city or in one part of the century. And for good measure, remember Bayreuth's 16:16:12:12:8 which neatly reduces to 4:4:3:3:2. But even this does not exactly agree with Wagner's figures for a Saxon National Theater, whose proposed string section was 11:11:6:6:5, which reduces more like 2:2:1:1:1.

Adding Wagner's figures to the morass above brings to mind ratios for winds vs. strings again. Wagner proposed for the Saxon theater 12 woodwinds, 10 brass, and 39 strings: a ratio of about 1:1:4; Bayreuth had 19 woodwinds, 22 brass, and 64 strings, or roughly 1:1:3. Combined winds vs. strings would come to 22 vs. 39 or about 1:2 for the Saxon theater, and 41 vs. 64 or 2:3 for Bayreuth. So even Wagner's ideas changed through the years and do not reduce to any "romantic" ratio. Strangely enough, while the string section for Strauss's *Heldenleben* is exactly the same as Bayreuth's, Strauss prescribed 16 woodwinds, 18 brass, which with the 64 strings comes to 1:1:4 or a combined winds vs. strings of 34 vs. 64 or 1:2. Both of these ratios are more like Wagner's earlier figures for the Saxon theater rather than equalling the Bayreuth ratios.

It seems unfair to have excluded Berlioz from these ruminations on possible proportions, but even he adds no clarity to the problem. His figures for the *Symphonie fantastique* and for *Le Carnaval romain* would reduce to ratios of about 1:1:6 for woodwinds vs. brass vs. strings, or 2:3 for combined winds vs. strings. The string section for both works reduces to about 5:5:3:4:3. But the string section for Miss Dolby's concert comes to exactly a ratio of 2:2:1:1:1. No consistency here! And if one looks at what might be called Berlioz's "Dream" orchestra no. 1,[16] one finds 14 woodwinds, 13 brass, and 84 strings or about 1:1:6, which amounts to 27 winds vs. 84 strings or 1:3. There are 21:20:18:15:10 in the string section which reduces to about 4:4:4–:3:2. But "Dream" orchestra no. 2[17] has 62 woodwinds, 47 brass, and 242 strings, or about 1+:1:5, which combines to 109 winds vs. 242 strings or about 1:2. The string section which splits to 60 firsts, 60 seconds, 40 violas, 45 cellos, and 33 basses, as well as allowing for other subdivisions (and omitting the 4 octobasses) would yield a ratio of about 5:5:3:4:3. So if one gives Berlioz the last word, it certainly cannot be reduced to any simple overall formula which can be universally applied.

If, then, one wants to produce a performance that is "faithful" as to orchestral size and proportions, probably the only recourse open would be to research the orchestra the composer was most familiar with at the time of composition. This can provide a close basis, provided the size of the hall is also taken into consideration. For example, the Leipzig Gewandhaus Orchestra in the 1830s and 1840s would provide some idea of the sound ideal familiar to Mendelssohn and Schumann, even young Wagner. But this must be tempered by the remembrance that Mendelssohn seemed pleased with the orchestra of 80 he had in the Munich concert of 1831, an orchestra more than twice the size of the one he conducted in Leipzig. The Bayreuth figures are easily available for the later music dramas of Wagner. But French composers must have been influenced by the larger orchestra at the Opéra, playing in a larger ambience.

Orchestra versus Chorus

A valid area for study in this connection would seem to be the proportions between orchestra and chorus. So often the orchestra in some modern performances has been treated as a bare accompaniment to an all-important chorus. But this was not always so. In the mid-eighteenth century, it seemed that the orchestra was invariably the larger. For example, in Berlin (*Oper und Musik des Königs*), there were 39 in the orchestra against 8 choristers in 1754,[18] a ratio of about 5:1. Dresden (Oper and Kapelle) in 1756 was less drastic with 51 players against 21,[19] about 5:2. In 1754, Breslau (Hochfürstl. Bischöflichen Capelle) with an orchestra of 15 against 7 singers[20] and Gotha (Hochfürstlichen Kammer- und Capellmusik) with 18 against 7[21] were more like 2:1. Meanwhile in Paris in 1754 the Opéra had an orchestra of about 51 against 38 in the chorus,[22] perhaps about 4:3, and in 1756 the *Concert spirituel* had 40 against 44,[23] close to 1:1.

The situation is not much changed later in the century. In 1770, the church of San Antonio in Padua had an orchestra of 24 against 16 singers,[24] 3:2. In 1772, Berlin (King of Prussia) had about 42 players against 24 singers;[25] in 1782 in the same city (Königl. Preussische Kapelle) there were 40 vs. 24,[26] both being about 2:1. In 1782, Cassel (Hof-Kapellmusik) had 24 players against 15 singers,[27] about a 3:2 proportion, and Dresden (Churfürstlich Sächsische Kapelle- und Kammer-Musik) had 46 against 25 singers,[28] roughly 2:1. In 1783 at Mainz (Churfürstlich Maynzische Capelle) there were 27 in the orchestra against only 8 in the choir,[29] about a 3:1 ratio. Meanwhile the *Concert spirituel* in Paris kept a 1:1 ratio in 1773 with 43 players against 42 singers.[30] Even the big Handel Commemoration in London in 1784 gave only a slight edge to the chorus with an orchestra of 251 against a chorus of 275.[31] But Handel's *Messiah* in the Domkirche in Berlin in 1786 gave a 3:2 advantage to the orchestra with 189 against the chorus's 119 (including the soloists).[32]

It is in the nineteenth century that choruses start to outnumber orchestras, and usually in large festivals. Thus in 1800 whereas a performance of Haydn's *Creation* at the Opéra in Paris kept a near 1:1 ratio with an orchestra of 159 and a chorus of 150,[33] the *Sing-Akademie* in Berlin gave the choir a better than 1:3 advantage in Mozart's *Requiem* with 33 in the orchestra against 115 singers.[34] And whereas in 1806 Napoleons's *Chapelle-Musique* in Paris gave a slight edge to the orchestra, 45 to 40,[35] the Antient Concerts in London in 1805 gave a slight advantage to the choir, 49 to 57.[36] In 1810, while the Thuringian festival at Frankenhausen conducted by Spohr (and including Haydn's *Creation*) gave a slight advantage to the orchestra with 106 to 98,[37] Righini's *Te Deum* was performed in Berlin, once (*im weissen Saale des königl. Schlosses*) with 172 players and 300+ singers,[38] another time (Opernhaus, *Concert spirituel*) with an orchestra of 93 and a chorus of 210+,[39] the latter giving the choir a better than 1:2 edge. Indeed, one's general impression is that it was in England that huge choruses were prevalent. The Birmingham Festival of 1820 with an orchestra of 81 outnumbered by a chorus of 134 would seem to confirm that impression,[40] offering about a 3:5 ratio; but the Niederrheinische Musikfest of 1821 in Cologne is more lavish than that with an orchestra of 159 against a chorus of 234,[41] or a proportion of 2:3. And if the Gloucester Festival of 1823 seemed modest with 47 players to 83 singers or almost 1:2,[42] the Yorkshire Grand Music Festival the same year had an orchestra of 177 to a choir of 269 or a ratio of 2:3.[43] Alongside these, the Liverpool Festival of 1823 with 72 players to 84 singers[44] and the Wakefield Musical Festival of 1824 with 85 to 86[45] are both close to 1:1. So again, generalities are just that. Paris also seemed to stay closer to 1:1 at this time. The coronation of Charles X at Reims Cathedral in 1825 had an orchestra of 94 to a choir of 96,[46] and in 1828 the Société des concerts du conservatoire under Habeneck had 85 players to 79 singers,[47] still giving the edge to the orchestra. A similar relationship obtained at Paris in 1830 in the *Chapelle Musique du Roi* with 48 players and 46 singers,[48] and the first complete performance of Beethoven's *Missa solemnis* at Warnsdorf the same year gave the edge to the orchestra with 47 vs. 36.[49]

In 1840 the Paris Conservatory Orchestra still remained close to 1:1, giving a slight advantage to the orchestra with 81 vs. 72.[50] In London in 1841, Jullien's *Concerts d'hiver* at Drury Lane showed a similar ratio with 98 players vs. 80 singers.[51] But even Haydn's *Creation* at the Opéra in Paris kept a similar ratio in 1844 with 241 in the orchestra and 250 in the chorus,[52] a slight advantage for the chorus. Opposed to these, the *Creation* at the Winterreitschule in Vienna in 1843 had 320 players and 660 singers,[53] more like 1:2; and at Cologne in 1844, the twenty-sixth Niederrheinische Musikfest with Dorn conducting was more like 2:5 with 167 in the orchestra and 417 in the chorus.[54] This would seem to indicate a preference for equality in France and a desire for choral dominance in the German-speaking countries as mid-century approached. Yet, perhaps this was more true of festivals than of smaller gatherings, although the *Concert spirituel* in Vienna showed about a 3:4 proportion in 1844 with 59 players and 80 singers,[55] the k. k. Hofkapelle in Vienna the same year was closer to 2:1 with 36 in the orchestra opposite 20 singers,[56] and the Beethoven Commemoration at Bonn in 1845 had nearly 80 in the orchestra and 80 in the chorus[57] for the Mass in D.

One sees a similar situation later in the century. While in 1859 the Société des concerts in Paris still gave a slight edge to the orchestra with 85 vs. 72,[58] the Handel Commemoration Festival in the Crystal Palace in London the same year conducted by Costa was almost 1:4 with an orchestra of 462 and a chorus of 2,700![59] And although Verdi conducted his *Requiem* at the Church of St. Mark in Milan in 1874 with 110 in the orchestra and 120 in the choir,[60] in

1875 he succumbed to British taste when he led the same work in Albert Hall in London with an orchestra of 150 against a chorus of 500 to 600![61] That would be in the vicinity of 1:4. But Theodore Thomas evidently liked even larger choruses. In 1882 he conducted the Biennial Musical Festival in Chicago with an orchestra of 174 against 900 voices,[62] something like 1:5. And that same year he conducted festivals in New York, Cincinnati, and Chicago with more like a 1:10 ratio: 300 players to 3,000 voices![63] So perhaps the American taste for large choruses that overwhelm the "accompaniment" came from Great Britain.

But what of the practices of some of the greater composers in this matter? Berlioz's *Requiem* calls for 166 players against 210 voices as a minimum.[64] And if these forces are increased he desires the same proportions of about 3:4. Yet with the satellite orchestras added, the figures amount to more like 1:1, that is 201 to 210.[65] What may be called his "Dream orchestra no. 1"[66] is close to 1:1 with a slight edge to the chorus: 119 to 126. And what might be called "Dream orchestra no. 2"[67] has more like a 4:3 ratio in favor of the orchestra with 465 to 360. This reinforces evidence of French taste for more or less equal forces. But look at the German side. When Mendelssohn conducted the Lower Rhenish Music Festival in Cologne in 1835, he had more like a 1:2 ratio favoring the chorus with 204 versus 476.[68] And Wagner even went further in his performance of Beethoven's Ninth Symphony at Bayreuth in 1872; his forces were at 1:3 with 100 players to 300 singers.[69] So the masters gave some precedence to this aspect of modern practice.

Part Four

Seating in the Nineteenth Century

11

Principles of Seating

It is worth reiterating at the outset that in many cases a "seating plan" could better be called a "standing plan," for the eighteenth-century practice of standing to play in concert situations still prevailed in many places in the nineteenth century. It is difficult to establish exactly how widespread the practice was, for it is seldom mentioned in accounts, probably being taken for granted. Richard Hoffman, the pianist, is one who did mention memories of his youth in Manchester in the 1830s and 1840s when his father was a violinist in the "Gentlemen's Concerts." He declared that he was always taken to these concerts and allowed to be on the stage near his father "whose chair I occupied while he was playing. The English orchestral players (except, of course, the 'cellos) always stood while they played; they were not allowed the privilege of sitting and crossing their legs in the listless manner which so often offends the eye in our modern performances."[1] And one of the oldest members of the Leipzig Gewandhaus Orchestra was quoted in an article in the *Leipziger Tageblatt* of October 1, 1893, as stating: "In the Gewandhaus we are wholly different people than in the theater; in black dress coat and standing erect at the desk, surrounded by the finely bedecked society in the hall, a different, higher spirit dominates us."[2] In fact, the violins and violas in Leipzig did not sit to play until about ten years after the advent of Artur Nikisch as conductor, which would be about 1905.[3] There are sketches of this orchestra which attest to this practice, for example, that shown in figure 20 from around 1840.

When Hanslick heard the Meiningen Court Orchestra under Hans von Bülow in 1884 he seemed to attribute their performing in the standing position to Bülow's desire for discipline. He called it a "much-discussed innovation" and "one which strikes me as of doubtful value" and found it a reversion to the older custom "possibly attributable in former times to the limited space of the old concert halls and the etiquette of court orchestras." He guessed that it was in Vienna that the fashion of playing in the seated position "first took hold," and referred to the story of Dittersdorf and the "Viennese custom" he adopted which was mentioned in an earlier chapter of this study. Hanslick's

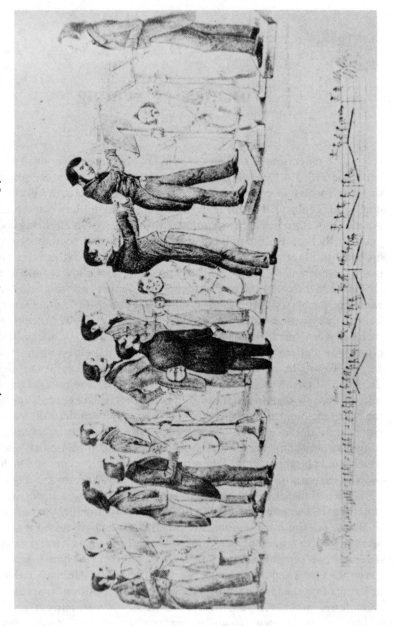

Figure 20. The Leipzig Gewandhaus Orchestra, ca. 1840
Reproduced from Mueller/AMERICAN, facing p. 311.

conclusions: "Standing is a kind of insurance against carelessness and easetaking on the part of the players; sitting conserves their strength. The first is more military, the latter more humane."[4]

David Wooldridge seemed to limit the practice to Germany: "It was of course customary for the German orchestra to perform standing until the last years of the nineteenth century."[5] But the description of Manchester above shows that the practice was at least known in England, and there is evidence that it was not uncommon in the United States. The New York Philharmonic was founded in 1842, and John Mueller has found that "at the inaugural concert the musicians stood before their desks in the approved Leipzig Gewandhaus manner—a pattern well-known in England and the United States too."[6] And a caricature of a concert of the Musical Fund Society in Philadelphia near mid-century shows the players standing (fig. 21).

The Chicago Philharmonic under Hans Balatka and Theodore Thomas' Orchestra played on consecutive evenings at Farwell Hall in Chicago in November 1869. According to one who was there: "Thomas's men remained seated during the performance. Balatka adhered to the old usage in Germany, requiring the men to stand while playing."[7] And the practice still survived in New York in 1853, for at least one critic was unable to "account for the necessity of the performers standing. Aside from being uncomfortable to them, this looks badly and impresses the spectators uncomfortably."[8] So if it is difficult to document just how widespread the practice was, it was by no means unusual. Even later in the century, "Gericke, Nikisch, and Paur in Boston and New York at times ordered their violins to stand, on the allegation that they thereby enhanced the volume of their tone."[9]

On Principles

Are there any basic, universally valid principles of placing the instruments on stage or in the pit? If so, on what factors do they depend; what circumstances would contribute to the necessity for slight or considerable changes? Mueller summed up the bases thus:

> (1) the relation of the various choirs to one another and to the conductor for mutual visual and aural coordination and support; (2) accoustical effect upon the listener; and (3) the aesthetic and visual impression upon the audience. There is, of course, no precise unanimity of opinion as to which detailed pattern best promotes these ends, although the general plan, proposed by Berlioz in his notable treatise, is still basic today.[10]

One would not be inclined to argue with these three principles but rather to emphasize the lack of "precise unanimity of opinion" as to how best to carry them out. One must question how "basic today" Berlioz's ideas on this subject are, but more on that later.

Figure 21. Philadelphia, Musical Fund Society, ca. 1845
Madeira / PHILADELPHIA, facing p. 144.

At the turn of the nineteenth century, Friedrich Rochlitz not only complained about the placing of instruments in his time but directly related the matter to compositional style. He found it "curious" that no one had realized that a "changed grouping" had become "essential" due to the changed use made of them at his time. As an example he suggested comparing the way "our forefathers" wrote for winds with the way they were composed for in his day. "And nevertheless one retains for the most part the now out-of-date places of the players." As a particular example, he pointed out that formerly one used trumpets and timpani seldom, only for "rejoicing" or "blaring," so that it made sense to place these instruments high up and conspicuous so that "they almost drown out the others." But then he asked: "how does one write for them now? Ah! hide your trumpets and timpani as far in a corner of your orchestra as possible—I am afraid too much noise still remains." He suggested bringing forth somewhat in their place the bassoons "which one formerly (with the exception of occasional obbligato passages) used only for martial music and for strengthening the basses."[11]

Interestingly, Rochlitz found fault not only with seating arrangements but also with such physical obstacles as music stands. He questioned the "usual *full* music stands—I mean such where the notes lie on an ordinary shelf. Cast them away, these shelves, and have instead the smallest possible ledges nailed there!" He pointed out that seldom does one realize "how detrimental" they can be to the sound, that they reflect it, especially in the case of violins and violas, and thereby "partly diminish the strength" of it for the listeners, and in large or not entirely full halls partly cause a "false reverberation and a resulting confusion."[12]

A bit later (1801–2) Georg von Unold complained that neither in his travels in Italy nor in Germany had he found what seemed to him perfection in placing an orchestra or in the construction and proportions of a music room. However, his prescription and the musical reasons for it sound more baroque than late classic. He proposed as a cardinal rule that the "quartet" which he named parenthetically as first and second violins, violas, basses and keyboard, should be kept together and near one another. Since all compositions were only in four parts, the other instruments, no matter how necessary they were, belonged to the "filling out, doubling and so forth or further coloring of the ideas." Therefore, "the above mentioned should be regarded as the center of the orchestra."[13]

By way of example Unold supposed a small orchestra of 25: 2 flutes, 2 oboes (or clarinets), 2 bassoons, 2 horns, 2 trumpets, timpani, keyboard, 5 first, 4 second violins, 2 violas, 1 cello, and 1 double bass. Such an orchestra might be set up in a room about 70 feet long and 40 feet wide. He proposed three elevations. The first should be a hollow floor one-half foot high; on it would be first and second violins, violas, bass, cello, keyboard, and bassoons.

The second elevation should be another half-foot higher; here the oboes (or clarinets) and flutes should be placed behind the first violins, the horns behind the second violins, and if vocal music is involved, the singers nearest the basses and keyboard. On the third elevation one foot higher, one should place the trumpets, trombones, and timpani. Unold felt that placing together the same types of instruments, "which according to their nature and even in conformity with the laws of the art of composition belong together," would facilitate performance and have the advantage of "communicating to the listener the harmonic sound at the same time and united as one."[14] It is too bad that Herr Unold was not more specific. For example, the strings would seem to be in a row without any separation between the two violin sections. The presence of a keyboard instrument, the placing of the bassoons with the lower strings, the willingness to substitute clarinets for oboes, all seem old-fashioned. As for the size, it must be remembered that Beethoven often had to be satisfied with not much more, even later.

While not giving any definite seating plan, an anonymous article of a few years later (1803–4) does give interesting advice, some of which indicates the fruit of practical experience. The article is on the duties of a theater conductor. Placing great importance on good placement of the instruments, the author first stipulated that the music director must take a place so that all the personnel can see him and so perceive the tempo instantly. The "standpoint" of the violin leader and of the best double bass player must be nearest to the director. As for the bass player, the director must test to find whether the place on which the bass rests is hollow or filled with beams or blocks or whatever. If so, the director must find a better place for fortifying the sound or even a place which he deems most appropriate for tearing up and making a cavity. "One can always assume as a rule that the tone of the contrabass becomes fuller and stronger by a third by means of a cavity beneath." He also advocated placing the basses so that the f-holes were aimed towards the audience. He noted that several instruments, for example, trumpets, timpani, trombones, etc., were often played by those who "with the best will" either through "bad habit or from lack of skill" were not able to restrain themselves in executing their parts. "These bad circumstances can only be helped to some extent if one tries to conceal these persons with their instruments as much as possible in a corner."[15] While there is no surprise in hearing of the noisy instruments or in the advice on directing the f-holes, the idea of finding a hollow spot to enhance the resonance of the double bass does seem a recommendation of which not everyone would have thought. The same writer also had advice as to the singers on stage as well as for players who must perform backstage. For the latter the music director must indicate a place suitable "so that the intended purpose of the composer be achieved." As for the singers, the director must see to it that decorations are so placed that when singers must be at a "distant, hidden, or raised place, the ensemble with the orchestra will not be impeded too much for the singers."[16]

I.F.K. Arnold also had definite ideas on orchestral layout, which were published in 1806. First he gave some general principles, stating that the differing relationships of the instruments to each other, their stronger or weaker tones, some quickly cutting through, others quickly covered, demand an "advantageous placing" of the orchestra if they are to produce "a total effect in which each makes itself heard without obscuring or being obscured.... On this above all depends the effect of the music."[17] Arnold also reiterated that it was absolutely necessary for the director to see and be seen by each individual member of the orchestra. On the position from which music should be heard, he offered the following three points: (1) the "standpoint" of the orchestra must be so chosen that neither the "physical nor esthetic effect" of the music fails for the listener; (2) the distance between the orchestra and the audience must be "so measured" that the music makes a "total impression" as would a piece performed by a single man on one instrument; and (3) the position of the more powerful instruments must be so chosen that they do not "drown out" the less powerful.[18] Arnold also found it desirable that the director understand physics or acoustics.[19]

Arnold elaborated on the above, reiterating the necessity that the music be "equally perfectly perceived" by all the listeners. He said that in order to disperse the "flood of tone" equally, it should be directed over all the heads of the audience by raising the place on which the musicians stand at least three feet; otherwise the tones would be "instantly absorbed" by the nearest listeners, deadening the resonance for the others. Therefore, the music must be placed "on such a standpoint" from which it is equally perceptible to all in its timbre and volume as well as its expression, and "none of its beauty becomes lost for the listeners." This end is served by "not only the raising of the orchestra but also the more or less acoustical form of the room in which the music is performed."[20] He even went so far as to say that the "more or less advantageous position" of the orchestra has a "superior influence" on the clarity of performance.[21] He could be sarcastic, as in warning against the practice of "Herr Choirmaster" who placed strings, winds, singers, and trumpets "nicely in a row" with the kettledrums, which usually made a display in velvet aprons on high holidays. The drums' golden trappings were hung over the heads of the "esteemed pious congregation" and "thus discharge their thunderstorm with all their might over the devout souls." He also pointed out "some *Maître des Plaisirs* at a certain court" who placed the horns at the head of the orchestra.[22]

Arnold got down to specifics, however, stipulating that the "stronger sounding instruments" must be placed so that their tones "get greater space for their air-vibration, and only indirectly strike the ear," discharging their sound more in the orchestra itself than directly among the audience, "so that they only be perceived *with the strings,* and *never stand out,* or cover the same at all." The timpani should maintain the back row "incontestably," well disposed of diagonally in the bend of the sidewall towards the backwall, protecting the listeners with a screen of taffeta against their tone as well as that of the trumpets "standing near them." In that way the sound is directed sideways and has "not so harsh an effect."[23] After warning against heavy pounding on the timpani and against wooden timpani, Arnold went on to reiterate that the "standpoint of the timpani must still be protected against this by a cover of taffeta or paper, so that the sound does not rise too harshly in intensity, but is more directed under the sounds of the other instruments." The horns must come in front of the timpani and trumpets "and with their singing tone moderate that shuddering." The oboes, clarinets, bassoons, and flutes follow in the same row. In front of them come the cellos, basses, and violas, and then the second violins. The forward place is maintained by the first violins in their "doubled or tripled setting."[24] One wishes that Arnold had been somewhat more clear here. There would seem to be no evidence of a desire to split the two violin sections, however, a practice which was to become so typical of the nineteenth-century orchestra. But otherwise, Arnold seems to suggest a quite sensible order. Several pages later he picked up this theme again and anticipated Berlioz's recommendation of a semicircle, as well as reiterating the importance of visibility; that is, all the musicians must "so stand" that they can "comfortably be overseen by the music director and see him." In the concert hall, "because the musicians here, like the actors, must show their faces to the audience, the semicircle or amphitheatrical disposition appears most advantageous." Arnold then postulated four or five "encircling arcs," with trumpets, timpani, and trombones forming the most posterior arc at the rear wall next to the horns, the latter being more prominent compared with the trumpets. In the second arc, enclosed by the first, should come at the "foremost end" the flutes, then the clarinets, "towards the middle" the bassoons, and "at the other end" the oboes. The third arc should have contrabasses at both ends, then cellos, and in the middle the violas. "In this amphitheater the music-director stands in the middle with the score." To his right should be the first violins and "somewhat back the second violins." The solo voices "step forward" and the violins "stand behind the music-director." The chorus singers "stand behind the solo voices."[25] Now first of all, here is an early version of double basses at both wings, a layout which will be seen quite often in the nineteenth century. But Arnold seems to have all the violins to one side, although it is not clear what he meant by "to his right," in that very often at this time the conductor had to face the audience, making it difficult to be sure whether the conductor's right is also the audience's right or left. Of course, it will be remembered that the strings were quite often to the right in the eighteenth-century orchestra, and perhaps Arnold still saw it that way.

Arnold allowed that a different layout was required in the theater because of the problem of space, if one were to "attain the purpose of the music" and be nearer to the singers to "more easily help them." Other problems mentioned are the fact that the acting often "draws the attention" of the players, and that the theater "absorbs a great many tones which are lost for the audience." Arnold felt that the following considerations had to be met: (1) the orchestra must be made "perfectly distinct" to the auditorium; (2) the orchestra must see and be seen by the director "comfortably"; (3) the players must not be disturbed by "gazing up at the stage" nor by the "spectators looking up there"; (4) as in the concert orchestra, the parts must be so dispersed that none cover the others and the ensemble is equally effective "from every standpoint." The "more circumscribed space" and the "relationship to the stage" requires a closer crowding together in which the "indicated order" cannot find "complete space."[26] He offered the plan shown in figure 22 as the most advantageous one for the theater in his opinion. In explanation, 1 is the "standpoint" of the conductor "with the score." From this point Arnold felt he could "oversee" the whole orchestra and the stage and be seen by all. Number 2 represents the first violins with their backs to the stage. Number 3 marks the position of the second violins also with their backs to the stage; together with the violas, 4, and the cellos, 5, and the basses, 6 (the basses "directly behind the music-director"), they form a circle around the conductor "which does not completely close, however, in order to accord view of the other instruments." Number 7 marks the clarinets with their backs to the stage, 8 indicates the oboes "crosswise," and 9, "somewhat behind the violas," marks the bassoons with their backs to the audience. Number 10 shows the flutes, backs to the stage, 11, the horns "crosswise," and 12, the trombones, "or even several violins for filling, if one can set them with supernumeraries." The "boundary points" at a and b are where the "balcony-boxes" are over the orchestra up to the stage. For damping, one should place trumpets and timpani at 13 and 14 under one side and opposite at 15, 16, and 17, percussion if needed. The space at 12 is also best for piano, harp, glockenspiel, and other similar instruments which may be needed, because from there these instruments "treated as obligato most easily join on the orchestra, and at the same time can hold to the harmony of the horns, to the melody of the flutes and violins, and to the foundational bass of the cellos and basses." And a final bit of wisdom: "In general each music-director must know how to use his terrain as advantageously as possible."[27]

This layout is remarkble for its division of the two violin sections, as well as the violas from the cellos and basses. The first violins are to the conductor's

Figure 22.   Arnold's Seating Plan for the Theater

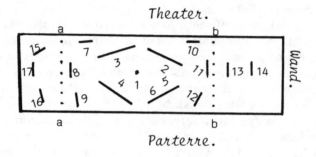

Redrawn from Arnold/MUSIKDIREKTOR, p. 311.

right, a fact which caused hesitation in his concert orchestra description. But why, one wonders, was not such a division recommended in the concert layout? It would seem every bit as important there, if not more so. Many players have their backs to the audience, a situation which will be encountered often later in this study when actual seating plans are perused. Also to be noticed in actual plans will be the use of the spaces under the balconies for louder instruments, just as Arnold has recommended here.

While Beethoven may not have left any detailed seating plan, some of his directions of December 1815 regarding the performance of *Wellingtons Sieg* are of interest in that they make use of spatial separation for dramatic effect. For example, two wind bands are required. The first march, *Rule, Britannia,* is to be played by the first; the second march, *Marlborough,* is played by the other. In the following movements both bands play together. The two bass drums for cannon shots must stand out of the sight of the audience "at some distance" from the orchestra as space permits, one on each side, one side representing the English army, the other the French. The cannon machines "must under no conditions" be in the orchestra, but at some distance. The "rattles" for musketry fire must also be on opposite sides, like the cannons, and close to them. The trumpets in E♭ and C are also to be on opposite sides, the E♭ on the English side, the C on the French side. There are also four more trumpets in the orchestra. There must also be on each side "two ordinary military drums" which will perform an *Entrade* before each march, if possible beginning at a distance and drawing nearer "to simulate with as much illusion as possible the approach of the troops."[28] While *Wellingtons Sieg* must be acknowledged to be a very special, even a peculiar, work, these indications show acute awareness of antiphonal possibilities, even if they are concerned with extramusical effects.

Wagner's report on Spontini's desires as to seating also sheds light on his own ideas. First of all, Spontini seems to have taken a "modern" position in the theater, that is, standing with the orchestra, excepting the oboes, as well as the stage in front of him, rather than standing at the foot of the stage with the orchestra behind him, as so often was the case in the nineteenth-century. As for the oboes, he for some reason wished them placed behind him.[29] But more important was the fact that he separated the two violin sections—a physical separation as typical of the nineteenth century as it had become in the late eighteenth, as will become increasingly evident. Spontini told Wagner, however, that he conducted the orchestra "only with his eyes." He claimed: "My left eye is the first violin, my right eye the second, and if the eye is to have power, one must not wear glasses (as so many bad conductors do), even if one is short-sighted." He admitted to Wagner in confidence that he could not see "twelve inches in front of me, but all the same I can make them play as I want, merely by fixing them with my eye." But Wagner found "irrational" the habit Spontini retained from "his old days in Paris" of placing the two oboists "immediately behind him," calling it a "fad which owed its origin to a mere accident," but one to which Spontini always adhered. Of course, the oboe was therefore averted from the audience, a situation which angered Wagner's Dresden "excellent oboist" when Spontini conducted there. But other than this, Wagner found his method to be "based upon the absolutely correct system (which even at the present time is misunderstood by some German orchestras) of spreading the string quartette over the whole orchestra." This system, according to Wagner, also divided the brass and percussion on both sides, thus preventing them from drowning each other out. The "more delicate wind instruments" were placed "at a judicous distance from each other" to form a "chain" between the violins. Wagner found this superior to the custom still prevalent in "some great and celebrated orchestras" which divided the orchestra into halves—strings and winds—"an arrangement that denotes roughness and a lack of understanding of the sound of the orchestra, which ought to blend harmoniously and be well balanced."[30] This division into strings on one side and winds on the other will be seen more in the theater than in concert seating plans as this study progresses. It will often seem due to physical characteristics of the allotted space. But Wagner was to follow much of Spontini's influence. After Spontini had introduced such a system at Dresden for his opera, Wagner found it an "easy matter to get the King's command to let the alteration stand." However, after Spontini's departure, he did "modify and correct certain eccentricities and arbitrary features in his arrangements; and from that moment I attained a high level of success with my orchestra."[31] One feels certain that the oboes no longer sat behind Wagner!

The extent of Wagner's adherence to these ideas will be seen later when the seating at Bayreuth is perused. However, further evidence of his realization of the importance of the physical aspects of performance is the fact that he had the stage rebuilt for the performance of the Beethoven Ninth at Dresden in 1846. In order to "ensure a good acoustic effect" he concentrated the whole orchestra in the center and surrounded it by a "steep amphitheater of seats" for the large chorus; "of extraordinary advantage to the massive effect of the choruses, this lent the finely-balanced orchestra great energy and precision in the purely symphonic movements."[32] Wagner showed similar concern for a concert in Zürich in 1853 when he had a special shell built; "and in the acoustical orchestra, constructed according to my indication, the tone of the instruments was most bright and beautiful."[33]

More detail is found in an anonymous article "On Concerts," published in a Boston periodical in 1839. The article states that the chief purpose in placement is to enable the *tutti* to "preserve the greatest unity in its effect upon the audience." The author also makes it "the chief condition, and a sine qua non" that every member of the orchestra be able to see the director as well as the leader. The orchestra should be amphitheatrical, with the director in front "turned towards the orchestra" and the leader or concertmaster at the "head of the first violins" immediately at his left with the second violins at his right. Behind the first violins he would place flutes and oboes; behind the seconds would come the clarinets and bassoons. In the middle between these "two files," the basses and cellos "must be extended down the whole length," and on the last platform behind all, the brass and timpani should be placed. "The Choir must by every means be placed before the orchestra, or at least as much so as can be; and the Solo singers must *on no account* stand behind the orchestra."[34] Notably lacking is mention of the violas, a not uncommon lacuna. The idea is simple enough; the two violin sections are separated by the basses and cellos with the woodwinds behind them and the brass to the rear. The emphasis on the position of the solo voices suggests that the writer had experienced the opposite. The necessity for the conductor to see and be seen is also evident in a later article in the same volume on "Uses and Duties of the Conductor and the Leader." It envisions the conductor as "beating" the time "with the full score before him," not only keeping the ensemble but "giving life to the whole." The next sentence suggests that the baton conductor should have arrived even in America by 1839, even if he had not: "He must therefore stand in front of the Choir and Orchestra, in such position that he can be seen by *each member*."[35] Such reiteration from author to author strikes the modern reader as needless but must be reflective of a widespread situation.

Again it is Berlioz who went into greater detail on what to him were certainly important matters. And he found the placing of musicians "of great importance," whether they were on a horizontal or an inclined stage, in a "space enclosed on three sides" or in the middle of the auditorium, whether there were reflectors, whether such had hard or soft surfaces, how close they were to the performers, "all this [was] of extraordinary consequence." He found reflectors "indispensable." He pointed out that they are found in every enclosed space in various forms. "The closer they are to the source of sound the greater is their effect. This is why there is no such thing as music in the open air." He pointed out that "the largest orchestra" performing in a space open on all sides "must remain completely ineffective." Using the Jardin des Tuileries as an example, he claimed that even if such an orchestra were placed close to the palace walls the reflection would be insufficient, the sound lost in all directions. "An orchestra of a thousand wind instruments and a chorus of two thousand voices, placed in an open plain, would be far less effective than an ordinary orchestra of eighty players and a chorus of a hundred voices arranged in the concert hall of the Conservatoire."[36] Anyone who has heard music in the open air can read of his own experiences here. Anyone who has heard microphones used to "improve" the situation knows that they usually serve to exacerbate it instead, only picking up high frequencies and perhaps extreme lows, leaving the middle like so much fluff—indeterminate and confused.

Berlioz continued, becoming gradually more specific: "The best way of placing an orchestra in a hall sufficiently large for the number of players used is to arrange them in rows one above the other on a series of steps in such fashion that each row can send its tones to the listeners without any intervening obstacles." And if the orchestra is on the stage of a theater, it should be enclosed by wooden walls not only on the sides and in the rear but also above.[37] In his revision, Strauss added to this that shells are "bad" if only half of the orchestra are enclosed while the remainder is in front. He also found "pear-shaped" concert halls "the best."[38] The last comment will come up again later, but to continue with Berlioz's arguments, he warned that if the orchestra was placed at one end of a hall or church where a massive wall reflected "with too much force and hardness" the instruments nearest to it, this "excessive reverberation" could be "easily" diminished by hanging draperies or "other suitable objects" there which serve to "break the sound waves." He admitted that theatrical architecture and dramatic requirements make the amphitheatrical layout impossible for opera. "Their members are condemned to play at the lowest point of the hall, on a horizontal plane, immediately in front of the footlights," thus depriving them of most of the benefits a concert orchestra gained arranged in the manner he had suggested. He related the loss of many effects and "fine shadings" to this situation, despite the "best execution" by opera orchestras. Berlioz found the problem so great that he advised composers not to score dramatic works in the same manner that they use in symphonies, masses, or oratorios.[39] This would seem a common experience when one stops to think about it, yet composers probably do not when in the throes of creation.

It was Berlioz who, if not specifically at least substantially, verbalized the reasons for the necessity for space between the two violin sections, as well as between any other sound sources when antiphony was desired. In discussing the dispersed brass bands in his *Requiem,* he singled out the importance of the "different points of origin of the tonal masses.... Certain groups of an orchestra are selected by the composer to question and answer each other; but this design becomes clear and effective only if the groups which are to carry on the dialogue are placed at a sufficient distance from each other." If only more composers had taken heed! As an example, he allowed that the percussion including the timpani could remain together when employed in the usual manner striking "certain rhythms simultaneously." But if they were to perform "an interlocutory rhythm, one fragment of which is given to the bass drums and cymbals, the other to kettledrums and drums," the effect would be not only "greatly improved" but "intensified" by locating the two groups at a distance from each other, even at "opposite ends" of the orchestra. Thus he found the "constant uniformity" in orchestral setups to be "one of the greatest obstacles to the creation of monumental and truly original works," a uniformity "preserved by composers more out of habit, laziness and thoughtlessness," though he allowed that the motive of economy was, "unfortunately, also a rather important one."[40] And Berlioz was not beyond taking his own advice. Examples of specific directions for the disposition of instruments can be found, in addition to those for the *Requiem,*[41] in such scores as *Roméo et Juliette,*[42] the *Te Deum,*[43] and *Harold en Italie,*[44] where specific directions are given for the placement of both harp and solo viola vis-à-vis the orchestra and public as well as each other. Other examples could be cited. In speculating on how "interesting" it would be to write a work for all the "musical forces available in Paris," Berlioz went even further:

> Where such an immense body is to be used, it is obviously of the greatest importance to consider the greater or smaller distance of the various groups from each other. This is indispensable if one wants to derive full advantage from this orchestra and to calculate with certainty the scope of the different effects.... The arrangement of the groups would be determined by the wishes and intentions of the composers. The percussion instruments, which exercise an irrestible influence on the rhythm and always lag when they are far from the conductor, should be placed as close to him as possible to be able to follow the slightest change of measure or tempo instantaneously and strictly.[45]

Certainly such a disposal of percussion would be an unusual one.

Berlioz commented on points of origin in another way in discussing the way scores were judged for the *Prix de Rome.* Although his comments were addressed to the situation in 1828, the complaints undoubtedly could have been raised in other years. His chief complaint was that the scenes which were composed with orchestra were played on a piano. Among the effects lost— such as "exquisite long-drawn notes" on wind instruments, "marvellous interweaving of flutes and clarinets," a "poignant, plaintive" oboe solo, the "piquant contrasts" brought on by the juxtaposition of strings and winds, the "characteristic tone-colours" distinguishing brass from woodwinds, the "mysterious power and grandeur" of percussion played softly and the "tremendous impact" of their forte—he also mentioned the "striking sonorities achieved when two sources of sound are placed at some distance from each other." He concluded that the piano "by destroying all sense of instrumentation, places every composer on the same level. The master of the orchestra is shrunk to the size of the fumbling incompetent who lacks the first idea of that branch of his art."[46] Clearly, tonal origin and the possible displacement of instruments and groups were important matters to Berlioz.

A detailed seating plan can be found in Berlioz's pamphlet on conducting which was appended to the treatise. It is worth close scrutiny. Like others before him, Berlioz also puts such grouping as "within the province" of the conductor, especially for concerts, though he admits it is impossible to indicate any arbitrary method since the shape and interior of any theater or concert hall would be an influencing factor, as well as the number of performers taking part and even the style of the works involved. As a general plan for concerts, he also recommended an amphitheater of eight if possible, but at least five, rows, semicircular in shape. He would put the first violins "in front on the right," the second violins "in front on the left," with the violas in the middle separating the two groups. However, it is difficult to be sure just what he meant by "right" and "left"; one translation adds "facing the public," but the original has no hint as to whether he meant stage right or the audience's right. One can easily understand this as advocating the disposal common in the eighteenth century of having the first violins to the right of the conductor. However, somewhat later Berlioz commented on the setup of the Paris Conservatory Orchestra which had the first violins to the conductor's left and he made no note of the discrepancy. And in the introduction to *Roméo et Juliette* he included a similar plan but there wrote, "the first-violins to the right of the stage with their profile to the audience,"[47] suggesting perhaps stage right rather than the conductor's right. At any rate here is another case of the violas being the separating agent. But returning to Berlioz's plan, he would place the flutes, oboes, clarinets, horns, and bassoons behind the first violins and a double rank of cellos and basses behind the seconds, with the trumpets, cornets, trombones, and tubas behind the violas. The remainder of the cellos and double basses would go behind the woodwind instruments. The harps would be in front near the conductor; the timpani and other percussion belong behind the brass. The conductor should have his back to the public and be at the base of the orchestra, near the first desks of the first and second violins. One notes that again the horns fall in with the woodwinds rather than with the louder brass and percussion. And the cellos and basses are on both wings of the orchestra—an arrangement which will be seen in a number of nineteenth-century plans, undoubtedly influenced by Berlioz. The importance of having the conductor in each performer's sight is everywhere implicit when not explicit.

Berlioz would have the chorus on a horizontal floor extending in front of the first rows of the amphitheater. He would place them "in form of a fan turned three-quarters towards the public" so that all can see the conductor. Though the inner grouping of the chorus would be influenced by whether the piece being performed was in three, four, or even six parts, the women should be seated in front, with the tenors standing behind the altos and the basses behind the sopranos. Solo singers should be in the center and foremost area of the stage, always placed so that "by slightly turning the head" they can see the baton. "For the rest, I repeat, these indications can be but approximate; they may be, for many reasons, modified in various ways."[48]

Berlioz added a few other precautions, such as the necessity for the chorus to be on a somewhat lower plane than the violins to avoid deadening the sound of the latter. For similar reasons if there were no other risers for the choir in front of the orchestra, he would have the women seated and the men standing so that the latter voices would proceed from a more elevated point. And finally when a chorus was not needed, they should be dismissed from the stage, "since this large number of human bodies injures the sonority of the instruments. A symphony performed by an orchestra thus more or less stifled, loses much of its effect."[49]

In his *Dirigent und Ripienist*, published shortly after the Berlioz *Traité* (in 1844), F. S. Gassner reiterated many of the dicta now becoming familiar, for example, that efficacy in performance depended above all on appropriate positioning and proportional setting [*"zweckmässiger Stellung und verhältnissmässiger Besetzung"*], and that one must take into account the stronger and weaker instruments so that neither one nor the other would stand out or be obscured. However, he also acknowledged that general norms to be followed without fail could not be laid down because of many other considerations such as the locality in which the performance was held, the space allotted to the performers, the space to be filled with sound, and the position of the audience. He counselled seeking to obviate inconveniences in locale through layout and setting according to possibilities.[50] He also saw a real difference in whether the music was to be performed in the open, in a church, in a concert hall, in the theater pit, or on the stage of a theater.

Gassner gave some general principles, many of which will also seem familiar. For example, the position of the performers should be so arranged that they could be perceived and heard equally well by all the listeners in both a physical and esthetic sense [*"in physischer und ästhetischer Hinsicht"*]. He recommended raising the orchestra at least three feet higher than the audience so that the flow of sound [*"Tonstrom"*] could disseminate equally well and unobstructed in all directions.[51] He sounded somewhat sarcastic and perhaps even bitter in his doubts that architects might pay heed to sound in new construction, and was without hope that any changes might be made in existing buildings. He admitted that it then became a necessity for a conductor to help himself by expedient use of existing space. The audience must not be too near the performers since the tones needed space to fully develop. The conductor must see and be seen by all, "because often a small sign, a nod of the head, even a mutual glance has very beneficial advantages." Since the conductor must watch over the whole ensemble, he must take care that the noisy instruments and any whose timbre drowns out others are not too near to him, a situation which would be especially detrimental in rehearsal. The same care should be taken with the more gentle instruments whose effect can be impaired by the vicinity of harsher instruments. Gassner seemed to recommend smaller ensembles within the larger group, so that the strings, woods, and brass keep some grouping as inner ensembles with some degree of independence. Along with that, each group should be able to hear its own underlying bass, but at the same time all must hear the double basses, which form "as it were an integrating part of the direction." The really strong instruments, especially the brass, must have sufficient room for vibration; thus they must be directed so that their force reaches more into the orchestra than towards the public, so that they are heard more indirectly and with the other instruments rather than directly and overwhelmingly. The timpani must be encircled by strong tone masses [*"Tonmassen"*] as much as possible so that they do not seem too deafening. He admitted their splendid effect when they are sensibly placed and played; but they "can however, misused by the composer or drummer, make deplorable disturbances."[52]

Gassner did not get much more specific because he felt that each case, each locale, offered specific demands. But he appended seating plans in an appendix, that is, plans of specific orchestras which will be taken up presently. Gassner felt that these offered further principles in a practical way to the thinking conductor, and it was for such, not for machines, that his writing was intended. "He who only wants to let others think for him is not suited for conducting and will also seek no guidance in conducting; to whom however it is a serious matter, hints proceeding from experience are enough."[53]

Somewhat later (1873) F. L. Schubert reiterated the need for adequate distance between orchestra and audience so that the sound waves have ample space to develop fully. He also advocated the conductor being on a raised platform so that all might see him well. As for placement, he offered that in the concert hall the strings stand nearest to the director, behind these the woodwinds, then the brass, and behind them the percussion. He also felt that each type must remain together in groups. Like Gassner, he warned that brass and percussion must have adequate room for their vibrations but their force must not extend directly on the audience, nor may it cover the resonance of the other instruments. In vocal works, he would, like Berlioz, have the chorus in front, with the solo voices in the immediate proximity of the conductor. He saw a different placing in the theater, since the space is more oblong and runs the width of the stage. Schubert's concert conductor must have faced the audience, because he wrote that in the theater he had "a different standpoint in that he does not turn his face to the public but to the stage so that he has the singers on the stage in sight."[54] He offered a plan for the theater, acknowledging it to be hinted at by the Dresden Opera Orchestra (fig. 23).

The basic idea is not different from those seen before and is one which Wagner warned against—that is, the orchestra is divided into two groups: strings and winds. Note that the heavy brass and percussion are where they would probably sit under boxes or balcony. The horns are separate from them. Note that the position of the conductor is different from that suggested by Spontini's arrangement or Arnold's plan: he is at the foot of the stage behind the spot where one would expect to find the prompter's box—actually a very common position in the nineteenth century, as will be seen. The players then must face the stage, rather than the audience, except for those to the sides who obviously face center. Not only did Schubert fail to indicate any separation between violin sections in his concert description, but his theater plan shows the strings all bunched together without antiphonal suggestion. This will also prove to have been quite common in many theaters in the nineteenth century, but rather rare in concert setups.

More of Wagner's ideas on this subject come to light in regard to the 1872 performance of the Beethoven Ninth Symphony at Bayreuth. Unfortunately they concern the singers more than the players, but they also highlight his concern about money. In a letter of April 7, 1872, he announced a "very simple expedient" for placing "my big body of singers" where there was not room enough on stage. He would place them in the front rows of the parquet. "In fact, this idea corresponds exactly and in the most perfect manner to my most ideal demands, according to which the public (just as the congregation in the church) shall join in the singing." Further, he proposed placing those choristers who desired "compensation in money rather than by a temporary art pleasure" in the parquet, thus paying them in the form of a ticket. Those performing "for art's sake" would presumably occupy the stage. "On the whole, I should like to have the entire parquet and stage reserved for us crazy musicians and singers, and relegate the listeners to the boxes and the

Figure 23.   Schubert's Seating Plan for the Theater

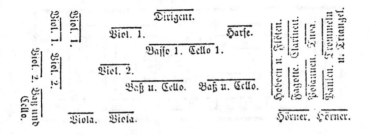

Source: Schubert/ MUSIKDIREKTOR, p. 48.

balconies."[55] He adamantly followed this up in another letter later the same month, demanding that "*nothing* shall be changed in the first plan," but now expecting to need the entire parquet as he had over three hundred at his disposal and did not want to reject any "for almost moral reasons." Thus the "real listening public" would be almost entirely in the galleries and boxes. "As the theatre is said to seat seven hundred, I count on placing two hundred in the parquet, in which number standing-room must probably also be included." The same letter later elucidated his feelings on this. "The chief thing is an inspiring *Musical Festival;* the chorus of the symphony should really be sung by the entire audience; in fact, it would be inspiring did they only seem to be doing so."[56] An example of imaginative positioning was an "innovation which he introduced, but one which seems not to be followed by present-day conductors," that is the placing of two smaller choirs of men's voices in the so-called trumpeters' boxes whence the "*Seid umschlungen Millionen*" was first sung, "as if a mystery were being announced to the body of the chorus."[57] Wagner's seating for the "invisible orchestra" at Bayreuth will be taken up later in conjunction with other actual seating plans for the theater.

Edouard Blitz, writing in 1887, reiterated familiar principles—the acoustics of the hall, the type of music to be performed (oratorio, opera, symphony)—adding to them the "preferences" of the conductor.[58] He then provided a seating plan for opera which he credited to the *Guide musical* (fig. 24). Again the conductor is at the base of the stage, his back to the orchestra. This obviously means that the players who are not sitting sideways must face the stage rather than the audience. Here the two violin sections are indeed separated for possible antiphonal effect. The cellos and basses are again divided on both wings of the orchestra, not too dissimilar to the situation in Berlioz's concert plan, with the basses well out of the audience's line of sight. While the horns are with the other brass, they are still in close proximity to the woodwinds.

Figure 24.   Blitz's Seating Plan for the Theater

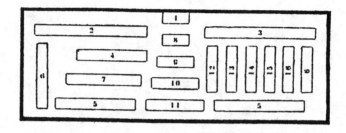

1. Le chef d'orchestre. — 2. Premiers violons. — 3. Seconds violons. —
4. Altos. — 5. Violoncelles. — 6. Contrebasses. — 7. Harpes. — 8. Flûtes.
— 9. Hautbois. — 10. Clarinettes. — 11. Bassons et Contrebasson. —
12. Cors. — 13. Trompettes et Cornets. — 14. Trombones. — 15. Trombone basse et Ophicléide. — 16. Timbales et Grosse-caisse.

Source: Blitz/CHEF, p. 40.

In 1881 Hermann Zopff also stated that positioning as well as locale exerts great influence on the effectiveness and accuracy of a performance. He reiterated familiar ideas: the placement "is conditioned (1) by the best and clearest possible efficacy of sound [*Klangwirkung*]: (2) by the baton being truly visible for each player; (3) by whether it is intended for the theater, the concert hall, for the church or for music being performed in open air."[59] Zopff acknowledged that opinions were divided as to which arrangement might be most advantageous and that only unauthoritative suggestions could be made, reviewing earlier developments. He attributed "the mechanical custom of placing strings and wind instruments separated from each other on different sides" to the earlier custom of having the director "in the middle of the orchestra" with harpsichords and harps before the days of baton conducting; the singers were "generally much more left to themselves" and "round about the last-named instruments all the others were placed." Thus gradually the separation

> got the upper hand. Homogeneous blending of both sound masses was thereby destroyed, the vibrations of one side could not be united with those of the other, in order to produce a full harmonic sound; on the contrary they seemed to repel each other, and especially the listener situated in the middle had to hear each of the two sound groups *separate* from the other.

Zopff claimed that such problems finally caused "individual intelligent" conductors in Berlin, Dresden, Vienna, and other places to place the trumpets, trombones, and timpani behind the strings and the horns along with the other percussion behind the woodwinds with some basses forming the center, and the remaining ones being dispersed to the corners. "The ensemble became in this way more truly astonishing and exceedingly rounded off, and especially the present placing of the basses proved particularly effective." However, he found separating the horns from the other brass to be "just as unfortunate" as their separation from the woodwinds, and thought it best to order things so that the horns "establish the connection between woodwinds and brass (round about the strings)." Zopff also warned that the bells of the horns should not be turned towards the public except "in moments where one wants to obtain therewith an especially vigorous effect."[60] The suggestion concerning the horns seems especially well taken, forming a compromise between their use with the woodwinds and their intrinsic nature as brass instruments. The suggestion that conductors make use of bell direction takes account of the increasing use of the horns with the other brass, as well as with the woodwinds. But Zopff provided further hints:

> Considering the first violins, many concertmasters are of the opinion that their effect is most favorable if they stand with their right hand turned towards the public; in truth however the sound-effect is more beautiful and rounded if the players turn themselves with their face (*en face*) to the listener like the solo players. In smaller orchestras, where one has perhaps at most three desks of basses, the director does best to place the first behind him, the second at a greater distance towards the left and the third even so off to the right. If however there are only two on hand, then he does best to concentrate both behind him. In smaller orchestras it is especially important that the strings, in order to come better into play, sit at least a step higher than the winds.[61]

This last suggestion would seem to at least partially block the winds from seeing the conductor. On the other hand, it would serve to dampen their sound somewhat. The point about the violinists facing the public is worth keeping in mind when perusing other plans later in this study. But the point about the basses behind the conductor is somewhat puzzling, unless Zopff is still thinking of the conductor as facing the public. And, of course, this all seems to take for granted the concert hall as the arena.

Many of Zopff's other ideas are also already familiar, for example, that in concert halls the performers should be on a raised platform so that the flood of sound ["*Tonstrom*"] can flow unobstructed over the audience. He recommended a hollow wooden platform about three feet high and found it even more important for vocal performances. On the other hand, where large theater orchestras were concerned, he thought it highly advisable that the space for the orchestra be much lower than usual so that the players and instruments would be out of the sight of the public as much as possible. A footnote adds that the new court theater at Munich had improved the sound for the audience by replacing the elongated form of space allotted to the over one hundred musicians with a round one. But Zopff admitted that Bayreuth had solved this problem most perfectly. He found a lowered orchestra for the most part advantageous. The stage "thus appears" more prominent and "as it were" brought nearer to the spectators. He felt that the acoustics suffered "not at all," but "on the contrary the sound-effect is beautified thereby, while the singers can hold their own much better." He admitted that care had to be taken that the "more delicate" instruments were not "too weak and deadened." Some conductors he called "intelligent" had recently "retreated with their desks" from a position at the prompter's box and placed the first basses and cellos between themselves and it.[62] Zopff's study also contains reminders that the performers should not sit too far from each other, that instruments belonging together be as near as possible to one another, that the strings have enough room to bow, trombones enough room to draw their slides, etc. He recommended Berlioz's layout as a starting point. He found it important that the director have at his elbow first desks of first and second violins as well as cellos and basses, especially in choral performances, "and indeed in the last case brought forward in a wedge shape."[63] If this seems unusual today, again familiar are the injunctions that the orchestra in no case be too near the public, since the sound waves need a certain amount of space to develop fully, and that the conductor always direct from a raised position in order to be seen by all. Zopff's remarks on performing out-of-doors are of less import.[64]

In 1889, Carl Schroeder repeated the warning that the conductor must take a position enabling him to see and be seen by each performer. He continued: "Entirely to be discountenanced is the practice, prevailing amongst many concert conductors, of turning the back to the orchestra, and conducting with the face towards the audience, coquetting with them when possible, as many Band conductors and Promenade Concert conductors are in the habit of doing." As to the disposition of the orchestra, he found it always advantageous to place the strings with the winds at the sides, and at concerts to also close ranks behind. A separation of the winds is difficult to avoid in the theater. There the woodwinds and horns sit behind the first violins to the conductor's left, the rest of the wind and percussion on the right behind the violas and cellos. Schroeder admitted "a little unsteadiness" between the horns and the other brass when they are "united in the orchestration." He found there was a tendency "to drag" in the trumpets which was caused "frequently by taking breath too late." He cautioned that in many works one of the winds must sit elsewhere, giving as an example the beginning of Act III of *Der Freischütz,* where the bass trombone "plays his part upon the side where the horns are located."[65] But as far as the problems arising from the separation of the horns from the other brass, Schroeder did not recommend a solution as did Zopff.

Schroeder would position choral forces differently from Berlioz. He would have the orchestra "close up in wedge shape between the choral masses," taking from the strings one or possibly two desks further forward. The remaining strings follow behind on each side with the woodwind between them, the brass and percussion "bringing up the rear."[66] He offered the illustration shown in figure 25. The complete disposal of the strings seems vague. One wonders if first desks of each are at the front with the others behind, or just how they are arranged. Certainly the illustration does not suggest the separation of first and second violins which one would expect at this time.

Schroeder continues: "At the Opéra, the conductor chooses his position so that only one row of desks is placed behind him, and in this way he is enabled to overlook nearly the whole orchestra." Again he offers an illustration (fig. 26). Here there is even less of an attempt at separating the two violin groups, and the distance between horns and the other brass, complained of above, is further exacerbated—a typical hindrance in opera seating. In his concert plan, some room for accommodation of this problem seems possible. The position of the basses right in the center would seem to indicate a pit deep enough to hide them from public view; however, some contemporary sketches show bass scrolls popping up into public view. Schroeder elaborated on the position of the conductor in the theater: "In small theatres, or where the company through a frequently changing ensemble is not very sure, the conductor will do better to take a position close to the stage, in order to render the utmost assistance in any failure of memory that may happen." And of course, such a position has already been alluded to in this study. In large theaters, he pointed out that placing the conductor in the middle of the orchestra or even nearer to the parquet would have the disadvantage that explanations to the singers at rehearsals become difficult. He recommended as remedy some sort of "speaking tube" between the conductor and somewhere behind the wings. "Without this, lowering the orchestra, at least half being hidden, is altogether inadvisable, as many disadvantages ensue thereby."[67] One can only wish that he had been clearer on the disadvantages of a lowered orchestra; Zopff had given so many good reasons in its favor. Schroeder's following remarks concern the chorus in the opera, and are of less interest here.

At first sight, H. Kling, publishing in 1890, seems to have much to say about principles of seating, but it all sounds so familiar that one is inclined to look back. And, lo! not only was it all said by Ferdinand Gassner forty-five years earlier, but Kling did not even bother to change Gassner's wording except here and there, omitting sections that no longer seemed à *propos.*[68]

Gustav Mahler certainly was concerned about the effects of positioning players. For example, in the First Symphony he wanted the trumpets off in the distance [*"In sehr weiter Entfernung aufgestellt"*] through measure 47 of the first movement, where he allowed them to resume their normal places [*"Die 3*

Figure 25. Schroeder's Concert Seating with Chorus

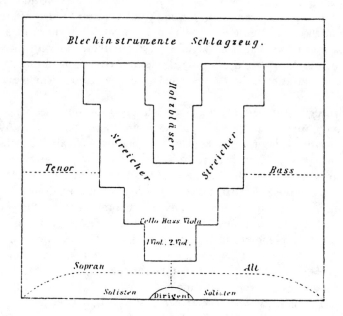

Source: Schroeder/KATECHISMUS, p. 66; or see Schroeder, HANDBOOK, p. 62.

Figure 26. Schroeder's Theater Seating

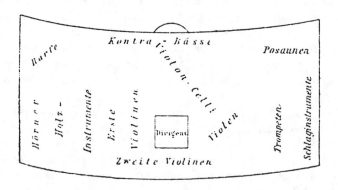

Source: Schroeder/KATECHISMUS, p. 66; or see Schroeder/HANDBOOK, p. 62.

Trompeten nehmen ihren Platz im Orchester ein"].[69] And in a letter to Julius Buths, who was obviously conducting a performance of the Second Symphony in 1903, Mahler offered the following advice:

> I advise letting the chorus (which had best been sitting up to here) to continue to sit further, and only at the E_b major passage: "With wings I have won for myself" (basses) to be allowed to stand. This was always of astonishing effect until now. Also very important is a well-considered disposition of the horns and trumpets in the "great summons." Horns and timpanists must be together and where possible set against the trumpets—the latter however again resound greatly distant from each other, flute and bass clarinet function in the orchestra so surely and trained that they hardly need the conductor any more, so that you do not beat *time* during the whole passage.[70]

This only whets the appetite and increases the wish that further data on Mahler's precise seating plan or plans might come to light. Perhaps further research might still turn up more information.

12

Concert Seating Plans

What about seating plans actually in use? What was the experience of the nineteenth century? It seems logical to consider plans for concert performance first, since there was less likelihood of the necessity to make compromises because of space, whereas the position of the organ and the space allotted to performers vis-à-vis the congregation in church and the pit in the theater have to exert considerable influence on seating in those localities.

First of all, the problems of music outdoors, the need for reflectors, and the desirability of risers, all discussed by Berlioz, were not unknown earlier. Spohr commented on the use of a shell for an outdoor concert under Jan Ladislav Dussek in Hamburg in 1802–3. "A kind of canvas shell had been set up, in which the orchestra, some hundred strong, was placed in tiers." A cantata composed by Dussek especially for the occasion "made a great impression" on Spohr, who found it "well written and splendidly prepared," but also gaining much because of a large organ situated behind the orchestra which "sounding through the stillness of the night, had such an effect of solemnity that I was entirely carried away."[1]

The following incident which happened in London in 1804 tells little more than that the oboe was near the bass. While this may seem surprising, such a position will be seen in at least one of the plans which follow. Evidently a "celebrated oboe player" named Fischer died during a performance. "He was seized with apoplexy whilst performing in a concert at Buckingham House, in the presence of their Majesties, and fell on the double bass instrument of the musician next to him."[2]

Much more concrete is the plan of the *Orchester des grossen Concerts und der grossen Oper in Paris,* obviously drawn up in concert formation (fig. 27). The date is 1810, five years before Habeneck's tenure as first violin. According to the anonymous writer, the plan was generally recognized as "superior" ["*vorzüglich*"]. Unlike many German orchestras, this one played seated and on risers: "The whole orchestra sits raised." The 11 cellists sitting highest and the 5 basses on opposite sides "envelop the whole orchestra." In opera performances, the violins moved back to the places occupied by the chorus and the cellos "enclose the whole in a half-circle."[3] One is struck not

Figure 27.   Paris, Orchester des grossen Concerts, 1810

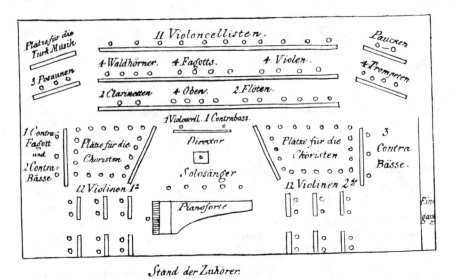

Source: AMZ, XII (1809/10), cols. 729–30. See also Hoffman/ ESECUZIONE, p. 97, and Haas/ AUFFÜHRUNGSPRAXIS, p. 253, for other drawings of the same plan, undoubtedly based on this one.

only by the separation between the two violin choirs, but also by the fact that they are separated from the rest of the orchestra by the chorus. The division of the chorus into two groups is also interesting, and one would guess that the sopranos and tenors were on opposite sides from the altos and basses. In addition to the piano, a cello and bass were close by for recitative. (Incidentally, perhaps it was such a solo bass player on whose instrument poor Mr. Fischer fell with apoplexy, seated in such an arrangement, in the incident described by Parke above.) The horns are more with the woodwinds than with the other brass which with the percussion are divided in the corners, although there is some proximity between horns and trombones which can share a similar mellowness. The basses are on the wings, as Berlioz later would have the cellos also, and the contrabassoon is with them, rather than with the other bassoons. Not marked above is the fact that the four places to the right of the two flutes are for four more violas: "Beside these sit on two rows 4 violists, hence altogether 8 violas."[4]

    A Paris orchestra in concert at the Théâtre Louvois in 1825, as described by Sir George Smart, presented a similar picture:

The orchestra on the stage was large and on one raised platform only, which was circular at the back and on this were the basses. Close to the front of the stage was the leader, behind him the first violins, opposite were the second violins. In the centre were the violoncello and bass, next behind them the row of wind instruments and behind these again five bassi and five, I suppose, 'celli.[5]

In the first place, this was most probably a smaller orchestra, if the wind instruments were all in one row. Presumably Sir George meant a violin leader like Habeneck, rather than a baton conductor; but what "behind" means is not clear. Nevertheless, the two violin groups were at opposite sides for antiphonal effect. It would seem that both cellos and basses formed a ring at the back here.

The plan which Habeneck used for the *Société des Concerts,* as given by Elwart, is shown in figure 28. Although he did not date the plan, Galkin in reproducing it[6] took it for granted that it dates from 1828, the date of the founding of the society. Since it is the only plan which Elwart presented, one can assume that Habeneck saw no reason to change it. Elwart, a staunch admirer as well as friend of Habeneck, found this to be an admirable setup. He noted the understanding of "sonorous effect" with which Habeneck had "disposed according to principle" the instruments and chorus. The percussion were "at the summit of the tiers" with all the brass forming "a homogeneous group"; the woodwinds are "joined together"; the cellos and basses "form a perfect triangle." The stage is "bordered" by the violas; the violins, "divided in two parts," form a "square elbow towards the footlights"; in the center are the harp, the bass voices, and the piano. The tenors and sopranos are on the two sides of the "proscenium," with the soloists separating them. The conductor, "who takes in with a glance the different divisions of his sonorous army, directs it with admirable ease and unity of movement."[7] What seems evident here (and should also have been pointed out in the 1810 Paris plan) is the fact that the solo singers must turn to see the conductor—a fact which would contradict Elwart's "ease and unity." Noticeably different from the earlier plan is the switch in positions between violins and the high choral voices, the violins now separated by the bass voices. Habeneck had gotten rid of the archaic cello and bass for recitatives formerly nearby, though he has retained the piano, now in front of him and slightly to his right. The violas form a connecting link between the two violin sections; the basses are no longer divided into two groups, but are interspersed with the cellos toward the right. The horns were placed where they could function with either the brass or the woodwinds, and formed a line with the trumpets, trombones, and ophicleide to the timpani and other percussion. Placed at the top, the trombones would presumably have room for their slides. The harp is to the front where it should be heard. Yes, it does seem to have offered a sonorous whole.

If Elwart's plan did indeed go back to 1828, then Habeneck retained it for some time, for the plan shown in figure 29 appeared in the *Musical World* for March 26, 1840. The harp, piano, ophicleide, and battery are missing (the English usually seem to mean timpani by drums), and there is one more second violin. Otherwise, it is pretty much the same. A possible defect which Carse pointed out: "Habeneck stood between two groups of choral singers, who would be obliged to turn their heads very considerably to see his beat."[8]

Figure 28.   Paris, Société des Concerts, Seating Plan, ca. 1828

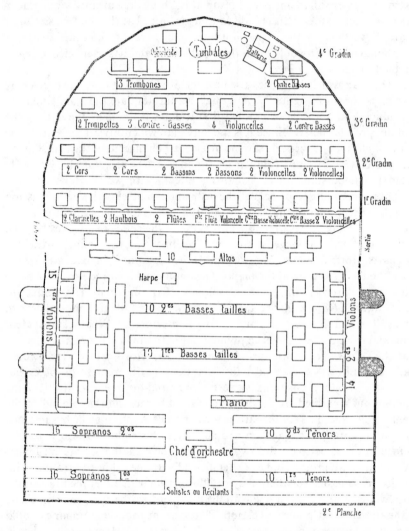

Source: Elwart/SOCIÉTÉ, between pp. 114–15; also reproduced in Galkin/CONDUCTING, p. 626, and in Kling/VOLLKOMMENE, p, 275.

Berlioz confirms this impression; in fact, his statement may have inspired Carse's observation:

> In the Paris Conservatoire, where the amphitheater has only four or five steps (not forming a semicircle), the violins and the violas are on the stage, and only the basses and wind instruments occupy the steps; the chorus is seated in the front of the stage, looking toward

Figure 29.   Paris, Société des Concerts, Seating Plan, 1840

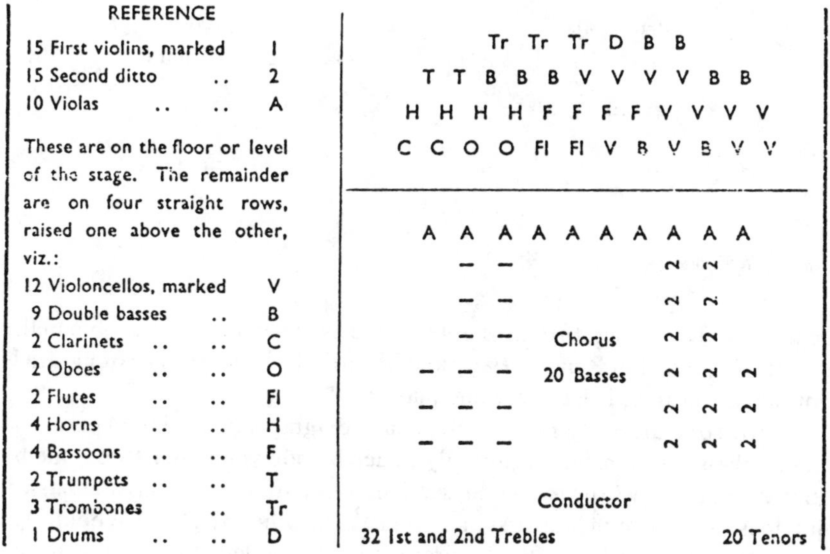

```
        REFERENCE
15 First violins, marked    I              Tr  Tr  Tr   D   B   B

15 Second ditto      ..     2          T  T  B  B  B  V  V  V  V  B  B

10 Violas        ..    ..   A          H  H  H  H  F  F  F  F  V  V  V  V

These are on the floor or level        C  C  O  O  Fl  Fl  V  B  V  B  V  V
of the stage.  The remainder
are  on  four  straight  rows,        ───────────────────────────────
raised one above the other,
viz.:                                  A   A   A   A   A   A   A   A   A   A
12 Violoncellos, marked     V              ─   ─                  2   2
 9 Double basses     ..     B              ─   ─                  2   2
 2 Clarinets    ..    ..    C              ─   ─       Chorus     2   2
 2 Oboes        ..    ..    O              ─   ─   ─   20 Basses  2   2   2
 2 Flutes       ..    ..    Fl             ─   ─   ─              2   2   2
 4 Horns        ..    ..    H              ─   ─   ─              2   2   2
 4 Bassoons     ..    ..    F

 2 Trumpets    ..    ..     T                       Conductor
 3 Trombones        ..     Tr
 1 Drums       ..    ..     D          32 Ist and 2nd Trebles          20 Tenors
```

Source: *Musical World*, March 26, 1840, p. 194, here reproduced from Carse/ BEETHOVEN, p. 476.

the audience. All the sopranos and altos are unable to see the movements of the conductor, since their backs are turned directly toward him. The arrangement is very inconvenient for this part of the chorus.[9]

Spohr described in general terms a rather interesting layout he experienced at a private concert in Rome in 1816. The "private institution" met every Monday at the home of a Signor Ruffini who owned "the great catgut factory." Operas were given in concert form by amateurs for an audience numbering from 200 to 250. "The orchestra, consisting of four violins, viola, cello, bass, two clarinets, two horns, and a bassoon, surrounds them on the floor level."[10]

Although it is not orchestral, the layout in figure 30 is interesting and revealing. It was witnessed by Smart at Cassel in 1825 for a performance of Spohr's Double Quartet. It reveals a desire to take advantage of antiphonal effects undoubtedly deriving from the concerto grosso and is not unlike the situating of the two violin groups in the nineteenth-century orchestra. It reminds one as well of Berlioz's dicta on separating instruments that are to answer each other.

Smart also reported on the concert room in the Schauspielhaus or Royal theater in Berlin in 1825, where he witnessed a concert by Moscheles. "It is large and beautiful and will hold, they say, with the galleries, sixteen hundred

Figure 30.   Cassel, Double Quartet Seating, 1825

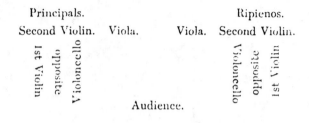

Source: Smart/JOURNALS, p. 214.

people.... This concert room is not so large as the great concert room in the palace of Vienna but is more neatly and beautifully fitted up. The orchestra is not much elevated, it has only one platform."[11]

Two comparatively recent books have diagrams of seating plans at the Gewandhaus in Leipzig, purportedly under Mendelssohn and 1835. One by John Mueller shows the two violin sections as separated by cellos and basses, but does not label either as first or second.[12] The other by David Wooldridge has a similar setup but with the first violins to the left, the seconds to the right.[13] The actual plan on which both are based is given in figure 31.

Here we see the first violins to the right, reminiscent of many eighteenth-century plans, the seconds to the left. The violas seem oddly off by themselves, almost as if an adjunct; but if one remembers the somewhat lowly position of the violas at this time, then perhaps this should not be too surprising. The horns are in a position where they could operate well with either brass or woodwinds or both, though somehow Wooldridge's diagram has them somewhat more distant from the other brass. One gets the impression that the original author made his visit to Leipzig in 1844 rather than 1835, though Zlotnik seems to date Schmidt's visit as 1846, the date of publication of his book.[14] But since Mendelssohn's tenure as conductor extended to 1843, perhaps this still reflects his layout. The violins seem to be on the floor rather than separated by the cellos and basses, which appear to be on risers. It is quite surprising that Schmidt seemed to consider David, the concertmaster, as director of the orchestra: "at the head of the orchestra stands Concertmaster David, one of the most excellent directors, whose prudence, skill and artistically refined taste is in equal proportion with his virtuosity on his instrument."[15] If one remembers that before Mendelssohn's arrival as conductor at Leipzig, purely orchestral pieces were conducted by the concertmaster or violin leader who was even then David, one will wonder if Schmidt made his trip even earlier. It certainly is strange that Schmidt did not even mention Mendelssohn's name.

Berlioz seemed pleased with the layout when he conducted at the

Figure 31. Leipzig Gewandhaus Seating, 1844

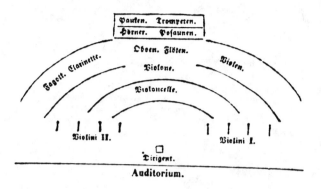

Source: Schmidt/REISE-MOMENTE, p. 46.

Gewandhaus in 1843. "The orchestral arrangement in this admirable hall is so good, communication between the conductor and each member of the orchestra is so easy, and the players, besides being capital musicians, have been trained by Mendelssohn and David to such a pitch of discipline and concentration that two rehearsals sufficed for putting on a long programme" which included "among other difficult works" the *King Lear* and the *Francs juges* overtures, as well as the *Symphonie fantastique.*[16]

Kling offered a plan for the Leipzig Gewandhaus Orchestra (fig. 32). Since he thanked the conductor Reinecke for it, and Reinecke's tenure as conductor there was from 1860 to 1895, and since Kling's book was published in 1890, it is probably safe to consider the plan as valid at least around 1880-90. Unlike the manner in which one must look at most plans, here the reader is looking in the direction of the audience rather than vice-versa. One must assume that the two different positions of the conductor's desk are for performances with large chorus and those either without chorus or with a smaller one. Whether three choirs were used at once also is not clear. One can count 340 voices plus the Thomaner-Chor of 40 plus the Pauliner Gesangverein of 150 which would make a total of 530. While this number might be used for festal occasions, why would they be kept separate as on the plan? The additional places at each side would seem to be for antiphonal choirs. At any rate, the chorus, when used, was placed in front of and around the orchestra, rather reminiscent of Habeneck's setup. Unlike Habeneck's case, however, the conductor evidently pulled back in this plan in order to see and be seen by all. The violins are split left and right, without any real separation evident, however. The two solo cellos suggest a role in recitatives as continuo instruments. The division of the basses from the cellos on the two wings is unusual. Also different here is the position of the horns with the brass,

Figure 32.   Leipzig Gewandhaus Seating, 1880-90

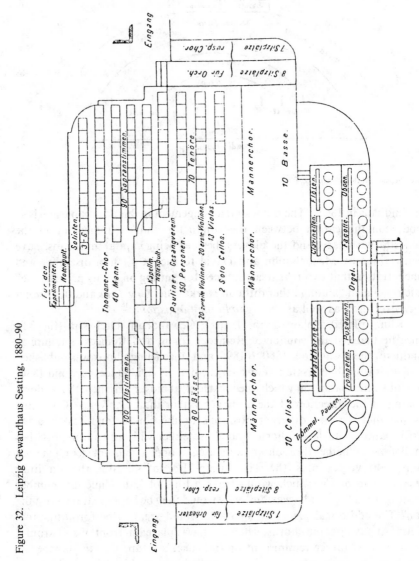

Source: Kling/VOLLKOMMENE, p. 276.

rather than adjacent to the woodwind instruments, suggesting the changing role of these instruments later in the century.

Artur Nikisch succeeded Reinecke as conductor of the Gewandhaus Orchestra in 1895. He adopted the plan shown in figure 33. Immediately striking is the fact that not only are the two violin sections separated antiphonally, but also the violas are set off from the cellos and basses. The four cellists immediately in front of Nikisch are perhaps unusual. The winds appear to be on risers, while the strings and percussion are on the floor. This would serve to differentiate further between the string sounds emanating from the two sides. Also differing from Reinecke's setup are the positions of the winds. Instead of bunching the woodwinds together and the brass as a group, Nikisch spread out the woodwinds in two rows on the first two risers. Where Reinecke gave the front row to flutes and clarinets, Nikisch gave it to flutes and oboes. The horns are spread out on the next riser, and the plan is unusually specific about the order, with the two high horns in the interior and the low horns on the flanks. The remaining brass are on the topmost riser. This again gives the horns the opportunity to blend well with either woodwinds or brass, depending on the piece or passage.

Although no Russian seating plans have come to light, Tchaikovsky must have envisioned something akin to Nikisch's plan in composing the famous passage which opens the last movement of his Sixth Symphony.[17] The melody begins in the second violins and alternates from one note to the next between them and the first violins, while at the same time the second harmonic/contrapuntal line does just the opposite, beginning in the first and alternating with the seconds. The two lines are evidently meant to create a "stereo" effect across the stage. At the same time the third and fourth lines act in like manner between the violas and cellos, the third line down starting in the cellos, the fourth in the violas. This would suggest perhaps the violas on the left and the basses and cellos on the right, opposite to Nikisch's plan. If the strings are not seated thus, then the music might just as well be rescored to match its reappearance in the recapitulation.[18]

It is difficult to visualize very much from the description given by Henry Phillips, reminiscing about his early days as a vocal soloist around London in the early 1820s:

> These performances, when I look back on them, were comparatively of a very primitive kind. A sort of painted theatrical front, of gothic pattern, was placed on the stage near the foot lights, there were a few chairs for the principal singers, a chorus of some eighty voices, an orchestra of about fifty performers, the conductor, with his back to us, looking the orchestra full in the face, and an old organ belonging to the theatre.[19]

Figure 33. Leipzig Gewandhaus Seating, 1896

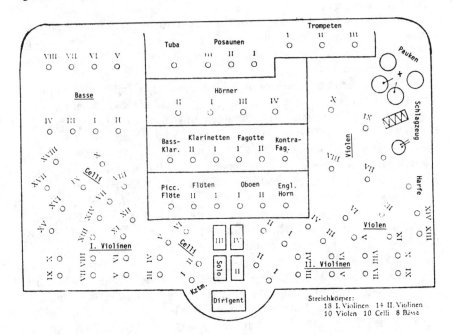

Source: Nösselt/GEWANDHAUS, p. 271. Also reproduced in Zlotnik/SCHUMANN, p. 669.

While it would not have been surprising if the conductor had been facing the audience at that period, the fact that he had his back to the singers tends to indicate that the voices were placed in front of the orchestra, and that the conductor took a position between them and the orchestra—a situation not too different from that at Paris under Habeneck.

Moscheles had some interesting remarks on a benefit concert at Covent Garden in 1826 in which he took part. While the first part consisted of sailors' songs and other light music, the second part was more serious. Yet the crowd was unruly during the overture to *Ruler of the Spirits*. "Could no one see that Weber himself was conducting?" Then Moscheles "sat down to my piano on the stage, and gave a sign to the band beneath me to begin my 'Recollections of Ireland'." But the crowd whistled and shouted and made further rumpus. "I stooped down to the leading violinist, and said, 'I shall continue to move my hands on the keyboard, as though really playing. Make your band pretend to be playing also; after a short time I will give you a signal and we will leave off together.' No sooner said than done."[20] Beyond documenting tremendous rudeness and lack of manners on the part of the London public, this passage paints a picture of a solo pianist on the stage while the orchestra—evidently in a subsidiary role—was down in the pit. With such a crowd and such a situation, no wonder poor Weber was a prophet without honor!

Fétis reported that when he saw the Philharmonic Society of London in 1829, they were placed in the semicircular form with risers later recommended by Berlioz in his treatise. Comparing the setup to those of the Paris Conservatory and *Concerts spirituels,* Fétis claimed that "this amphitheater has an elevation much more rapid and more approaching the perpendicular." Some of the performers were in a semicircular gallery placed "almost above the heads of the others." He found the situation "faulty in that it scarcely permits the performer to hear what is going on above and below him. The niceties of performance have to suffer much from that, it seems to me." After complaining about the fact that the conductor here faced the audience rather than the orchestra and the problem concomitant to that, he pointed out "another peculiarity" which "without doubt, will arouse astonishment with French musicians"; this was the placing of all the basses in the front of the orchestra but lower than the other instruments. Although he found such an arrangement "would seem contrary to all acoustical principles," he was forced to admit that its effect was "much less disagreeable than one would think" and that the sonority of the violins seemed not to be affected by it, probably owing to the fact that the violins were much more elevated.[21] Fétis had undoubtedly seen the orchestra in the Argyll Rooms, for when the Society moved its concerts to the Hanover Square Rooms in 1833, Moscheles commented that the orchestra was arranged differently in the new locale, the basses being separated and placed more in the background.[22] The illustration in figure 34 shows how the orchestra was arranged in 1840, confirming Moscheles's observations. It suggests that the basses were on both wings of the orchestra, a situation encountered before in Paris, as well as in the plan of Berlioz. Carse imputed the change to the modification in conducting, claiming that when baton conducting became the norm in London, it was no longer so important to have a prominent bass to keep the "ensemble intact." He claimed that "in 1840 the Philharmonic took an important step when the whole orchestra in the Hanover Square Rooms was rearranged, and the violins were placed in front of the basses, and to the left and right of the conductor in the same way as was usual in Paris"; however, the leading cello and bass remained in the center as the illustration shows but on an "elevated platform" right behind the piano.[23] Carse also suggested that the position of the basses had not remained

Figure 34. London Philharmonic Society Seating, 1840

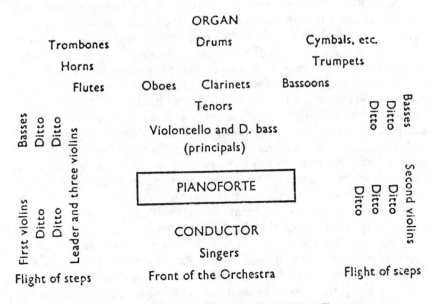

Source: *Musical World,* Feb. 6, 1840, p. 83; here reproduced from Carse/BEETHOVEN, p. 478.

stable since 1833, quoting a description from 1839 that the Philharmonic basses were "invariably in front."[24] Notice the great space between first and second violins as at Paris. The fact that, other than the principal cellist, no others are shown suggests that they are somehow with the basses. The violas ("tenors") seem to form a line between the basses on the two wings. The brass present still another layout, with the horns and trombones in one corner, separated from the trumpets who are with the percussion in the other corner.

The situation in London is further complicated by the picture shown in figure 35, purporting to be an orchestra in the Hanover Square Rooms in 1843. Here the basses are in front on both sides, most of the orchestra is seated rather than standing, and the conductor is in the middle, facing the audience. Certainly the situation in London must have been a motley one! The Philharmonic Society was performing in the Hanover Square Rooms at this time, and this picture does give one an idea of the physical setup of the risers, especially the two corners for brass and percussion.

In 1846, Sir Michael Costa became conductor of the Philharmonic Society and made considerable modifications in the seating plan. Nettel has quoted a critic's reactions:

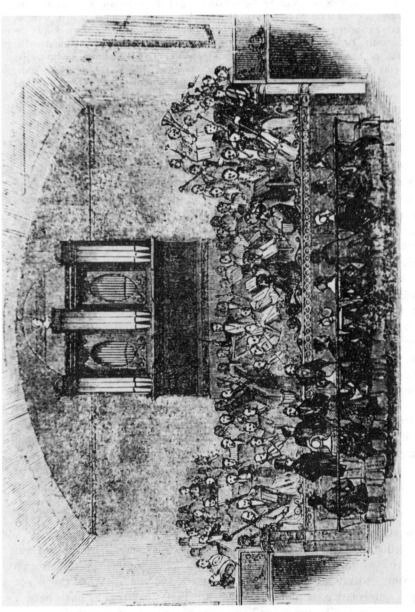

Figure 35. A London Orchestra, 1843
Reproduced from Carse/BEETHOVEN, p. 221.

A greater triumph never prevailed. The oldest members of the Society frankly admitted, that never before in this country had the great symphonies and overtures been so marvellously executed; and the critics have one and all handsomely acknowledged the genius of Costa in the management of his forces. It is necessary to enquire into the secret of such an important result, and the first point to be considered is the disposition of the orchestra. To persons acquainted with the general arrangement of an orchestra, it will be seen that a complete revolution has been effected. The rapid and almost perpendicular rise of the old plan was long a matter of complaint—now, the elevation is reduced considerably; players with drums and trombones, etc., are no longer perched up in the roof to drown the stringed instruments, which are in a valley, with a formidable array of double basses in front, effectively to stifle the melody of the first violins. Costa has got rid of such monstrosities; and studying the principles of acoustics, he has sought, and successfully, to blend the various tones.[25]

It is informative for us that the critic credited so much of Costa's success to this seating plan. Carse also quoted the same source, which informs us that "the conductor faced his troops, instead of fronting the audience."[26] In Costa's plan (fig. 36) the principal bass and cello are prominent in their old-fashioned positions. Violas and some cellos serve to separate first from second violins. Once again horns are more with the woodwinds than with the other brass. But oddest of all is the sprinkling of the cellos and basses throughout the orchestra. It would seem to harken back to Rousseau's dictum that the basses must be heard by all because they carry the beat. Nettel seemed convinced of the efficacy of Costa's plan, claiming that for the first time "Londoners heard an orchestra that was a single musical instrument instead of a body of individuals. Costa's personality dominated the performance, and although he never pretended to impose his own 'reading' of a score on his audience, the effect he produced was distinctive."[27] Of course, these remarks also reflect Costa's dominating and commanding personality.

The reader might want to check Wooldridge's illustration of Costa's plan, which differs slightly in details from that presented here.[28] The two violin sections seem more grouped together there and the violas seem to extend straight across the orchestra. The central cellos are behind the violas, rather than flanked by them. The rear basses are in front of the organ rather than to the sides of it. Where Wooldridge got these details of this "absurdly complex arrangement" is not disclosed.

Costa also became conductor of the Sacred Harmonic Society in 1848, stipulating complete authority there as in the Philharmonic Society. A detailed seating plan for the sacred group under Costa has not been found, but one critic wrote that "there were always, high up among the men-singers, two 'serpents,' which led the attack in that exalted region."[29] While this is not highly informative, it does suggest again that Costa might have been a different martinet in one group from what he was with the other. Of course, there is always the possibility that he was adjusting to the strengths and/or weaknesses of the players in the two ensembles, as well as being guided by

Figure 36. London Philharmonic, Costa, Conductor

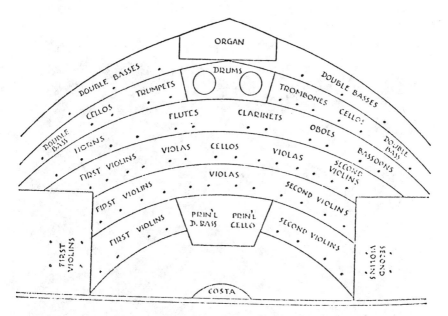

Source: Nettel/ENGLAND, p. 174. It is also available in Carse/BEETHOVEN, p. 479, Mueller/AMERICAN, p. 302, and Wooldridge/CONDUCTOR'S, p. [342].

differing repertoires. Henry Phillips gave a somewhat fuller description, calling the "re-arrangement" of this orchestra under Costa a "very important one" with reforms which "added materially to the effect of the whole." First of all, Costa did away with the violin leader, leaving only a first violin; the whole responsibility then fell to the conductor. Phillips also felt that the instruments were placed better, "more graduated and more concentrated." He remembered "very well when the principal double bass and violoncello were placed together at the same desk, and others of less note, in a totally different part of the orchestra, with perhaps half-a-dozen violins between them and the audience. How could they hear, see, or understand the precision required to create a perfect whole?" But Phillips claimed that "now" all the basses and cellos were "in a row in front" with the "more acute" violins "immediately behind," the winds "ranged in equal progression. This was a great step towards rendering all more perfect."[30] This would seem to show a reversion at the Sacred Harmonic Society in 1848 to a plan used earlier at the Philharmonic Society, quite different from the latter group's later setup under the same conductor. It all even makes one wonder as to the accuracy of Phillips's recollections; somehow it seems unlikely that Costa would use the 1846 setup with one group but one so different in conception with another

Figure 37. Promenade Concert, Covent Garden, 1847
Source: Carse/ORCHESTRA, p. 67.

Figure 38.   Promenade Concert, Covent Garden, 1846
Source: Carse/BEETHOVEN, p. 232.

group only two years later. But then again, there was no mention of serpents with the Philharmonic Society either!

The two pictures in figures 37 and 38 show different perspectives of the very popular Jullien's Promenade Concerts at Covent Garden Theater toward mid-century in London. A special platform was evidently built for this purpose in front of the stage. The audience was free to walk around the orchestra, hence the name "promenade." The orchestra was on risers, in fact, rather steep ones. Most of the players seem seated, with Jullien conducting in their midst. Here again, the basses were in front. This positioning was evidently not universally abandoned in London after Costa's example, and one can easily see here why the violins might have been "stifled" by the basses. The cartoon presented earlier of Jullien conducting may even be more faithful to the spirit of these concerts. When Jullien came to the United States in 1853, bringing with him an orchestra of from 45 to 50,[31] he evidently used much the same layout. Ryan provided a good description of Jullien in the United States:

> He had a dais built in the centre of the orchestra, the floor of which was covered with white cloth having a gold-lace border. On the dais he had a splendid arm-chair of white and gold. When he directed, he stood up and faced the audience, his string forces being on either hand, part way between him and the audience, but leaving him in full view; and the wood and wind were on each side, with the brass in the rear.[32]

The fact is that when Sir Charles Hallé came to England to accept conductorship of the Gentlemen's Concerts in Manchester, the position of basses in front was still to be encountered. Sir Charles had accepted with the condition that the "band" was to be dismissed and reorganization was to be completely up to him. "It is hard to imagine today that one major change should concern the position of one of the instruments: the double-bass had hitherto been placed standing in the front!"[33] Nettel stated that the results were approved by the subscribers and that Manchester's place in the history of the orchestra in England may be said to date from this event.[34] Another writer claimed that Hallé's improvements in the "standard of playing astounded subscribers."[35]

Returning to Germany, figure 39 depicts a concert seating plan at Dresden according to Gassner, probably in the early 1840s. The position of the chorus in reference to the conductor is similar to that under Habeneck in Paris, suggesting the same visual problems for them and the soloists. However, the bunching together of the strings, especially the two violin sections, with the woodwinds to the right is different. The horns seem to be neither with the other brass nor with the woodwinds, but almost by themselves behind the strings. Yet the timpani and trumpets are separated, perhaps suggesting that they were no longer thought of as "noise" instruments.

Gassner also provided a plan for a "stable orchestra in the old opera house in large performances" (fig. 40). This is not too different from the

Figure 39.   Dresden, a Concert Orchestra, 1840s

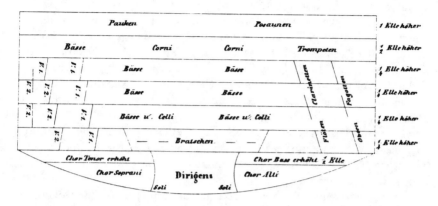

Source: Gassner/DIRIGENT, Beilage no. 4. Same, based on Gassner, also in Schünemann/DIRIGIERENS, p. 308.

Figure 40.   Dresden, "Stabiles Orchester," Old Opera House, 1840s

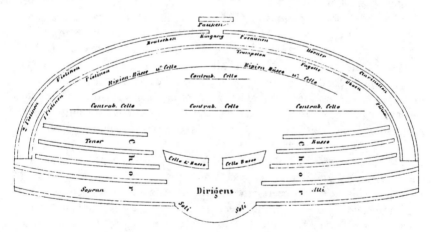

Source: Gassner/DIRIGENT, Beilage no. 3.

previous plan; the chorus and soloists are in similar positions; the strings are pretty much on one side, extending across the middle; the brass and woodwinds are together on the right, if more to the rear. Where in the first plan, the oboes and bassoons are to the rear, here the clarinets are. It is, perhaps, strange that the horns are to the rear here, while the trumpets are in front of the trombones. With the strings, the violas are at the back; in the other plan they were in front of the basses and cellos. The cello and bass desks at the center remind one of Costa's principals in a similar position for recitatives. Elsewhere Gassner made the following additions to the situation in the old opera house: from the third row of the chorus on, the platform is moderately elevated. The third and fourth row of basses and the last choral rows are likewise again elevated. The row of first violins, violas, and wind instruments running around in a circle is one and one half yards higher. The row of second violins, violas, and winds behind them "withdrawing" under the boxes of the first tier is again a yard higher, "so that all can comfortably look over and follow the director over the chorus when they sing standing."[36] Berlioz commented on the situation at Dresden in 1843 when he was there for concerts. "In addition to the distinguished artists I have mentioned, the Dresden orchestra includes the excellent teacher Dotzauer. He leads the cellos and has also to be acting leader of the double basses, for the ancient bass player who shares the desk with him can no longer play some of the notes and indeed barely support the weight of his instrument."[37]

Turning to Munich, Gassner gave the following plan for the Hofkapelle there. Here again is a plan which "faces" the audience (fig. 41). It also is another case where it would seem that the chorus would have problems in seeing the director. The position of the upper woodwinds in front of the strings is interesting. But unlike the Dresden plans, the strings are not bunched together; the violin sections are left and right. This seems like a small orchestra—only two violas, two cellos, and two basses. Commenting on the separated positions of bassoons, cellos, and basses, Schünemann found the weakness to lie "obviously" in the position of the basses "which must remain in touch with the conductor directly through the cellos." But he found the strings and basses to be grouped very well around the organist's position. "To be sure the latter cannot exclusively lay claim to the direction, and so the putting-back of bassoon and basses remains a disadvantage which is further augmented by the woodwinds shoved in between."[38]

In Gassner's plan for the Odeon in Munich (fig. 42), again the plan faces the audience. Here is another case where the chorus and soloists would experience difficulties in seeing the conductor. The form is semicircular, that recommended by Berlioz. The placement of the basses front and center mirrors the situation found in London at the same period. Can one assume that London was influenced by Germany in this? The violins are left and right, separated by the violas as was more and more common in the nineteenth century. The timpani seem to be strangely placed among the woodwinds; on the other hand the brass are rather well placed with the horns so that they can function with either woodwinds or brass or both, as the situation demands. Schünemann had some comments on this plan. He found the semicircular setting and the "radiant dispersion" of the violins "very aptly" realized, "yet the last violins have no favorable place next to the trombones." He also found the concertmaster too far removed from the director and from the sopranos.[39]

F. L. Schubert also gave a description of the Hofkapelle in Munich in 1873. He described five rows. In the first row the conductor was in the middle.

Figure 41.　Munich, Hofkapelle, 1840s

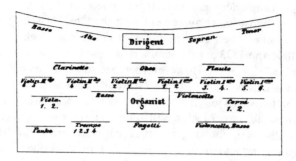

Source: Gassner/DIRIGENT, Beilage no. 15.

Figure 42.　Munich, Odeon, 1840s

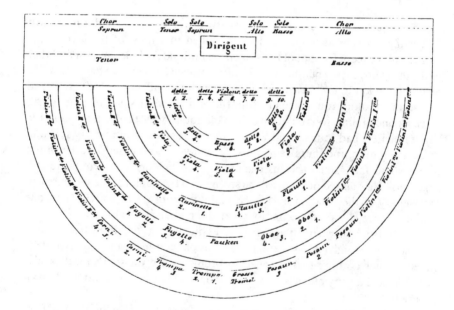

Source: Gassner/DIRIGENT, Beilage no. 13.

To his right were the sopranos and altos; to his left, the tenors and basses. In the second row the oboes were in the middle "behind the conductor," with the flutes to the right and the clarinets to the left. In the third row were first violins to the right and seconds to the left. The fourth row had the organist in the middle, cellos and horns to the right, and violas and basses to the left. The bassoons were in the fifth row in the middle with another cello and bass to the right, and trumpets, trombones, and percussion to the left.[40] Schubert's description points up once again the dangers inherent in this research. First of all one notices almost exact agreement with the plan Gassner gave for the Munich Hofkapelle. Then one reasons that either not much had changed between ca. 1844 and 1873 or that Schubert had used Gassner's book and plan as a basis for his description. However, there are subtle differences. Schubert has the altos and tenors in opposite places. He also adds trombones, which did not appear in Gassner's plan, and suggests other percussion instruments besides the timpani Gassner included. However, if one did not have Gassner's plan at one's disposal, showing a view, as it were, from the back of the orchestra toward the audience, one would interpret Schubert's description entirely differently. One would imagine the first violins to be at the audience's right, rather than on their left, and so on through the orchestra. This brings to mind again the problem of interpreting Berlioz's description of the ideal seating plan for the orchestra. There are other similar questionable cases as well.

Schubert also discussed the seating at Munich's Odeon—again suggesting Gassner as a source. He mentioned that most of the layout was semicircular except for that of the singers on both sides of the director and that of the ten cellos sitting behind him. The first semicircle included ten basses; the second from left to right a second violin, ten violas and a first violin; the third two second violins, four clarinets, four flutes, and two first violins; the fourth three second violins, four bassoons, timpani, four oboes, three first violins; the fifth semicircle had four second violins, four horns, four trumpets, bass drum, three trombones, and four first violins. "This layout is seemingly motley, but it is not so in fact, since the instruments which belong to a group are still together." He pointed out that all the strings join the points of the semicircle in the vicinity of the conductor.[41] Once again, without the aid of Gassner, one would picture the first violins to be at the audience's right, etc. The only difference from Gassner's plan here is that his suggests ten desks respectively of first and second violins, rather than ten of each instrument as Schubert stated. Either nothing had changed in Munich since Gassner's time, or else Schubert had a copy of Gassner's book and was describing that rather than an experience.

Gassner also mentioned the concerts in Hessen Cassel in the 1840s. There the concerts were given in the theater with the orchestra so arranged on the stage that the basses were all together in the middle with the violins and violas on both sides. The winds were on two elevations behind the strings.[42] This would suggest the "modern" manner of splitting the first from the second violins.

A picture of Verdi conducting his *Requiem* (fig. 43) in 1873 shows a space between orchestra and chorus, which are on opposite sides of the stage, with Verdi and the soloists in between. Verdi is facing the audience and would seem to have little contact with the members of the orchestra who in turn would have great difficulties in seeing him. The chorus seems to be standing on risers, while most of the orchestra is seated.

On the other hand, a sketch of Dvořák's "New World" Symphony being premiered at Carnegie Hall in 1893 (fig. 44) shows conductor Anton Seidl facing a seated orchestra. Most of the orchestra is seated on the floor; only the last two rows seem to be on risers. But one notes that the basses are here at the left rear.

Mueller provided a seating plan for the newly formed Boston Symphony Orchestra under Georg Henschel in 1881 (fig. 45). He observed that it was quite close to Berlioz's plan, noting that Henschel "inexperienced in conducting, was probably happy to adopt the recommendation of the most authoritative text on orchestration of that day."[43] The plan is reminiscent of Berlioz's, even down to the position of the harp at the conductor's right hand, as well as the cellos and basses divided on the two wings.

Mueller seems to have based his drawing mainly on a photograph (fig. 46). One also notices, though, in the photograph, a cello and bass perched up to the left of the timpanist. But this is evidently not the only seating plan that Henschel used with the Boston orchestra, even that first year. He told himself of experiments "dividing, for instance, the strings into equal halves on my right and left with the object of enabling the listeners on either side of the hall to have the full effect of the whole string-quintet."[44] In fact, for all that the eye can tell, such could possibly be the case in the photograph. Mueller described a somewhat different seating for the opening concert:

> However, the strangest detail of Henschel's seating for the first concert consisted in ranging the string sections (first and second violins and viola) in concentric semicircles around the podium. The first violins occupied the first semicircle, the second violins the second semicircle, and the violas, the third. Aside from the eccentricity of this system, the Boston habitués seemed to be most disturbed by the familiar faces peeking out of the most unaccustomed places. Well-known viola players sat apparently ready to play first violin, and some first violinists were stationed where one had been accustomed to look for the seconds. Since all the strings were thus divided, the complete orchestra was spread over the whole stage, the right half duplicating the left half.[45]

Aside from the fact that one wonders why a new orchestra would be disturbing with "familiar" faces, Henschel in both of these cases destroyed any antiphonal effect with his intent to give the same fullness to both sides of the audience. Wooldridge presented a drawing of the latter plan (fig. 47). This plan shows oboes and trumpets, too, somehow lacking in Mueller's drawing. Wooldridge, however, assumed that it became permanent with Henschel, a questionable conclusion, as is that inferring that the plan "persisted in America." While Thomas and Seidl utilized the idea of cellos and basses on the wings, there is no evidence that they set the upper strings in this design.

Figure 43. Verdi Conducting His *Requiem*, 1873
Source: Lang & Bettmann/PICTORIAL, p. 154.

Figure 44.   Premiere of Dvořák's *New World* Symphony Carnegie Hall, 1893
Source: Lang & Bettmann/PICTORIAL, p. 186.

Figure 45.   Boston Symphony, 1881

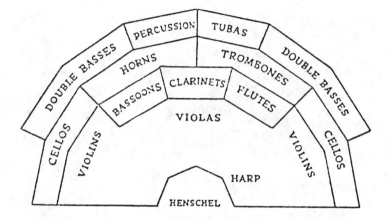

Source: Mueller/AMERICAN, p. 302.

Henschel evidently sent a couple of possible seating plans to his friend Brahms for comment during the time of his experimentation, for he received a letter from Brahms marked "Vienna, 1882," which included the following:

> Your experiments in regard to the placing of an orchestra look very good and interesting. I should almost give preference to the first of the two drawings on account of the horns; the violas, however, seem to give trouble up to now?
>
> By far the best feature in both arrangements, however, is the fact that no committee will be sitting in front of them. There is not a Kapellmeister on the whole of our continent who would not envy you that![46]

According to Henschel, Brahms preferred the plan shown in figure 48. In this plan, the separation of the two violin sections is restored. But now the cellos are divided from the basses on the two wings by wind instruments, a questionable feature. The harp has receded to the left and behind the first violins. What Brahms liked about the position of the horns is not clear, since we lack the second of the two plans which Henschel had sent to him. As far as the division of the cellos and basses on the two wings was concerned, Mueller claimed that Henschel "soon abandoned it after having evoked this criticism" after the opening concert: "We think it a mistake to divide the cellos and basses into two bodies, separated by the entire width of the stage." But the "arrangement of the brasses at the back of the strings seem to be an improvement."[47] But in addition to Seidl in New York and Thomas in Chicago using such a positioning of the lower strings, Mueller claimed that Wagner used it at least once, evidenced by a letter "of advance instruction" to

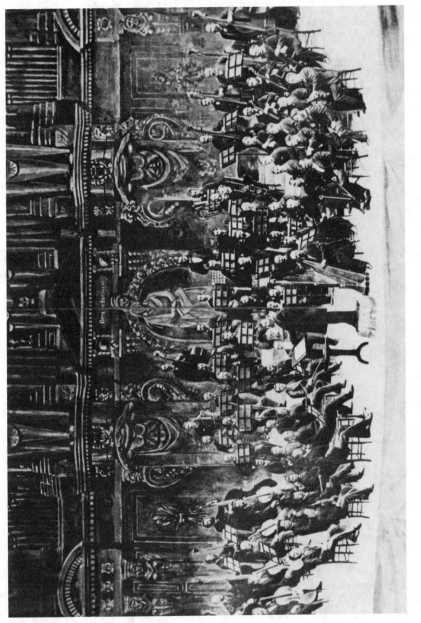

Figure 46.   Boston Symphony, Henschel, Conductor
Source: Howe/BOSTON, between pp. 66-67.

Figure 47. Henschel's Experimental Seating, Boston Symphony, 1881

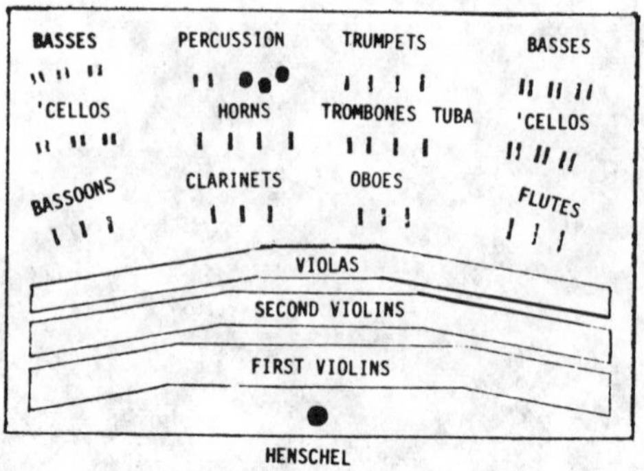

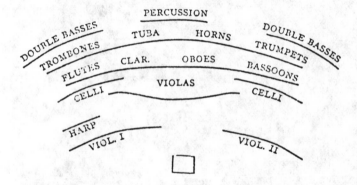

Source: Wooldridge/ CONDUCTOR'S, p. [342].

Figure 48. A Plan Approved by Brahms

Source: Henschel/ BRAHMS, p. 84.

Heckel in Mannheim, December 6, 1871, in which he requested that the basses be placed on the left and right front wings of the orchestra.[48]

A picture of the Boston Orchestra in 1891 under Artur Nikisch (fig. 49) has the basses across the back of the orchestra. The sides are apparently cut off in the picture, but the cellos seem to be at the left behind the first violins. The harp has been restored to the front on the conductor's right. Of course, these pictures show a much smaller Boston Orchestra than is the case at present. Here the brass are all on the right, the four horns being in front of the two basses on the right.

The placement of the various instruments was of enormous importance to Theodore Thomas. According to one biographer "he had the place of every performer's chair fixed to an inch; he himself designed the decorations back of

Figure 49.　Boston Symphony with Nikisch, 1891
Source: Wooldridge/CONDUCTOR'S, plate IV, following p. 240.

them so as to obtain the best sound effects from the material used."[49] He was also an experimenter. According to Mrs. Thomas's memoirs, he ceaselessly experimented with sounding boards, platforms, and layout during the thirteen years he conducted in the Auditorium in Chicago.

> The timpani traveled all round the semicircle, and back again—the double basses collected in the middle, divided on either side, strung themselves out in a row and finally bunched together at the left—the violins advanced out on to extra platforms built over the front rows of seats in the parquet, and retreated again behind the proscenium arch; while the wood-winds, brasses, and harps were equally restless in their wanderings over the stage. As for sounding-boards; sometimes the stage was enclosed tightly, at others a space six feet wide would be left open at the back; again, a broken sounding-board, made like great slats, with an open space between each one, would be used. The orchestra sat on two sounding boards besides the regular flooring of the stage, and Thomas was incessantly tinkering at the varying heights at which each man should be elevated above the floor level. In short, the fine effects achieved by the orchestra in the Auditorium were due quite as much to the work of Thomas in adjusting the orchestra and stage, as to the good acoustics of the theater itself.[50]

Thomas was most careful as to visibility, disliking the practice of rapping on the desk for attention. He had the stands placed so that each player could see him over the top of his stand. He required each one to look at him at least once in each measure of music. The result was that he could stop the music just by dropping his arms, "which was signal enough."[51]

As for sounding boards, Thomas found one an absolute necessity for his Chicago concerts in the huge Exposition Building from the 1870s.

> The first maddening problem was about sound. How could seventy men be heard in that huge cavern? He had recourse to his studies in acoustics and all alone devised and made a sounding board that commanded the wondering attention of all acoustic engineers and experts and is still standard in technical works on this subject. It was a vast contrivance of wood erected at a certain angle immediately back of the players. With potted trees and shrubs he marked off the concert space from the rest of the gigantic building, and so effectually that one never noticed the gloomy void beyond. With other plants and shrubs he made a garden, cool and sweet and attractive.
>
> The sounding board worked incredibly well; in that great building one could actually get as good effects as in any ordinarily sized hall.[52]

Thomas was not surprised when a copy of his sounding board did not work for some eastern architects. "Of course not" was his response. "They have overlooked a vital point. There must be an open space of eighteen inches at the bottom and my angle has not been observed."[53] A diagram of the one he used in Chicago appears below (fig. 50). The floor seems to slant slightly toward the audience, with three rows rising at the rear. There is space beneath it, which would certainly have some effect on resonance.

A seating plan which Thomas used with the Chicago Orchestra follows (fig. 51). The two violin sections are split on both sides, as would be expected.

Figure 50. Thomas's Sounding Board

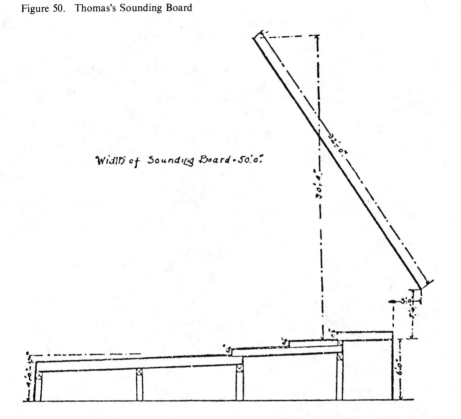

Width of Sounding Board · 50′.0″

Source: Thomas/ MEMOIRS, p. 125.

The harp is left front, not too different from Berlioz's recommendation. One has to wonder if the cello desk at front is still a hangover from continuo practice, as Costa's plan suggested. Here there are basses on both wings, but the remaining cellos are placed together at the left. Again horns are where they can function both as brass and with the woodwinds. The conductor is back where he can be easily seen by all, especially with the slanting stage and the rear risers. As to Thomas's method of seating a chorus, only a hint can be gleaned from a description by Otis of a performance of Berlioz's *Faust* during the first Chicago Orchestra season in 1892. Otis writes that Thomas had the tenors and basses "directly in front of him and in the center of the chorus."[54] However, as indicted above, Thomas had experimented with seating, and this plan had not always been used by him. That he had used at least one differing

Figure 51.   Thomas's Seating Plan

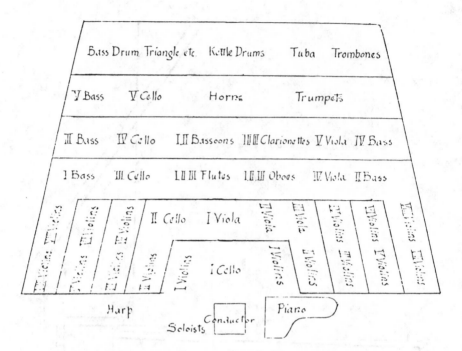

Source: Thomas/MEMOIRS, facing p. 372.

plan with the earlier Thomas Orchestra which was based in New York but toured widely is evidenced by the influence this orchestra had on the Orchestra of the Harvard Musical Association. Mueller found that the conductor of this group, Carl Zerrahn, "imitated Thomas' seating order, by grouping the cellos together in a solid body in middle front, the basses behind them, and the wind band—raised in two long rows above—in the extreme rear."[55] Pictures of the earlier Thomas Orchestra and the later Chicago Orchestra also suggest that Thomas's ideas on seating were not static (figs. 52 through 55).

Though not very specific, Felix Weingartner did indicate a general plan for seating the chorus and orchestra for Beethoven's Ninth symphony. He said that the orchestra "must as far as possible take its accustomed place and be surrounded by the chorus in a broad semicircle. The podium must rise in the form of a terrace."[56] For a wide stage, he suggested the plan shown in figure 56.

Figure 52.   Thomas Orchestra, Gilmore's Garden, New York City
Source: Thomas/AUTOBIOGRAPHY, II, facing p. 134.

Figure 53.   Thomas Orchestra, Steinway Hall, New York City
Source: Thomas/AUTOBIOGRAPHY, II, facing p. 82.

Figure 54. Chicago Orchestra in the Auditorium
Source: Thomas/AUTOBIOGRAPHY, I, facing p. 172.

Figure 55.   Chicago Orchestra in Orchestra Hall
Source: Thomas/AUTOBIOGRAPHY, I, facing p. 216.

Figure 56. Weingartner's Seating for Beethoven's Ninth Symphony

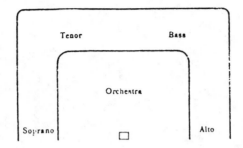

Source: Weingartner/BEETHOVEN, p. 176.

He elucidated on it further: "If however it is long and narrow, so that with the above arrangement the greater part of the orchestra would be pushed too far back, it is advisable to fill all the front room with the violins and, if possible, with some of the viola- and violoncello-desks, and then to let the chorus take its place behind on a distinctly raised platform."[57] Mr. Weingartner's remarks were made in 1906.

Seating in the Church

Since the physical layout of a church can offer special problems, even if only because of the position of the organ, it seems well to devote some separate space to a few plans as a separate topic. Extreme conditions prevailed at Paris during the early years of the consulate of Napoleon due to the destruction of the chapel of the Tuileries—probably around 1800–1804. Eight singers and 27 "symphonists" under the direction of Paisiello formed the group of musicians "sufficing" for the "areas" where the service took place. The chapel of the Tuileries had been destroyed, so the divine office was celebrated in the hall of the state council where only the singers and piano could be placed. The violins played in two rows behind the singers on a small balcony facing the altar; the basses and winds were relegated to the next room. "The musicians had much trouble maneuvering in a terrain so disadvantageous for ensemble."[1] Indeed, one would wonder about any ensemble at all in such quarters. But this was an extreme case.

The problem caused by the organ is suggested by Smart's observations in St. Michael's Church in Vienna in 1825: "We went up into the orchestra, which was crowded. The organist, Mr. Schmidt, was placed in the centre with the keys facing the altar. The organ was of bad tone and was placed on the sides to the right and left of him."[2] This suggests that the console as well as the organ proper can be obstacles around which the orchestra must be arranged. Here the organist faced away from the altar, if one reads Smart correctly, a circumstance which one suspects was very common.

Gassner gave a plan for a Dresden church, probably around 1844 (fig. 57). Schünemann assumed it was the court or *Hofkirche*.[3] Here the organ formed a separation between the strings on one side and the winds and chorus on the other. Basses and cellos are on both wings; basses also seem to be to the front on both sides of the conductor. The direction in which the conductor faced is addressed by Schünemann, though whether by inference or discovery is not clear. He claimed that the conductor turned his back to the main body of instruments, "since in the performance of a Mass he had to see the celebrating

Figure 57. Dresden, Hofkirche Seating

Source: Gassner/DIRIGENT, Beilage no. 5.

clerics. The choir stood to his right, while trumpets and timpani were placed on side-balconies."[4] Here "to his right" clearly meant as he faced the altar and not from the audience standpoint; this question has already been alluded to before. Schünemann also stated that the main points of this setup were still to be seen in his time.

Gassner also provided a plan for the royal court chapel in Vienna in the 1840s (fig. 58). Here again the strings and winds are on separate sides of the organ console. Trumpets and timpani are in this case to the rear of the orchestra, in front of the organ pipes. The upper strings and the choir face each other. It is difficult to be sure what differentiates between "Kapellmeister" and "Director" in this plan. Could "Director" mean really the concertmaster or violin leader? The conductor or "Kapellmeister" is on a raised platform. Here again, Schünemann read this plan with the conductor facing out towards the congregation or altar. He saw the existing space as requiring "an elongated arrangement of the strings, which were conducted by the concertmaster (on the right hand of the director). The choir sang close by the conductor on the left side." He found the placement of the cellos and basses to be in conformity with the "Dresden principle."[5] But Schünemann seemed to understand "Director" here to mean concertmaster.

The orchestra of the *Concert spirituel* in Vienna is suitably considered here, since it performed either in a church or a like structure containing an organ. Gassner provided the plan appearing in figure 59. Only the position of the chorus differentiates this from the Dresden plan or that of the Viennese Hofkapelle. But here is another case where both the solo singers and the chorus cannot see the conductor unless they turn their heads.

According to Gassner, the seating in the Garnisonskirche in Berlin was

Figure 58.   Vienna, k. k. Hofkapelle

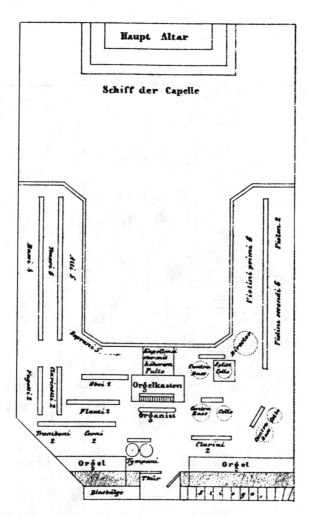

Source: Gassner/DIRIGENT, Beilage no. 12.

about the same as that in the Berlin Opera in the 1840s.[6] That plan will be considered in the proper chapter.

    A different solution was found for the performance of Beethoven's C major Mass at Bonn in 1845, during the festivities celebrating the unveiling of Beethoven's statue. Sir George Smart described the event:

Figure 59. *Concert spirituel*

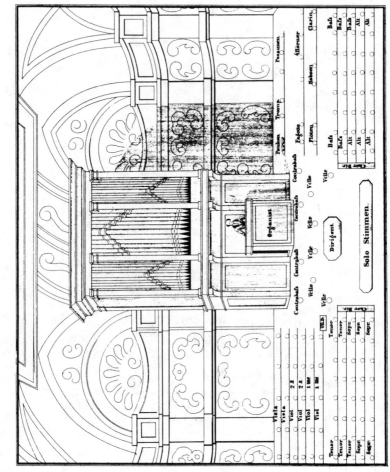

Source: Gassner/DIRIGENT, Beilage no. 16.

In the afternoon we went to a rehearsal in the Münster, or principal church, of Beethoven's Mass in C.... The band and chorus were behind the high altar, out of sight to us in a pew about the middle of the church, which was prettily decorated with flowers and green garlands.... The chorus was strong and good.... The band was good, the wind instruments played excellently, but the band was not strong enough for the voices. I suppose there was not room for a larger band. Dr. Breidenstein conducted, we could not see him.... Many parts of this beautiful mass were unsteady, the fault seemed to be with the worthy conductor who may not have had sufficient experience, besides this there was a small echo in the part where the band was placed.[7]

Echoes were probably as common as other problems of available space in church performances. But Elwart felt that the above performance produced an "*effet merveilleux*": "Never had I had the occasion to hear Beethoven in church, and in this place, vast and of a style entirely catholic, the religious work of the composer seemed to me quite superior to the other mass (no. 2) performed at the first concert."[8] As to the work itself, probably not many would agree as to its merits relative to the great *Missa solemnis*.

Opera Seating

The great spatial problems of the opera pit have already been noted. They have not always been solved in the same way nor probably with the same degree of success. Indeed, often the placement of certain instruments would seem awkward vis-à-vis the action on the stage. For example, Sir George Smart reported that he saw a Grétry opera in Paris at the theater in rue Feydeau; of four double basses, one was in the center of the orchestra.[1] Now unless the orchestra pit was very deep, this would seem an obstruction to the audience. Nor was this an isolated case. At Stuttgart in 1825 Smart made a similar observation: "There were only four double basses, these with the 'cellos were in the centre exactly behind the leader."[2] And a sketch of a performance of Wagner's *Rienzi* at Dresden in 1842[3] shows four basses all in the row nearest the audience; two are at the left, but the other two are in the middle, one to the left of center, the other to the right. If one refers back to the seating plan offered by F. L. Schubert in 1873 for the theater, two basses and cellos are in the middle of the orchestra.[4] He admitted that such was the placement at the Dresden Opera. He also mentioned that at Leipzig, the basses and cellos were all behind the conductor. And in the court theater at Stuttgart, two basses stood directly in front of the conductor, and four at the left in front of the stage, "however so that they turn their faces to the public."[5]

The position of the conductor also changed during the nineteenth century. Although this problem was discussed earlier in this study, it is worth some consideration here also. Around 1820, Castil-Blaze claimed that at the Opéra-Comique and most provincial theaters, the *maître de musique* ordinarily took his place at the center, facing the stage, and sometimes at the "very end" of the orchestra, with the stage to his left. He said that Lahoussaye had such an arrangement at the Feydeau and that Grasset had adopted such for the Italian Opera.[6] But in 1825 at the Feydeau, Mendelssohn found the conductor standing in the middle.[7] In 1825 at Ghent, Smart found the conductor in the middle: "The conductor beat time in the centre, close to the lamps, but he and the leader did not seem very good friends."[8] In Darmstadt later the same year, Smart took note of "Mr. Mancolt, the director of this band, who sat sideways with his little stick and could therefore see the Grand Duke on his right and the singers on his left."[9] Later Smart was in Stuttgart: "The conductor stood in the center facing the stage beating time with his violin bow and occasionally playing the violin."[10] In Vienna at the theater in the Leopoldstadt, "the conductor sat at a queer-toned long pianoforte and beat time with a roll."[11] But at the Josephstadt-Theater, "the conductor beat time at a desk in the centre even with the violins."[12] At Cologne the conductor was an elder brother of Weber. "He beat time at the usual place in the centre with his violin bow, only using his violin once."[13]

At Leipzig the director sat "immediately in front of the stage in order to lead the vocal ensemble."[14] And in the sketch of Wagner's *Rienzi* at Dresden in 1842 mentioned above, the conductor was in the center right at the base of the stage, his back to the orchestra.[15] When the new opera house at Vienna opened in 1869, the conductor was at the base of the stage.[16] But Mahler made changes when he took over. He had the podium "raised and pushed close up to the strings." His predecessor Jahn had sat on a chair in the middle of the orchestra, and before him the conductor was "right up in front of the footlights." The orchestra was, of course, behind him and "he busied himself almost exclusively with the singers" and the stage action. A cleared space behind him enabled him to turn to the orchestra when necessary. The present position of the conductor in most theaters, which "seems to us to be its classical, one might almost say its natural place, has only been customary since the time of Mahler's successor Felix von Weingartner."[17] Marcel Prawy, who provided this information, embroidered on Weingartner's innovation further: "For all his shortcomings, Weingartner took his duties at the Opera very seriously and left at least one indelible mark on orchestral procedure: he was the first to conduct from the position we know today, before the railing which separates the pit from the audience. There he could see and be seen."[18] F. L. Schubert's theater plan shown previously illustrates the former position at the base of the stage. He indicated that such was the position taken at Dresden, Leipzig, and Stuttgart at that time.[19] The sketch in figure 60 shows such a position at London's Covent Garden in 1889.

When Carl Maria von Weber became conductor at Breslau in 1804, he showed an immediate interest in the seating arrangements. On the right side he seated the first violins, oboes, horns, a double bass and a cello; on the left he placed the second violins, clarinets, and bassoons, next to them the violas, and behind them the trumpets and timpani. Evidently before this the winds had been in front and the strings together behind them. The musicians complained because they could not hear themselves too well with the new arrangement; the public complained that the new sound effect was good only for the boxes and the last rows of the parterre. But Weber held his ground.[20]

Figure 60. Covent Garden Opera, 1889

Source: Nettel/ENGLAND, p. 255.

At Dresden, Weber again met with a situation which caused him dissatisfaction and which resulted in his making changes. The year was 1817 when he assumed his duties there. His son described the process, claiming that Weber was immediately "uncomfortably aware" that the way in which the orchestra was arranged would make it impossible for him to direct the opera productions as a whole: orchestra, singers, chorus, and even the decor. The orchestra space there was a rectangle whose longish sides went along the parquet and stage. On the right and left it extended with "cavernous, 7-foot high" recesses under the court boxes which bordered on the stage apron. The left recess contained a staircase leading down to the orchestra, but the right one housed the timpani, trumpets, and percussion which were "cooped up" there. From this "cavern" these instruments could neither sound forth effectively nor clearly see the conductor who sat at a keyboard in the middle of the orchestra. The isolated position of the conductor also made it impossible for him to help the singers, keep the orchestra with the stage action, give any signals to the prompter, or see and motion to anyone in the wings.

While this arrangement might have worked for Italian opera, in Weber's mind such conditions were untenable, since he wished to control the whole action "by a nod of his head, a glance of his eye, or a movement of his baton." For example, a cello and bass sat behind the conductor (an obvious holdover from the eighteenth century), even reading from his score, and also obstructing his ear for nicety and balance of sound. Moreover, their reading was hampered by his movements. In front of the conductor were another bass and cello, adding to the deep sounds. The third bass was posted in the corner at the right near the king's box. If a fourth was needed for a full orchestra, a "little piece" of the parquet was partitioned off for him. To the right of the director sat the first and second violinists at the same desk, in front of them were two violas, and left of these four more first and four second violins. Between the strings and the stage sat alto, tenor, and bass trombones which not only greatly "harrassed" the strings but also much impaired the efficacy of their sound. Left of the director sat first two flutes and two oboes, then two clarinets and two bassoons, and finally two horns and two trumpets. If four horns were needed, the trumpets were banished to the recess under the right box.

Weber studied the situation for eight months until he was convinced that it was unsuitable, especially for the goals of German opera. He then determined what rational transformation could be made with little trouble and without cost. The performance of Weber's Italian cantata *L'Accoglienza* and Mozart's *Titus* for the nuptial festivities of the princess provided an opportunity to try the desired changes. In rehearsals Weber pushed his desk up behind the prompter's box so that he could tap on it and speak with its inhabitant. Behind him and to his right he set the first and second violins; then at the wall of the parquet he set the violas, cellos, and basses. The trombones were set among the other brass, with the woodwinds to his left. Thus the conductor was visible even to the players under the king's box. These changes proved themselves to practical musicians and conductors and were adopted almost unchanged when the theater was rebuilt. However, at a performance of Spontini's *Vestalin,* the king noticed the changed look of the orchestra and was offended by the sound of the trombones close to his box.[21] This was quite different from Weber's Breslau plan where he had antiphonal effects from the split violin sections. Here strings were massed together and woodwinds and horns were placed together to his left. The objections raised mushroomed, however, and Weber had to abandon his changes for a time. Eventually he won out, thanks to the "express desire of the Queen"; in 1820 his changes were adopted, most of them even by Morlacchi for the Italian opera.[22]

Wooldridge gave a plan for Weber in Dresden, giving the year as 1817 (fig. 61). Once again one has to wonder at the source of his information. First of all, he has Weber in the modern position, close to the audience. A conjecture that perhaps the plan faces away from the stage cannot be

Figure 61. A Questionable Drawing of Weber's Dresden Seating

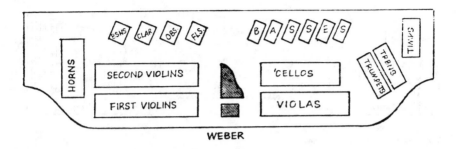

WEBER

Source: Wooldridge/CONDUCTOR'S, p. [341].

sustained, because directly above this plan, Wooldridge presented the Rousseau plan of the orchestra under Hasse, and the shape of the orchestral space is the same and facing the stage. Not only that, but why would the keyboard player face the audience instead of the stage? Also, note that this plan correctly has the heavy brass and timpani on the right under the king's box, though Weber seemed to put the two trumpets behind the horns when only two horns were used. But in general, this plan does not conform to young Weber's description, albeit that description is not a model of clarity (the English translation is even less so, omitting most of the detail).

Wolfgang Becker confused things somewhat further in stating that the royal box and the brass and percussion under it were on the left. Could he have been picturing the plan from the stage out? He pointed out that the seating Weber had found in 1817 still conformed to that used by Hasse with only a few changes occurring through the years, such as a few violins migrating to the same side as the winds. But Becker also felt that Weber had gained enough room with his changes to "bring the timpani and trumpets out from the cavity under the royal box."[23] Perhaps this explains even better the king's displeasure with the trombones; if they were near his box rather than under it, they would be less muffled.

Siegfried Borris's discussion also adds to the confusion. He claimed that Weber's seating was managed "according to new viewpoints" with the winds no longer in front of the orchestra. He described first violins, oboes, horns, basses, and cellos on the right, second violins, flutes, clarinets, bassoons, and violas on the left, with trumpets and timpani behind the violas.[24] Borris seems to have confused the Dresden and Breslau situations, though he did not mention Breslau in his text, only Prague and Berlin in addition to Dresden. But his description matches Max Weber's delineation of the Breslau seating adopted by Weber. Robert Haas's description supports the idea that Weber

Figure 62. Dresden, Opera Seating, 1840s

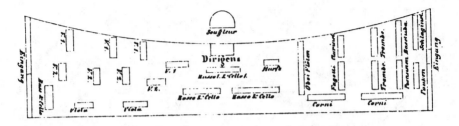

Source: Gassner/DIRIGENT, Beilage no. 2.

moved the winds from a position near the public to the rear near the stage wall at Breslau, but he did not mention the divided violins there; so he cannot have misled Borris.[25] But Sir George Smart, who visited Dresden in 1825 and saw Weber conduct, supports Max Weber's description rather closely: "All the strings were on the right and all the wind instruments on the left of the conductor, who beat time with a roll at a square pianoforte. The tromboni were one behind the other, each in the centre of the oboe desks."[26] It seems strange, however, that Smart did not mention Weber's position at the stage, especially if it was unusual at that time. He also saw another conductor at the theater for an Italian opera. "Marschner, I suppose, directed at the square pianoforte, which was brought nearer the pit this evening."[27] This does suggest by inference that Weber had it in a different position, perhaps nearer the stage. But Smart's text does seem to lend credence to Max Weber's description.

Gassner's plan for the Dresden opera is shown in figure 62. Weber's seating seems to have been reversed—strings left and winds right. This also confirms the positions of the basses in the sketch of Wagner's *Rienzi* referred to earlier. In addition it shows that in 1844 the conductor was still in Weber's position near the prompter's box. And unless F. L. Schubert was merely copying Gassner's plan, the situation was still the same in Dresden in 1873.[28]

A description of the orchestra of La Scala at Milan in 1814 had this numerous group set in only two rows: "They stand in two rows: in one the strings, in the other the winds and percussion; the basses and cellos stand at both extremities."[29] This does suggest the kind of separation which was to come under Weber at Dresden. But the plan of La Scala shown in figure 63 from 1825 suggests three rows of instruments. Again strings and winds are divided, and cellos and basses are on both wings as in 1814. Note, however, that there is no attempt to utilize the two violin sections antiphonally. Here is another case where the horns are with the woodwinds rather than the other brass. The same communication containing this plan was also sent to an English periodical and appears in figure 64. One notes some discrepancies between the two, first of all the less elongated shape of the English example.

Figure 63. Milan, La Scala, 1825

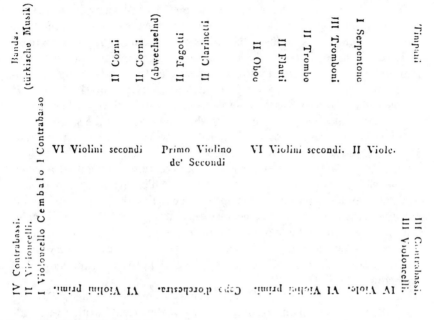

Banda. (türkische Musik) II Corni II Corni (abwechselnd) II Fagotti II Clarinetti II Oboe II Flauti II Trombo III Tromboni I Serpentone Timpani

VI Violini secondi   Primo Violino de' Secondi   VI Violini secondi. II Viole.

IV Contrabassi.   II Violoncelli.   I Violoncello Cembalo 1 Contrabasso

IV Viole. VI Violini primi.   Capo d'orchestra.   VI Violini primi.

III Contrabassi.   III Violoncelli.

Source: AMZ, XXVII (1825), cols. 131–32.

Figure 64. La Scala, 1825, Another Version

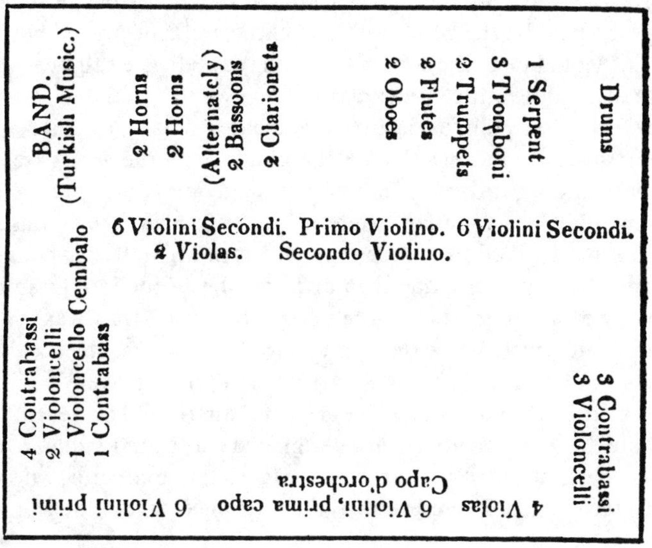

BAND. (Turkish Music.) 2 Horns 2 Horns (Alternately) 2 Bassoons 2 Clarionets 2 Oboes 2 Flutes 2 Trumpets 3 Tromboni 1 Serpent Drums

6 Violini Secondi. Primo Violino. 6 Violini Secondi.
2 Violas.   Secondo Violino.

4 Contrabassi 2 Violoncelli 1 Violoncello Cembalo 1 Contrabass

3 Contrabasi 3 Violoncelli

4 Violas   6 Violini, prima capo   Capo d'orchestra   6 Violini primi

Source: HARMONICON, III (1825), p. 140.

The positions of the basses and cellos in relation to the first violins on the left and those on the right vis-à-vis the violas is somewhat different. Whereas in the German version the conductor or leader is in the modern position near the audience, in the English one six first violins and their leader are behind him. Also, the leader of the seconds in the center of the German plan appears to be two separate players in the English. The German example would seem to be the more reliable. But note that in both versions, the winds on the left are facing towards the right; those on the right are facing left. This is also the case with the cellos and basses as well as the percussion on both sides. The second violins seem to be facing the audience, while the first face the stage.

By 1890 much had changed at La Scala, as is evident in the plan in figure 65. First of all the conductor is at the base of the stage, not in the modern position. The woodwinds and horns are in the center of the orchestra. They and the violas divide the two violin sections which are now in a typical nineteenth-century separation. It seems strange to find the harps way over on the left with the louder brass and percussion. Although the cellos are all on the right, the basses are split on both wings. But one bass is still in a position which would seem to interfere with audience vision. Incidentally, this is a very up-to-date orchestra, with cornets, bass clarinet, English horn, tuba, and numerous percussion.

What if Kling was wrong, however, in indicating that the stage ["*Bühne*"] was to the rear in this plan? What if instead it really faced the other way with the audience farthest from the reader? The shape of the stage would suggest this. Then the conductor's position would agree with the earlier La Scala plans; the harps and strings would be forward, nearer the audience as one would expect; and the brass and percussion would be nearer the stage. But note that if such may be the case—and it would seem to be a good bet—then the first violins would be to the conductor's and the audience's right as was the case in so many eighteenth-century plans.

Figure 66 gives the plan for the then new theater of San Carlo in Naples in 1818. It is reminiscent of the 1825 La Scala plan in that the winds are in two groups, each facing inward, although here each group is much more to the side. The conductor is in a similar "modern" position, while the violins are on both sides, but not be section—there are again as in Milan firsts and seconds on each side. Carse pointed out that dividing the lower strings into two groups, posting each group at opposite sides of the orchestra, "was evidently an Italian custom which was extended to the violas, no doubt because the instruments so often played the bass part in the upper octave."[30]

A picture from 1821 shows the pit of the Kärtnerthor Theater in Vienna (fig. 67). While the instruments are not designated for the individual places, it is possible to note how the rows near the stage faced the conductor, who was at the base of the stage. Those nearest the audience faced the stage and conductor.

Figure 65. La Scala, ca. 1890

Besetzung des Streichquintetts: 16 erste Violinen.
14 zweite Violinen.
10 Bratschen.
11 Violoncellos.
11 Kontrabässe.

Source: Kling/VOLLKOMMENE, p. 277.

Figure 66. Naples, San Carlo, 1818

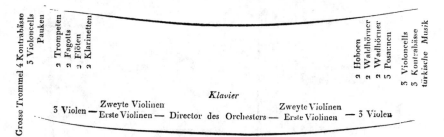

Die Anzahl der Violinen ist mir unbekannt: wahrscheinlich sind ihrer 24.

Source: AMZ, XX (1818), cols. 495-96.

A plan for the Vienna Court Opera in the 1840s is given in figure 68. Here the conductor is in the center of the orchestra with the strings clustered around him. But the double basses are also in the center—right in the line of audience view, one would think. The woodwinds and horns are to the right, facing inward; the brass and percussion are to the left facing inward also. There is some slight division between the two violin sections, with the first to the right—perhaps unusual for this late date.

Evidently pit levels varied from place to place, for when the new opera house opened in Vienna in May 1869, much experimentation had been done. After many rehearsals in search of the right level, the one finally agreed on was

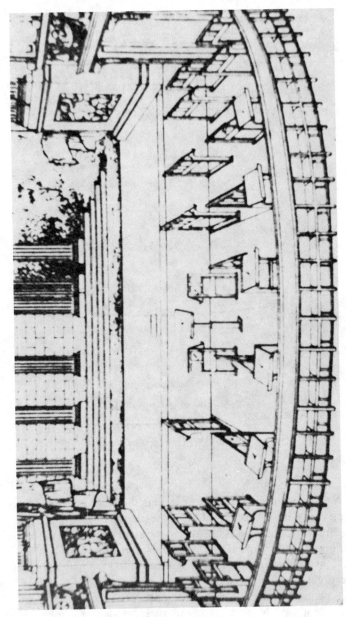

Figure 67. Vienna, Kärntnerthor Theater, 1821
Source: Carse/ORCHESTRA, p. 28.

Figure 68.   Vienna, Court Opera, 1840s

Source: Gassner/DIRIGENT, Beilage no. 10.

"somewhat below the Italian, but above the German level."[31] Marcel Prawy has reproduced a memorandum on this subject written by the conductor Otto Dessoff on May 2, 1869. It outlines many of the problems encountered. He found that the rehearsal of May 1 had confirmed his feeling that the level was too low. He found the tone "muffled," the first violins sounding "thin and shrill," the second violins and cello "inaudible when playing forte," little to be heard from the basses "beyond the strike of the strings on the finger-board but no healthy tone," and the winds proceeding to "smother all the rest." He felt that raising the platform would "achieve an enhanced clarity" and "at least restore some measure of that sonority" which was felt to be a "specialty" of that orchestra. He therefore requested the platform be raised by nine inches. Dessoff also wanted to place the bass drum and cymbals "in the niche beneath the archducal box" to mollify the "most unpleasant" effect produced when these instruments were in open space. Also, with the trumpets and trombones "compressed" against the stage wall and second violins and cellos in front of them, the brass sound would be subdued. He even thought that it might be an advantage to seat the trumpets and trombones "at a slightly lower level (1-1/2 to 2 inches)" than the rest of the orchestra.[32] While it might have been nice to lower the orchestra below audience view, this could at the same time have served to muffle tone. And Dessoff evidently had to have permission to place noisy instruments under the royal box. Remember that at Dresden Weber had raised opposition by moving instruments.

Kling's plan for the Vienna Court Theater around 1890 is given in figure 69. While at first glance it seems similar to that in the 1840s—the conductor in the center, the strings around him, with the basses in the center against the stage—closer perusal shows some significant changes. There is a more pronounced division between first and second violins, with the firsts on the left now, seemingly more normal for the nineteenth century. The woodwinds and horns are on the left now, with harp at the extreme left; the harp had been closer to the strings but on the brass side in 1840 or so. The brass and

Figure 69. Vienna, Court Theater, ca. 1890

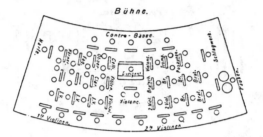

Source: Kling/VOLLKOMMENE, p. 274.

percussion are here on the right. But one notes that most of the violins are still facing the stage and conductor; no wonder that Dessoff found their tones muffled. It will be remembered that Mahler moved the conductor's rostrum and then Weingartner moved it to the "modern" position.

When Smart visited Stuttgart in 1825, he found the then more normal theatrical arrangement of strings on one side, winds on the other.

> The conductor stood in the centre facing the stage beating time with his violin bow and occasionally playing the violin.... There were only four double basses, these with the 'cellos were in the centre exactly behind the leader, all the stringed instruments were on his left and all the wind instruments and drums were on his right. I do not like this arrangement which occasioned a want of blending, the wind instruments were not always in time together. The oboe was tolerable but rather loud, the fagotto cutting.[33]

While the last remarks may have been directed more at the players than at the arrangement, it is clear that Smart found fault with this plan from the point of view of ensemble. Again the basses were in the center of the orchestra.

By the 1870s this plan had been just about reversed. According to F. L. Schubert, at that time the strings were "almost all" on the right with the winds and percussion on the left. Two cellos sat behind the director, two to his right and two to his left "next to him." Two basses were "directly in front" of him and four at the left "in front of the stage, however so that they turn their faces to the public." But he found that having the violins and violas all on the right was perhaps "less practical," since as a result their sound was "thrown" more to the stage, because their F-holes were not "turned to the public."[34]

The position of the conductor at the Königstadt Theater in Berlin in 1827 sounds much like the "modern" one. The director, Carl Blum, would seem to have been influenced by a trip to Italy, according to the following description.

Since the return of this gentleman from Italy, he has introduced several alterations for the better, and particularly in the arrangement of the orchestra. The leader, instead of being seated as formerly, low in the centre, is raised and stationed with his back immediately to the pit, so as to have a full command not only of the whole orchestra, but of the singers also, whom it is one great point of duty to guide and correct; the contrabasses are ranged round him like a rampart, the violins on both sides, with their faces to the stage, while the wind instruments, and those of a noisier character, are distributed in the two wings of the orchestra.[35]

Placing the violins "on both sides" almost suggests the antiphonal setup usual in concert orchestras in the nineteenth century. This and the conductor's position suggest a very "modern" condition in Berlin at an early date. Gassner claimed the seating was the same as in the opera house, whose seating plan is shown in figure 70.[36]

Berlioz mentioned the German Opera when he was in Berlin in 1843. He found the theater, which had been burned to the ground only three months previous to his visit, "a rather gloomy and ramshackle place, but well designed from the point of view of musical effect, with fine resonant acoustics." He described the orchestra pit as not extending as far into the auditorium as in Paris, but extending much farther on either side with the "more vehement" instruments—trombones, trumpets, timpani, bass drum—"partly overhung" by the first row of boxes, which cut off "their extreme reverberations."[37] Such a position for the brass and percussion has already been noticed in other German theaters.

Gassner's plan for the Berlin Opera House (fig. 70) was replicated in another source which dates it as 1840.[38] Still another source dates it as ca. 1845 under Meyerbeer.[39] The shape of the orchestral area suggests that here is another plan where the audience is furthest from the reader, the stage closest to him. The conductor here is near the audience; the first violins are to the right; the seconds to the left. (Could such a disposition have influenced Wagner's much later Bayreuth placement?) The percussion are under the boxes as in Berlioz's description, with the harp to the front where it can be easily heard. But the cellos are oddly dispersed throughout the orchestra, as are also the basses—a relic of former practices. It is in some ways reminiscent of Berlioz's concert plan with cellos and basses on both wings. But again there is a bass position right in the center, as has so often been seen. In many ways this anticipates the La Scala plan of ca. 1890.

Kling provided the plan shown in figure 71 for the Royal Opera House in Berlin in 1887. The shape of the stage makes it obvious that this is not the same building as is depicted in Gassner's plan, unless Gassner erred in picturing a straight instead of a curved stage. Here the conductor is not so far back as in

Figure 70.   Berlin, Opera House, 1840s

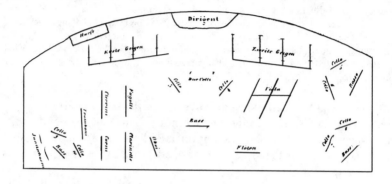

Source: Gassner/DIRIGENT, Beilage no. 9.

Figure 71.   Berlin, Royal Opera, 1887
For the centennial anniversary performance of *Don Giovani* the strings
numbered 12 first and 10 second violins, 8 violas, 8 cellos and 6 double basses.

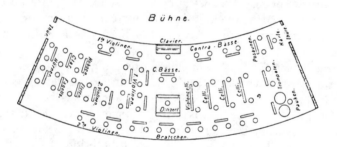

Source: Kling/VOLLKOMMENE, p. 272.

the previous plan, and there are violas behind him. The violins are all on one
side, suggesting another reversion from the plan tin the 1840s. If the brass and
percussion are placed for muffling by boxes here, one has to wonder why the
harp would also be with them. One notes the horns on the far left side from the
other brass, with the woodwinds, as had so often been the case. Here again the
basses are in the center and along the stage wall, suggesting some depth to the
pit.

Nösselt provided three plans for the theater at Leipzig for the first half of
the century (fig. 72). In all three plans the conductor is in about the same
position at the base of the stage—a position common in many places at this
time. The two earlier of the three plans show the type of division between

Figure 72. Leipzig, Three Plans, 1830s and 1840s

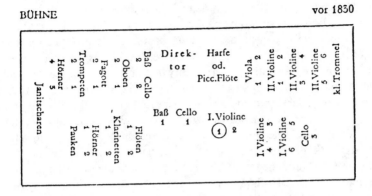

BÜHNE   vor 1830

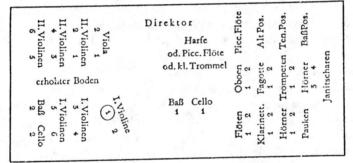

BÜHNE   neue Plazierung durch Dorn: 15.6.1830

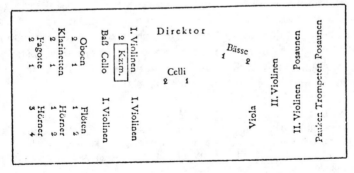

BÜHNE   neue Plazierung: 1844

Source: Nösselt/GEWANDHAUS, p. 269.

strings and winds one has become used to in opera seating at this time. But where the strings were at the right before 1830, the positions were reversed under Dorn in 1830, probably in an attempt to turn their f-holes more towards the audience. In the first two plans the first chairs of cello and bass are in the center, probably for continuo use in recitative. The seating of the second chairs of these instruments to the left with the woodwinds is unusual: they are divorced from the other strings—probably to help spread the beat around, an idea that still reflects Rousseau's stressing of the importance of the bass instruments for such a purpose. If the distance between the piccolo and the other flutes in the first plan seems odd, it is undoubtedly because the harpist doubled on piccolo. The choice was either to seat him with the strings or with the winds, perhaps depending on which instrument demanded his services with the greater frequency. Doubling also probably explains the positioning of the small drum behind the strings on the right; a violinist most likely filled in in on this instrument when needed. Note that under Dorn in 1830, the harpist doubled on drum as well as piccolo and was then seated with the other woodwinds.[40] Particularly noticeable in the 1844 plan is the division between first and second violins, putting Leipzig in a more up-to-date position in this respect. But basses and cellos are still spread around. One also notes that horns are on the left with the woodwinds rather than with the brass and percussion on the right.

Puzzling in the above regard is F. L. Schubert's comment in 1873 concerning the Leipzig theater. After discussing the problem with the F-holes when violins and violas were seated on the right, he went on to say, "It was earlier also thus but was later changed; violins and violas now sit on the left side of the director."[41] While this problem offers the most logical reason for Dorn's changes in 1830, it makes one wonder if Schubert was unaware of the changes in 1844, or if later changes reverted to an earlier setup. Concert plans from Leipzig in these later years would make one doubt that the separation between the violin sections had been given up in the theater.

The likelihood that the 1830 plan with strings to the left and even more so the 1844 plan with divided violins were "modern" for German opera houses at this time is suggested by Berlioz's remarks on Frankfurt in 1842. He had been discussing the makeup of the Frankfurt orchestra.

> The identical force of 47 players is, with minor variations, found in every German town of the second rank. So is the arrangement of the orchestras: violins, violas and cellos together on the right; basses in a straight line in the middle against the footlights; flutes, oboes, clarinets, bassoons, horns and trumpets grouped on the left opposite the strings; and drums and trombones by themselves at the back on the right.[42]

Elliott Galkin has drawn a layout based on Berlioz's remarks (fig. 73). The sections probably were not so concentrated and did not leave such a gap in the

Figure 73. Frankfurt Layout, 1841

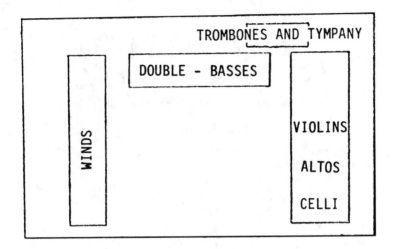

TROMBONES AND TYMPANY

DOUBLE - BASSES

WINDS

VIOLINS

ALTOS

CELLI

Source: Galkin/CONDUCTING, p. 628.

center of the pit. One also wonders if the violins would have been close to the audience, reversing the positions with the cellos as drawn.

Gassner's plan for the Court Theater at Darmstadt in the 1840s is shown in figure 74. Since the print is somewhat unclear in places and difficult to read, perhaps it is well to present Schünemann's redrawing of it also (fig. 75). Again the conductor is at the base of the stage. (Smart had him sitting sideways facing right in 1825.)[43] Here strings are left for good f-hole direction and winds are on the right, with the louder brass and percussion on the far right. But the first violins and violas would seem to be facing the stage, obviating any f-hole advantage. There is a hint of the "modern" positions of first and second violins, that is, towards opposite sides, but with the firsts taking more of an archaic position here on the right.

Gassner's plan for the theater orchestra at Hessen-Kassel in the 1840s is given in figure 76. Again the conductor is at the stage with the orchestra all presumably facing him. The strings are to the left except for the cellos and basses which spill over to the right side, another case of basses in the center of the pit. The percussion is to the left behind the strings with the exception of the timpani which are on the right with the heavy brass. The horns are interestingly in a position bridging either brass or woodwinds, and yet almost off by themselves.

Gassner also provided a plan for the Court Theater in Munich (fig. 77). Here the conductor is in the middle of the orchestra. The basses lined up

Figure 74.   Darmstadt, Court Theater, 1840s

Source: Gassner/DIRIGENT, Beilage no. 11.

Figure 75.   Darmstadt, Another Drawing

Source: Schünemann/DIRIGIERENS, p. 313.

against the stage seem to face out, while the piccolo, cellos 3 and 4, and first violins 1 and 2 face the stage. All the other players face the conductor from either side. This case is almost the exact opposite to Kassel; the strings are on the right here, despite any f-hole problem. The cellos and basses spread across towards the opposite side. But the horns here are integrated more with the woodwinds, though still adjacent to the heavier brass. Note that in smaller operas, the trombones would move into the places of the third through sixth trumpets. But here is another case where the curve of the stage would make one wonder whether this should be seen from the opposite direction, that is, with the stage in the same position as the reader. Then everything pointed out would be reversed. However, Heinz Becker incorporated a sketch in his article for MGG,[44] based on a drawing left by the Munich clarinetist Carl Baermann which was prepared for Meyerbeer and used by him to reorder the Berlin Court Opera Orchestra. That sketch is almost exactly the same as this, except

Figure 76. Hessen-Kassel, Hoftheater, 1840s

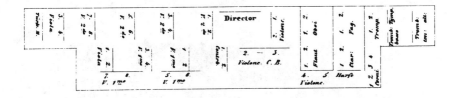

Source: Gassner/DIRIGENT, Beilage no. 8.

Figure 77. Munich, Hoftheater, 1840s

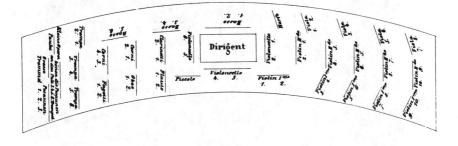

Source: Gassner/DIRIGENT, Beilage no. 14.

for small details such as a tuba in the lower left-hand corner, but the curve is the opposite way, suggesting that the stage is away from the reader. Once again one is alerted to the possibilities of inaccuracy in research of this type. In the latter sketch, the trombones also replace the fifth and sixth trumpets, as marked in the Gassner plan for small operas.

A picture of the London Royal Theater in 1843 (fig. 78) perhaps makes a bit clearer how elevated the conductor might be in his position behind the prompter's box, as well as the way the players faced in order to see him. The picture of Costa conducting at Covent garden in 1847 (fig. 79) shows a similar situation from the side. Quite obviously the British did not share the German propensity for placing double basses in the middle to obscure audience view. A picture of Castle Garden in New York in the mid-nineteenth century (fig. 80) suggests that the European—probably mostly British—influence was strong in the United States. Here the conductor is greatly elevated and probably could easily be seen by the orchestra as well as the singer/actors on stage. The picture of Verdi conducting a performance of *Aïda* in Paris (fig. 81)

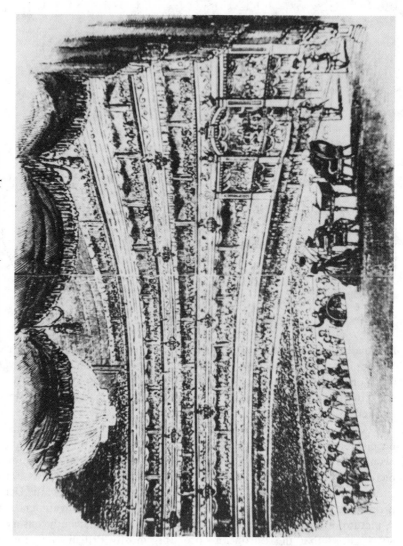

Figure 78. London, Royal Theater, 1843
Source: From Carse/BEETHOVEN, p. 170.

Figure 79.   London, Covent Garden, 1847
Source: From Carse/BEETHOVEN, p. 386.

Figure 80.   New York, Castle Garden, Mid-Century
Source: Schonberg/CONDUCTORS, p. 76.

Figure 81. Verdi Conducting *Aïda* in Paris
Source: Lang & Bettmann/ PICTORIAL, p. 152.

once again illustrates the position of the conductor at the base of the stage: here he turns to control the orchestral players, while they are facing him rather than the audience.

Kling's plan for the Opéra in Paris, shown in figure 82, was sent to him by Ernest Eugène Altès, who was deputy-conductor at the Opéra from 1871 and chief conductor from 1879 to 1887. In this plan, the first and second violins are left and right, as might be expected. But the cellos and basses are at the center in front of the audience, and the basses are at both wings as well. The violas at the left might lend some antiphonal effect in contrast to the cellos, though such was probably not as important as the fact of the two violin sections. The

Figure 82. Paris, Opéra, 1870s and 1880s
In this orchestra, the strings numbered 12 first and 11 second violins, 8 violas, 10 cellos and 8 double basses.

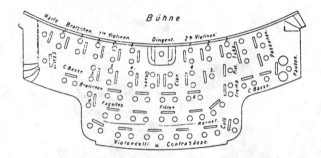

Source: Kling/ VOLLKOMMENE, p. 273.

harp is at the far left with the strings. One wonders whether the heavy brass and percussion at the far right were damped by any overhang. The horns have an interesting position across the front. Since the conductor was still at the base of the stage—this not having changed since Habeneck's time—one would presume that the bassoons and flutes, horns and cellos and basses faced the stage, while the others faced inwards.

That Wagner's music dramas represent the paragon of nineteenth-century orchestral writing, the fulfillment of the romantic ideal, should find little argument. In a similar way the arrangement of the orchestra in the *Festspielhaus* at Bayreuth can be considered an ideal example of orchestral seating as well as of orchestral size. Wagner had already spent a creative lifetime mulling over and wrestling with problems of the orchestra, from a practical as well as a creative standpoint. His interest in the arrangement of the orchestra has already been alluded to in the discussion of Spontini's seating, as well as the 1872 performance of the Beethoven Ninth Symphony at Bayreuth. Presumably in designing the *Festspielhaus*, Wagner could not only have had whatever size orchestra he desired, but he was also in a position to design the ideal seating for it. It has already been seen that the size and makeup of the Bayreuth orchestra became decisive for Richard Strauss, and one can assume its influence on major orchestras and conductors—Theodore Thomas stands out as a "local" example. It is a cause for lament that Wagner's Bayreuth seating has not had more of a continued influence on twentieth-century performances of romantic music outside Bayreuth.

Back in 1844 Wagner had complained of the seating for concert purposes in Dresden. He found "inconceivably stupid" the way the orchestra was arranged "in a long, thin, semicircular row round the chorus." He was told that these arrangements dated from the period of the late Italian composer/conductor Morlacchi, Weber's old nemesis, who Wagner felt had "no true realization of the importance of the orchestra." Wagner was made to realize the difficulties Weber had had and warned that even then after so many years had passed since the deaths of both men, he would not easily prevail against these practices, "because the opinion still prevailed in the highest circles that he [Morlacchi] must have understood best what he was about."[45] Poor Weber! Even in death he had not won out at Dresden.

But in 1846 Wagner evidently had his own way for a performance of the Ninth Symphony, even extending to a "complete reconstruction of the hall" in order to "obtain good acoustic conditions for the orchestra" which he arranged "according to quite a new system of my own." With a "totally new construction of the platform" he was able to "concentrate the whole of the orchestra towards the centre, and surround it, in amphitheatre fashion, by the throng of singers" who were placed on "seats very considerably raised." He found it "not only of great advantage to the powerful effect of the choir, but it also gave great precision and energy to the finely organised orchestra in the purely symphonic movements."[46] And in 1848 Wager went to great lengths to improve orchestral concerts in the theater. "By a special device of my own the stage of the theatre was made into a concert-hall (afterwards considered first-class) by means of a sounding-board enclosing the whole orchestra, which proved a great success."[47] And in 1860 in Paris, Wagner ran into problems preparing a concert in Herz Hall, problems which he attributed to a "faulty setting up of the orchestra." In correcting it he arrived at the hall early and "superintended the arranging of the desks myself."[48] So by the time Bayreuth was designed, Wagner had had much experience and had devoted considerable thought and experiment to the matter of orchestral seating. In her editorial comments on some Wagner letters, Caroline Kerr suggests that such thought and experience were not without fruits.

> On the 1st of August, 1875, the orchestral and ensemble rehearsals began.
> It was then that the effect of the invisible orchestra was tested. Wagner assigned his musicians their place in the "mystic abyss," according to the arrangement which to-day is so convincing. The strings were placed under the upper sounding-board, the harps and woodwinds in the uncovered space, in order that their delicate quality might assert itself, and the brasses and instruments of percussion were relegated to a position under the stage projection, in order that the aggressiveness of their tone might be modified. The results justified in the highest degree the expectations of Wagner and the assembled listeners. The volume of sound surprised by its ideal tonal beauty; everything material seemed to have been fully eliminated, and every figuration, even in the middle voices, came out with startling distinctness. The most painstaking effort was expended upon every detail of the performance.[49]

Figure 83.   Bayreuth, Section of the Orchestra

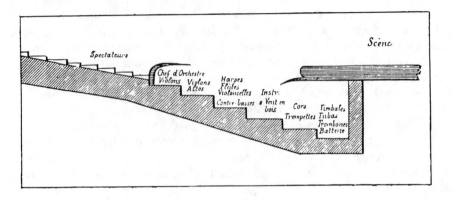

Source: Lavignac/BAYREUTH 1, p. 85; also available in Lavignac/BAYREUTH 2, p. 61.

The idea of an invisible orchestra does not seem to have been entirely new with Wagner. Haas quoted Gassner as claiming that an invisible orchestra in church would be very "edifying" and in the theater would "undoubtedly contribute to an elevation of the expression."[50] Haas also stated that Karl Friedrich Schinkel desired a sunken orchestra for Berlin as early as 1817, even providing a sketch for it.[51] Haas also claimed that Verdi showed himself in favor of a lowered orchestra in a letter on *Aïda* to Ricordi in 1871, and that even before Schinkel a certain L. Catel recommended such in 1802 for improving the Schauspielhaus in Berlin. Also, de Marette had suggested lowering the orchestra in a memoir in Paris in 1775! And according to Schinkel, Count C. di Benevello in Turin had put forth a plan for lowering the orchestra entirely under the stage floor in 1841.[52]

The sketch appearing in figure 83 shows the sunken space at Bayreuth better than words can describe it. The same source also provides a clear verbal description.

> The orchestra, which is made invisible by means of a double screen, which partly covers it, is arranged upon steps, which are a continuation of those of the spectators, and descend a long way under the stage as into a kind of cave, which has received the name of the "mysterious space," or the "mystic abyss." There the instruments are grouped by families, exactly as at large symphony concerts, except that things are reversed, the conductor and violins being above, and the noisy instruments below at the back; moreover, the first violins are to the right, and the second to the left; it is simply an ordinary orchestra reversed.[53]

Figure 84. Bayreuth, Seating Plan

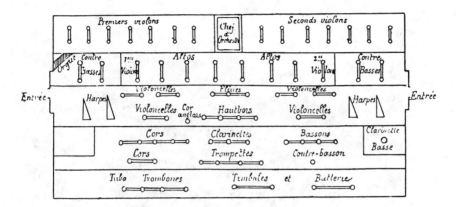

Source: Lavignac/BAYREUTH 1, p. 86; also available in Lavignac/BAYREUTH 2, p. 62.

One can see in the sketch that the heavier brass and percussion are under the overhang of the stage. One can only wonder why Wagner chose to reverse the positions of the two violin sections from that which had become common in his time; if he ever stated his reasons, they have not come to light. But conversations with Dr. Joel Sheveloff have suggested a probable basis. When in concert orchestras the first violins are to the audience's right with the seconds to the left, the seconds are afforded a chance for their usually lower parts to come through by the more advantageous positioning of their f-holes. But in the case of Bayreuth, Sheveloff points out that the f-holes of the first violins would be aimed at the opening above, making them more brilliant, while the f-holes of the seconds would be aimed more at the overhanging shield. It makes much sense.

Lavignac has provided a very detailed seating plan for the orchestra (fig. 84). Indeed, the first violins are to the right of the conductor. But no antiphonal separation between violas and the lower strings is evident; instead the cellos and basses are on both wings in a manner reminiscent of Berlioz's plan. The harps have been treated likewise. The horns once again take a position linking them to both woodwinds and brass. For the interested reader, Lavignac's fine little report has other sketches which further elucidate the way the orchestra is situated in relation to the structure as a whole.[54] The cartoon in figure 85 gives one a better spatial idea of the orchestral arrangement at Bayreuth.

Figure 85. Bayreuth, Cartoon of Seating
Source: Lang & Bettmann/PICTORIAL, p. 138.

Figure 86. Bayreuth, Seating for *Parsifal*

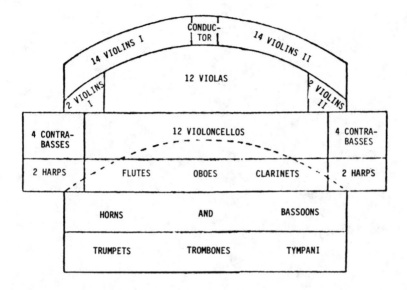

Source: *New York Herald,* 1882, here reproduced from Galkin/CONDUCTING, p. 630.

That there was room for some spatial variation from one performance to another is suggested by a plan for a performance of *Parsifal* (fig. 86). If this sketch is correct, the cellos have been spread right across the third row, the flutes, oboes, and clarinets taking the row behind them, while the horns and bassoons share the next one. The trumpets have dropped back with the trombones and timpani which have moved to the conductor's left, an arrangement which would seem superior anyway.

15

Festival Seating

Seating an orchestra and chorus for a festival might at first thought seem to be just an extension of concert seating. But even the size such forces usually take and the ensuing necessity for spreading them out would seem to offer special problems. Just the problem of the choir alone raises questions: should they be behind the orchestra, surrounding them, off to one side, or even in front of the players? Many variants will be found in festival seating, as has been the case heretofore.

Perhaps the first performance of Haydn's *Creation* at the Imperial Burgtheater in Vienna is a good place to start, although strictly speaking it did not take place in the nineteenth century. Johan Fredrik Berwald and his father, cousins of the composer Franz, were in Vienna at the time and Johan left the following description of the performance.

> When we entered, we saw that the stage proper was set up in the form of an amphitheatre. Down below at the fortepiano sat *Kapellmeister* Weigl, surrounded by the vocal soloists, the chorus, a violoncello and a double bass [as continuo]. At one level higher stood Haydn himself with his conductor's baton. Still a level higher on one side were the first violins, led by Paul Wranitzky and on the other the second violins, led by his brother Anton Wranitzky. In the centre: violas and double basses. In the wings, more double basses; on higher levels the wind instruments, and at the very top: trumpets, kettledrums and trombones. That was the disposition of the orchestra which, together with the chorus, consisted of some 400 persons. The whole went off wonderfully.[1]

This passage suggests that Haydn was conducting in the modern manner, with a baton, although as noted previously, it was not uncommon even in the baroque for someone to beat time in performances including chorus and orchestra, especially when these forces were numerous and spread out. The two violin sections were in the "modern" manner, on each side. The double basses make one think of the Berlioz plan which perhaps was derived from setups such as this.

There is a rather extended description of a festival at Frankenhausen which was conducted by Spohr on June 20-21, 1810, featuring the *Creation* by

Haydn as well as another concert. According to the description, the group occupied an arch formed by two galleries "in front of and under" the organ, "thus the whole width of the church." On the lowest gallery which projected "a good bit" a special platform was built for the instruments "in stepwise elevation" with Spohr at the mid-point. On his right stood the first violins in two rows, taking up half the width of the church. To his left were the three solo singers near the keyboard, followed by the "whole wind choir of 27 artists," also in two rows, with the clarinets and flutes forward, the oboes, bassoons and "basshorn" in the rear row. This took up the other half of the church's width, so the trumpets and horns stood "directly on the flutes" at the beginning of the side gallery. The second violins and violas formed the third line of the orchestra across the whole width of the church with the second violins behind the first and the violas behind the winds. A fourth line behind the violins accommodated the rest of the second violins. Directly behind Spohr in the middle of this line on the first riser were the two leaders of the basses (probably one as cellist, the other as double bass). The remaining basses (undoubtedly including the cellos) were behind them on a second riser divided in two rows. To the left of the basses behind the winds were the timpani. The chorus occupied the upper organ gallery across the whole width of the church, with the altos and basses to Spohr's right above the violins and the "descants" and tenors to the left, "each part raised in two rows behind one another." The trombones followed the descants and tenors, but on the side gallery directly over the horns and trumpets. "This beautiful and practical placing, whereby each one had enough space around himself and the director constantly before his eyes had unquestionably no little bearing on the excellent performance of so big, partly new and most difficult works after only one rehearsal, as were performed especially on the 2d day."[2] Of course, one difficulty here is trying to guess which way Spohr was facing. The conductor at this time seldom turned his back on the audience, so if the first violins were on his right, it may have meant on the audience's left. In any case, the two violin sections were on the same side, the seconds behind the firsts. But if they were on the right, they probably faced forward so that there was little if any resonance problem resulting from f-hole direction, unlike in the opera. All in all, this arrangement seems to have included strings on the right, then woodwinds on their right, followed by brass and timpani on the far left. By "basses" the author undoubtedly meant cellos and double basses, since elsewhere the author named the leader of the cellos and that of the contrabasses.[3] The chorus here was behind the orchestra on a higher elevation.

Figure 87 shows a seating plan for an 1812 performance of Handel's *Timotheus* in Vienna involving 590 performers. Here the choir was in front of the orchestra, in contrast to the situation at Frankhausen. The wind groups at the front do suggest concertino use; besides cellos and basses, that on the right

Figure 87. Vienna, Handel's *Timotheus*, 1812

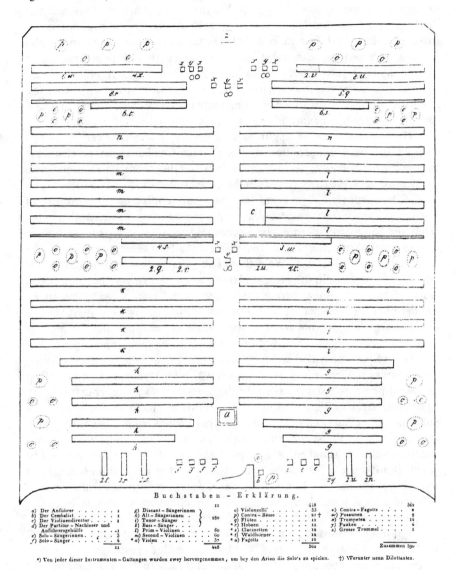

Buchstaben - Erklärung.

a) Der Anführer 1
b) Der Cembalist 1
c) Der Violinendirector 1
d) Der Partitur – Nachleser und
   Anführersgehülfe 1
e) Solo – Sängerinnen 5
f) Solo – Sänger 4
                          ‾‾11

g) Discant – Sängerinnen ⎫
h) Alt – Sängerinnen . . ⎬ 280
i) Tenor – Sänger . . . ⎭
k) Bass – Sänger . . . .
l) Prim – Violinen 60
m) Second – Violinen 60
*n) Violen 57
                          ‾‾448

o) Violoncelli 53
p) Contra – Bässe . . . . . . 27 †
q) Flöten 10
*r) Hoboen 12
*s) Clarinetten 12
*t) Waldhörner 12
*u) Fagotts 12

v) Contra – Fagotts 2
w) Posaunen 9
x) Trompeten 12
y) Pauken 4
z) Grosse Trommel 1

                    Zusammmen 590

*) Von jeder dieser Instrumenten – Gattungen wurden zwey hervorgenommen, um bey den Arien die Solo's zu spielen.   †) Worunter neun Dilettanten.

Source: AMZ, XIV (1812), facing cols. 853–54.

is also supported by two violas. Cellos and basses are sprinkled around the orchestra, reminding one of eighteenth century Dresden and Rousseau; but then why not? The work dates from an earlier period, deserving idiomatic treatment. But there is here a definite separation between the two violin sections with the first on the right, still in an eighteenth century manner, but in that of the later classic rather than baroque setting, counteracting any real idiomatic baroque treatment! However, there are also violas on both sides, and wind groups are sprinkled here and there throughout the orchestra, as are timpani. This is a very interesting and quite unusual arrangement.

The interested reader might want to peruse an alternate version of this same concert plan as reproduced by Haas.[4] It has small discrepancies from the present plan, especially spatial discrepancies, but they seem to be minor. Some easily noticed: Were there four as in the present plan or five male solo singers at the left front? The spacing of the small concertino-like groups of instruments at the front varies from one plan to the other, as well as that of the cellos and basses on the front wings at both sides; the present plan has them as distinct groups; the other makes two cellos and a bass seem more a part of the "concertino" on each side. Were there five rows of first violins and one of violas on the right as in the present plan, or was it four rows of first and two of violas? One sees a similar problem with the second violins and violas on the left between the two plans. And most obviously, the present plan has the overall shape longer from front to rear, while in the other one the width is longer in measurement. And both plans seem to be contemporary.

Louis Spohr provided an interesting report of an open-air concert during the Congress of Vienna in 1814, a concert which took place as a festival affair for the emperor's guests. It was an evening program in a palace courtyard with a platform setup for the orchestra and chorus in the middle, surrounded by tall buildings. The Court and retinue faced the performers from a balcony with the general public in the space remaining in the courtyard. Spohr was to play a concerto but was "shocked" at the space and crowd, fearing he would not be heard. But it went "better than I had expected." The tall buildings acted as a sounding board and Spohr's violin "had its usual strength and brilliance" and "every nuance could be heard plainly" with the effect being "most favorable."[5] A most unusual and perhaps unique success for music outdoors!

Spohr also reported on a Swiss Music Festival held at Fribourg in 1815. While he does not go into detail, his description does point up the problem that can arise from the physical inflexibility of the organ. It was a performance of Haydn's *Creation* in mid-afternoon. The "auditorium was satisfactory, and the orchestra well placed, the only disadvantage being that the organ, situated at the opposite end, could not be used." Spohr also noted that at former festivals the performers had numbered at least three hundred, but that on this occasion there were "hardly two hundred" with more than half in the chorus.

He claimed that the orchestra, "particularly in the big choral episodes, was much too weak. Indeed, it was at times inaudible."[6]

Of course, even the sparsest description of Mendelssohn's famous performance of the *St. Matthew Passion* in 1829 has to be of interest. That left by Eduard Devrient is not very detailed but somewhat informative. He says that when the orchestra was in place, a piano was placed across the stage between the two choirs, for "it was then not yet customary for the conductor to turn his back to the audience." This would suggest that Mendelssohn must have conducted from a position at the piano, on which he probably also played the secco recitatives (one wonders about continuo while he was conducting). This placed the first choir behind him while he faced the second and the orchestra. The winds were at the back, "above the semicircular [*"amphitheatralischen"*] platform" and extending "towards the small concert-room through three open doors. The task of keeping steady this waving mass devolved upon Eduard Rietz."[7] This sounds as though the winds flowed over into an adjoining room, perhaps an effective way of offering some muffling. According to Ferdinand Hiller, Mendelssohn turned his right side to the orchestra.[8] This would have put the first choir to the right and the orchestra on the left, it would seem. It is too bad that this description is not more explicit. One would have expected, for example, that the orchestra also would have been divided in two for antiphonal effect.

Ignaz Moscheles described the 1834 Handel Festival in Westminster Abbey as taking place in the nave, which was covered with boards. The orchestra was opposite the Royal box, with the solo singers in front, then the small chorus of 40 voices, with Sir George Smart, the director, close to this choir at a piano. Behind him the orchestra was in tiers with the cellos on either side, the violins in the center, and then the winds. There was a "magnificent" organ built for the occasion arranged so that the organist faced the director instead of the organ. The large chorus was packed in the side "aisles and niches" so that "to a part of the audience" it was "smothered" by the orchestra. In other sections of the Abbey "the effect was reversed, and the performance as a whole could only be enjoyed in a small part of the vast building."[9] This is another case of an orchestra being behind a chorus that was spread around the sides.

The festival concert in Paris in 1840 organized and conducted by Berlioz brings to the fore problems of distance which can arise in such an undertaking. Berlioz had a combined chorus and orchestra of six hundred. On the program were the first act of Gluck's *Iphigénie en Tauride,* a scene from Handel's *Athalia,* the *Dies irae* and *Lacrymosa* from Berlioz's own *Requiem,* the Apotheosis from his *Symphonie funèbre et triomphale,* the adagio, scherzo, and finale from *Roméo et Juliette,* and an unaccompanied work for chorus by Palestrina. At the final rehearsal, all went "reasonably well" except for the

Queen Mab scherzo which was "rashly" included on the program. "The piece is too swift to be performed by an orchestra of this size, nor should it be." He found it "virtually impossible" to keep the extremities of such huge forces together. The players farthest from the conductor kept getting behind the "very rapid beat." Berlioz said he was so agitated that it never occurred to him to have the piece performed by a "small picked orchestra which, concentrated near me in the middle of the stage, could have carried out my intentions without difficulty." After the "most fearful struggles" the piece was removed from the program. He also noticed that the "little cymbals in B flat and F" dragged when they were at a distance from him. "I had stupidly left them at the back of the stage, next to the drums, and despite everything I could do they were sometimes as much as a bar behind." After that experience, Berlioz was careful "to place them right beside me, and the difficulty has vanished."[10]

Gassner provided a detailed plan for a performance of Haydn's *Creation* in Vienna in 1843 (fig. 88). Here is a case of the chorus being in front of and surrounded by the orchestra instead of vice-versa. It would seem that the solo voices and at least a good part of the choral altos and sopranos would have great difficulty in seeing the "Erster Director," The cellos and basses surrounding him were undoubtedly for continuo use in the recitatives. Other cellos and basses are on the wings as well as along the rear wall. Neither are the brass or woodwinds concentrated in one place, but they also appear in clusters here and there. The two horns at the left front are with trumpets and brass, but the ten at the rear seem to be aligned with clarinets and flutes. The first violins are right, the seconds left; both they and the violas have ripieno strength evidently saved for the big places. The violas run right across the orchestra with no apparent attempt at concentration.

Gassner also gave a setup for the festival at Darmstadt in 1844 (fig. 89). Elsewhere he stated that the personnel were placed amphitheatrically.[11] Here is another case of the chorus surrounding the orchestra. As for the orchestra, although the violins are placed left and right, there is no real separation between them. "Basso" here undoubtedly includes both cellos and basses. One finds a pair in front for recitative work; the remainder range towards the rear on the right side from the audience's point of view. The horns join the heavy brass with the woodwind choir.

Sir George Smart was at the festival in Bonn in 1845 for the unveiling of Beethoven's statue. He gave a plan of the then new *Festhalle,* which was built in eleven days (fig. 90). Of course, this is completely lacking in detail, but fortunately Smart did give some clues in his text. In fact, the following is quite explicit on some points.

Figure 88.   Vienna, Haydn's *Creation*, 1843

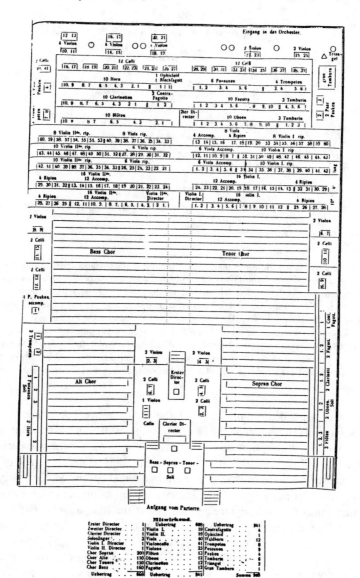

Source: Gassner/DIRIGENT, Beilage no. 1 (here reduced in size).

Figure 89. Darmstadt, Festival, 1844

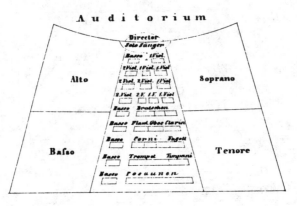

Source: Gassner/DIRIGENT, Beilage no. 6.

The following description is taken when looking to the orchestra, which was much too low, and the platform did not rise sufficiently, indeed it was more of a slope than rising. All the chorus were in the front, which was bad, for the band could not penetrate through them, being too low and too far back. The conductor was in a handsome pulpit, his desk was placed to face the primo side. The leader was not situated as at the Philharmonic but nearly according to our former plan, not elevated. The four principal singers were on the secondo side, much elevated and rather behind the conductor, who had to turn round to them and to turn to the secondo side when necessary. The principal singers should have been on the primo side and the conductor should have been a little in advance, with his back to the public.[12]

Elwart, who seemed more pleased with the performance, confirmed much of this description. He said that the chorus numbered four hundred. But he felt that the violins, violas, and basses, "although very numerous, were still not strong enough." He gave the number of instruments as nearly four hundred. He claimed to have "never heard so perfect a vocal ensemble. Germany had sent the flower of her singers." He described them as on the proscenium and encircling the conductor, in front of whom sat the solo singers. The "choirs, among whom the prettiest eyes in the world were casting quick flashes, performed with a warmth, a charm and a stunning brilliance!"[13] Smart had earlier commented on a rehearsal of Beethoven's *Mass in C* and a cantata by Liszt, conducted respectively by Spohr and Liszt: "They both conducted from a tall closed-up pulpit, the conductor's back to the secondo side, a bad plan this."[14] This is reminiscent of Mendelssohn's position for the *St. Matthew*

Figure 90. Bonn, Beethoven Festival, 1845

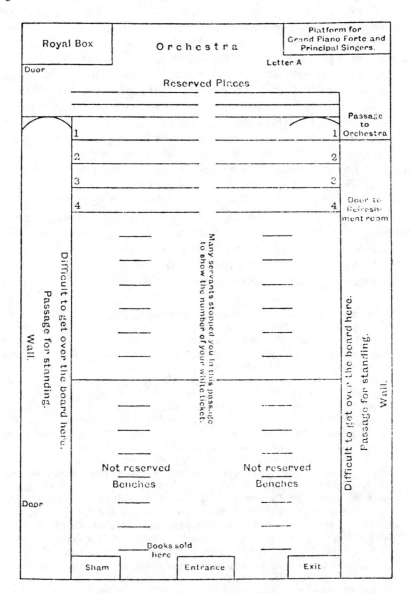

Source: Smart/JOURNALS, p. 313.

Passion; Spohr and Liszt evidently had their right side to the performers also. But "primo" and "secondo" also suggest that the first violins were to the left and the seconds to the right.

A picture of a performance of Beethoven's *Choral Fantasy,* though not detailed, does give a general picture of practice around 1850 (fig. 91). The conductor has his right side to the orchestra, which is "draped" around him and the piano soloist. Some of the players at the right face him rather than the audience in order to see. The chorus is on a lower level; one has to wonder if they can see the conductor at all!

Berlioz told how positioning and seating had an effect on a festival performance he conducted in 1855. Prince Napoleon had put him in charge of organizing a "vast concert" to be held at the Exhibition in the Palace of Industrial Products. "I had twelve hundred performers, accommodated in a gallery behind the throne. In this position they made little effect.... We had moved the orchestra down into the lower part of the hall and arranged it in proper fashion, and the effect was excellent."[15]

The following excerpts from a description of Gilmore's Peace Jubilee of 1869 which was held in Boston may not contribute anything of solidity to this discussion, but perhaps the reader will be at least amused.

> Gilmore was just the sort of man into whose head would come buzzing the idea that the nation should have a big, rollicking family jubilee to celebrate the happy state of the country. Boston was the place above all places in which to hold it. . . . Accordingly a wooden building of good acoustic properties was promptly erected on the Back Bay lands, near or on the site of the present Art Museum,—a building capable of holding fifty thousand persons, including a big chorus of ten thousand and a great orchestra of one thousand. . . . A great organ was built for the occasion; also a bass drum, the head of which might have been ten or twenty feet in diameter. . . . Returning to details, it will surprise many to know that the orchestra numbered quite a thousand—with the patriotic Ole Bull at the head of the violins, and Carl Rosa playing at the same desk. Gilmore had engaged all the principal sopranos of Boston, constituting a "bouquet of artistic singers." These were placed on a special raised balcony between the orchestra and the chorus, and they sang in unison the *obbligato* parts as they occurred in the choral pieces. . . . But a chorus of ten thousand persons would naturally occupy a wide space, and they would inevitably drag the *tempo.* Mr. Zerrahn often had to show good generalship by rushing up the aisle which separated the two divisions of the big choral army in order to get near enough to beat the laggards into time.
>
> Mr. Gilmore was a modest and a wise man, and conducted but little of the music himself; but that little was great,—for did he not direct the "'Anvil Chorus"? Will Boston, or at least its Jubilee participators, ever forget the sensation it had when the one hundred firemen— each in his belt, helmet, and red flannel shirt, carrying a long-handled blacksmith's hammer at "right shoulder shift" like a musket—marched into the hall and onto the stage in two files of fifty, and then separated far enough to form a red frame for two sides of the orchestra, which meanwhile was playing the introduction to the "Anvil Chorus"? Reaching their special *real* anvils, the firemen faced the audience, lifted their hammers to the proper position, and at the right musical moment of time began to pound the anvils,—right, left, right, left,—while the great orchestra and chorus played and sang the melody.
>
> If ever "the welkin rang" it did then![16]

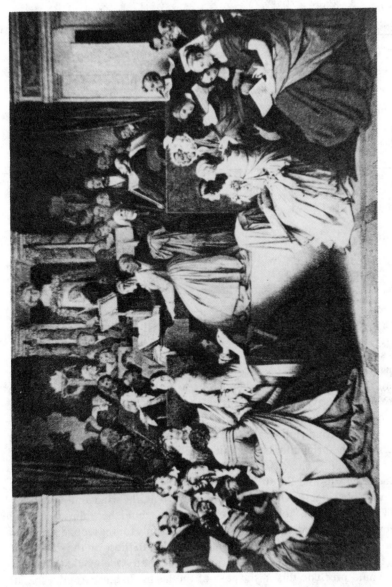

Figure 91. A Performance of Beethoven's Choral Fantasy, 1852
Source: Carse/ORCHESTRA, p. 35.

Figure 92. Gounod's *Rédemption*, Birmingham Festival, 1882

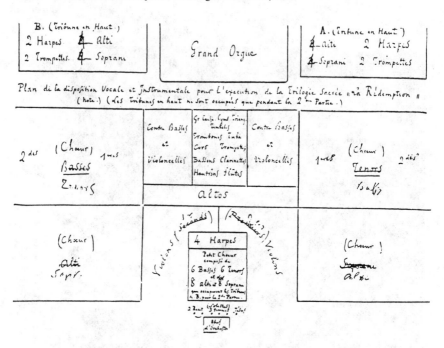

One is sure it did! While nothing of import is to be learned from this excerpt, perhaps it warns one what to avoid if one is serious about music.

Gounod provided his own sketch for seating the forces for a performance of *La Rédemption* at the Birmingham Festival of 1882 (fig. 92). It is interesting that he considered the first violins, sopranos, and tenors to belong on the same side, while the second violins, altos, and basses were to be on the opposite side. Furthermore, he originally had the first violins to the right and changed his mind at some point. There is a definite spatial division between the two limbs of the large chorus and the smaller choir which is right before the conductor behind the solo singers. The cellos and basses flank the wind and percussion on both sides, while the violas run across the stage behind the violins. Since the forces on the two raised galleries were to be there only for the second part, one wonders if the harps and trumpets were in addition to those on the stage, or if the latter were supposed to move during intermission. One would think that tuning would preclude this in the case of the harps. In any case, the spatial effect of the differing "points of origin," as Berlioz would have it, is obvious.

Figure 93. Rhine Festival Plan, 1880s

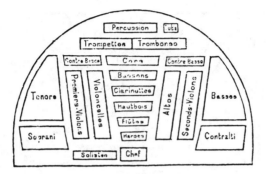

Source: Blitz/CHEF, p. 43.

Blitz found the plan, shown in figure 93, evidently that used for the Rhine festivals, at least in the 1880s, preferable to that propounded by Berlioz in the *Traité*. He felt it had better "homogeneity of sound." The stage was amphitheatrical with the percussion above, the conductor below, "but on a platform elevated enough so that he can dominate the whole orchestra and be seen by each musician."[17] The arrangement of the chorus around the orchestra, or more properly, separated in two by the orchestra is similar to that seen in Gounod's plan, with the sopranos and tenors on the same side as the first violins. But here, the violas and cellos are also separated by the woodwinds and horns; only the basses are in a position similar to that in Gounod's plan. Both harps and soloists are convenient to the conductor. This would seem a suitable plan for small forces, as well as admirable for large festivals.

Theodore Thomas placed seating among his highest priorities in preparing for a festival. "Finally, the orchestra must be prepared, scores corrected, bowing marked, extra parts copied, and diagrams made of platforms for both chorus and orchestra, and the seating arrangements required for the various concerts."[18] He used a novel arrangement for a festival in New York in 1882 which included an orchestra of three hundred and a chorus of three thousand. Speaking of the orchestra, he noted:

> I arranged them so that they formed a triple orchestra, similar to the three manuals of an organ, which I could play on singly or in combination at my pleasure. Of course the orchestra parts were all marked, and had been rehearsed accordingly, but in such an immense hall as that in which the festival was given, the difference in the acoustics when it

Figure 94. New York Festival, Thomas, 1882

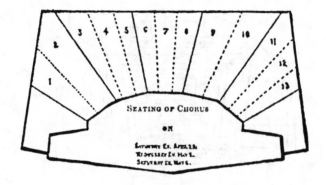

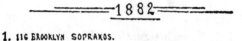

1. 116 BROOKLYN SOPRANOS.
   2. 112 NEW YORK SOPRANOS.
      3. 104 BROOKLYN 2². SOPRANOS.
         4. 80. NEW YORK 2². SOPRANOS.
            5. 47. BROOKLYN 2². TENORS.
               6. 46. NEW YORK 2². TENORS.
                  7. 35 BROOKLYN, 26 NEW YORK TENORS.
                     8. 42. BROOKLYN, 58. NEW YORK BASSOS. (2ᵈ)
                        9. 69. BROOKLYN, 66 NEW YORK BASSOS. (1ˢᵗ).
                           10. 75 BROOKLYN 1ˢᵗ. ALTOS.
                              11. 62 NEW YORK 1ˢᵗ ALTOS.
                                 12. 53. NEW YORK 2² ALTOS.
                                    13 40. BROOKLYN 2² ALTOS.

Source: Thomas/MEMOIRS, p. 226.

Figure 95. New York Festival, 1882, Alternate Plan

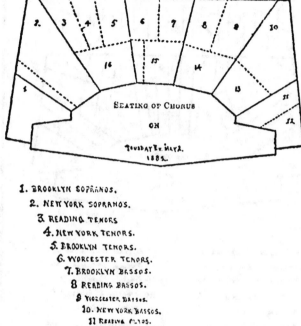

1. BROOKLYN SOPRANOS.
2. NEW YORK SOPRANOS.
3 READING TENORS
4. NEW YORK TENORS.
5. BROOKLYN TENORS.
6. WORCESTER TENORS.
7. BROOKLYN BASSOS.
8 READING BASSOS.
9 WORCESTER BASSOS.
10. NEW YORK BASSOS.
11 READING ALTOS.
12 WORCESTER ALTOS.
13. NEW YORK ALTOS.
14. BROOKLYN ALTOS.
15. READING SOPRANOS.
16. WORCESTER SOPRANOS.

Source: Thomas/MEMOIRS, p. 227.

Figure 96. New York Festival, 1882, Handel Seating

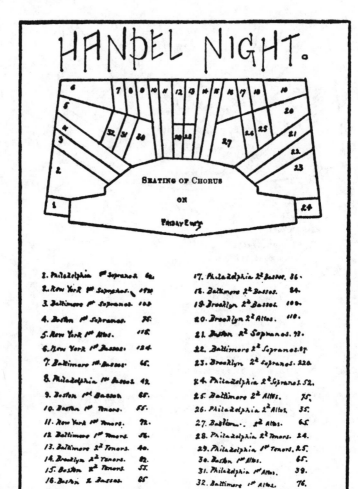

Figure 97.   Chicago, Festival, 1882

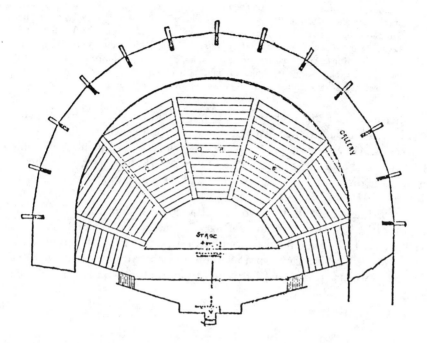

Source: Thomas/MEMOIRS, p. 238.

Figure 98.   Mainz, Handel Festival, 1895/97

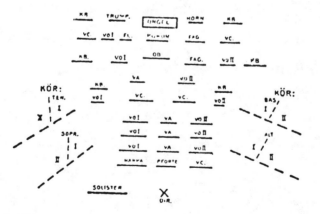

Source: Norling/DIRIGERINGS, p. 62.

was empty or when it was full of people was so great that I had to be prepared for any emergency. In the concerts I made good use of my combinations and accomplished some unusual shading by manipulating my triple orchestra, even in such works as the Jupiter Symphony of Mozart. Some of the works were given with overpowering effect, but others again, for instance the Beethoven Mass [*Missa solemnis*], disappointed me. The greatest and most enduring effect was made by the Wagner programme. This performance created the greatest excitement I ever witnessed in a concert. Considered from every point of view this festival was one of these unusual occasions which rarely come twice in a lifetime.[19]

Further details of this orchestral seating are unavailable, but several plans show the different arrangements he made for the huge chorus for differing programs. They were on graded platforms. Three plans for this New York festival are shown in figures 94-96. In all cases, Thomas spread the chorus behind the orchestra. Also included in his plan for a Chicago festival, also in 1882 (fig. 97).

And finally, a plan is shown for a Handel festival in Mainz late in the century (fig. 98). Here the chorus is again at the sides of the orchestra. The violas serve to separate the two violin sections. Again the high choral voices are at the left beside the first violins, the low choral voices right with the seconds. A cello, piano, and harp are at the front, obviously for continuo purposes.

16

Summary of Seating Practices

It is safe to conclude that there was great, even bewildering variety in manners of seating or standing in the nineteenth century orchestra. One would most probably expect the concert orchestra to represent the ideal disposition of the times, because space presented such serious, sometimes insurmountable problems in church and opera house. The outstanding exception to this is, of course, the Bayreuth Festspielhaus where Wagner was able to plan all details from below the ground upwards. The acoustical qualities of the hall in any particular case have often been put forward as an important factor in determining disposition. But perhaps even more important was the nature of the music to be performed, though it is far more difficult to isolate and articulate the pertinent data here that would affect disposition of performers; Berlioz was less than totally specific about these points, though he insisted that the music was central to the decisions concerning numbers of players as well as their arrangement on the stage.

Yet in the midst of all this diversity, some conclusions can be drawn, though with some caution. First of all, the conductor of the concert orchestra did not generally face the orchestra until late in the century. He was turned instead towards the public, or, like Mendelssohn, faced diagonally to one side, so that at least some of the performers were behind him. As a result, at any one time many players had an obstructed view of the beat and thus the conductor undoubtedly had to pivot a great deal. The awkwardness of this situation caused it to be changed in time, but with remarkable slowness.

In the opera house, the conductor seemed most often to be at the base of the stage near the prompter's box, with his back to the orchestra, facing the singers on the stage. This forced the players to face the stage as well, a practice which must have inhibited the possibility of optimum sound for the audience. Of course, it is quite possible that composers, used to such disposition, may have taken all this into account when scoring their works, adjusting balances within the orchestra and between orchestra and singers in accordance with this practice. It was only slowly and gradually that conductors moved back to the position at which they are presently located, the players at the same time gradually turning to face the public.

As described above, Berlioz emphasized "points of origin" as a basic principle of orchestral scoring. This study has led to the conviction that behind the diversity of the plans encountered, such a principle is a basic premise, though it is not possible at this time to elaborate on this matter in all points. But one fact stands out with clarity: the nearly universal separation of the two violin sections is the most important illustration of this principle, since the scores of the time are replete with dialogue between these two groups. However, the question of which is placed to the left and which to the right of the conductor, however basic it may appear to us now, must remain in doubt as a universal principle, since the Mendelssohn and Berlioz specifications are quite definite in placing the seconds to the left, a situation also encountered at Bayreuth (even though there the "mystic abyss" produced different results from such a setup). This is a question worthy of further study, both of scores as well as of secondary data surrounding actual performances. It seems quite probable at this time that a particular score as well as particular historical data will be needed to determine a given case, rather than reliance on a static disposition.

Individual locations are difficult to establish with certainty; some individual instruments and groups of instruments were often located in areas that seem bizarre by today's standards. Double basses in concert orchestras were often placed on the wings of the stage, or dispersed with the cellos around the orchestra, as if to preserve the eighteenth-century ideas of keeping the beat or having all players in close contact with the bass line. Such ideas strike us today as being anachronistic in the absence of a continuo and with a time-beating conductor. One is horrified to find basses even at the front of the stage or, even worse, at the front of the pit at the opera, certain to obstruct the audience's view of the stage as well as of the rest of the instrumental ensemble.

Some plans separate the violas from the cellos in a manner analogous to that of the placement of the two violin sections, but in the next rank. Again, which side belongs to the violas or cellos cannot be ascertained as a static principle; different plans show different solutions. But there are scores— Beethoven's *Eroica* Symphony and Tchaikovsky's *Pathétique* Symphony are outstanding examples—which demand such treatment from the lower as well as the upper string sections if the contrapuntal thematic wanderings are to have great effect.

The woodwinds present less controversy, though there are some divergences in location within the group as well as in relation to the brass. The brass and percussion instruments can only be said to be farthest from the audience; any further description of their relative weight or location cannot be reduced to a simple statement. The horns present an interesting case though.

They seem to be more often with or near the woodwinds, though in some plans they take a position linking the woodwinds and brass.

The question of these practices and twentieth-century performances of nineteenth-century music will be dealt with in the concluding part of this book. But it can be stated here that current performances seldom seem aware of or concerned with the rich diversity of location of sound sources and "points of origin" as practiced in the last century. And if recent scholarship in early performance practices has taught us that the sound-ideal of music at the time of its composition is worthy of restoration, often revealing the essence of the music in a way unavailable to modern practice, then one ought to think carefully about the orchestral dispositions of the romantic era as a resource rather than as an obstacle to imparting the message of the music. In other words, a conductor would do well to be cognizant of these ideas and have them in mind when preparing programs and making decisions about seating. Seating should be supple instead of static, reflecting the work performed, just as the make-up and size of the orchestra should be fluid, even if this means moving forces between pieces, unless each program is put together around the idea of a particular seating plan and even a particular core orchestra. For it seems clear that only by reflecting such principles can current performances recreate the sound-ideals of the composer at the time of composition—a condition one has already come to expect in the case of baroque, renaissance, or medieval music.

Part Five

Nineteenth-Century Music and Current Performance Practices

17

Toward a "Standard" Orchestra

Great strides have been taken in attempting to rediscover and put into use valid performance practices proper to music of the middle ages, the renaissance, and the baroque period. Many excellent recordings abound as the fruits of this search. One even sees elements of such an attempt beginning to extend to music of the later eighteenth century. But somehow the idea seems to prevail that since the nineteenth century is closer to us in time, we still know how best to perform and interpret that music; the tradition has never been lost. But is this true, particularly of the first half of the century?

There has been a tendency to standardize the orchestra in the twentieth century. Perhaps a random list of selected orchestras will tend to prove this, allowing for a larger string contingents in the United States. Here is such a list.

1904   Chicago Symphony Orchestra, Thomas, conductor:
  2 flutes, 1 piccolo, 2 oboes, 2 English horns, 2 clarinets, 1 bass clarinet, 2 bassoons, 1 contrabassoon;
  4 horns, 2 trumpets, 2 cornets, 3 trombones, 1 bass trombone;
  1 timpanist, 3 percussion, 2 harps, 1 organ;
  15 1st violins, 15 2d violins, 10 violas, 10 cellos, 9 basses
    Total = 91[1]

1906-7   Boston Symphony Orchestra, Karl Muck, conductor:
  4 flutes, 3 oboes, 1 English horn, 3 clarinets, 1 bass clarinet, 4 bassoons;
  6 horns, 5 trumpets, 3 trombones, 1 tuba;
  16 1st violins, 14 2d violins, 10 violas, 11 cellos, 8 basses
    Total = 96[2]

1908   Manchester, Hallé Orchestra:
  4 flutes, 4 oboes, 4 clarinets (including bass clarinet), 4 bassoons (including contrabassoon);
  4 horns, 2 trumpets, 2 cornets, 3 trombones, 1 tuba;
  1 timpanist, 3 percussion, 2 harps, 1 organ;
  16 1st violins, 16 2d violins, 11 violas, 12 cellos, 10 basses
    Total = 100[3]

1922   Dresden, State Opera (in concert):
5 flutes, 5 oboes, 1 English horn, 6 clarinets, 1 bass clarinet, 6 bassoons, 1 contrabassoon;
12 horns, 4 trumpets, 6 trombones, 1 tuba;
1 timpanist, 4 percussion, 2 harps, 1 piano;
16 1st violins, 14 2d violins, 10 violas, 10 cellos, 10 basses
Total = 116[4]

1933   Manchester, Hallé Orchestra:
4 flutes (including piccolo), 4 oboes (including English horn), 4 clarinets (including bass clarinet), 4 bassoons (including contrabassoon);
4 horns, 4 trumpets, 3 trombones, 2 tubas;
1 timpanist, 3 percussion, 2 harps, 1 organ;
16 1st violins, 14 2d violins, 12 violas, 12 cellos, 10 basses
Total = 100[5]

1935   Leipzig, Gewandhaus Orchestra in the theater:
3 flutes, 2 oboes, 1 English horn, 2 clarinets, 1 bass clarinet, 3 bassoons;
4 horns, ? trumpets, 3 trombones, 1 tuba;
1 timpanist, 1 percussion, 2 harps;
10 1st violins, 10 2d violins, 6 violas, 6 cellos, 7 basses
Total = 63 + trumpets[6]

1950   Philadelphia Orchestra:
4 flutes, 3 oboes, 1 English horn, 4 clarinets, 4 bassoons;
8 horns, 4 trumpets, 4 trombones, 1 tuba;
1 timpanist, 3 (?) percussion, 2 harps, 1 piano;
18 1st violins, 16 2d violins, 12 violas, 12 cellos, 9 basses
Total = 107 (?)[7]

1960   Berlin Philharmonic:
4 flutes, 5 oboes, 4 clarinets, 4 bassoons;
6 horns, 4 trumpets, 4 trombones, 1 tuba;
4 timpani & percussion, 1 harp;
19 1st violins, 15 2d violins, 13 violas, 11 cellos, 9 basses
Total = 104[8]

1960   Dresden Sächsische Staatskappelle:
6 flutes, 5 oboes, 5 clarinets, 5 bassoons;
8 horns, 5 trumpets, 6 trombones, 1 tuba;
5 timpani & percussion, 2 harps;
21 1st violins, 17 2d violins, 12 violas, 11 cellos, 8 basses
Total = 117[9]

1960   Milan, La Scala:
4 flutes, 4 oboes, 4 clarinets, 4 bassoons;
4 horns, 4 trumpets, 4 trombones, 1 tuba;
1 timpanist, 4 percussion, 1 harp, 1 piano, 1 organ;
16 1st violins, 16 2d violins, 12 violas, 10 cellos, 6 basses
Total = 97[10]

1960   London, BBC Symphony Orchestra:
3 flutes, 3 oboes, 3 clarinets, 3 bassoons;
5 horns, 3 trumpets, 3 trombones, 1 tuba;
1 timpanist, 3 percussion, 1 harp;
16 1st violins, 14 2d violins, 12 violas, 10 cellos, 8 basses
Total = 89[11]

1960   New York Philharmonic:
    4 flutes, 3 oboes, 4 clarinets, 4 bassoons;
    7 horns, 4 trumpets, 4 trombones, 1 tuba;
    1 timpanist, 3 percussion, 1 harp;
    18 1st violins, 16 2d violins, 12 violas, 12 cellos, 9 basses
      Total = 103[12]

1960   Paris, Orchestra Lamoureux:
    3 flutes, 3 oboes, 4 clarinets, 3 bassoons;
    5 horns, 5 trumpets, 5 trombones, 1 tuba;
    1 timpanist, 4 percussion, 2 harps;
    18 1st violins, 17 2d violins, 13 violas, 10 cellos, 8 basses
      Total = 101[13]

1961   Cleveland Orchestra:
    4 flutes, 4 oboes, 5 clarinets, 4 bassoons;
    6 horns, 4 trumpets, 3 trombones, 1 tuba;
    1 timpanist, 4 percussion, 2 harps, 2 keyboard;
    18 1st violins, 17 2d violins, 12 violas, 11 cellos, 9 basses
      Total = 107[14]

1961   Tel Aviv:
    4 flutes, 4 oboes, 4 clarinets, 4 bassoons;
    6 horns, 4 trumpets, 4 trombones, 1 tuba;
    1 timpanist, 3 percussion, 1 harp, 1 keyboard;
    15 1st violins, 14 2d violins, 11 violas, 10 cellos, 9 basses
      Total = 96[15]

1964   Düsseldorf, Symphoniker:
    5 flutes, 5 oboes, 5 clarinets, 5 bassoons;
    6 horns, 5 trumpets, 5 trombones, 1 tuba;
    5 timpani & percussion; 2 harps;
    18 1st violins, 12 2d violins, 11 violas, 8 cellos, 7 basses
      Total = 100[16]

1970   Boston Symphony Orchestra:
    4 flutes, 4 oboes, 4 clarinets, 4 bassoons;
    6 horns, 4 trumpets, 3 trombones, 1 tuba;
    1 timpanist, 4 percussion, 2 harps, 1 piano;
    18 1st violins, 15 2d violins, 12 violas, 12 cellos, 9 basses
      Total = 104[17]

It is not difficult to see a growing tendency towards a "standard" orchestra. While the need for such an orchestra as an available force is obvious to accommodate the varied repertoire, the tendency to use it as a constant is to be lamented. Also evident is a large number of orchestras with greater strength in the first violins over the seconds—a situation comparatively rare in the nineteenth century. Trumpets seem to find exclusive use; there is no sign of cornets after the first two decades.

New Ideas on Seating

Perhaps of even greater effect has been the trend away from the principles of seating which had evolved from the classic era well through the romantic. Sir Adrian Boult seemed to give Sir Henry Wood credit for being the instigator in this rapid development:

> Until 1910 it was the custom all over the world to have the "layout" of the orchestra as far as possible on a principle of balance, by which the high instruments (e.g., violins) were not all placed to the left of the platform, but were distributed, firsts on the left and seconds on the right. Violas and 'cellos were opposed to each other in the same way. When Sir Henry Wood changed this, and placed all his violins together, I remember an old friend of mine, who had always sat in the middle of the Queen's Hall circle, saying that he couldn't sit there any longer: all the bass came into his right ear and all the treble to his left, and he had to sit round at the side to get a blend.[18]

Wood's views were quoted in the *Musical Times* of March 1911. He acknowledged that the arrangement in Queen's Hall was unusual in that all the violins were on the left, with the violas on the right in the "customary place of the second violins." The woodwinds were in the center of the orchestra with the brass and percussion "ranged above them." The cellos and basses were on the right near the violas.

> This arrangement is explained by the desirability of grouping the instruments that generally work together in an ensemble, and, besides, it facilitates the giving of cues and economizes time at rehearsals. The underlying justification for any rational disposition of the orchestral forces is that it enables the conductor to control and the players to work in unity. If there were no conductor to consider, and no desire for perfect ensemble, something might be said for Spontini's suggestion that the string and wind players should mix miscellaneously in order that the tone might blend.[19]

However, Wood's ideas did not immediately gain universal acceptance. In April of 1910 the *Musical Times* reported of Landon Ronald that he preferred "to adhere to the customary plan" with first violins on the left and seconds on the right of the conductor. "The arrangement of 1st and 2nd violins all on the left side has some advantages, but it sometimes destroys antiphonal effect designed by a composer."[20]

But Wood must have later changed his mind concerning the relative positions of violas and cellos, for in his book on conducting which was published in 1945 he provided the plan which he had earlier furnished Boosey & Hawkes with for a book on *The Orchestra and its Instruments* (fig. 99). It would seem to enable the cellos and basses, who so often play the same line in octaves, to blend well. Also the horns are admirably placed so as to blend well with either or both woodwinds and trombones who also often fill the middle

Figure 99. Wood's Seating Plan

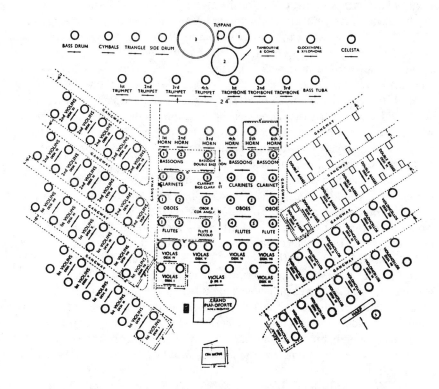

Source: Wood/CONDUCTING, front end-papers.

of the texture. Wood had further justifications for his plan. He preferred all the violins together on the left because he found that "better ensemble is assured, and volume and quality of tone improved with all the S holes facing the auditorium." He liked cellos and basses on the right because "they too are of a colour, and ensemble is better assured by placing together instruments of the same family." He felt that the "fan-shaped" layout allowed the "eye of the conductor" to take in "practically all" the violins "(a very important point to obtain a perfect ensemble)" and all the cellos and basses and most of the violas. "Looking straight in front of his nose," he can observe the winds and timpani; the horns on the left should have their bells towards the audience. He counselled drawing a "straight line from the nose of the conductor to the tympani" and placing the first woodwind players on either side of this "central line" so that there would be three each on either side. He claimed that thus arranged the woodwinds and horns can hear each other and "feel in touch with one another," ensuring ensemble and "certainly better chordal playing." He would place harp(s) in the center of the orchestra if possible, "just in front of the first flute and first oboe, dividing slightly the violas from the second violins." Thus they can hear all woodwind and string solos. He found placing the harp at the side of the orchestra to be "a grave error" not always possible to avoid, as they cannot hear well from there to accompany any solos as they must often do.[21] However, a glance at Wood's plan shows the violas right in front of the conductor, where he certainly can have them in sight, and the harp at the side. Another discrepancy is the position of the horns in the plan, straight across the middle rather than at the left as in his description. The plan also does not suggest that the first-chair players of the woodwinds are at the center but rather to the conductor's left.

Wood also had something to say about the layout when a chorus is involved. He found it "unfortunate that in Great Britain our choirs are always placed *behind* the orchestra, so that a lot of their work does not tell." Acknowledging that seating a chorus is "always a problem" he wished it were possible to seat full orchestra and chorus of about three hundred as in the "rough sketch" shown in figure 100.[22] As can be seen, the chorus rather surrounds the orchestra—the sopranos and altos coming around to the sides. But Wood also provided a plan which included a large chorus and orchestra, a plan also initially furnished for *The Orchestra and its Instruments* (fig. 101). Again there would seem to be contradiction. The only logical explanation for the chorus being behind the orchestra in this plan might be that when Wood originally drew up the plans, he was showing what was usual rather than what he would like.

But Boult had other objections to Wood's plan and others like it.

This modern practice has now been adopted by almost all conductors on both sides of the Atlantic—it is no doubt easier for players and conductor, and it might seem better that the second violins should play with their instruments turned *towards* the audience. It is also suitable for certain types of orchestration, such as Tchaikovsky's, for example, which so frequently requires first and second violins to play the same part in octaves or in unison, and it may well be thought advantageous that the sound should come from the same direction, though it is not impossible that the composer wished the sound to come from all parts of the orchestra. But, on the other hand, in almost every orchestral work there are passages where firsts and seconds *answer* each other, and the obvious expectation of the composer was that the sounds should come from opposite sides of the platform.

I have repeatedly found when conducting as a guest (when I am unwilling to alter the orchestra's normal seating just for a concert or two) that these answering passages when taken up by second violins sound like a pale reflection of the firsts instead of a vigorous rejoinder. No placing of the orchestra is perfect for everybody, but I claim (and I have Toscanini and Bruno Walter on my side) that a first-class orchestra should not choose the easy way, but that which gives its audience the most completely balanced whole; and the second violins can always be reminded not to turn too far away from the audience.[23]

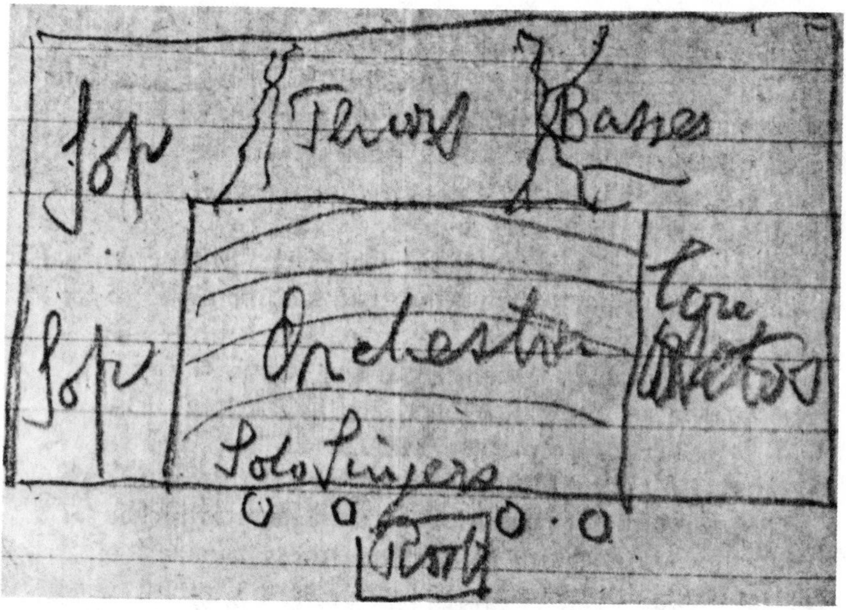

Figure 100.   Wood's Sketch for Placing a Choir
Source: Wood/CONDUCTING, p. 94.

However, one must question Boult's reference to Tchaikovsky above, at least as far as the Sixth Symphony is concerned. The reader will remember the reference in an earlier chapter to the last movement where the first theme flits back and forth between first and second violins, while the lower two harmonic strands flash back and forth between violas and cellos. To play this passage with seating like Wood's is tantamount to reorchestrating it in the manner of the recapitulation. In fact, it would seem more sensible and perhaps even more honest to actually rescore the passage in question, using the recapitulation as a model.

Boult had more, perhaps later, thoughts on this subject. Perhaps it is worth including them here at some length. Acknowledging that there is no perfect plan without any disadvantages, he proposed some general points. He would always place the woodwinds first, the four first chairs together in the middle, the others "radiating outwards in two rows." Then he would place the horns to the left of the woodwinds but not too near a wall, "for their tone emerges behind them, and will be powerfully thrown back if the wall is too close." The other brass he would put to the right (from the conductor's

Figure 101. Wood's Plan for Orchestra and Chorus

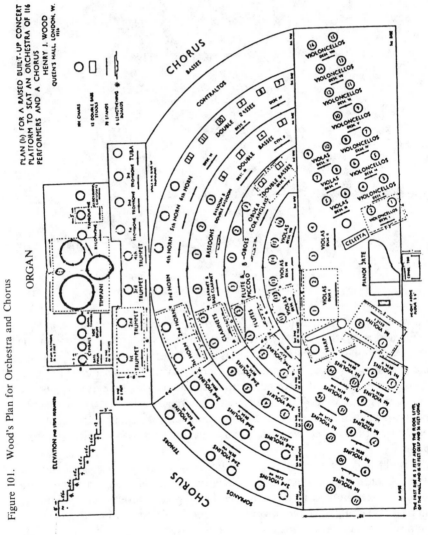

Source: Wood/CONDUCTING, rear end-papers.

viewpoint) with the trombones playing "rather at an angle towards the middle and not straight down the hall. Their tone will blend better in that way." He liked the double basses "in a row at the back, Vienna-fashion," but he realized that this was impossible in many halls, where they would have to "go away in some corner." He found this unfortunate, since "the string foundation should be central." He remembered that Hans Richter placed four in each corner of the stage, feeling it better to separate them than to leave them unbalanced. (This reminds one of Berlioz and many other plans.) As for the other strings, he reiterated his objections to having all the treble left and the bass right. Again he preferred the firsts to the left and the seconds to the right, "so that the treble of the string sound reaches the audience from the whole width of the front of the platform. This must have been in Rimsky-Korsakov's mind when he wrote the slow movement of *Scheherazade.*"

Boult admitted that when guest-conducting he insisted on changing the seating for "this balance." To the argument that the seconds cannot be heard well when "their bridges are on the inward side," he countered that it would only be true if they sat "hunched up with their backs to the audience." But he claimed that if they sit "squarely" facing the conductor, no listener with his eyes shut will find them in a weaker position. He was sure that Hans Richter would have been "horrified" at the idea of all his violins together on one side. Boult acknowledged that the position of the seconds on the right made problems for ensemble, especially when a piano separated them still further, but found that players liked the challenge and he had "very rarely had to complain of slackness in that quarter."

He would fit the remaining players where space was available—"usually not over-generous." With choruses, the "numerical weakness of the men nowadays often demands a closely packed centre with the tenors well forward. The stronger ranks of women stretch out each side as the platform allows."[24]

Sir Adrian actually contradicted the usual assertion that the second violins were weaker on the right because their f-holes faced in, finding them actually weaker on the left because of an inferior position behind the firsts. One conductor of acquaintance found instead problems of intonation between the two sections when he tried the split positions with a student orchestra. A layout such as Boult recommended comes from a record jacket on the orchestra narrated by Sir Adrian (fig. 102).

The impact of the new seating was gradually to become quite widespread. Wood, of course, adopted it with the London Philharmonic in 1911.[25] Though the Dresden State Opera orchestra used a quite traditional plan for performances in 1922,[26] Koussevitzky is credited with using a different layout in Boston in 1925 (fig. 103). This plan appears in David Wooldridge's book on conducting, and once again one must be hesitant in accepting his evidence, for in discussing such a layout with the cellos on the right front, Mueller stated

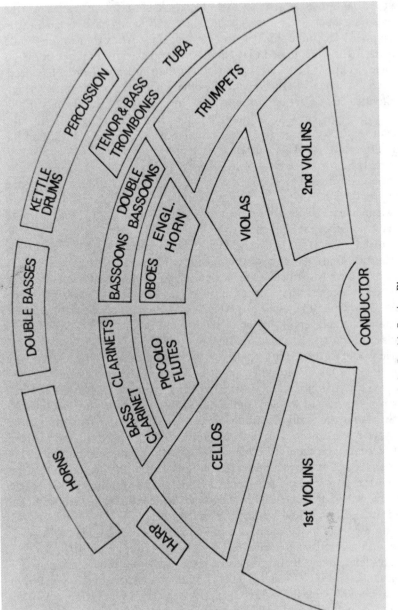

Figure 102.   Boult's Seating Plan
Source: SERAPHIM GUIDE, jacket.

Figure 103. Boston Symphony, Koussevitzky, 1925

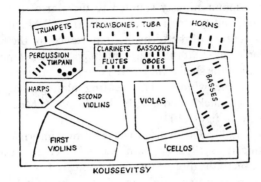

KOUSSEVITSY

Source: Wooldridge/CONDUCTOR'S, p. [342].

that a "slight variation" on this where the violas "occupy the old front location of the second violins" was introduced by Goossens and Koussevitzky, "a seating which corresponds to the usual string quartet sequence."[27] This has been corroborated by a conversation with a member of the Boston Orchestra whose tenure dated back to Koussevitzky's time; he remembered the violas as being on the right front. Of course, it is also possible that Koussevitzky used the plan in figure 103 in 1925, but later switched the violas and cellos.

In the late 1920s Stokowski was experimenting widely in Philadelphia. As one writer described it, audiences were never sure where players would be seated, "for Stokowski decided at a fairly early stage that the traditional orchestral floor plans no longer suited modern needs." He would place the double basses on the left to face the audience. He shifted the brasses, seeking a better blend "in relation to one another." He tried the woodwinds in front of the strings, then set them back again. He tried a flat stage as well as risers. "And there were positive achievements to come out of the constant moving and shifting." The writer gave Stokowski credit for breaking up the traditional seating plan and setting the second violins to the left, violas in the center, and cellos on the right, a plan which "in recent years has become the standard deployment of most American orchestras."[28] But such a plan dates back at least to Sir Henry Wood, as has been shown. And even if Stokowski moved the cellos to front right before Wood did (remember he had violas in that position early on), Koussevitzky preceded him in that by a year or two, if Wooldridge is at all correct. Perhaps Mueller showed more clarity in this regard. He gave Stokowski credit for the placement of cellos on the right front, not for the whole plan.[29] He also noted that in 1931 Eugene Ormandy adopted the "Stokowski shift" with the Minneapolis Symphony Orchestra.[30]

But more striking was Stokowski's so-called "upside-down" orchestra which Mueller described as "sprung upon the audience" in 1939-40, a layout in which the "strings were ignominiously shunted to the rear of the stage, and the woodwinds, brass, and tympani moved to the front." Mueller claimed that this was in part because of the "growing importance" of the winds in recent scoring and a conjecture that the strings might be "reflected more effectively" from the rear wall of the shell if they were nearer to it, thus giving them more strength vis-à-vis the winds. "This seating plan gained no adherents whatsoever and was quickly and quietly abandoned."[31] Mueller's drawing of that plan is shown in figure 104.

Once again Wooldridge seemed to have his own information and offered a drawing, dating it as 1932![32] Again one is forced to wonder about his sources. In addition to the discrepancy in the date, he has the horns in front of the cellos which are at extreme right and the trombones in front of the harps which are extreme left. But Mueller inferred that Stokowski was not so original with this plan after all.

Nearly ten years previously, the conductor of the Milwaukee Symphony Orchestra had anticipated this reshuffle on another theory—that the prominence of the strings was an anachronism in a period when modern instrumentation featured wind and percussion. These theoretical demands were satisfied by placing the woodwinds to the immediate frontright and retaining the strings at left.

Stokowski's "upside-down" orchestra not only was not imitated, but actually aroused universal aversion. It offended the visual habits of the audience, and was deemed unnecessary by musicians and critics, who reasoned that a good conductor had at his command many less circuitous ways of attaining balance. The pithy comment that, in this new order, the "front rows did not keep busy enough to put up a good show" epitomized the public verdict with more finality than any esoteric analysis.[33]

As a matter of fact, what Wooldridge labeled the "current Stokowski seating plan" most closely resembled that described by Mueller as having been tried in Milwaukee. Wooldridge's drawing appears in figure 105. Perhaps the great one was not so original after all! Wooldridge claimed that this plan led to "greatly improved ensemble in—and within—every section, and to a broad antiphonal effect between string and wind choirs." He also claimed that it had been used by other groups, including the Beirut Symphony Orchestra, "with unvarying success."[34] Actually it is reminiscent of many nineteenth century opera plans, such as that of Weber.

Meanwhile changes continued to spread. An example is the plan used in the theater in Leipzig from 1935 (fig. 106). One notes that there the violas hold the right front position, while horns are at the left with the woodwinds. One looks in vain for the trumpets which must have been omitted inadvertently. Perhaps they might have been in the corner to the left of the harps, behind the woodwinds and horns.

Figure 104. Stokowski's "Upside-Down" Seating

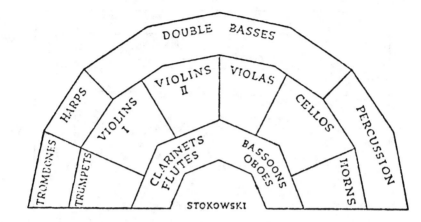

Source: Mueller/AMERICAN, p. 308.

Figure 105. "Classic" Stokowski Plan

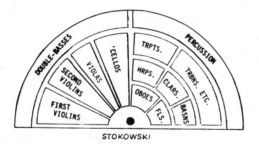

Source: Wooldridge/CONDUCTOR'S, p. [343].

In the 1940s, while the Vienna Philharmonic and the Amsterdam Concertgebouw, whose plans are shown in figures 107 and 108, adhered to the traditional positions for the two violin sections (though differing in other respects), the New York Philharmonic employed the "Stokowski shift" (fig. 109). Yet at least one author showed a plan (fig. 110) which he deemed the traditional plan typical in American opera houses. And if the Orchestre National of Paris retained a traditional disposition in their seating plans in the 1940s (figs. 111, 112), the Philadelphia Orchestra under Ormandy in 1950 retained the "Stokkowski shift."[35] But Charles Munch preferred a layout with the violas on the right front, as for instance with the Boston Symphony

Figure 106. Leipzig, Theater Plan, 1935

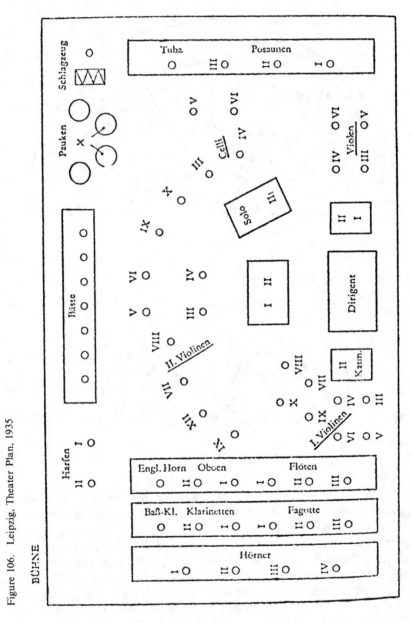

Figure 107. Vienna Philharmonic, 1940s

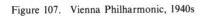

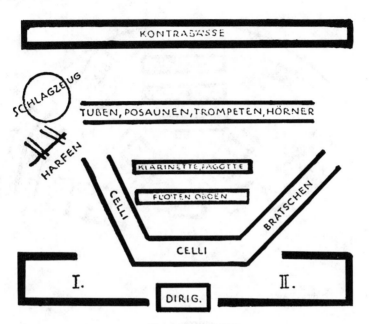

Source: Jerger/ WIENER, p. [110].

Figure 108. Amsterdam, Concertgebouw, 1940s

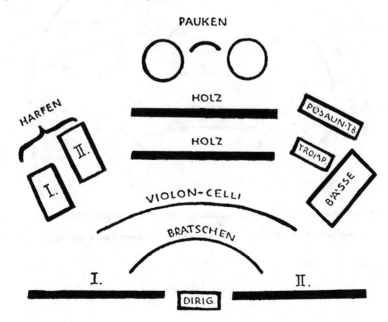

Source: Jerger/ WIENER, p. [110].

Figure 109. New York Philharmonic, 1940s

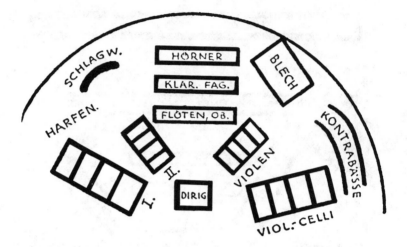

Figure 110. "Typical" American Opera Plan, 1940s

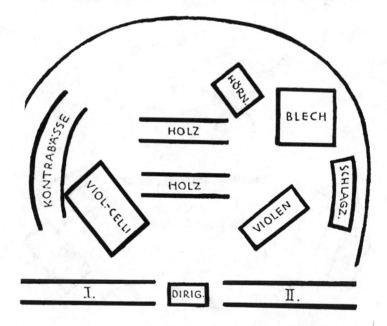

Figure 111.   Paris, Orchestre National, 1940s

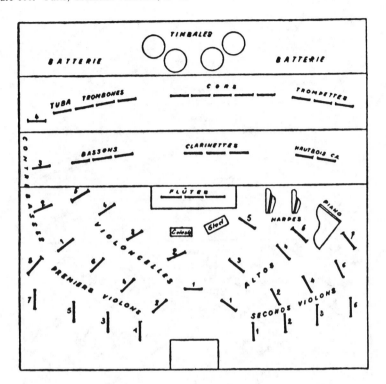

Source: Inghelbrecht/CHEF, p. 136; or see Inghelbrecht/CONDECTOR'S, p. 120.

Orchestra in 1951.[36] Wooldridge claimed that this layout was also used by Sir John Barbirolli and several other conductors, including himself.[37] And in the 1950s the Hamburg Orchestra is credited with performing the Symphony No. 39 of Mozart with seating certainly not in keeping with eighteenth-century principles (fig. 113)! While the effort to effect stylistic balance with a reduced string section is evident and maybe even laudable in the Hamburg arrangement, the completely unstylistic seating of the strings counteracts it. The La Scala Orchestra was using the "shift" for concerts in 1960,[38] and by 1970 the Boston Symphony had returned to positioning the cellos at the right front.[39]

And yet many writers on the orchestra or on conducting continued to present the "traditional" type of seating plan. For example, Alfred Thienemann gave two plans for the theater and concert hall respectively (fig. 114, 115). Note that Thienemann chooses the cellos to be the separating agent,

Figure 112.   Orchestre National with Chorus, 1940s

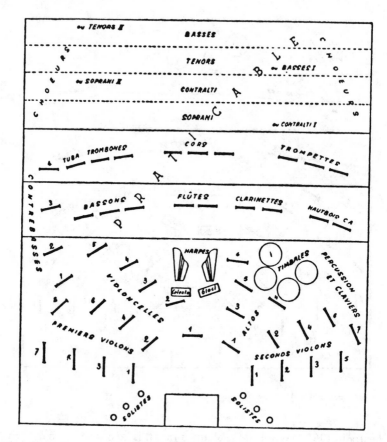

Figure 113.   Hamburg Orchestra Playing Mozart, Jochum Conducting, 1950s

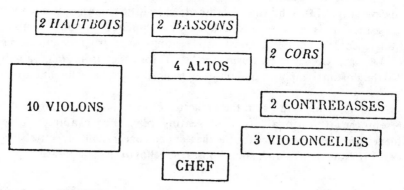

Figure 114. Thienemann's Theater Plan

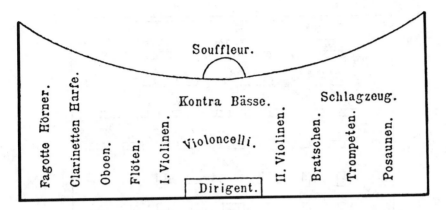

Source: Thienemann/DIRIGIERENS, p. 94.

Figure 115. Thienemann's Concert Plan

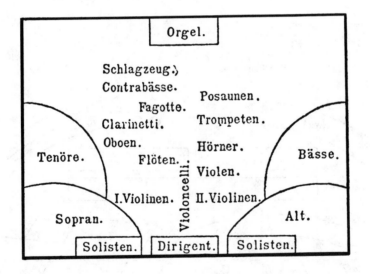

Source: Thienemann/DIRIGIERENS, p. 94.

which is rather unusual in the plans seen before. Also to be noted is the way the chorus is "draped" around the front part of the orchestra in the second plan. Here the chorus presses the orchestra together, apparently causing the cellos to be strung out in a straight line, difficult for ensemble, one would think. In 1910, Fritz Volbach presented a plan for a "modern orchestra" (fig. 116). Here the cellos are rather similarly placed as in Thienemann's plans. Even in 1943, a book on conducting could recommend the plan shown in figure 117.

Figure 116. Volbach's "Modern Orchestra"

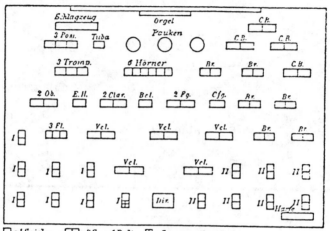

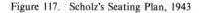

Source: Volbach/ORCHESTER, p. 111.

Figure 117. Scholz's Seating Plan, 1943

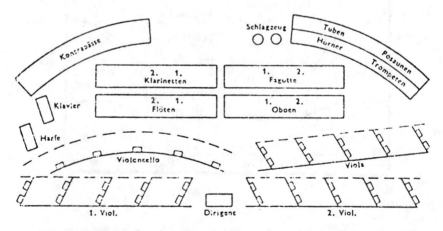

Source: Scholz/DIRIGIERLEHRE, p. 100.

Like Boult and Inghelbrecht, Toscanini preferred the nineteenth-century type of seating, yet with flexibility, as evidenced by one of his biographers:

> He likes the old-fashioned way of seating an orchestra, with the first violin section to his left and the second violins to his right. "The first and second violins," he says, "are like a pair of shoulders, and like shoulders they must be strong and equal." He rails at conductors who fool around with the seating of the orchestra, insisting that they are throwing out the balance sought by the composer. When he saw a younger conductor's reseating of an orchestra, Toscanini muttered, "The trouble with some conductors is they conduct by eye instead of by ear."
> And yet he does not hesitate to be inconsistent. He, too, makes slight rearrangements in seating if he thinks they will benefit the balance of a composition. In "La Mer" he moves the harps close to the woodwinds because he wants to clarify and blend the texture of the music more effectively.[40]

On the other side is Wooldridge who defended the "Stokowski shift" and discounted allegations of antiphony.

> There is, too, a supreme logic behind his layout of the orchestra, which was the fruit of many years of experimentation in Philadelphia, and is patently more logical than the division of first and second violins to the left and right of the conductor. (A number of illustrious persons have recently deplored the passing of this practice—which is supremely *illogical*—maintaining that without it, the element of antiphony between first and second violins is lost. I have searched my scores of Haydn, Mozart and Beethoven in vain to discover more than the most fleeting examples of this alleged "antiphony," which in any case is surely the antithesis of "symphony." By extension, one surely achieves a greater element of antiphony between strings and winds by separating *them*—the principle which governs Stokowski's practice.[41]

One has to wonder how thoroughly Mr. Wooldridge perused his scores, and whether he included Tchaikovsky in his search. Besides, did not the nineteenth-century type of plan offer antiphony between winds and strings in that the former were usually bunched together and elevated on risers?

But perhaps it is only fair to let Stokowski offer his own rationale for his actions:

> Something very simple and strangely overlooked is that every instrument in the orchestra emits a tone in a certain direction. For example, the tone of the French horn goes to the right of the player and downward. From the tuba, the tone goes to the left of the player and upward—exactly the opposite. Now this direction of tone from the instrument is a fact, a very important fact, that is often overlooked. As a further example, in the double bass the tone goes to the right of the player and outward. The cello looks like a small double bass, but the tone goes from the cello forward. From the violin, the tone rises upward and to the right. The flute's tone goes directly upward from the instrument. The tone of the trombone and trumpet goes forward from the instrument. So, obviously all these instruments have different directions of tone, and it is my idea that we should so place the players and the

instruments on the stage that the tone goes to the listener in the audience, because the concerts are for the listeners and not for us. What we conductors enjoy most, frankly, is rehearsing. I like the rehearsals more than the concerts. There is something tremendously interesting in gradually forming things in the rehearsal. In a concert, however, the tone should go to the listeners in the audience. The tone waves should blend in the air. They travel from the stage and from the orchestra toward the listeners, and this can best be done if one studies the direction of tone from each instrument. That is why I do not place the players on the stage in what is known as the "classical" way, the way our grandfathers and great grandfathers did. There is a foolish attitude of resistance to new ideas which we find in every form of life, not only in music. The moment someone comes along with a new idea, there are always people who resist it merely because it is new, not because it is not good. It is simply a matter of good sense to seat the players and their instruments on the stage in such a way that the instruments' tone goes to the audience and blends in the air as it travels.[42]

While acousticians might find matter for argument with Stokowski's "fact"—his theory of directions of tone—it would seem that there are other considerations to be observed in addition to tonal direction, for example, the strength of the tone, which differs from instrument to instrument—the reason why Boult liked the trombones facing diagonally rather than straight at the audience. And then, would not "classical" composers have taken all this into consideration when composing, with the "normal" seating in mind as they proceeded? But in all fairness, Stokowski did take power into consideration in his most recent seating:

Often the woodwind instruments, which are very delicate instruments, are placed in the back center of the stage. That makes if difficult for the tone of those instruments to penetrate out into the hall and they are sometimes inclined a little to force the tone; therefore I brought them forward. On the left side of the stage are the strings, on the right side are the woodwinds so that they can play even the most delicate passages without forcing the tone. The brasses we place in the back of the stage because they easily come out, the same way with the battery. The percussion instruments are in the back of the stage because they have great power, but the harp and the celesta are put forward on the stage because they are delicate instruments.[43]

This all sounds very logical and perhaps benefits certain modern works. In fact, in the manner of Berlioz, it might be well for contemporary composers to have such a plan in mind—and specify it in a preface to the score—when composing orchestral works. But there can be no possibility that eighteenth- and nineteenth-century composers could have been thinking of such a plan when they imagined their orchestral sounds. Why would they have had such dreams for their works without articulating them in order to realize them in performance? In fact, as noted before, Tchaikovsky's *Pathétique* cries out for just the opposite treatment from Stokowski's.

The fact is that, despite professions of faith in the idea of fidelity to the score and to the composer's intentions—such professions have been heard time and time again in various quarters—the tendency has been in our time to put a standard orchestra on stage in one seating plan without change regardless of the works being performed, unless one calls change not using an English horn where none is indicated, etc. Where period instruments are now in use for much early music extending even to the baroque, the same instruments are used for music from Haydn to Boulez. And most conductors are probably more concerned with suiting the seating to the hall, rather than to the work in hand. This would seem to have been the case with Josef Krips, who admitted to trying different ways of seating. Indicating that every orchestra had a different plan, he stipulated: "It all depends on the hall where an orchestra is playing. You have to adjust to the acoustical condition." He felt he had a "most satisfactory" seating plan in the San Francisco Opera House with its acoustical shell. "First of all, it is no longer possible for the brass or percussion to drown out the rest of the orchestra."[44] Of course, this is not a new concept; C.P.E. Bach inferred that his father took building design into account when placing a group.[45] But need such considerations negate the demands of the score in hand? One would think not.

But quests for authenticity, at least in some aspects of performance, have been noted from time to time. For example, a critic could rail at the New York Philharmonic for its performance of Mozart's *Eine kleine Nachtmusik* in 1906:

> To set the eighty-odd Philharmonic string players in Carnegie Hall to playing this guileless and graceful little piece which Mozart doubtless intended for ten or a dozen musicians in a chamber of moderate dimensions, seemed like a perversion of its obvious intention, based on a strange insensibility to the requirements of style in music. It was well played, with a wide variety of light and shade, yet in many passages with a heavier touch then the music could well endure.[46]

But the same critic found much to praise in the efforts of Sam Franko in 1904:

> Mr. Franko is a student of earlier periods of composition and of the true methods of performing the music belonging to them. He always succeeds in presenting something worthy of the attention of music lovers. Furthermore, the circumstances and the forces employed are such as to reproduce measurably the effects as the composers intended them. A small auditorium such as the New Lyceum Theatre, and a small orchestra, based upon six first violins and five seconds, with the wind instruments as prescribed, gives the tonal effect of such a symphony as the early one of Mozart's in G minor and the first of Bach's Brandenburg concertos as they may have sounded to Mozart and Bach.[47]

And such partial efforts have not ended there. The quest for the "return to authority" has reared its head time and again, even if sometimes it has met with depredation.

Toscanini, in performing the Haydn Symphony in G [almost certainly the 88th], once reduced the strings by half in order to recapture the "balance" of Haydn's day. This was no doubt interesting and instructive, in a museum sense, but balance is more than a count of instruments and is unsuccessful unless many other acoustical and technical matters are considered. Furtwängler, like Berlioz, Nikisch, and other romantic conductors, protests against this scholastic antiquarianism.[48]

And more recently, Kurt Masur conducted the last three Mozart Symphonies with the Boston Symphony Orchestra with the strings reduced to 8 - 8 - 5 - 4 - 4. But more encouraging is the recent project which recorded the complete symphonies of Mozart with "original" instruments by a group calling themselves the Academy of Ancient Music.[49] This should have much more impact than just reducing size alone.

Perhaps even more encouraging is the incursion into the early nineteenth century with an eye to somewhat more authentic performances. Even though restricted to the parameter of size, Michael Tilson Thomas began recording the symphonies of Beethoven in a "Beethoven with Chamber Orchestra" series not only with reduced strings but keeping to single woodwinds.[50]

As indicated previously, there have been those who have adhered to nineteenth-century principles of seating, so that the efficacy of its variegated points of origin can be experienced today. One need go no further than one's turntable or cassette deck. A few years ago RCA released a stereo version of the Franck Symphony conducted by Guido Cantelli with the NBC Symphony Orchestra.[51] In comparing it with the monaural version available many years ago, Harris Goldsmith had the following to say:

> The distribution of the orchestra is faithfully reproduced—double basses lined up along the left wall; first and second violins divided left and right (Toscanini once said that the violins in the orchestra were like a pair of shoulders); cellos center left; violas center right; timpani to the rear right; woodwinds, brasses, and harp in the center—and innumerable details in the scoring are clarified by these spatial relationships. Moreover, the prevailing sonority, while retaining its original clarity and (in the brasses and timpani) biting impact, is warmer and more sensual than the harsh, dry mono disc. This is, of course, all to the advantage of the music.[52]

And even on a car stereo radio, the recording of the Beethoven *Eroica*[53] conducted by Wyn Morris[54] immediately struck the listener with its separation of first and second violins. Closer listening showed the violas to be center-left and the cellos center-right with the basses also bordering on the right—just opposite to Cantelli's layout as described above. The entire recording is testimony to the benefits of such a plan, but the skeptic should check places like m.232-43 in the development section of the first movement where the spatial separation clearly helps to delineate the imitative four-part counterpoint in the strings. The coda is replete with instances: m.567f. with the motive of the first theme in the second violins coming from the right while a quicker motive is heard from the first violins at the left; the tossing back and forth of a motive in m.595f., and m.639f., where the first theme motive is now in the first violins while a faster motive in the second violins clearly comes from below, soars over the firsts and back down. Many other places could be cited from the other three movements, but that might be to beg the point.

Earlier the idea of composing for such a setup as Stokowski's was mentioned. Many recent composers have composed for special seating plans which they have specified in their scores. But too often, it would seem, conductors do no pay attention to proper seating even then. For example, Bela Bartók provided a seating plan for his *Music for String Instruments, Percussion, and Celesta* which is quite novel, having the violins divided into four groups, the violas into two, the cellos into two, as also the double basses, these groups being spread over the stage in a specified manner.[55] Yet this writer can remember during a seminar on nineteenth-century music taking part in an inquiry as to how many of the then available stereo recordings of this work could be heard to have used Bartók's plan. Not one, seemed to be the answer, if memory does not err. This attitude does not hold out hope for compliance when the guidelines for correct seating in nineteenth-century works are more tenuous.

What hope can be held for truer performances of nineteenth-century music then? Perhaps conductors will gradually be influenced by hearing the fruits of such few attempts as are being made recently, for example, those just-mentioned recordings of Mozart and Beethoven. Perhaps they can be encouraged to keep at the back of their minds the advice of Berlioz when preparing a work for performance: each work should have its own orchestra and its own seating. In other words, the conductor should not only study the work for notes, cues, tempi, phrasing, and general interpretation, but also for size of string section, possible doubling of woodwinds, and above all, seating.

A Model of Procedure

Perhaps a model of procedure can be suggested, taking the works of Mendelssohn, Schumann, and even early Wagner as a basis for this purpose. Since all three men spent much time in Leipzig and knew the Gewandhaus Orchestra which probably supplied much of their orchestral experience—it might not be an exaggeration to suggest that it may have formed the basis and model of their orchestral thinking and auralizing when composing—this orchestra as it existed in the 1830s and 1840s could be used as a point of departure for the size and seating for a modern performance. It will be remembered that in 1830 the orchestra used in the theater was quite small:

piccolo, 2 flutes, 2 oboes, 2 clarinets, 2 bassoons;
4 horns, 2 trumpets, 3 trombones;
1 timpanist, 1 percussion, 1 harp (doubling on piccolo or small drum);
6 1st violins, 6 2d violins, 2 violas, 2 cellos, 2 basses
    Total = 39[56]

In 1831, the concert orchestra had the same total of 39, although its makeup was somewhat different—stronger in strings, weaker in winds—probably reflecting differing demands of the repertoire.

2 flutes, 2 oboes, 2 clarinets, 2 bassoons;
2 horns, 2 trumpets;
1 timpanist;
8 1st violins, 8 2d violins, 4 violas, 3 cellos, 3 basses
    Total = 39[57]

Strangely, Nösselt gave an even smaller group for 1833:

2 flutes, 2 oboes, 2 clarinets, 2 bassoons;
2 horns, 2 trumpets, 3 trombones;
1 timpanist;
5 1st violins, 5 2d violins, 4 violas, 2 cellos, 2 basses
    Total = 34[58]

This resembles the orchestra used for the theater in 1830 more than a concert group. In 1836, Mendelssohn used an orchestra of 65 for a performance of Handel's *Israel in Egypt*,[59] but that must have been assembled especially for that occasion, for in 1838-39, besides the "usual winds," the Gewandhaus had the following string section: "9 first violins, 8 second violins, 5 violas, 5 cellos, 4 basses."[60] Even in 1850 when the orchestra had grown to 56 men, there were only 22 violins.[61]

These figures should give one a starting point in deciding how large an orchestra to put on stage to begin with. Other factors, such as the size and acoustics of the hall used, might necessitate some changes, but such an aggregation should be close to correct. On the other hand, small chamber groups are constantly playing in large halls without being "swallowed up"—at least in halls with good acoustics to begin with. As far as seating this orchestra is concerned, it should seem obvious that the Gewandhaus plan shown previously[62] must be again at least a point of departure. This plan, it will be remembered, had the first violins to the right, the cellos and basses in the center, bassoons and clarinets left on risers, oboes and flutes center on risers, with violas to their left (audience right), and the brass to the rear center even higher up. Such an orchestra must have been the basis of the inner-aural image Mendelssohn, Schumann, and even young Wagner experienced when thinking in orchestral terms.

This should at least provide a starting point for performances of the music of that group. (Of course, the later Wagner works would reflect later thinking, his Beethoven performances and the Bayreuth situation, for example.) Now if "original" instruments can be resurrected with players willing to learn how to manage them, the situation will be even truer. Is this too much to hope? Not too long ago it would have seemed so, but with Mozart symphonies appearing with "original" instrumentation and Beethoven with reduced orchestra, perhaps romantic works can in the near future receive proper treatment also. If each work is treated as an individual demanding an individual orchestra in its own seating plan, we can come close to realizing that music as it appeared to contemporary audiences.

18

Postscript

There are other areas which could properly be considered under the category of physical aspects of performance practices, but since the scope of this study has already assumed quite large proportions and other areas would open up even more vast bibliographies, they cannot be included here in detail. Salient among them would be the matters of halls and/or opera houses, and pitch or, more properly, tuning—both having great influence on performance.

Halls

It seems obvious that the size and shape of a hall is going to have some effect on the performance of an orchestra of a certain size which is seated in a particular way. In fact, one could argue that it should be the other way around: the orchestral size and its arrangement on the stage should be decided on according to the hall in which the performance is to take place. In 1817 when Beethoven was responding to Ferdinand Ries concerning a projected trip to London with two new symphonies for the Philharmonic Society, he not only asked about the size of the orchestra but also the hall: "How powerful is the Society's orchestra, how many violins and so forth; and are there *one or two of each wind-instrument?* Is the hall large and resonant?"[1] It will also be remembered that in his performance directions for *Wellingtons Sieg* he had written: "the larger the hall, the more players."[2] In fact, it can be strongly argued that the increase in orchestral size in the nineteenth century is directly related to the increased number of public concert halls, halls which were increasingly larger in size in order to accommodate a growing middle-class audience. Dart went even further in relating musical style to proposed acoustical surroundings. He claimed that the forms used by Haydn and Mozart in their works for chamber combinations and orchestra are identical, but that "details of style (counterpoint, ornamentation, rhythm, the layout of the chords, and the rate at which harmonies change) will vary according to whether they are writing room-music, concert-music, or street-music."[3] And as was pointed out earlier in this work, Berlioz directly related size, seating, and style of composition to the hall in which performance should take place in his speculations on writing for huge forces.[4]

In the eighteenth century, orchestral music was usually performed in a court salon; in fact, the line between chamber music and orchestral music is not always easy to draw. Haydn's London Symphonies were first performed in the Hanover Square Rooms which also served the Philharmonic Society after 1833. The principal concert room there was 90 feet long by 30 feet wide; it could seat eight or nine hundred people.[5] The opera house in Berlin was somewhat larger in the 1780s, measuring 300 feet in length by 100 feet in width.[6] This presents quite a discrepancy; 2700 square feet versus 30,000 square feet!

Since the Leipzig Gewandhaus Orchestra has figured prominently in this study, perhaps the hall itself will be of interest. The old Gewandhaus was built in 1780 and stood until 1894; it was the home of the orchestra during Mendelssohn's illustrious reign as conductor (1835-47). August Schmidt, who visited the hall in the 1840s, probably paced it off and gave its dimensions: "the length of the whole hall is roughly 42, the width 21 paces."[7] More precise is the citation by Dörffel as of 1870: 106 feet long, 40 feet wide, and 35 feet high.[8] According to Beranek, it seated about 400 until 1842 when side-balconies increased its capacity to about 570.[9] This would suggest a smaller seating capacity than the Hanover Square Rooms which had a smaller hall. But there is discrepancy here: Beranek gave the volume as 75,000 cubic feet,[10] while Dörffel's figures would multiply out to 148,000 cubic feet! At any rate, the need for a larger hall resulted in the Neues Gewandhaus which was built in 1886 (and unfortunately lost to bombing during World War II). It was about twice as long as it was wide with rounded corners.[11] It seated 1,560, had a 50-foot ceiling, and measured 375,000 cubic feet in volume.[12] Even with the large discrepancy above, this is a sizeable increase!

The possible inadequacy of an eighteenth-century hall for the forces required in mid-nineteenth-century scores is pointed up by the following:

> The Hanover Square Rooms were never adequate for the performance of music requiring large forces. This inadequacy was strikingly shown up in 1856, when Schumann's cantata *Paradise and the Peri* was performed by the Philharmonic Society, with Jenny Lind singing the chief soprano part and with Queen Victoria, the Prince Consort and many royal personages from abroad in the audience. The body of the hall had seating room for six hundred, just enough to provide one seat apiece for the Society's subscribers, but a hundred extra tickets were sold for a special occasion such as this, and a big space had to be reserved for the royal visitors. The platform, designed to accommodate an orchestra with reasonable comfort, had to find room for eighty chorus singers and six soloists as well, with the result that the string players could hardly use their bows.[13]

One suspects that such would have been as true of other concert halls in London and elsewhere at the time. In 1858, St. James's Hall was opened in London for concerts on a large scale, supposedly exceeding "nearly all" halls in the kingdom in length and height, though not in width. Scholes cited the *Musical Times* as providing the measurements as 134 feet by 60 feet by 60 feet high.[14] Elkin had it as 139 feet by 60 feet by 60 feet, and seating about 2,500.[15] But another discrepancy shows up where Scholes elsewhere gave the area as 1,271 square feet;[16] it has to be at least 8,040 square feet, if not 8,340! Such variances, even involving such a study as Beranek's, are indicative of the problems which would beset a detailed study of halls and opera houses. Besides, one has to wonder whether it was the need to accommodate a larger audience rather than a larger sound which was the root cause of the increase in hall size.

But there is no question that grow in size they did! Perhaps just a few figures will suffice to give evidence to what is popular assumption anyway.

> London, Royal Albert Hall (1871): 3,060,000 cubic feet in volume; 5080 seats plus 1000 standees.[17]
> New York, Metropolitan Opera House (1883): 690,000 cubic feet; 3639 seats.[18]
> New York, Carnegie Hall (1891): 857,000 cubic feet in volume; 2760 seats.[19]
> Boston, Symphony Hall (1900): 662,000 cubic feet in volume; 2631 seats.[20]

Then there are the questions of shape and materials. For example, it might be surprising that I. F. K. Arnold in 1806 considered the most advantageous form of a music hall to be an oval.[21] He claimed that this is the form in which tones are allowed to come to the most perfect formation.[22] And lest one think that such a view was but a curiosity, almost forty years later Gassner was content to extensively quote his "friend" Arnold on this topic within the larger context of halls in general.[23] And even in 1890, Kling paid probably unknowing tribute to Arnold's ideas on the oval as being the best form in his slightly edited but unacknowledged cribbing from Gassner.[24] Zopff was also of the same opinion, quoting *"der grosse Akustiker Chladni u. A."* in what reads like Gassner's version of Arnold.[25]

Oddly enough, the hall of the Leipzig Gewandhaus did fit this prescription. Kufferath wrote in 1909: "There was, in this ancient building of the drapers' corporation, today demolished, an oval-shaped room of an exquisite sonority, where already concerts were given from the time of Mozart and Beethoven."[26] Spohr agreed with Kufferath as to the sonority of the hall when he visited Leipzig in 1804. His diary recalled that the "hall in which these concerts are given is very beautiful, and most favorable to the musical effect."[27] Perhaps the success of the oval influenced the building of the Neues

Gewandhaus in 1886 "with rounded corners."[28] Yet this shape does not seem to find favor in other more modern halls.

But if the increase in the size of halls is related to the larger performing forces and audiences, the reverse does not seem to be necessarily true. That is, a large hall can often be filled adequately by a reduced orchestra. It is not uncommon to hear so-called "chamber" orchestras perform in a hall like Boston's Symphony Hall. The performance of the three last Mozart Symphonies with greatly reduced strings referred to in the last chapter did not seem lost there. In fact, it has not been unusual to hear quartets or trios or even solo pianists play in such a hall. So one has to wonder if the excuse that Haydn and Mozart must be played with enlarged string sections in order to fill up a modern hall has absolute validity; the same doubt would apply to Beethoven, Schubert, and even Mendelssohn.

Pitch

Pitch is another topic which would require a full-scale study to do it justice. There has never been any universal standard of absolute pitch. That, aside from the problems of *Kammerton* and *Chorton,* pitch varied widely in the eighteenth century is attested to by the fact that the flute had interchangeable middle pieces to accommodate deviations in pitch from one locale to another. This fact prompted Quantz to further divide the middle piece in two to facilitate carrying, with two or three extra upper of these two pieces, each varying by a semitone![29]

Castil-Blaze found pitch variances between Paris and the provinces in the early nineteenth century. He claimed that the pitch at the Opéra was more than a semitone lower than elsewhere.[30] Later he made the claim that the rise in French pitch began in 1759, and he attributed it to Rameau by a process of deduction. His conjecture was that when Rameau wanted to bring the *cors de chasse* into the orchestra, he found that they were more than a semitone above the other instruments. Rather than diminish the brightness of their sound by making them lower (crooks were not yet in use), he preferred to make the strings and woodwinds retune.[31] However, one has to wonder how much leeway woodwinds could have had for retuning!

Nettel pointed out a drastic rise in pitch between mid-eighteenth century and mid-nineteenth century in England: "Handel's English tuning-fork stands at A 422.5, which is almost the same as the pitch first adopted by the Philharmonic Society in 1813—A 423.7. By Costa's time, however, the pitch in use at this Society's concerts was A 452.5—a difference of over a semitone above the classical pitch."[32] Indeed, Schindler suggested that when Beethoven was still able to hear, the pitch was a semitone lower than at the time of his writing his biography (1840).[33] In fact, it seems worth quoting editor MacArdle's footnote to this statement:

According to Grove 6-793, Mozart's piano in 1780 was tuned to A = 422 cps. When Sir George Smart visited Vienna in September 1825, he carried with him a fork tuned to A = 433 cps, and reported that at several of the theatres of the city and at the private performance of opus 132 for Schlesinger the pitch was "rather above" his fork [see Smart/JOURNALS, pp. 99, 100, 110]... Grove reports "Vienna, high pitch (1859) "as A = 456 cps. Smart's fork was about 0.4 semitones above Mozart's pitch, and the Vienna standard of A = 440 cps is about a quarter of a semitone above the pitch that Smart found in Vienna in 1825.[34]

As a matter of fact, Smart found a motley situation throughout Europe during his visit of 1825. At the Cologne Cathedral, the "pitch was exact with London."[35] At the theater in Stuttgart it was "exact to my fork."[36] At the cathedral in Munich, the "organ was my pitch," although at the theater there it was "very little above my fork."[37] In Dresden at the theater the "pitch was exact to mine, though at the cathedral it was rather lower."[38] But at a Catholic church in Dresden it was "exact to my fork."[39] At the theater in Leipzig the pitch was "exactly that of my fork."[40] At the theater in Hanover the "pitch of my fork was exact with that of the orchestra."[41] And at a concert in the Théâtre Louvois in Paris it was "exact to my fork."[42] But there were other variances. At a play in Frankfurt it was "a comma above my fork."[43] At a theater in Berlin it was "a little sharper than my fork";[44] at Berlin's Königstadt Theater it was "above my fork."[45] And at a concert in Cassel which had Spohr for conductor, the pitch was a "comma above my fork."[46] A motley situation indeed!

Exchanges on the subject appeared as letters to the editor of *The Harmonicon* in 1824. One writer, signing himself as "Gallicus," blamed the rise in pitch on the open-air celebrations in Paris after the revolution. He cited the need for "constant excitement" which the open-air performances helped to fill:

Two, and sometimes three, concerted choirs, with as many orchestras, were established in the *Champ de Mars*, which had to combine their means at a considerable distance from each other. For the purpose of producing an effect in such a space, nay even in order to hear each other, these choirs and orchestras were reduced to the necessity of raising their pitch. Now the musicians of the opera took a part in these performances, and after having screamed the whole morning, it was not easy for them to quit the same habit in the evening, and therefore they continued to sing in the same tone....

Meanwhile the players on wind instruments found that their horns, clarinets, etc., had gained more *éclat;* the evil was too seductive not to make its impression, and immediately led to pernicious consequences.[47]

Another writer signing himself as "X," cited a report of a committee which studied the subject of pitch at the Paris Conservatory concerts as a result of an order from Buonaparte in 1812. The Committee noted that the "extreme height of Concert-pitch *(élévation du ton)* in use at the concerts of the Conservatoire, strains the voices of the pupils, and endangers their being forced beyond their natural means," so that the Committee "adopted a medium between those of the Imperial Academy of Music, the Opéra Buffa, the chapel of His Majesty, and the Conservatoire." Yet X found that "last year" in Paris the pitch at the Opéra was "still rather higher than that fixed by custom in London."[48] But yet another writer, John Farey, took issue with both Gallicus and X—with the former for avoiding technical terms and mathematical calculations, with the latter for assuming that a change of pitch took place as a result of an "undefined, and almost laughable, order." Letting drop that he had prepared the articles on pitch for *Dr. Rees' Cyclopaedia* (1807) and the *Edinburgh Encyclopaedia* (1813), and after lengthy technical deductions, he pointed out that in "most full concerts now" there is an organ and piano, "the tuning of which keyed instruments, is invariably conducted by tempered or *flattened* FIFTHS, upwards and downwards *from* C." He went on: "All the best comparable experiments, made from twenty to thirty years ago, concurred very nearly . . . in fixing the concert-pitch of this C, at 240 v."[49] Of course, he was referring to middle C and seemed to suggest that variances might be due to the other instruments tuning from the piano's (or organ's) A, thereby introducing some small error. But he was in error himself in giving an overall reason for such tuning in the "violins, violoncellos, etc., having no open string C," since both cellos and violas do.

In 1858, a commission, after deliberating on problems of pitch, established A = 435 as the "official" French pitch. During the deliberations of this commission, Berlioz wrote an article on the matter, pointing out reasons for the necessity of an inquiry:

> The Minister of State, uneasy respecting the future, more and more alarming, of musical execution in lyric theatres; astonished at the shortness of the singer's career; and rightly persuaded that the progressive elevation of pitch is a cause of the ruin of the best voices; has just appointed a commission, carefully to examine into this question, ascertain the extent of the evil and discover a remedy for it.[50]

He blamed "recent" composers to a great extent for singers' problems:

> At the time when they commenced to write dramatic music in France, and to produce operas, as, for example, at the time of Lulli, the pitch, being established though not fixed (as we shall shortly see), the singers, whoever they might be, experienced no trouble in singing the parts written within the limits then adopted for voices. When, later on, the pitch had become appreciably higher, it was both the duty and interest of composers to recognize the fact by writing slightly lower; but they did not do so. Notwithstanding that, the parts written for Paris theatres by Rameau, Monsigny, Grétry, Gluck, Piccini and Sacchini, at a time when the pitch was about a tone lower than it is now, remained for a long time singable. The greater part of them are so still; which shows what an amount of prudence and reserve these masters exhibited in the use of voices.[51]

But along with the rise in pitch, composers asked for higher and higher notes more frequently:

> Twenty-five years later, during which the pitch had rapidly risen, high notes for tenor and sopranos became more frequent....
>
> On the whole, these excessively high intonations became so frequent, that the singer could no longer *emit* them, but was obliged to *extract* them, with violence; after the manner of a vigorous operator extracting a decayed tooth. After full consideration, the evidence allows us no alternative but to adopt the strange conclusion that grand opera in France was written for, higher and higher, whilst the pitch was also gradually rising. One can easily become convinced of this by comparing the scores of the last century with those of the present day.[52]

He went on to cite examples to prove his thesis. But it was not only the singers who suffered as a result of this problem:

> Horn, trumpet and cornet players can no longer be sure of certain notes which were formerly in general use; the majority not being even able to attack them.... At every moment, frayed and broken notes, vulgarly called *couacs,* appear to the detriment of an instrumental ensemble, sometimes composed even of the most excellent artists. Thus we hear it said:
>
> "Trumpet and horn players have no longer any *lip?* Why? Surely, human nature has not changed."
>
> No; human nature has not changed, but the pitch has; and many modern composers seem to ignore the new conditions.[53]

Berlioz went on to blame wind-instrument makers for this rise in pitch.[54]

An international conference in Vienna in 1885 established the norm as A equal to 435 (or 870 for the octave above as Haas put it), but there has never been universal acceptance.[55] While it had already been introduced in the Leipzig Gewandhaus in 1875,[56] it was not adopted by the Philharmonic Society in London until 1895[57] and has never become universal, A equal to 440 and even higher being common in the United States.[58]

Obviously, it would take extensive research to disentangle the complexities of pitch. But this subject will also have to be left to another day and another hand for further exploration.

Notes

Chapter 1

1. A good example of an attempt to revive classic-era performance practices is the series of Mozart symphonies recorded by the Academy of Ancient Music on L'Oiseau-Lyre, vols. 1–7, D167D3–D173D3.

Chapter 2

1. Rockstro/HÄNDEL, p. 259.

2. Carse/18TH, p. 117.

3. Dart/INTERPRETATION, pp. 67–68.

4. See Quantz/FLÖTE 1, p. 185, or Quantz/FLUTE, p. 214.

5. Cucuel/ETUDES, p. 12.

6. Bobillier/CONCERTS, p. 251. Even in 1783, Forkel considered the setting or assigning of the parts an important duty of the leader; see Forkel/BEGRIFFE, pp. 1058–61.

7. Spohr/LEBENSERINNERUNGEN, p. 8; trans. Spohr/JOURNEYS, p. 4.

8. Carse/HISTORY, p. 9.

9. Mozart/VIOLONSCHULE, p. 3; trans. Mozart/TREATISE, p. 11.

10. Quantz/FLÖTE 1, p. 212; trans. Quantz/FLUTE, p. 241.

11. Adam/SOUVENIRS, p. 67.

12. Blaze/ACADEMIE, II, p. 342.

13. Ibid., II, p. 340.

14. Galkin/CONDUCTING, pp. 48–49.

15. Dr. Murray Lefkowitz claims he has been able to play a sforzando attack on members of the viol family.

16. Dittersdorf/LEBENSBESCHREIBUNG, p. 60; trans. Dittersdorf/AUTOBIOGRAPHY, p. 47.

17. Mozart/BRIEFE, II p. 517; trans. Mozart/LETTERS, II, p. 638.

18. Parke/MEMOIRS, I, pp. 42–43.

19. Stamitz/SYMPHONIES, facsimile reproduced in liner notes; orig. in French. See also Carse/18TH, pp. 34, 126 for more insight on this point.

20. Mozart/BRIEFE, I, p. 408; trans. Mozart/LETTERS, I, p. 174.

21. Adam/DERNIERS, p. 67.

22. Cucuel/ETUDES, p. 16.

23. Walter/LEXIKON, p. 168.

24. C.L. Junker, quoted in Galkin/CONDUCTING, p. 43.

25. Mozart/BRIEFE, II, p. 517; trans. Mozart/LETTERS, II, p. 638.

26. In discussing the theater orchestra in Brussels in 1882, Burney considered the first clarinet to be serving as oboe; see Burney/GERMANY, I, p. 24.

27. Galkin/CONDUCTING, p. 43.

28. Haas/AUFFÜHRUNGSPRAXIS, p. 218.

29. Cucuel/ETUDES, p. 14.

30. Carse/18TH, p. 36, including note 1.

31. Mee/OLDEST, p. 35.

32. Parke/MEMOIRS, I, p. 11.

33. Landon/SYMPHONIES, p. 112.

34. Nettel/ENGLAND, p. 85.

35. Cramer/MAGAZIN, I, pp. 179–80.

36. Carse/18TH, p. 39.

37. Carse/HISTORY, p. 113.

38. Blaze/ACADEMIE, II, p. 345; however, Marpurg/BEYTRAGE, I, p. 194, credits the Opéra orchestra with two horns in 1754.

39. Cucuel/ETUDES, p. 23.

40. Ibid., p. 27.

41. Carse/HISTORY, p. 45; a D trumpet could be changed into a C by means of a crook; see ibid., p. 19. The English conductor Sir George Smart, who visited Beethoven in 1825, reported the latter's opinion: "He believes—I do not—that the high notes Handel wrote for trumpets were played formerly by one particular man." Smart/JOURNALS, p. 114. Praetorius had considered the D instrument normal and the 8-foot C trumpet to be more recent. Werner Menke reported that of seven sixteenth- and seventeenth-century trumpets he examined, five were in D, one from D to D♭, and one in F; see Menke/TRUMPET, p. 107. This makes one wonder about Bach's Second Brandenburg Concerto for the shorter F trumpet, where the note d‴ appears at least three times (in measures 76, 80, and 81 of the first movement)—a note equalling a sounding g‴! An authority to whom Percy Scholes submitted his article on trumpet regarded the work even in "respect" as "an unjustifiable and unaccountable freak"; see Scholes/OXFORD, pp. 958–59, notes 1 & 2. Although the false 11th and 13th harmonics could be "lipped" in tune (see Monk/BRASS, p. 287), a slide

for correcting these problems was prescribed by a John Hyde in 1798. "Mr. Hydes' [*sic*] ingenious invention" is mentioned in Parke/MEMOIRS, I, p. 41. However, it seems to be a resurrection of the "flat trumpet" used by Purcell; see Monk/BRASS, p. 189.

42. Terry/ORCHESTRA. pp. 25–26.

43. The decline of *clarino* playing has been explained in some quarters as the result of a change in taste, but perhaps Menke puts forth better reasons. He suggests that the skill was lost because of the use of more crooks for more keys and a shortened tube. Later trumpets were crooked in almost all keys from 6-foot F down to low B♭; see Carse/18TH, p. 43. *Clarino* technique is less possible on the shorter instruments, and the constant changing of crooks caused intonation problems and made impossible the greater skill founded on *one* instrument in *one* tuning. Then to provide a fuller tone, the players altered the mouthpiece, thus voiding the higher notes altogether. So one set of limitations was traded for another. See Menke/TRUMPET, pp. 58–59. But might not the decline be explained by so simple a cause as trumpet players wanting longer careers than the strain of *clarino* would allow?

44. Menke/TRUMPET, p. 59.

45. See the letter of George Case of 12:11:02 printed in Bennett/FORTY, pp. 202–4. Case claims that "in Handel's time the six sacbuts of the Royal Chapel were the only trombones in England, no one but the King being allowed to use them." Handel had them only for the London performances of his oratorios. Case further claims that the names of the trombone players are not in orchestral lists in Handel's time, because "being thoroughly trained artists, they played string-parts when not playing trombone-parts in the Choruses." But the program for the 1784 Handel Commemoration at Westminster Abby lists the six King's Sacbuts both with the strings and as trombones.

46. Quoted in Cucuel/ETUDES, p. 34–35. However, Blaze/ACADEMIE, II, p. 348, claims they entered the *Académie* with Gluck's *Iphigénie en Aulide* on April 19, 1774.

47. Nettel/ENGLAND, p. 69.

48. Cucuel/ETUDES, p. 34.

49. See Carse/HISTORY, pp. 16–17.

50. Blaze/ACADEMIE, II, p. 349.

51. Dart mentions evidence that the harp saw some use as a continuo instrument; see Dart/INTERPRETATION, p. 53.

52. The interested reader should consult Cucuel/ETUDES, pp. 29–34, for rather extensive information.

53. Blaze/ACADEMIE, I, pp. 332–33, and II, p. 349; he seems to suggest that it replaced the keyboard which then disappeared.

54. Parke/MEMOIRS, I, p. 120.

55. Landon/SYMPHONIES, p. 126.

56. Carse/HISTORY, p. 170.

57. Blaze/ACADEMIE, II, p. 349.

58. Bach/VERSUCH, II, p. 2; trans. Bach/ESSAY, p. 173.

59. "Further, I assume that another instrument is playing the bass with the keyboard." Bach/VERSUCH, I, p. 5; trans. Bach/ESSAY, p. 33.

60. Bach/VERSUCH, II, p. 1; trans. Bach/ESSAY, p. 172.

61. Quantz/FLÖTE 1, p. 185; trans. Quantz/FLUTE, p. 214.

62. Landon/SYMPHONIES, p. 118. He also includes extensive advice on the proper method of realizing the continuo in Haydn's symphonies on pp. 118-21.

63. See Dart/INTERPRETATION, p. 71, where he cites Haydn as stating that he had grown out of the habit of using the harpsichord by the 1790s.

64. Quantz/FLÖTE 1, p. 184; Quantz/FLUTE, p. 212.

65. For example, see Quantz/FLÖTE 1, p. 183, or Quantz/FLUTE, p. 212; or Rousseau/DICTIONNAIRE, plate G, facing p. 224.

66. Handel's concerti grossi were originally issued with two continuo parts according to Dart/INTERPRETATION, p. 53.

Chapter 3

1. Available in Bach/DOKUMENTEN, pp. 102-6; translation in David & Mendel/BACH, pp. 120-24.

2. Bach/DOKUMENTEN, p. 103; trans. David & Mendel/BACH, p. 121.

3. Quantz/FLÖTE 1, p. 185; trans. Quantz/FLUTE, p. 214.

4. Rousseau/DICTIONNAIRE, article "Orchestre," p. 354.

5. Forkel/ALMANACH, 1783, pp. 100-101.

6. Pohl/HAYDN, I, p. 227.

7. Landon/SYMPHONIES, p. 111.

8. Ibid., p. 111.

9. Reproduced in facsimile in Somfai/HAYDN, p. 59.

10. Dittersdorf/LEBENSBESCHREIBUNG, p. 141; trans. Dittersdorf/AUTOBIOGRAPHY, p. 144.

11. Reproduced in facsimile in Somfai/HAYDN, p. 106.

12. Landon thinks probably 6-5-2; see Landon/SYMPHONIES, p. 112.

13. Reproduced in numerous sources, including Haas/AUFFÜHRUNGSPRAXIS, facing p. 240; Schonberg/CONDUCTORS, p. 49; Bernstein & Picker/INTRODUCTION, p. 253.

14. Pohl/HAYDN, II, p. 15.

15. Cf. Carse/18TH, p. 41.

16. Mennicke/HASSE, p. 273.

17. The pantaleon was a dulcimer improved and enlarged by Pantaleon Hebenstreit at the beginning of the 18th century. It survived in use by itinerant players until the 1780s. See Geiringer/INSTRUMENTS, pp. 130, 159.

18. Zaslaw/REVIVAL, p. 179. When in Eisenstadt, Haydn's *Kammermusiker* also performed with the *Chormusiker*; see Gerlach/HAYDNS, p. 35. For the possibilities of doubling on various instruments and voices, see the table in ibid., p. 47.

19. Pierre/CONCERT, p. 76.

20. Ibid., p. 77.

21. Bobillier/CONCERTS, p. 242.

22. Blaze/ACADEMIE, I, p. 181.

23. Cucuel/ETUDES, p. 15.

24. Pierre/CONCERT, p. 78.

25. Cucuel/ETUDES, p. 14.

26. Pierre/CONCERT, p. 78.

27. *Almanach historique du Théâtre ou Calendrier historique et chronologique de tous les Spectacles,* Paris, 1783, cited by Carse/18TH, p. 25.

28. Ibid., 1791, cited by Carse/18TH, p. 26.

29. See, for example, Adam/SOUVENIRS, p. 143ff.

30. The poem, *"Nos concerts ne touchent plus/Si le monstrueux assemblage/De vingt instruments superflus/N'y fait un bachique tapage,"* is quoted in Bobillier/CONCERTS, p. 210.

31. J.J.H.R. in Cramer/MAGAZIN, I, pp. 732–34.

32. Pohl/LONDON, II, p. 121. Since Pohl gives "etwa 40" as total, it is assumed that winds were in pairs.

33. Quoted in Pohl/HAYDN, III, p. 10.

34. Dart/INTERPRETATION, p. 55.

35. Haydn/BRIEFE, p. 60; trans. Haydn/CORRESPONDENCE, pp. 10–11.

36. Rosen/CLASSICAL, p. 144.

37. Carse/18TH, pp. 36–37.

38. Rockstro/HÄNDEL, p. 259.

39. Ibid., p. 259.

40. Zaslaw/REVIVAL, p. 181.

41. Ibid., pp. 182–83.

42. Cf., for example, Dart/INTERPRETATION, p. 68.

43. Dart/INTERPRETATION, pp. 55–56.

44. See, for example, Dart/INTERPRETATION, p. 68.

45. Carse/18TH, p. 38.

46. Haydn/BRIEFE, p. 59; trans. Haydn/CORRESPONDENCE, p. 10.

47. Carse/18TH, p. 38.

48. Ibid., p. 40.

49. Mozart/BRIEFE, III, p. 106; trans. Mozart/LETTERS, II, p. 724.

50. Rosen/CLASSICAL, p. 143.

51. Blaze/ACADEMIE, I, p. 212. Cucuel/ETUDES, p. 34, quotes Gossec, giving the date as 1762, also describing "the terrible and sinister effect of three trombones united to four clarinets, four trumpets, four horns and eight bassoons hidden in the distance and in an elevated part of the church...."

52. Dittersdorf/LEBENSBESCHREIBUNG, p. 121; trans. Dittersdorf/AUTOBIOGRA-PHY, p. 120. The translation would suggest to the American reader a total of 240 instead of 160.

53. Dittersdorf/LEBENSBESCHREIBUNG, pp. 197-98; or Dittersdorf/AUTOBIOG-RAPHY, p. 214.

54. Elkin/LONDON, pp. 69-70.

55. Burney/HANDEL, pp. 16-21, after 56p.

56. Cramer/MAGAZIN, II, pp. 171-73. His earlier announcement gave 268 instruments and 225 later corrected to 245 voices; see ibid., p. 162 & 165.

57. Carse/18TH, pp. 46-47.

58. Haas/AUFFÜHRUNGSPRAXIS, p. 196.

59. Burney/HANDEL, pp. 16-21, after 56p.

60. Cramer/MAGAZIN, II, p. 162, 165, & 171-73.

61. Parke/MEMOIRS, I, pp. 98-99.

62. Ibid., I, p. 147.

63. Ibid., I, pp. 220-21.

64. Hiller/NACHRICHT, pp. 21-27.

65. *Schlesische Zeitung für Musik* (Mehwald), Breslau, 1835, p. 262, cited in Schreiber/ORCHESTER, p. 112.

66. Dittersdorf/LEBENSBESCHREIBUNG, p. 257; Dittersdorf/AUTOBIOGRAPHY, p. 288. Again the original suggests that about 230 is a total figure.

Chapter 4

1. Bach/DOKUMENTEN, p. 197; trans. David & Mendel/BACH, p. 278.

2. See Walther/LEXIKON, frontispiece; also in Lang & Bettmann/PICTORIAL, p. 44. A plan drawn from this picture appears in Schünemann/DIRIGIERENS, p. 195. A plan offered as suitable for a work by Bach but without historical justification, rather suggesting modern baton-style conducting can be seen in Hoffmann/ESECUZIONE, p. 86.

3. Dart/INTERPRETATION, p. 53.

4. Bach/VERSUCH, I, p. 7; trans. Bach/ESSAY, p. 35.

5. Quantz/FLÖTE 1, pp. 183-84; trans. Quantz/FLUTE, pp. 211-12.

6. Appearing in Quantz/FLÖTE 2. p. 134.

7. See Schünemann/DIRIGIERENS, p. 200.

8. Rousseau/DICTIONNAIRE, p. 354.

9. Rousseau/DICTIONNAIRE, p. 354.

10. Certain remnants of these practices can be seen in some nineteenth-century orchestras. For example, Michael Costs in 1846 with the London Philharmonic Society, though baton conducting with no keyboard, still kept the principal cello and bass right in front of him and positioned the others on both wings of the orchestra. George Henschel with the Boston Symphony in 1881 had the basses on both wings. The Berlin Opera orchestra in 1840 had some cellos and basses in the center, the others on both wings.

11. Schünemann/DIRIGIERENS, p. 203, note 1.

12. BEMERKUNGEN, pp. 56–57.

13. See Becker/ORCHESTER, col. 178.

14. Quoted in Zaslaw/REVIVAL, p. 162.

15. Quantz/FLÖTE 1, p. 184; trans. Quantz/FLUTE, pp. 212–13.

16. See Schünemann/DIRIGIERENS, p. 190.

17. *Bibliothek der schönen Wissenschaften,* X (1763), pp. 51–53, as translated in Quantz/FLUTE, pp. xxxi–xxxii.

18. Dörffel raises questions about this also, in fact, some of these raised here. See Dörffel/GEWANDHAUS, p. 5.

19. Nösselt/GEWANDHAUS, p. 268.

20. Schünemann/DIRIGIERENS, p. 187.

21. BEMERKUNGEN, p. 15.

22. For example, the eighteenth-century court orchestra in Lang & Bettmann/PICTORIAL, p. 69; Frederick the Great and his orchestra in Carse/ORCHESTRA, p. 21.

23. Dittersdorf/LEBENSBESCHREIBUNG, p. 141; trans. Dittersdorf/AUTOBIOGRAPHY, p. 143.

24. Junker/KAPELLMEISTERS 1, reprinted with corrections and elimination of some regionalisms in Cramer/MAGAZIN as Junker/KAPELLMEISTERS 2.

25. See Junker/KAPELLMEISTERS 1, pp. 12–14; or Junker/KAPELLMEISTERS 2, pp. 747–49.

26. Junker/KAPELLMEISTERS 1, pp. 14–18; Junker/KAPELLMEISTERS 2, pp. 749–52.

27. Junker/KAPELLMEISTERS 1, p. 18; Junker/KAPELLMEISTERS 2, p. 752.

28. Mozart/BRIEFE, II, p. 101; trans. Mozart/LETTERS, I, pp. 355–56.

29. Junker/KAPELLMEISTERS 1, p. 18; Junker/KAPELLMEISTERS 2, p. 753.

30. Junker/KAPELLMEISTERS 1, p. 18; Junker/KAPELLMEISTERS 2, p. 752.

31. Junker/KAPELLMEISTERS 1, p. 19; Junker/KAPELLMEISTERS 2, p. 753.

32. See Junker/KAPELLMEISTERS 1, pp. 18–20, Junker/KAPELLMEISTERS 2, pp. 752–54, for the description of the Mannheim orchestra.

33. BEMERKUNGEN, p. 15.

34. See Schünemann/DIRIGIERENS, pp. 192-93 for Petri's comments.

35. Cf. p. 27.

36. In Burney/HANDEL, pp. 16-21 (after 56); Cramer/MAGAZIN, II, pp. 171-73.

37. Carse/18TH, p. 45.

38. Quoted in Zaslaw/REVIVAL, p. 164.

39. Carse/18TH, p. 46.

Chapter 5

1. Terry/ORCHESTRA, pp. 11-12.

2. Bach/DOKUMENTEN, pp. 72-73; trans. David &,Mendel/BACH, p. 231. Originally in Latin.

3. Bach/DOKUMENTEN, p. 196; trans. David & Mendel/BACH, p. 277.

4. Quantz/FLÖTE 1, pp. 178-79; trans. Quantz/FLUTE, pp. 207-8.

5. Bach/VERSUCH, I, p. 6; trans. Bach/ESSAY, p. 33.

6. Bach/VERSUCH, I, pp. 7-8; trans. Bach/ESSAY, pp. 34-35.

7. Carse/18TH, p. 93.

8. Forkel/BEGRIFFE, pp. 1057-62. As earlier pointed out, Forkel also considered assigning the parts as an important duty of a leader.

9. Mozart/BRIEFE, III, p. 239; trans. Mozart/LETTERS, II, p. 828.

10. Zaslaw/REVIVAL, p. 162.

11. Mozart/BRIEFE, II, p. 388; trans. Mozart/LETTERS, II, pp. 557-58.

12. Forkel/ALMANACH, 1783, pp. 100-101.

13. Haydn/BRIEFE, p. 58; trans. Haydn/CORRESPONDENCE, p. 9.

14. Creuzburg/GEWANDHAUS, p. 14.

15. Dart/INTERPRETATION, pp. 92-93.

16. Dittersdorf/LEBENSBESCHREIBUNG, p. 59; trans. Dittersdorf/AUTOBIOGRA-PHY, pp. 46-47.

17. Parke/MEMOIRS, I, p. 94.

18. Ibid., I, p. 143.

19. Ibid., I, p. 151.

20. Ibid., I, pp. 220-21.

21. Ibid., I, p. 147.

22. See Rousseau/DICTIONNAIRE, article "Bâton de Mesure," p. 50.

23. Ibid., article "Orchestre," p. 355.

24. For example, *batteur de mesure* in 1671 is defined in Blaze/ACADÉMIE, II, p. 358; Lulli gave the "bâton de mesure" to Marais in 1687, ibid., II, p. 339.

25. Bobillier/CONCERTS, p. 39.

26. Carse/ORCHESTRA, p. 39.

27 .Zaslaw/REVIVAL, p. 162.

28. Ibid., pp. 162–63.

29. Bobillier/CONCERTS, p. 277.

30. Blaze/ACADEMIE, I, p. 335.

31. Burney/GERMANY, I, pp. 22–23. "There was no harpsichord, which, as there were but two pieces of recitative, and those accompanied, was, perhaps, not wanted." Ibid., p. 26.

32. Parke/MEMOIRS, I, pp. 71–72.

33. Ibid., I, p. 98.

34. Ibid., I, pp. 39–40.

35. Burney/HANDEL, p. 14 (after 56).

36. "...Mr. Glösch, who beat time to some choruses on the organ loft," Hiller/NACHRICHT, p. 21.

37. Quoted in Haas/AUFFÜHRUNGSPRAXIS, p. 165.

38. See Creuzburg/GEWANDHAUS, pp. 35–36.

39. "Then Vachon spoke for the rest. *'Voilà ce qu'on appelle diriger l'Orchestre, sans faire tant de bruit et des grimasses inutiles, qui ne servent qu'à barbouiller l'Orchestre!'* " Dittersdorf/AUTOBIOGRAPHY, p. 284.

40. Carse/18TH, p. 102.

41. BEMERKUNGEN, pp. 16, 26, & 56–57.

42. Letter in AMZ. I, col. 728.

43. Carse/18TH, pp. 106–7.

Chapter 6

1. Arnold/MUSIKDIREKTOR, p. 8.

2. Ibid., p. 13.

3. Ibid., pp. 17–18.

4. Ibid., pp. 74–75.

5. Ibid., pp. 137–38.

6. Ibid., pp. 138–39.

7. Ibid., p. 139.

8. Ibid., pp. 139–40.

9. Ibid., p. 141.

10. Gassner/DIRIGENT, p. 6.

11. Ibid., p. 16.

12. Ibid., p. 12.

13. Ibid., p. 26/ It is very difficult to find a suitable English word for the German *Besetzung*; "setting" is perhaps as close as one can come.

14. Ibid., p. 99. Beat patterns and associated problems are discussed on pp. 106–19.

15. Rochlitz/BRUCHSTUCKE, cols. 17–19.

16. Quoted in Elkin/ROYAL, p. 15.

17. Ibid., p. 12.

18. See also Nettel/ENGLAND, pp. 90–92.

19. Parke/MEMOIRS, II, pp. 150–1.

20. Moscheles/LEBEN, I, p. 74; trans. Moscheles/RECENT, p. 51.

21. Moscheles/LEBEN, I, p. 228, or Moscheles/RECENT, p. 166.

22. HARMONICON, III (1825), p. 19.

23. Ibid., III (1825), p. 19.

24. Ibid., III (1825), p. 20.

25. Ibid., III (1825), pp. 131–33.

26. Bennett/FORTY, pp. 34–35.

27. Fétis/CURIOSITES, pp. 186–88.

28. Madeira/PHILADELPHIA, p. 76.

29. Ibid., p. 140.

30. Parke/MEMOIRS, II, p. 195.

31. Mendelssohn/BRIEFE, I, p. 110; trans. Mendelssohn/ITALY, p. 100.

32. Smart/JOURNALS, p. 90.

33. Ibid., pp. 98–99.

34. HARMONICON, III (1825), p. 185.

35. Smart/JOURNALS, pp. 227–28.

36. Parke/MEMOIRS, I, p. 290.

37. Smart/JOURNALS, p. 31.

38. See biographical sketch in Berlioz/MEMOIRS, p. 546; also Carse/ORCHESTRA, p. 39.

39. See Wagner/DIRIGIREN, p. 338. or Wagner/CONDUCTING, p. 15.

40. Chorley/MUSIC, I, p. 20.

41. Elwart/SOCIETE, pp. 360–61.

42. Ibid., pp. 325–26, note 1.

43. See Berlioz/SOIREES, pp. 166–70; Berlioz/EVENINGS, pp. 127–31 for translation.

44. Berlioz/MEMOIRES, II, p. 10; trans. Berlioz/MEMOIRS, p. 231.

45. See, for example, Kennedy/HALLE, p. 14.

46. See Berlioz/MEMOIRES, II, pp. 10, 15, & 40; or Berlioz/MEMOIRES, pp. 231, 235, 254, 594-95.

47. Spohr/LEBENSERINNERUNGEN, I, p. 245; trans. Spohr/JOURNEYS, pp. 145-46.

48. Spohr/LEBENSERINNERUNGEN, II, p. 106; trans. Spohr/JOURNEYS, pp. 238-39.

49. Spohr/LEBENSERINNERUNGEN, II, p. 110; trans. Spohr/JOURNEYS, p. 243.

50. Smart/JOURNALS, p. 110.

51. Ibid., pp. 227-28.

52. Ibid., p. 80.

53. Ibid., p. 221.

54. Parke/MEMOIRS, II, p. 263.

55. Berlioz/MEMOIRES, II, p. 128; trans. Berlioz/MEMOIRS, p. 324.

56. Ryan/RECOLLECTIONS, p. 15.

57. Ibid., pp. 36-37; see also p. 201 on Gilmore Jubilee; "Strauss, violin in hand, conducted the orchestra daily."

58. Ibid., p 201.

59. Ibid., p. 56.

60. Ibid., p. 57.

61. Schonberg/CONDUCTORS, p. 198.

62. Letter from F. Edward Bache to George Ingram, from Rome, Dec. 29, 1856, quoted in Bache/BROTHER, pp. 91-92.

63. Phillips/RECOLLECTIONS, I, pp. 153-54.

64. Nösselt/GEWANDHAUS, p. 121.

65. Berlioz/MEMOIRES, II, p. 52; trans. Berlioz/MEMOIRS, p. 264.

66. Wooldridge/CONDUCTORS, p. 14.

67. HARMONICON, III (1825), p. 103.

68. Deldevez/CHEF, pp. 2-3.

69. Ibid., Chapter One, "Du Chef d'orchestre compositeur-violoniste," pp. 7-18, explores this further, adding other, not necessarily new, arguments.

70. Ibid., p. 12.

71. Ibid., pp. 28-29.

72. Blitz/CHEF, pp. 47-48.

73. Phillips/RECOLLECTIONS, I, p. 130.

74. Creuzburg/GEWANDHAUS, p. 14.

75. Moscheles/LEBEN, I, p. 31; trans. Moscheles/RECENT, pp. 18–19.

76. Mueller/AMERICAN, p. 41.

77. Weber/BEMERKUNGEN, cols. 805–7.

78. HARMONICON, III (1825), p. 129.

79. AMZ, XII (1809/10), col. 714.

80. See, for example, Elkin/LONDON, p. 120.

81. Moscheles/LEBEN, I, p. 120; trans. Moscheles/RECENT, p. 82.

82. Moscheles/LEBEN, I, p. 121; trans. Moscheles/RECENT, pp. 82–83.

83. Hiller/MENDELSSOHN 1, p. 178, or Hiller/MENDELSSOHN 2, p. 212.

84. Creuzburg/GEWANDHAUS, pp. 56–57.

85. Moscheles/LEBEN, I, pp. 280–81; trans. Moscheles/RECENT, pp. 203–4. See also Galkin/CONDUCTING, p. 312.

86. Quoted in Davison/MENDELSSOHN, pp. 48–49.

87. Scholes/MIRROR, I, p. 377.

88. Elkin/LONDON, p. 136.

89. Quoted in Nettel/ENGLAND, p. 142.

90. Moscheles/LEBEN, II, p. 95; trans. Moscheles/RECENT, p. 292.

91. Moscheles/LEBEN, II, p. 139; trans. Moscheles/RECENT, p. 314.

92. Quoted in Moscheles/RECENT, pp. 280–81.

93. Smart/JOURNALS, pp. 76–77.

94. Ibid., p. 148.

95. Ibid., p. 163.

96. Smart/JOURNALS, p. 66.

97. Ibid., p. 100.

98. Dorn/LEBEN, I, pp. 27–28.

99. Phillips/RECOLLECTIONS, I, p. 139.

100. Wagner/LEBEN, p. 72; trans. Wagner/LIFE, I, pp. 69–70.

101. Berlioz/MEMOIRES, II, p. 78; trans. Berlioz/MEMOIRS, p. 285.

102. Berlioz/MEMOIRES, II, p. 272; trans. Berlioz/MEMOIRS, p. 434.

103. Berlioz/TRAITE, p. 300; trans. Berlioz-Strauss/INSTRUMENTATION, p. 411, or see Berlioz/CONDUCTOR, p. 4.

104. Bülow/NEUE, p. 470, or Bülow/LETTERS, p. 237.

105. Wooldridge/CONDUCTORS, p. 92.

106. Prawy/VIENNA, p. 86.

107. Nettel/ENGLAND, p. 213.

108. Zopff/DIRIGENT, p. 60.

109. A chorus of 5,500, an orchestra of 200, 2 large military bands, and 2 drum corps of 50 each, according to Thomas/MEMOIRS, p. 381.

110. Thomas/MEMOIRS, p. 382.

111. Russell/THOMAS, p. 210.

112. Borris/ORCHESTER, p. 258.

113. Kufferath/DIRIGER, pp. 98–100.

114. "Le chef d'orchestre Rey, qui, depuis trente-six ans, tenait le baton de mesure à l'Opéra, le cède à Persuis, prend sa retraite, et meurt la même année, à l'âge de septante-six ans, 15 juillet 1810." Blaze/ACADEMIE, II, p. 129.

115. MUSIKDIREKTOR, col. 167.

116. ZUGE, cols. 392–93.

117. Berlioz/MEMOIRES, I, p. 260; trans. Berlioz/MEMOIRS, p. 196.

118. Mendelssohn/BRIEFE, I, p. 162; trans. Mendelssohn/ITALY, p. 151.

119. Wagner/LEBEN, p. 82; trans. Wagner/LIFE, I, pp. 79–80.

120. MUSICAL MAGAZINE, I (1839), p. 128.

121. Blaze/OPERA, I, pp. 431–32.

122. Ibid., I, pp. 445–46.

123. MUSICAL MAGAZINE, I (1839), pp. 164–66.

124. Ibid., I (1839), pp. 269–70.

125. Berlioz/TRAITE, p. 310; trans. Berlioz-Strauss/INSTRUMENTATION, p. 418, or see Berlioz/CONDUCTOR, p. 16.

126. Deldevez/CHEF, pp. 135–38.

127. See Weber/WEBER 1, I, p. 434, & II, p. 59; trans. Weber/WEBER 2, I, p. 323, & II, p. 42.

128. Neumann/WAGNER 1, p. 16; trans. Neumann/WAGNER 2, p. 17.

129. Walter/MAHLER, p. 98.

130. Blaze/ACADEMIE, II, p. 327.

131. Borris/ORCHESTER, p. 126.

132. See Galkin/CONDUCTING, p. 414, & Devrient/MENDELSSOHN 1, p. 63, or Devrient/MENDELSSOHN 2, p. 59.

133. Hiller/MENDELSSOHN 1, p. 134; trans. Hiller/MENDELSSOHN 2, pp. 157–58. See also Devrient/MENDELSSOHN 1, pp. 63–64; trans. Devrient/MENDELSSOHN 2, p. 59.

134. Ryan/RECOLLECTIONS, p. 70.

135. Smart/JOURNALS, p. 302.

136. Borris/ORCHESTER, p. 126.

137. Zopff/DIRIGENT, p. 37.

138. Schroeder/KATECHISMUS, p. 65; trans. Schroeder/HANDBOOK, p. 61.

139. Schroeder/HANDBOOK, p. 99; from translator's appendix, not in original.

140. Blaze/ACADEMIE, II, pp. 327–38.

141. Borris/ORCHESTER, p. 126.

142. Berlioz/MEMOIRES, II, pp. 236–37, including note 1; trans. Berlioz/MEMOIRS, p. 406, including note 1. For a description of a violin-conductor's score with its system of cues, see Fuld/OPERATIC. Berlioz discusses other desirable studies for the would-be conductor, such as instrumentation; Berlioz/MEMOIRES, II, pp. 234–37, or Berlioz/MEMOIRS, pp. 404–6. See also Berlioz/TRAITE, p. 310; trans. Berlioz-Strauss/INSTRUMEN-TATION, p. 418, or Berlioz/CONDUCTOR, p. 16. Berlioz does not seem to have been taken with the idea of conducting from memory.

143. Deldevez/CHEF, pp. 139–47.

144. Blaze/ACADEMIE, II, p. 362.

145. Berlioz/MEMOIRES, II, p. 334; trans. Berlioz/MEMOIRS, p. 483, where the editor gives the inventor's name as Verbrugghen in note 4.

146. See Thompson/CYCLOPEDIA, p. 1493.

Chapter 7

1. Wood/CONDUCTING, p. 23.

2. Blitz/CHEF, p. 80.

3. Borland/BALANCE, pp. 18–19.

4. Carse/WIND, pp. 91–94; see also Baines/WOODWIND, pp. 316–17.

5. Carse/WIND, pp. 98–100; see also Baines/WOODWIND, p. 322.

6. Gassner/PARTITURKENNTNISS, I, pp. 17–18.

7. Berlioz/TRAITE, p. 152; trans. Berlioz-Strauss/INSTRUMENTATION, p. 227.

8. Berlioz-Strauss/INSTRUMENTATIONSLEHRE, II, pp. 242–43; trans. Berlioz-Strauss/INSTRUMENTATION, p. 227.

9. Berlioz/TRAITE, p. 151; trans. Berlioz-Strauss/INSTRUMENTATION, p. 227.

10. Berlioz/MEMOIRES, II, p. 123; trans. Berlioz/MEMOIRS, p. 321.

11. Blitz/CHEF, pp. 79–80.

12. Zopff/DIRIGENT, pp. 14–15.

13. Berlioz-Strauss/INSTRUMENTATIONSLEHRE, II, p. 242; trans. Berlioz-Strauss/INSTRUMENTATION, p. 227. A footnote adds: "In France, there are also Boehm clarinets, bassoons and oboes in use."

14. Carse/ORCHESTRA, p. 26.

15. Gassner/PARTITURKENNTNISS, I, p. 16; Berlioz/TRAITE, p. 158; trans. Berlioz-Strauss/INSTRUMENTATION, p. 236; Zopff/DIRIGENT, p. 15.

16. Gassner/PARTITURKENNTNISS, I, pp. 16–17.

17. Berlioz/TRAITE, p. 158; trans. Berlioz-Strauss/INSTRUMENTATION, p. 236.

18. Zopff/DIRIGENT, p. 15.

19. Galkin/CONDUCTING, p. 41; Bate/OBOE, pp. 60–83; Baines/WOODWIND, pp. 325–29; Carse/WIND, pp. 136–41.

20. Gassner/PARTITURKENNTNISS, I, p. 18; Berlioz/TRAITE, p. 103; trans. Berlioz-Strauss/INSTRUMENTATION, p. 163; Zopff/DIRIGENT, p. 14.

21. Mendelssohn/BRIEFE, I, p. 313; trans. Mendelssohn/ITALY, pp. 317–18.

22. Berlioz-Strauss/INSTRUMENTATIONSLEHRE, I, p. 177; trans. Berlioz-Strauss/INSTRUMENTATION, p. 163.

23. Berlioz/TRAITE, p. 104; trans. Berlioz-Strauss/INSTRUMENTATION, p. 164.

24. Zopff/DIRIGENT, p. 14.

25. Blitz/CHEF, p. 80.

26. Mueller/AMERICAN, p. 164.

27. Blaze/ITALIEN, p. 223.

28. Carse/ORCHESTRA, p. 26.

29. Blaze/ACADEMIE, II, pp. 349–50.

30. Mendelssohn/BRIEFE, I, p. 296; or Mendelssohn/ITALY, p. 300.

31. Berlioz/MEMOIRES, II, p. 78; trans. Berlioz/MEMOIRS, p. 285.

32. Berlioz/MEMOIRES, II, p. 83; trans. Berlioz/MEMOIRS, p. 289.

33. Berlioz/MEMOIRES, II, p. 91; trans. Berlioz/MEMOIRS, pp. 295–96.

34. Berlioz/MEMOIRES, II, p. 103; trans. Berlioz/MEMOIRS, p. 305.

35. Berlioz/MEMOIRES, II, p. 109; trans. Berlioz/MEMOIRS, p. 310.

36. Berlioz/MEMOIRES, II, p. 115; trans. Berlioz/MEMOIRS, p. 315.

37. Berlioz/MEMOIRES, II, p. 156; trans. Berlioz/MEMOIRS, p. 346.

38. Russell/THOMAS, p. 48.

39. Mueller/AMERICAN, p. 162.

40. See Gassner/PARTITURKENNTNISS, I, p. 19; Berlioz/TRAITE, p. 122; trans. Berlioz-Strauss/INSTRUMENTATION, pp. 183–84; Zopff/DIRIGENT, pp. 13–14.

41. Blaze/OPERA, I, p. 353. See also Fétis/REVOLUTIONS, p. 196, Fétis/CURIOSITES, p. 288, and Berlioz/TRAITE, p. 150, or Berlioz-Strauss/INSTRUMENTATION, p. 226.

42. See Carse/WIND, pp. 157–65; Baines/WOODWIND, pp. 331–33.

43. Gassner/PARTITURKENNTNISS, I, p. 20; Berlioz/TRAITE, p. 134; or Berlioz-Strauss/INSTRUMENTATION, p. 199; and Zopff/DIRIGENT, p. 12.

44. Berlioz/TRAITE, p. 134; trans. Berlioz-Strauss/INSTRUMENTATION, p. 199.

45. Gassner/PARTITURKENNTNISS, I, p. 20, and II, p. 11, no. 33.

46. Zopff/DIRIGENT, p. 12.

47. Blaze/OPERA, I, pp. 352–53.

48. Berlioz/TRAITE, p. 136; Berlioz-Strauss/INSTRUMENTATIONSLEHRE, I, pp. 216, 220; Berlioz-Strauss/INSTRUMENTATION, pp. 201, 205.

49. Berlioz/TRAITE, p. 137; Berlioz-Strauss/INSTRUMENTATIONSLEHRE, I, p. 221; trans. Berlioz-Strauss/INSTRUMENTATION, p. 206.

50. Blitz/CHEF, p. 81.

51. Schubert/MUSIKDIREKTOR, p. 33. See also Zopff/DIRIGENT, p. 62, for a similar complaint.

52. Blitz/CHEF, p. 80.

53. See Carse/ORCHESTRA, p. 26.

54. Blaze/ACADEMIE, II, p. 348.

55. See Wagner & Liszt/BRIEFWECHSEL, I, pp. 55, 63, 290; trans. Wagner & Liszt/CORRESPONDENCE, I, pp. 70, 79, 349.

56. Nösselt/GEWANDHAUS, p. 183.

57. Berlioz/TRAITE, p. 148; Berlioz-Strauss/INSTRUMENTATION, p. 222.

58. Zopff/DIRIGENT, pp. 12–13.

59. Berlioz/TRAITE, p. 148; trans. Berlioz-Strauss/INSTRUMENTATION, p. 222.

60. Berlioz/TRAITE, pp. 149–50; or Berlioz-Strauss/INSTRUMENTATION, p. 226.

61. Gassner/PARTITURKENNTNISS, I, p. 24.

62. See for example Schroeder/KATECHISMUS, p. 92.

63. Zopf/DIRIGENT, p. 13.

64. Berlioz/MEMOIRES, II, pp. 230–31; trans. Berlioz/MEMOIRS, p. 402.

65. Smart/JOURNALS, p. 162.

66. Berlioz-Strauss/INSTRUMENTATIONSLEHRE, II, p. 241; trans. Berlioz-Strauss/INSTRUMENTATION, p. 226.

67. MacGillivray/WOODWIND, p. 269; see also Carse/WIND, pp. 191–99; Galkin/CONDUCTING, pp. 44–45; Baines/WOODWIND, pp. 336–37.

68. Gassner/PARTITURKENNTNISS, I, pp. 25–26.

69. Berlioz/TRAITE, p. 128.

70. Berlioz-Strauss/INSTRUMENTATIONSLEHRE, I, p. 204; or Berlioz-Strauss/INSTRUMENTATION, p. 189.

71. Zopff/DIRIGENT, pp. 11–12.

72. Schroeder/KATECHISMUS, p. 92.

73. Berlioz-Strauss/INSTRUMENTATIONSLEHRE, I, p. 204; trans. Berlioz-Strauss/INSTRUMENTATION, p. 189.

74. Gassner/PARTITURKENNTNISS, I, p. 25.

75. Berlioz/TRAITE, p. 128; trans. Berlioz-Strauss/INSTRUMENTATION, p. 190.

76. Carse/ORCHESTRA, p. 26.

77. Jerger/WIENER, p. 83.

78. Thomas/MEMOIRS, p. 37; the work was Verdi's *Don Carlos*.

79. Berlioz/TRAITE, p. 133; trans. Berlioz-Strauss/INSTRUMENTATION, p. 198.

80. Zopff/DIRIGENT, p. 11. Schroeder/KATECHISMUS, p. 93, also agrees in range.

81. Berlioz-Strauss/INSTRUMENTATIONSLEHRE, I, p. 213; trans. Berlioz-Strauss/INSTRUMENTATION, p. 198.

82. Berlioz/TRAITE, p. 133, or Berlioz-Strauss/INSTRUMENTATION, p. 198.

83. Gassner/PARTITURKENNTNISS, I, p. 37.

84. Berlioz/MEMOIRES, II, p. 231; trans. Berlioz/MEMOIRS, p. 402.

85. Berlioz/TRAITE, p. 284; trans. Berlioz-Strauss/INSTRUMENTATION, p. 400.

86. See letter in Davison/MENDELSSOHN, p. 216.

87. Haas/AUFFÜHRUNGSPRAXIS, p. 255.

88. Ibid., pp. 255-56.

89. Blitz/CHEF, pp. 78-79.

90. Berlioz/CHANTS, pp. 296-98; trans. Berlioz/ESSAYS, pp. 103-5.

91. Mendelssohn/BRIEFE, I, p. 313; trans. Mendelssohn/ITALY, p. 317.

92. Berlioz/MEMOIRES, II, p. 123; trans. Berlioz/MEMOIRS, p. 321.

93. Berlioz/MEMOIRES, II, p. 141; trans. Berlioz/MEMOIRS, p. 334.

94. Berlioz/MEMOIRES, II, pp. 60-61; trans. Berlioz/MEMOIRS, p. 271.

95. Fétis/CURIOSITES, p. 194.

96. Galkin/CONDUCTING, p. 46; also Blaze/ACADEMIE, II, p. 347.

97. See Jerger/WIENER, pp. 83-84, note. Weingartner wondered why this was entrusted to the fourth horn and recommended giving it to the first or third, "according to their respective merit." See Weingartner/RATSCHLAGE, I, p. 179, or Weingartner/BEETHOVEN, p. 169.

98. Elwart/SOCIETE, p. 131.

99. Berlioz/MEMOIRES, II, pp. 67-68; trans. Berlioz/MEMOIRS, p. 277.

100. Berlioz/MEMOIRES, II, p. 103; trans. Berlioz/MEMOIRS, p. 306.

101. Berlioz/MEMOIRES, II, pp. 119-20; trans. Berlioz/MEMOIRS, p. 318; see also Berlioz/TRAITE, p. 185; trans. Berlioz-Strauss/INSTRUMENTATION, p. 260.

102. For example, Schroeder/KATECHISMUS, pp. 94–95.

103. For example, Schubert/MUSIKDIREKTOR, p. 34; Zopff/DIRIGENT, p. 62.

104. Berlioz/TRAITE, p. 185; trans. Berlioz-Strauss/INSTRUMENTATION, pp. 259–60.

105. Gassner/PARTITURKENNTNISS, I, p. 45.

106. Ibid., I, pp. 26–29; II, p. 15, no. 42.

107. Berlioz/TRAITE, pp. 170–73; trans. Berlioz-Strauss/INSTRUMENTATION, pp. 247–49.

108. Zopff/DIRIGENT, pp. 15–16.

109. Schroeder/KATECHISMUS, pp. 93–94.

110. Blitz/CHEF, pp. 67–69, 96.

111. See, for example, Berlioz/MEMOIRES, II, pp. 68, 103; trans. Berlioz/MEMOIRS, pp. 277, 306.

112. Berlioz/MEMOIRES, II, p. 120; trans. Berlioz/MEMOIRS, pp. 318–19.

113. Smart/JOURNALS, p. 84.

114. Ibid., p. 90.

115. Ibid., p. 301.

116. Blitz/CHEF, p. 64.

117. Ibid., pp. 76–77.

118. Galkin/CONDUCTING, pp. 46–47.

119. Berlioz/TRAITE, p. 188; trans. Berlioz-Strauss/INSTRUMENTATION, p. 282.

120. Blaze/ACADEMIE, II, p. 350.

121. Gassner/PARTITURKENNTNISS, I, pp. 30–31, II, p. 17, no. 49.

122. Berlioz/TRAITE, pp. 186–88; can also be seen in Berlioz-Strauss/INSTRUMEN-TATION, pp. 281–82.

123. Schroeder/KATECHISMUS, p. 95.

124. Zopff/DIRIGENT, pp. 17, 62.

125. Berlioz-Strauss/INSTRUMENTATIONSLEHRE, II, p. 301; trans. Berlioz-Strauss/INSTRUMENTATION, p. 282.

126. Gassner/PARTITURKENNTNISS, I, p. 44.

127. Berlioz/TRAITE, p. 191; trans. Berlioz-Strauss/INSTRUMENTATION, p. 288.

128. Menke/TRUMPET, p. 60.

129. See Widor/ORCHESTRE, p. 62, or Widor/ORCHESTRA, p. 54. He uses the cornet as the modern example, but the result would be even more exaggerated in that case.

130. Forsyth/ORCHESTRATION, p. 93.

131. Berlioz/TRAITE, pp. 192–93, 196–97; can also be seen in Berlioz-Strauss/INSTRUMENTATION, p. 292, 294–95.

132. Schroeder/KATECHISMUS, p. 95.

133. Volbach/ORCHESTER, p. 95.

134. Widor/ORCHESTRE, pp. 89–90; or Widor/ORCHESTRA, p. 73.

135. Forsyth/ORCHESTRATION, pp. 102–3.

136. Carse/ORCHESTRA, p. 26.

137. Smart/JOURNALS, p. 90.

138. Bennett/FORTY, p. 335.

139. Gerber/MUSIKFESTE, col. 750.

140. Madeira/PHILADELPHIA, p. 84.

141. See, for example, Galkin/CONDUCTING, pp. 47–48.

142. See Menke/TRUMPET, pp. 186–87.

143. Blaze/OPERA, I, p. 365.

144. Gassner/PARTITURKENNTNISS, I, pp. 32–33, 39–43.

145. Berlioz/TRAITE, pp. 199–202; trans. Berlioz-Strauss/INSTRUMENTATION, pp. 298–300; Berlioz-Strauss/INSTRUMENTATIONSLEHRE, II, p. 324.

146. Schroeder/KATECHISMUS, pp. 95–96.

147. Zopff/DIRIGENT, pp. 19–21.

148. Berlioz/MEMOIRES, II, p. 79–80; trans. Berlioz/MEMOIRS, p. 287.

149. Berlioz/MEMOIRES, II, p. 145; trans. Berlioz/MEMOIRS, pp. 337–38.

150. Hiller/MENDELSSOHN 1, p. 39; trans. Hiller/MENDELSSOHN 2, p. 47.

151. Carse/ORCHESTRA, p. 26.

152. Adam/SOUVENIRS, pp. 62–63.

153. Mendelssohn/BRIEFE, I, p. 312; trans. Mendelssohn/ITALY, p. 316.

154. Bennett/FORTY, pp. 335–36. See also Nettel/ENGLAND, pp. 142, 185.

155. Gassner/PARTITURKENNTNISS, I, p. 38.

156. Berlioz/TRAITE, p. 230; trans. Berlioz-Strauss/INSTRUMENTATION, p. 348.

157. Carse/ORCHESTRA, p. 26.

158. Blaze/ACADÉMIE, II, p. 350.

159. Berlioz/MEMOIRES, II, pp. 80, 83, 91, 103, 109, 121, 156; trans. Berlioz/MEMOIRS, pp. 287, 289, 295–96, 306, 310, 303–5, 346.

160. Berlioz/MEMOIRES, II, pp. 115, 159; trans. Berlioz/MEMOIRS, pp. 315, 348.

161. Blitz/CHEF, pp. 11–12, 78–79.

162. Ryan/RECOLLECTIONS, p. 20.

163. Thomas-Stein/AUTOBIOGRAPHY, pp. 26–27.

164. Kennedy/HALLE, pp. 24, 110.

165. *Illustrated London News,* Dec. 10, 1842, quoted in Carse/BEETHOVEN, p. 235.

166. Hoffman/RECOLLECTIONS, p. 71.

167. Gassner/PARTITURKENNTNISS, I, pp. 38-39.

168. Berlioz/TRAITE, pp. 226-27; trans. Berlioz-Strauss/INSTRUMENTATION, p. 337.

169. Volbach/ORCHESTER, p. 84.

170. Berlioz/MEMOIRES, II, p. 142; trans. Berlioz/MEMOIRS, p. 335.

171. See, for example, Howes/FULL, p. 58; Zopff/DIRIGENT, pp. 21-22.

172. See, for example, Carse/WIND, p. 302; Widor/ORCHESTRE, pp. 117-22, or Widor/ORCHESTRA, pp. 94-97; & Pegge/HORN, p. 314.

173. Pegge/HORN, p. 315. See also Volbach/ORCHESTER, pp. 95-97.

174. See Berlioz/TRAITE, , p. 230; trans. Berlioz-Strauss/INSTRUMENTATION, p. 348.

175. Blaze/OPERA, I, p. 366.

176. Ibid., I, pp. 366-68.

177. Blaze/ACADÉMIE, II, pp. 350-51.

178. Fétis/CURIOSITES, p. 194; Berlioz/MEMOIRES, II, p. 76; trans. Berlioz/MEMOIRS, p. 284.

179. Berlioz/MEMOIRES, II, p. 122; trans. Berlioz/MEMOIRS, p. 320.

180. See, for example, Berlioz/MEMOIRES, II, p. 231-32; trans. Berlioz/MEMOIRS, p. 403.

181. See Gassner/PARTITURKENNTNISS, I, pp. 113-14.

182. Ibid., I, p. 46, & II, p. 34, nos. 80-81.

183. Berlioz/TRAITE, p. 254; trans. Berlioz-Strauss/INSTRUMENTATION, p. 371.

184. Berlioz-Strauss/INSTRUMENTATIONSLEHRE, II, p. 397; trans. Berlioz-Strauss/INSTRUMENTATION, p. 371.

185. Zopff/DIRIGENT, p. 22.

186. Hanslick/KRITIKEN, p. 416; trans. Hanslick/VIENNA, p. 272, including note.

187. See Schroeder/KATECHISMUS, p. 97.

188. Berlioz-Strauss/INSTRUMENTATIONSLEHRE, II, p. 397; trans. Berlioz-Strauss/INSTRUMENTATION, p. 371.

189. Carse/ORCHESTRA, pp. 26-27.

190. Nösselt/GEWANDHAUS, p. 62.

191. Smart/JOURNALS, p. 148.

192. HARMONICON, III, (1825), p. 133.

193. Beethoven/WELLINGTONS, p. 124; trans. Beethoven/NEW LETTERS, pp. 162-63, also note 7 on p. 164.

194. Blaze/OPERA, I, p. 369.

195. Gassner/PARTITURKENNTNISS, I, pp. 45–49.

196. Berlioz/TRAITE, pp. 268–83; trans. Berlioz-Strauss/INSTRUMENTATION, pp. 385–99.

197. See, for example, Berlioz/MEMOIRES, II, pp. 122, 156–57; trans. Berlioz/MEMOIRS, pp. 320, 346.

198. Berlioz/MEMOIRES, II, p. 274; trans. Berlioz/MEMOIRS, p. 435.

199. Berlioz/MEMOIRES, II, p. 346; trans. Berlioz/MEMOIRS, p. 493.

200. Berlioz/MEMOIRES, II, p. 232; trans. Berlioz/MEMOIRS, p. 403.

201. Zopff/DIRIGENT, p. 23.

202. Schroeder/KATECHISMUS, p. 98.

203. Aubert & Landowski/ORCHESTRE, p. 82.

204. Rochlitz/BRUCHSTUCKE, cols. 19–20.

205. Fétis/CURIOSITES, p. 188.

206. Gassner/PARTITURKENNTNISS, I, p. 56.

207. Berlioz/TRAITE, pp. 97–100; or trans. Berlioz-Strauss/INSTRUMENTATION, pp. 157–60.

208. Zopff/DIRIGENT, p. 9.

209. Blaze/ITALIEN, p. 224.

210. Carse/ORCHESTRA, p. 26.

211. Blaze/ACADEMIE, II, p. 349.

212. Blaze/OPERA, I, p. 338.

213. Smart/JOURNALS, pp. 207–8.

214. Gassner/PARTITURKENNTNISS, I, p. 57.

215. Berlioz/TRAITE, pp. 77–78; or Berlioz-Strauss/INSTRUMENTATION, pp. 138–39.

216. Berlioz-Strauss/INSTRUMENTATIONSLEHRE, I, p. 155; trans. Berlioz-Strauss/INSTRUMENTATION, p. 144.

217. Berlioz/MEMOIRES, II, pp. 66–67; trans. Berlioz/MEMOIRS, p. 276.

218. Berlioz/MEMOIRES, II, p. 73; or Berlioz/MEMOIRS, p. 281.

219. Berlioz/MEMOIRES, II, p. 83; or Berlioz/MEMOIRS, p. 289.

220. Berlioz/MEMOIRES, II, p. 91; trans. Berlioz/MEMOIRS, p. 296.

221. Berlioz/MEMOIRES, II, p. 115; trans. Berlioz/MEMOIRS, p. 315.

222. Berlioz/MEMOIRES, II, p. 157; trans. Berlioz/MEMOIRS, p. 346.

223. Berlioz/MEMOIRES, II, pp. 108–9; trans. Berlioz/MEMOIRS, p. 310.

224. Berlioz/MEMOIRES, II, p. 159; trans. Berlioz/MEMOIRS, p. 348.

225. Berlioz/MEMOIRES, II, p. 102; trans. Berlioz/MEMOIRS, pp. 304–5.

226. Berlioz/SOIREES, p. 418; or Berlioz/EVENINGS, p. 331.

227. Berlioz/MEMOIRES, II, p. 240; trans. Berlioz/MEMOIRS, p. 409.

228. Berlioz/MEMOIRES, II, pp. 345–46; or Berlioz/MEMOIRS, p. 493.

229. Russell/THOMAS, p. 48.

230. Zopff/DIRIGENT, pp. 8–9.

231. Schroeder/KATECHISMUS, p. 99.

232. Galkin/CONDUCTING, p. 48.

233. Dart/INTERPRETATION, p. 34.

234. Galkin/CONDUCTING, p. 48.

235. Ibid., p. 49.

236. Berlioz/MEMOIRES, II, p. 123; trans. Berlioz/MEMOIRS, p. 321.

237. Schonberg/CONDUCTORS, p. 67.

238. Parke/MEMOIRS, II, p. 257. "Although this gentleman, who was a great pigeon-fancier, did not go aloft on the fiddle, he went every day up to the top of his house to see his pigeons fly..."

239. Gassner/PARTITURKENNTNISS, I, p. 9.

240. Berlioz/TRAITE, p. 3; Berlioz-Strauss/INSTRUMENTATIONSLEHRE, I, p. 3; trans. Berlioz-Strauss/INSTRUMENTATION, p. 2.

241. Berlioz/MEMOIRES, II, p. 230; trans. Berlioz/MEMOIRS, pp. 401–2.

242. Fétis/CURIOSITES, p. 284.

243. *Monthly Chronicle,* quoted in Carse/BEETHOVEN, p. 201.

244. MUSIKDIREKTOR, col. 182.

245. Ernest Reyer, *Notes de musique,* pp. 76–77, quoted by ed. in Berlioz/MEMOIRS, p. 402, note 2.

246. Wagner/DIRIGIREN, p. 329; trans. Wagner/CONDUCTING, pp. 3–4.

247. Berlioz/MEMOIRES, II, p. 230; trans. Berlioz/MEMOIRS, p. 402.

248. Berlioz/MEMOIRES, II, p. 346; trans. Berlioz/MEMOIRS, p. 493.

249. See Blaze/OPERA, I, p. 344, note 1.

250. Gassner/PARTITURKENNTNISS, I, pp. 10–11.

251. Berlioz/TRAITE, p. 37; trans. Berlioz-Strauss/INSTRUMENTATION, p. 74.

252. Berlioz-Strauss/INSTRUMENTATIONSLEHRE, I, p. 81; trans. Berlioz-Strauss/INSTRUMENTATION, p. 74.

253. Hanslick/KRITIKEN, p. 416; trans. Hanslick/VIENNA, p. 272.

254. Gassner/PARTITURKENNTNISS, I, pp. 11–12.

255. Phillips/RECOLLECTIONS, I, p. 128.

256. Berlioz/TRAITE, p. 41–42; trans. Berlioz-Strauss/INSTRUMENTATION, p. 77.

257. See Schubert/KONTRAVIOLONS, cols. 187–91.

258. Blaze/OPERA, I, p. 346, plus note 3.

259. Schubert/KONTRAVIOLONS, cols. 189–90.

260. Smart/JOURNALS, p. 213.

261. Gassner/PARTITURKENNTNISS, I, p. 13.

262. Berlioz/TRAITE, p. 53; Berlioz-Strauss/INSTRUMENTATION, p. 96.

263. Zopff/DIRIGENT, p. 8.

264. Carse/BEETHOVEN, p. 254.

265. Berlioz-Strauss/INSTRUMENTATIONSLEHRE, I, pp. 104–5; trans. Berlioz-Strauss/INSTRUMENTATION, p. 97.

266. Hanslick/KRITIKEN, p. 416; or Hanslick/VIENNA, p. 272.

267. Phillips/RECOLLECTIONS, I, pp. 129, 310.

268. Smart/JOURNALS, p. 112.

269. Nettel/ENGLAND, p. 151.

270. Berlioz/MEMOIRES, II, p. 123; trans. Berlioz/MEMOIRS, p. 321.

271. Gassner/PARTITURKENNTNISS, I, p. 59; Berlioz/TRAITE, pp. 39–40; Berlioz-Strauss/INSTRUMENTATION, pp. 75–76; Blitz/CHEF, p. 11.

272. Blaze/ACADÉMIE, II, p. 351.

273. Berlioz-Strauss/INSTRUMENTATIONSLEHRE, I, p. 84; Berlioz-Strauss/INSTRUMENTATION, p. 76.

274. Gassner/PARTITURKENNTNISS, I, p. 57; Berlioz/TRAITE, pp. 83–86; Berlioz-Strauss/INSTRUMENTATION, pp. 145–50.

275. Gassner/PARTITURKENNTNISS, I, pp. 57–58.

276. Ibid., I, p. 58; Berlioz/TRAITE, pp. 87–88; Berlioz-Strauss/INSTRUMENTATION, pp. 151–52; Schoeder/KATECHISMUS, p. 99.

277. Gassner/PARTITURKENNTNISS, I, p. 60.

278. Ibid., I, p. 61.

279. Blitz/CHEF, p. 80.

280. Ibid., pp. 82–83.

281. Ibid., p. 95.

282. Berlioz/SOIREES, pp. 422–23; trans. Berlioz/EVENINGS, pp. 355–56.

Chapter 8

1. Unold/STELLUNG, col. 783.

2. Weber/BEMERKUNGEN, col. 823.

3. Letter to Archduke Rudolph, Oct. 1811; Beethoven/BRIEFE 1, II, p. 46. Wooldridge/CONDUCTORS, p. 35, gives this request as in 1813 for the Seventh Symphony, but the date of the letter would preclude that, the Seventh having been composed in 1812.

4. Ms. Anderson translates this as: "four violins, four seconds, four first, two double basses, two violoncellos"; see Beethoven/LETTERS, I, p. 343.

5. Haas/AUFFÜHRUNGSPRAXIS, p. 253.

6. Memo of Beethoven, quoted in Thayer-Forbes/BEETHOVEN, I, p. 576.

7. See Zlotnik/SCHUMANN, p. 54.

8. See, for example, Borris/ORCHESTER, p. 250.

9. See Beethoven/WELLINGTONS, p. 124; trans. Beethoven/NEW LETTERS, p. 162.

10. Beethoven/BRIEFE 1, III, p. 178; trans. Beethoven/LETTERS II, p. 688.

11. According to Haas/AUFFÜHRUNGSPRAXIS, p. 253.

12. Beethoven/BRIEFE 2, p. 712; trans. Beethoven/LETTERS, III, p. 1119.

13. Beethoven/NEW LETTERS. p. 445, note 3.

14. Borris/ORCHESTER, p. 92.

15. Schindler/BEETHOVEN 1, I, p. 149; trans. Schindler/BEETHOVEN 2, pp. 141–42.

16. Spohr/LEBENSERINNERUNGEN, I, p. 8; trans. Spohr/JOURNEYS, p. 4.

17. Spohr/LEBENSERINNERUNGEN, I, p. 46; trans. Spohr/JOURNEYS, p. 33.

18. Spohr/LEBENSERINNERUNGEN, I, p. 48; trans. Spohr/JOURNEYS, p. 34.

19. Spohr/LEBENSERINNERUNGEN, I, p. 18; trans. Spohr/JOURNEYS, pp. 14–15.

20. Gerber/MUSIKFESTE, col. 747–48.

21. Spohr/LEBENSERINNERUNGEN, I, pp. 197–98; trans. Spohr/JOURNEYS, pp. 123–24.

22. Spohr/LEBENSERINNERUNGEN, I, p. 203; trans. Spohr/JOURNEYS, pp. 125–26. Incidentally, Spohr found many faults with the work as a symphony; see further on LEBENSERINNERUNGEN, I, p. 203, or JOURNEYS, on to p. 127. Another source reported that ca. 1811, the Munich orchestra under Winter's direction "when at its full complement...amounted to as many as eighty-seven performers." See Weber/WEBER 1, I, p. 260; trans. Weber/WEBER 2, I, p. 199.

23. Spohr/LEBENSERINNERUNGEN, I, pp. 236–37; trans. Spohr/JOURNEYS, pp. 139–41.

24. Spohr/LEBENSERINNERUNGEN, I, p. 245; trans. Spohr/JOURNEYS, p. 145.

25. Spohr/LEBENSERINNERUNGEN, I, p. 277; trans. Spohr/JOURNEYS, pp. 160–61.

26. Smart/JOURNALS, p. 38.

27. Ibid., p. 80.

28. Ibid., p. 90.

29. Ibid., p. 192.

30. Ibid., pp. 167–68.

31. Ibid., p. 122.

32. Ibid., p. 133.

33. Ibid., pp. 139–40.

34. Ibid., p. 209.

35. Ibid., p. 221.

36. Dorn/LEBEN, I, p. 20.

37. Wagner/LEBEN, p. 330; trans. Wagner/LIFE, I, p. 337.

38. See seating plan in Gassner/DIRIGENT, Beilage 2.

39. Wagner/LEBEN, p. 336; trans. Wagner/LIFE, p. 344.

40. Gassner/DIRIGENT, Beilage 2.

41. Berlioz/FANTASTIC, pp. 49, 81, 106, 122, 143.

42. Berlioz did have an orchestra of 130 assembled for a proposed performance which had to be abandoned, principally because of lack of space and desks, etc., in the Théâtre des Nouveautés. See Berlioz/MEMOIRES, I, pp. 168–69, or Berlioz/MEMOIRS, pp. 126–27.

43. Berlioz/REQUIEM, pp. 1, 19.

44. Ibid., p. 1, note, which also includes translation.

45. Berlioz/CARNAVAL, p. 1.

46. See Paris Conservatory/ARCHIVES, Box 4.

47. Letter in Bennett/FORTY, pp. 158–59.

48. Berlioz/NOUVELLES, pp. 164–65, or see Bennett/FORTY, p. 160.

49. Berlioz/MEMOIRES, I, pp. 70–71; trans. Berlioz/MEMOIRS, pp. 54–55.

50. Berlioz/MEMOIRES, II, pp. 47–48; trans. Berlioz/MEMOIRS, pp. 259–60. Another writer claims there were only 450 performers: "Berlioz is sometimes a little exuberant in his *Memoirs*." See Schonberg/CONDUCTORS, pp. 112–13.

51. Berlioz/MEMOIRES, II, pp. 172–73; trans. Berlioz/MEMOIRS, p. 358, Schonberg/CONDUCTORS, p. 113, has it as 1200; Berlioz seems none too "exuberant" here!

52. Berlioz/MEMOIRES, II, p. 173; trans. Berlioz/MEMOIRS, p. 358.

53. Berlioz/MEMOIRES, II, p. 177; trans. Berlioz/MEMOIRS, p. 361.

54. Berlioz/MEMOIRES, II, p. 178; trans. Berlioz/MEMOIRS, p. 362.

55. Berlioz/NOUVELLES, pp. 62–67.

56. Ibid., pp. 96–97.

57. Ibid., pp. 106–9.

58. Letter & translation in Davison/MENDELSSOHN, pp. 180–81.

59. Berlioz/NOUVELLES, pp. 236–37.

60. Berlioz/TRAITE, p. 294; trans. Berlioz-Strauss/INSTRUMENTATION, p. 406.

61. Seating plan, *Musical World,* 3/26/1840, p. 194, reproduced in Carse/BEETHOVEN, p. 476.

62. Schindler/PARIS, pp. 10–18.

63. Berlioz/TRAITE, p. 294; trans. Berlioz-Strauss/INSTRUMENTATION, p. 407.

64. Berlioz/TRAITE, p. 294; trans. Berlioz-Strauss/INSTRUMENTATION, p. 407.

65. Berlioz/TRAITE, p. 294, trans. Berlioz-Strauss/INSTRUMENTATION, p. 407.

66. Berlioz/TRAITE, p. 295; trans. Berlioz-Strauss/INSTRUMENTATION, p. 407. See also Berlioz/MEMOIRES, II, pp. 51–52, or Berlioz/MEMOIRS, pp. 263–64, for similar speculation on this subject.

67. Berlioz/TRAITE, pp. 295–97, where instrumental total is incorrectly given as 467; here from Berlioz-Strauss/INSTRUMENTATION, pp. 408–9.

68. Berlioz/SOIREES, p. 301; trans. Berlioz/EVENINGS, p. 235.

69. Berlioz/MEMOIRES, II, p. 188; trans. Berlioz/MEMOIR, p. 370.

70. Berlioz/TRAITE, p. 297; trans. Berlioz-Strauss/INSTRUMENTATION, p. 409.

71. Berlioz/MEMOIRES, II, p. 200; trans. Berlioz/MEMOIRS, p. 379.

72. Berlioz wondered why Habeneck, among others, was conspicuous by his absence. See Berlioz/SOIREES, p. 415, or Berlioz/EVENINGS, p. 239.

73. Elwart/SOCIETE, p. 347.

74. Smart/JOURNALS, p. 304.

75. Berlioz/SOIREES, pp. 417–18; trans. Berlioz/EVENINGS, pp. 331–32.

76. Haas/AUFFÜHRUNGSPRAXIS, p. 266.

77. Berlioz/SOIREES, p. 418; trans. Berlioz/EVENINGS, p. 332.

78. Smart/JOURNALS, p. 322.

79. Elwart/SOCIETE, p. 355.

80. Fétis/CURIOSITES, pp. 286–89; trans. Fétis/REVOLUTIONS, p. 196.

81. Fétis/CURIOSITES, p. 228.

82. Ibid., p. 239.

83. Ibid., p. 285.

84. Moscheles/LEBEN, I, p. 35; or Moscheles/RECENT, p. 22.

85. Mendelssohn/BRIEFE, I, p. 297; or Mendelssohn/ITALY, pp. 300–301.

86. Werner/MENDELSSOHN, p. 254.

87. Haas/AUFFÜHRUNGSPRAXIS, p. 198.

88. Mendelssohn/BRIEFE, II, p. 201; trans. Mendelssohn/LETTERS, p. 157.

89. Creuzberg/GEWANDHAUS, pp. 85–86.

90. Zlotnik/SCHUMANN, p. 52.

91. Ibid., p. 53. See Hedler/DUSSELDORFER, pp. 22–23, for a breakdown of these figures.

92. Thomas-Stein/AUTOBIOGRAPHY, p. 27.

93. Davison/MENDELSSOHN, p. 110.

94. Elkin/LONDON, p. 139.

95. Ryan/RECOLLECTIONS, p. 66.

96. Mueller/AMERICAN, p. 33.

97. Davison/MENDELSSOHN, p. 217.

98. Ibid., p. 218.

99. Quoted in Schonberg/CONDUCTORS, p. 129.

100. In Bayreuth/GEBURTSTAG, pages unnumbered.

101. Wagner/DIRIGIREN, p. 329; trans. Wagner/CONDUCTING, p. 3.

102. Wagner/DIRIGIREN, p. 330; or Wagner/CONDUCTING, pp. 4–5.

103. Wagner/NEUNTEN, p. 53; trans. Wagner/CHORAL, pp. 243–44.

104. Wagner/NEUNTEN, pp. 53–54; trans. Wagner/CHORAL, p. 244. See also description in Wagner/LEBEN, p. 389, or Wagner/LIFE, I, p. 400.

105. Wagner/NEUNTEN, pp. 54–55; or Wagner/CHORAL, pp. 245–46.

106. Wagner/NATIONAL 1, pp. 264–66; or Wagner/NATIONAL 2, pp. 350–52.

107. Berlioz/MEMOIRES, II, p. 83; trans. Berlioz/MEMOIRS, p. 289.

108. Raabe, *Liszt,* I, p. 104, cited in Carse/BEETHOVEN, p. 59, & in Schreiber/ORCHESTER, p. 111; and Beckett, *Liszt,* p. 39, cited in Zlotnik/SCHUMANN, pp. 27–28.

109. Schonberg/CONDUCTORS, p. 158.

110. Wagner & Liszt/BRIEFWECHSEL, I, p. 55; trans. Wagner & Liszt/CORRESPONDENCE, I, p. 70.

111. Wagner & Liszt/BRIEFWECHSEL, I, p. 63; trans. Wagner & Liszt/CORRESPONDENCE, I, p. 79.

112. Wagner & Liszt/BRIEFWECHSEL, I, p. 45; trans. Wagner & Liszt/CORRESPONDENCE, I, pp. 58–59.

113. Wagner/LEBEN, p. 533; trans. Wagner/LIFE, II, p. 553.

114. Schonberg/CONDUCTORS, p. 134.

115. Wagner & Liszt/BRIEFWECHSEL, I, p. 234; trans. Wagner & Liszt/CORRESPON-DENCE, I, pp. 282–83.

116. Wagner & Liszt/BRIEFWECHSEL, I, p. 238; trans. Wagner & Liszt/CORRESPON-DENCE, I, pp. 286–87.

117. Wagner & Liszt/BRIEFWECHSEL, I, p. 153; trans. Wagner & Liszt/CORRESPON-DENCE, I, p. 192.

118. Wagner & Liszt/BRIEFWECHSEL, I, p. 245; trans. Wagner & Liszt/CORRESPON-DENCE, I, pp. 296–97.

119. Wagner & Liszt/BRIEFWECHSEL, I, p. 273; trans. Wagner & Liszt/CORRESPON-DENCE, I, p. 332.

120. Wagner & Liszt/BRIEFWECHSEL, II, p. 105; trans. Wagner & Liszt/CORRESPON-DENCE, II, p. 130.

121. Wagner & Liszt/BRIEFWECHSEL, II, p. 139; trans. Wagner & Liszt/CORRESPON-DENCE, II, pp. 169–70.

122. Reported in Wooldridge/CONDUCTOR'S, p. 61.

123. Wagner/LEBEN, p. 732; trans. Wagner/LIFE, II, p. 761.

124. Wagner/LEBEN, pp. 824–25; trans. Wagner/LIFE, II, p. 855.

125. Wagner/LEBEN, p. 829; trans. Wagner/LIFE, II, p. 860.

126. Reported in Wooldridge/CONDUCTOR'S, p. 99.

127. In Wagner/BAYREUTH, p. 93.

128. See Wagner/BAYREUTH, pp. 79, 93.

129. See Wagner/BEETHOVEN'S 1 or Wagner/BEETHOVEN'S 2, *passim*.

130. Reproduced in Kufferath/DIRIGER, pp. 59–60.

131. Kufferath/DIRIGER, p. 61.

132. Lavignac/BAYREUTH 1, p. 519; or Lavignac/BAYREUTH 2, p. 484.

133. Lavignac/BAYREUTH 1, p. 518; trans. Lavignac/BAYREUTH 2, p. 483.

134. Lavignac/BAYREUTH 1, p. 519; trans. Lavignac/BAYREUTH 2, p. 484.

135. Hanslick/STATIONEN, p. 229; trans. Hanslick/VIENNA, p. 152.

136. Neumann/WAGNER 1, p. 157; trans. Neumann/WAGNER 2, p. 151.

137. Davison/MENDELSSOHN, p. 516.

138. Ibid., p. 515.

139. Borris/ORCHESTER, p. 222.

140. Zlotnik/SCHUMANN, pp. 54–55.

141. Newman/WAGNER, IV, p. 312.

142. Boult/CONDUCTING, p. xii, cited in Zlotnik/SCHUMAN, p. 55.

143. Galkin/CONDUCTING, pp. 114–15.

144. Strauss/HELDENLEBEN, p. 2.

145. See Borris/ORCHESTER, pp. 366–67.

146. Thomas/MEMOIRS, p. 498.

147. Thomas/MEMOIRS, p. 499, where it is called "Mass in D minor"; whoever started the error, it was compounded; Thomas-Stein/AUTOBIOGRAPHY,pp. 211–12, also refers to "the great D minor Mass."

148. Russell/THOMAS, p. 288.

149. Thomas-Stein/AUTOBIOGRAPHY, pp. 350–51.

150. Ibid., p. 212.

151. Thomas/MEMOIRS, p. 500.

152. Ibid., p. 500.

153. Ibid., p. 500.

154. See Wagner/MEISTERSINGER, pp. 1–64.

155. Bülow & Strauss/CORRESPONDENCE, p. 27.

156. Ibid., p. 24.

157. Ibid., p. 84.

158. Hanslick/KRITIKEN, pp. 415–16; trans. Hanslick/VIENNA, p. 271.

159. Hanslick/KRITIKEN, p. 417; trans. Hanslick/VIENNA, p. 273.

Chapter 9

1. Smart/JOURNALS, pp. 167–68.

2. Berlioz/MEMOIRES, II, p. 119; or Berlioz/MEMOIRS, p. 318.

3. Gassner/DIRIGENT, Beilage 9.

4. AMZ, VIII (1805/6), cols. 137–39.

5. Wagner/NATIONAL 1, p. 264; trans. Wagner/NATIONAL 2, p. 351.

6. Carse/BEETHOVEN, p. 141.

7. See Berlioz/MEMOIRES, II, p. 91; or Berlioz/MEMOIRS, p. 296.

8. Burney/FRANCE, p. 353.

9. See Spohr/LEBENSERINNERUNGEN, I, p. 277; trans. Spohr/JOURNEYS, pp. 160–61.

10. Ibid.

11. Blaze/ACADEMIE, II, p. 349.

12. Elkin/LONDON, p. 101.

13. AMZ, II (1799/1800), cols. 846–47.

14. NZFM, XIII (1840), p. 153.

15. Smart/JOURNALS, p. 38,

16. AMZ, V (1802/3), cols. 277–79.

17. Blaze/ACADÉMIE, II, p. 374.

18. AMZ, XXV (1823), cols. 237–38.

19. AMZ, XXV (1823), cols. 317–18.

20. Smart/JOURNALS, p. 77.

21. AMZ, XXVII (1825), cols. 131–32.

22. List in Paris Conservatory/ARCHIVES, Box 4.

23. AMZ, XXVIII (1826), col. 342.

24. Blaze/ACADÉMIE, II, p. 374.

25. Nösselt/GEWANDHAUS, p. 167.

26. Kennedy/HALLE, p. 27.

27. Nettel/ENGLAND, p. 151.

28. Elwart/SOCIÉTÉ, p. 95.

29. Blaze/ITALIEN, pp. 474–75.

30. Seating plan in Lavignac/BAYREUTH 1, p. 86, or Lavignac/BAYREUTH 2, p. 62.

31. Howe/BOSTON, p. 250.

32. Dörffel/GEWANDHAUS, p. 181.

33. Kennedy/HALLE, p. 67.

34. Seating plan in Kling/VOLLKOMMENE, p. 272.

35. Kling/VOLLKOMMENE, p. 277.

36. Otis/CHICAGO, p. 415.

Chapter 10

1. See MUSIKDIREKTOR, cols. 181–83.

2. Nettel/ENGLAND, p. 93.

3. Ibid., pp. 93–94.

4. See Borris/ORCHESTER, p. 78.

5. MUSICAL MAGAZINE, I (1839), p. 126.

6. Ibid., I (1839), p. 166.

7. See, for example, Berlin in 1823 or 1825, Dresden in 1817 or 1819, Munich in 1820 and 1827, to name just a few cases.

8. Thomas-Stein/AUTOBIOGRAPHY, p. 45.

9. Ibid., pp. 100–101.

10. Schubert/MUSIKDIREKTOR, pp. 38–40.

11. Blitz/CHEF, p. 12.

12. Cf. Dart/INTERPRETATION, p. 55.

13. Zopff/DIRIGENT, pp. 56–57.

14. Deduced from 8 vs. 30+; cf. Carse/18TH, pp. 36–37.

15. Dart/INTERPRETATION, pp. 55–56.

16. Berlioz/TRAITÉ, p. 294, or Berlioz-Strauss/INSTRUMENTATION, p. 407.

17. Berlioz/TRAITÉ, pp. 295–97, where instrumental total is incorrectly given as 467; or Berlioz-Strauss/INSTRUMENTATION, pp. 408–9.

18. Marpurg/BEYTRÄGE, I, pp. 75–78.

19. Fürstenau/DRESDEN, II, pp. 294–95.

20. Marpurg/BEYTRÄGE, I, pp. 445–47.

21. Ibid., I, pp. 269–71, 560–61.

22. Ibid., I, pp. 193–96.

23. Pierre/CONCERT, p. 78.

24. Burney/FRANCE, p. 136.

25. Burney/GERMANY, pp. 96–100.

26. Forkel/ALMANACH, 1782, pp. 146–48.

27. Ibid., 1782, p. 139–40.

28. Ibid., 1782, pp. 143–45.

29. Cramer/MAGAZIN, I, pp. 748–50.

30. Pierre/CONCERT, p. 78.

31. Burney/HANDEL, pp. 16–21 (after 56).

32. Hiller/NACHRICHT, pp. 21–27.

33. Blaze/ACADEMIE, II, pp. 372–73.

34. Borland/BALANCE, p. 5.

35. Blaze/CHAPELLE, pp. 171–76; see also Blaze/ITALIEN, pp. 325–26.

36. Borland/BALANCE, p. 4.

37. Gerber/MUSIKFESTE, cols. 746–48.

38. AMZ, XII (1809/10), col. 425.

39. Ibid., XII (1809/10), col. 494.

40. Borland/BALANCE, p. 5.

41. AMZ, XXIII (1821), col. 632.

42. Borland/BALANCE, p. 5.

43. HARMONICON, I (1823), pp. 152–54.

44. Borland/BALANCE, p. 5.

45. HARMONICON, III (1825), p. 19.

46. Blaze/CHAPELLE, pp. 240–41.

47. Elwart/SOCIETE, pp. 98–103.

48. Blaze/CHAPELLE, pp. 225–32.

49. Program in Haas/AUFFÜHRUNGSPRAXIS, p. 254.

50. Seating plan, *Musical World,* 3/26/1840, p. 194, reproduced in Carse/BEETHOVEN, p. 476.

51. Nettel/ENGLAND, p. 133.

52. Blaze/ACADÉMIE, II, pp. 372–73.

53. Gassner/DIRIGENT, Beilage 1.

54. Dorn/LEBEN, I, p. 21.

55. Seating plan, Gassner/DIRIGENT, Beilage 16.

56. Ibid., Beilage 12.

57. Elwart/SOCIETE, p. 347.

58. Ibid., pp. 103–8.

59. Davison/MENDELSSOHN, pp. 229–30.

60. Borland/BALANCE, p. 5; on p. 9 the same source gives 100 players vs. 120.

61. Ibid., p. 14.

62. Otis/CHICAGO, p. 17.

63. Russell/THOMAS, p. 145; also Thomas/MEMOIRS, p. 221.

64. See Berlioz/REQUIEM, p. 1.

65. Ibid., pp. 1, 19.

66. Berlioz/TRAITE, p. 294, or Berlioz-Strauss/INSTRUMENTATION, p. 407.

67. Berlioz/TRAITE, pp. 295–97, or Berlioz-Strauss/INSTRUMENTATION, pp. 408–9.

68. Werner/MENDELSSOHN, p. 254.

69. See Wagner/BAYREUTH, pp. 79, 93.

Chapter 11

1. Hoffman/RECOLLECTIONS, pp. 63–64.

2. Quoted in Creuzburg/GEWANDHAUS, p. 122.

3. Ibid., p. 122, note 1.

4. Hanslick/KRITIKEN, pp. 416–17; trans. Hanslick/VIENNA, pp. 272–73. The Coleridge translation of Dittersdorf's Autobiography misses the implication of playing seated, so clear in the German: "During that time I ordered long desks and benches to be made, for I introduced the Viennese plan of using these for the orchestra, which was so arranged that every player fronted his audience." Dittersdorf/AUTOBIOGRAPHY, p. 143. But Dittersdorf/LEBENSBESCHREIBUNG, p. 141, agrees almost exactly with Hanslick/KRITIKEN.

5. Wooldridge/CONDUCTOR'S, p. 112.

6. Mueller/AMERICAN, p. 300.

7. Otis/CHICAGO, p. 11.

8. *Willis Musical World and Times,* Dec. 3, 1853, quoted in Mueller/AMERICAN, p. 300.

9. Mueller/AMERICAN, p. 300.

10. Ibid., pp. 301–3.

11. Rochlitz/BRUCHSTÜCKE, col. 59.

12. Ibid., cols. 59–60.

13. Unold/STELLUNG, col. 782.

14. Ibid., cols. 783–84.

15. MUSIKDIREKTOR, cols. 183–84.

16. Ibid., col. 184.

17. Arnold/MUSIKDIREKTOR, pp. 259–60.

18. Ibid., pp. 262–63.

19. Ibid., p. 266.

20. Ibid., pp. 280–81.

21. Ibid., p. 294.

22. Ibid., pp. 294–95.

23. Ibid., pp. 295–96.

24. Ibid., p. 297.

25. Ibid., pp. 307–9.

26. Ibid., pp. 309–11.

27. Arnold/MUSIKDIREKTOR, pp., 312–14.

28. Beethoven/WELLINGTONS, p. 124; trans. Beethoven/NEW LETTERS, pp. 162–63.

29. Wagner/LEBEN, p. 331; trans. Wagner/LIFE, I, p. 339.

30. Wagner/LEBEN, pp. 334–35; trans. Wagner/LIFE, I, pp. 342–43.

31. Wagner/LEBEN, p. 335; trans. Wagner/LIFE, I, p. 343.

32. Wagner/NEUNTEN, p. 55; trans. Wagner/CHORAL, pp. 245–46.

33. Wagner & Liszt/BRIEFWECHSEL, I, p. 238; trans. Wagner & Liszt/CORRESPON-DENCE, I, p. 287.

34. MUSICAL MAGAZINE, I (1839), pp. 165-66. Again the capitalization and punctuation as well as the mispelling suggest translation from the German.

35. Ibid., I (1839), p. 269. Here translation from the German is acknowledged.

36. Berlioz/TRAITÉ, p. 293; trans. Berlioz-Strauss/INSTRUMENTATION, p. 406.

37. Berlioz/TRAITÉ, p. 293; trans. Berlioz-Strauss/INSTRUMENTATION, p. 406.

38. Berlioz-Strauss/INSTRUMENTATIONSLEHRE, II, p. 434; trans. Berlioz-Strauss/INSTRUMENTATION, p. 406.

39. Berlioz/TRAITÉ, pp. 293-94; trans. Berlioz-Strauss/INSTRUMENTATION, p. 406.

40. Berlioz/TRAITÉ, p. 295; trans. Berlioz-Strauss/INSTRUMENTATION, p. 407.

41. Berlioz/REQUIEM, p. 19.

42. Berlioz/ROMEO, pp. 3-4.

43. Berlioz/TE DEUM, p. 3.

44. Berlioz/HAROLD, p. 1.

45. Berlioz/TRAITE, p. 295; trans. Berlioz-Strauss/INSTRUMENTATION, pp. 407-8.

46. Berlioz/MEMOIRES, I, pp. 148-49; trans. Berlioz/MEMOIRS, pp. 111-12.

47. Berlioz/ROMEO, p. 4.

48. Berlioz/TRAITE, p. 310; trans. Berlioz/CONDUCTOR, pp. 16-17. Berlioz-Strauss/INSTRUMENTATION, p. 418, has omissions in these passages.

49. Berlioz/TRAITE, p. 310; trans. Berlioz/CONDUCTOR, p. 17.

50. Gassner/DIRIGENT, pp. 73-74.

51. Ibid., p. 86.

52. Ibid., pp. 91-95.

53. Ibid., p. 95.

54. Schubert/MUSIKDIREKTOR, pp. 47-48.

55. Wagner/BAYREUTHER, pp. 70-71; trans. Wagner/BAYREUTH, p. 74.

56. Wagner/BAYREUTHER, pp. 74-77; trans. Wagner/BAYREUTH, pp. 78-81.

57. Ed. in Wagner/BAYREUTH, pp. 94-95.

58. Blitz/CHEF, p. 39.

59. Zopff/DIRIGENT, p. 53.

60. Ibid., pp. 53-54.

61. Ibid., pp. 54-55.

62. Ibid., p. 55.

63. Ibid., pp. 55-56.

64. Zopff/DIRIGENT, p. 56.

65. Schroeder/KATECHISMUS, p. 65; trans. Schroeder/HANDBOOK, p. 61. The translation is inexact in regard to the winds.

66. Schroeder/KATECHISMUS, p. 65; trans. Schroeder/HANDBOOK, p. 61. Again there are problems in the translation.

67. Schroeder/KATECHISMUS, p. 67; trans. Schroeder/HANDBOOK, p. 63.

68. Compare Kling/VOLLKOMMENE, pp. 265–70, with Gassner/DIRIGENT, pp. 86–96.

69. See Mahler/SYMPHONY 1, pp. 11–17.

70. Mahler/BRIEFE, p. 316.

Chapter 12

1. Spohr/LEBENSERINNERUNGEN, I, p. 18; trans. Spohr/JOURNEYS, pp. 14–15. The discrepancies in the translation seem minor here. Some passages are from Spohr's own diary.

2. From Parke/MEMOIRS, I, p. 334.

3. AMZ, XII (1809/10), col. 731.

4. Ibid., XII (1809/10), col. 731.

5. Smart/JOURNALS, p. 234.

6. Galkin/CONDUCTING, p. 626.

7. Elwart/SOCIETE, p. 115.

8. Carse/BEETHOVEN, p. 475.

9. Berlioz/TRAITE, p. 310; trans. Berlioz-Strauss/INSTRUMENTATION, p. 418.

10. Spohr/LEBENSERINNERUNGEN, I, p. 290; trans. Spohr/JOURNEYS, p. 167.

11. Smart/JOURNALS, p. 174.

12. See Mueller/AMERICAN, p. 301.

13. See Wooldridge/CONDUCTOR'S, p. [342].

14. See Zlotnik/SCHUMANN, pp. 46–47.

15. Schmidt/REISE-MOMENTE, p. 45.

16. Berlioz/MEMOIRES, II, p. 92; trans. Berlioz/MEMOIRS, p. 296.

17. Tchaikovsky/SYMPHONY 6, pp. 211–13, m. 1–4, 19–23.

18. See ibid., pp. 222–23, m. 90–93, 103–7.

19. Phillips/RECOLLECTIONS, I, pp. 74–75.

20. Moscheles/LEBEN, I, p. 121; trans. Moscheles/RECENT, pp. 82–83.

21. Fétis/CURIOSITÉS, pp. 186–88.

22. Moscheles/LEBEN, I, p. 264; or Moscheles/RECENT, p. 192.

23. Carse/BEETHOVEN, p. 477.

24. *Musical World,* May 2, 1839, quoted in Carse/BEETHOVEN, p. 477.

25. *Illustrated London News,* May 21, 1846, quoted in Nettel/ENGLAND, pp. 145–46.

26. Ibid., quoted in Carse/BEETHOVEN, , p. 478.

27. Nettel/ENGLAND, p. 146.

28. See Wooldridge/CONDUCTOR'S, p. [342].

29. Bennett/FORTY, p. 335.

30. Phillips/RECOLLECTIONS, II, p. 5.

31. Ryan/RECOLLECTIONS, p. 66.

32. Ibid., pp. 69–70.

33. Rees/HALLE, p. 21.

34. Nettel/ENGLAND, p. 165.

35. Kennedy/HALLE, p. 27.

36. Gassner/DIRIGENT, p. 160.

37. Berlioz/MEMOIRES, II, p. 103; trans. Berlioz/MEMOIRS, p. 305.

38. Schünemann/DIRIGIERENS, p. 307.

39. Schünemann;DIRIGIERENS, p. 311.

40. Schubert/MUSIKDIREKTOR, pp. 48–49.

41. Ibid., p. 49.

42. Gassner/DIRIGENT, p.160.

43. Mueller/AMERICAN, p. 303.

44. Henschel/MUSINGS, pp. 273–74.

45. Mueller/AMERICAN, pp. 303–5.

46. Henschel/BRAHMS, pp. 84–85.

47. *Musical Record,* October 29, 1881, quoted in Mueller/AMERICAN, p. 305.

48. Mueller/AMERICAN, p. 305.

49. Russell/THOMAS, p. 142.

50. Thomas/MEMOIRS, pp. 536–37.

51. Russell/THOMAS, p. 265.

52. Ibid., pp. 105–6.

53. Ibid., pp. 105–6.

54. Otis/CHICAGO. p. 33.

55. Mueller/AMERICAN, p. 79.

56. Weingartner/RATSCHLÄGE, I, p. 187; trans. Weingartner/BEETHOVEN, p. 176.

57. Weingartner/RATSCHLÄGE, I, p. 188; trans. Weingartner/BEETHOVEN, p. 176.

Chapter 13

1. Blaze/CHAPELLE, p. 166.

2. Smart/JOURNALS, p. 112.

3. Schünemann/DIRIGIERENS, p. 306.

4. Ibid., pp. 305-6.

5. Schünemann/DIRIGIERENS, pp. 306-7.

6. Gassner/DIRIGENT, p. 160.

7. Smart/JOURNALS, pp. 303-4.

8. Elwart/SOCIETE, p. 353.

Chapter 14

1. Smart/JOURNALS, p. 38.

2. Ibid., p. 80.

3. In Bayreuth/GEBURTSTAG, pages not numbered.

4. See Schubert/MUSIKDIREKTOR, p. 48.

5. Ibid., p. 48.

6. Blaze/OPERA, I, pp. 446-47.

7. Letter, April 20, 1825, in Hensel/MENDELSSOHN 2, p. 126.

8. Smart/JOURNALS, p. 66.

9. Ibid., pp. 76-77.

10. Ibid., p. 80.

11. Ibid., p. 99.

12. Smart/JOURNALS, p. 100.

13. Ibid., p. 221.

14. Nösselt/GEWANDHAUS, p. 121.

15. Bayreuth/GEBURTSTAG, pages not numbered.

16. See Prawy/VIENNA, cartoons, p. 28, pictures between pp. 32-33.

17. Ibid., p. 63.

18. Ibid., p. 86.

19. Schubert/MUSIKDIREKTOR, p. 48.

20. Weber/WEBER 1, I, pp. 96-97; the translation Weber/WEBER 2, I, p. 58, omits most of the detail.

21. Weber/WEBER 1, II, pp. 138–41; again the translation Weber/WEBER 2, II, pp. 99–102, omits detail.

22. Weber/WEBER 1, II, pp. 148–49; trans. Weber/WEBER 2, II, p. 106.

23. Becker/WEBER, p. 47.

24. Borris/ORCHESTER, p. 124.

25. Haas/AUFFÜHRUNGSPRAXIS, p. 256.

26. Smart/JOURNALS, p. 140.

27. Ibid., p. 148.

28. See Schubert/MUSIKDIREKTOR, p. 48.

29. AMZ, XVI (1814), col. 252.

30. Carse/BEETHOVEN, p. 473.

31. Prawy/VIENNA, p. 27.

32. From Prawy/VIENNA, p. 30; orig. German in handwriting difficult to decipher.

33. Smart/JOURNALS, p. 80.

34. Schubert/MUSIKDIREKTOR, p. 48.

35. HARMONICON, V (1827), p. 211.

36. Gassner/DIRIGENT, p. 160.

37. Berlioz/MEMOIRES, II, pp. 118–19; trans. Berlioz/MEMOIRS, pp. 317–18.

38. Becker/ORCHESTER, col. 181.

39. Norlind/DIRIGERINGS, p. 53.

40. See the Leipzig concert plan for 1746–48 (fig. 9) for the many doublings used in that orchestra at that time.

41. Schubert/MUSIKDIREKTOR, p. 48.

42. Berlioz/MEMOIRES, II, p. 60; trans. Berlioz/MEMOIRS, p. 270.

43. Smart/JOURNALS, pp. 76–77.

44. Becker/ORCHESTER, col. 182.

45. Wagner/LEBEN, pp. 323–24; trans. Wagner/LIFE, I, p. 330.

46. Wagner/LEBEN, p. 391; trans. Wagner/LIFE, I, p. 402.

47. Wagner/LEBEN, p. 420; trans. Wagner/LIFE, I, p. 433.

48. Wagner/LEBEN, p. 699; trans. Wagner/LIFE, II, p. 727.

49. Wagner/BAYREUTH, pp. 224–25.

50. Quoted in Haas/AUFFÜHRUNGSPRAXIS, p. 267. The present author could not locate these passages.

51. Ibid., p. 267, with sketch which is not too clear.

52. See ibid., pp. 279–80.

53. Lavignac/BAYREUTH 1, p. 84; trans. Lavignac/BAYREUTH 2, pp. 64–65.

54. See Lavignac/BAYREUTH 1, pp. 87, 89; or Lavignac/BAYREUTH 2, pp. 64, 67.

Chapter 15

1. From Landon/HAYDN CHRONICLE, IV, p. 455.

2. Gerber/MUSIKFESTE, cols. 749–50.

3. See ibid., col. 748.

4. In Haas/AUFFÜHRUNGSPRAXIS, p. 257.

5. Spohr/LEBENSERINNERUNGEN, I, pp. 181–82; trans. Spohr/JOURNEYS, pp. 107–8.

6. Spohr/LEBENSERINNERUNGEN, I, p. 236; trans. Spohr/JOURNEYS, pp. 139–40.

7. Devrient/MENDELSSOHN 1, pp. 63–64; trans. Devrient/MENDELSSOHN 2, p. 59.

8. Hiller/MENDELSSOHN 1, p. 134; or Hiller/MENDELSSOHN 2, p. 158.

9. Moscheles/LEBEN, I, pp. 280–81; trans. Moscheles/RECENT, pp. 203–4.

10. Berlioz/MEMOIRES, II, pp. 46–48; trans. Berlioz/MEMOIRS, pp. 259–60.

11. Gassner/DIRIGENT, p. 160.

12. Smart/JOURNALS, p. 310.

13. Elwart/SOCIÉTÉ, p. 347.

14. Smart/JOURNALS, p. 302.

15. Berlioz/MEMOIRES, II, pp. 333–34; trans. Berlioz/MEMOIRS, pp. 482–83.

16. Ryan/RECOLLECTIONS, pp. 190–94.

17. Blitz/CHEF, p. 43.

18. Thomas/MEMOIRS, p. 247.

19. Ibid., p. 222; for a similar quotation see also Thomas-Stein/AUTOBIOGRAPHY, p. 90.

Chapter 17

1. Thomas-Stein/AUTOBIOGRAPHY, pp. 377–78.

2. Howe/BOSTON, p. 251.

3. Kennedy/HALLÉ pp. 395–96.

4. Seating plan in Becker/ORCHESTER, col. 185.

5. Kennedy/HALLE, pp. 397–98.

6. Seating plan in Nösselt/GEWANDHAUS, p. 270. Trumpets are not shown, undoubtedly by error or omission.

7. Seating plan in Mueller/AMERICAN, p. 306.

8. MGG, X, p. III between col. 192 & 193.

9. MGG, X, p. IV between col. 192 & 193.

10. Seating plan, Becker/ORCHESTER, col. 190.

11. MGG, X, p. X after col. 192.

12. MGG, X, p. XVI after col. 192.

13. MGG, X, p. XI after col. 192.

14. MGG, X, p. XVI after col. 192.

15. MGG, X, p. XI after col. 192.

16. Hedler/DÜSSELDORFER, pp. 67–68. The author noted that two places in the second violins were empty as were one each in the cellos and horns.

17. Seating plan in Machlis/ENJOYMENT, p. 45.

18. Sir Adrian Boult in introduction to Carse/ORCHESTRA, p. 11.

19. Scholes/MIRROR, I, p. 376.

20. Ibid., I, p. 376.

21. Wood/CONDUCTING, pp. 53–54.

22. Ibid., p. 94.

23. Introduction to Carse/ORCHESTRA, p. 12.

24. Boult/CONDUCTING, pp. 22–24.

25. See drawing in Galkin/CONDUCTING, p. 637.

26. See plan in Becker/ORCHESTER, col. 185.

27. Mueller/AMERICAN, p. 307.

28. Kupferburg/PHILADELPHIANS, pp. 57–58.

29. Mueller/AMERICAN, p. 130.

30. Ibid., pp. 141–42.

31. Ibid., p. 130.

32. See plan in Wooldridge/CONDUCTOR'S, p. [343].

33. Mueller/AMERICAN, pp. 307–8.

34. Wooldridge/CONDUCTOR'S, p. [343].

35. See plan in Mueller/AMERICAN, p. 306.

36. See plan in Wooldridge/CONDUCTOR'S, p. [343].

37. Ibid., p. [343].

38. See plan in Becker/ORCHESTER, col. 190.

39. See plan in Machlis/ENJOYMENT, p. 45.

40. Taubman/MAESTRO, p. 291.

41. Wooldridge/CONDUCTOR'S, pp. 122–23.

42. Stokowski/INNOVATIONS, pp. 120–21.

43. Ibid., pp. 121–22.

44. Krips & Frankenstein/SAN FRANCISCO, pp. 36–37. The passage refers to the San Francisco Opera House and its acoustical shell.

45. Bach/DOKUMENTEN, p. 197; or David & Mendel/BACH, p. 278.

46. Aldrich/NEW YORK, p. 158.

47. Ibid., p. 55.

48. Mueller/AMERICAN, p. 327.

49. On L'Oiseau-Lyre, vols. 1–7, D167 D3–D173 D3. See the review of vol. 3, the first to appear as D 169 D3, by Nicholas Kenyon in HF, XXX, 5 (May 1980), pp. 61–62.

50. See review of vol. 1, Symphony No. 6, on Columbia M 35169, by Harris Goldsmith in HF, XXX, 4 (April 1980), pp. 78–80.

51. Disc as ARL 1-3005 or cassette as ARK 1-3005.

52. In HF, XXIX, 3 (March 1979), p. 86.

53. On Peters PLE-020, disc, or PCE-020, cassette.

54. Abram Chipman recently referred to Morris's "stately, rounded lyrical style, consistent stereo separation of first and second violins" in reviewing recent Mahler recordings in HF, XXX, 4 (April 1980), p. 71.

55. See Bartók/MUSIC, p. [ii].

56. Nösselt/GEWANDHAUS, p. 269.

57. Dörffel/GEWANDHAUS, p. 78. Nine more men might be used as required.

58. Nösselt/GEWANDHAUS, pp. 118–19.

59. Döeffel/GEWANDHAUS, p. 90.

60. Creuzburg/GEWANDHAUS, pp. 85–86.

61. Nösselt/GEWANDHAUS, p. 161.

62. See figure 31, or Schmidt/REISE-MOMENTE, p. 46.

Chapter 18

1. Beethoven/BRIEFE 1, III, p. 178; trans. Beethoven/LETTERS, II, p. 688.

2. Beethoven/WELLINGTONS, p. 124; or Beethoven/NEW LETTERS, p. 162.

3. Dart/INTERPRETATION, pp. 57–58.

4. See Berlioz/TRAITE, pp. 294–97, or Berlioz-Strauss/INSTRUMENTATION, pp. 407–9; Berlioz/MEMOIRES, II, pp. 51–52, or Berlioz/MEMOIRS, pp. 263–64.

5. Elkin/LONDON, p. 93. Nettel/ENGLAND, p. 173, gives 95′ by 35′. Scholes/MIRROR, I, between pp. 184–85, gives area as 943 ft., presumably square feet!

6. Cramer/MAGAZIN, II (1784–87), p. 317.

7. Schmidt/REISE-MOMENTE, p. 46.

8. Dörffel/GEWANDHAUS, p. 251.

9. Beranek/ACOUSTICS, p. 47, 273.

10. Ibid., p. 273.

11. Ibid., p. 273.

12. Ibid., p. 276.

13. Elkin/LONDON, pp. 100–101.

14. Scholes/MIRROR, I, p. 206.

15. Elkin/LONDON, pp. 149–50.

16. Chart in Scholes/MIRROR, I, between pp. 184–85.

17. Beranek/ACOUSTICS, p. 323.

18. Ibid., p. 163.

19. Ibid., p. 151.

20. Ibid., p. 97.

21. Arnold/MUSIKDIREKTOR, p. 290.

22. Ibid., p. 282.

23. Gassner/DIRIGENT, p. 87, 90.

24. Kling/VOLLKOMMENE, pp. 266–67.

25. Zopff/DIRIGENT, pp. 51–53.

26. Kufferath/DIRIGER, p. 116, note 1.

27. Spohr/LEBENSERINNERUNGEN, I, p. 78; Spohr/JOURNEYS, p. 50.

28. Beranek/ACOUSTICS, p. 273.

29. See Quantz/FLUTE, pp. 31–32, including notes.

30. Blaze/OPERA, I, p. 437.

31. Blaze/ACADEMIE, II, pp. 346–47.

32. Nettel/ENGLAND, p. 207.

33. Schindler/BEETHOVEN 1, II, p. 81; or Schindler/BEETHOVEN 2, p. 286.

34. Schindler/BEETHOVEN 2, p. 351, note 212.

35. Smart/JOURNALS, p. 69.

36. Ibid., p. 80.

37. Ibid., p. 90.

38. Smart/JOURNALS, p. 140.

39. Ibid., p. 142.

40. Ibid., p. 158.

41. Ibid., p. 205.

42. Ibid., p. 234.

43. Ibid., p. 75.

44. Ibid., p. 167.

45. Ibid., p. 177.

46. Ibid., p. 212.

47. HARMONICON, II (1824), p. 128.

48. Ibid., II (1824), p. 150.

49. Ibid., II (1824), pp. 176–78.

50. Berlioz/CHANTS, p. 290; trans. Berlioz/ESSAYS, p. 95.

51. Berlioz/CHANTS, p. 293; trans. Berlioz/ESSAYS, p. 99.

52. Berlioz/CHANTS, pp. 293–94; trans. Berlioz/ESSAYS, pp. 100–101.

53. Berlioz/CHANTS, pp. 196–97; trans. Berlioz/ESSAYS, pp. 103–4.

54. See Berlioz/CHANTS, pp. 297–98; or Berlioz/ESSAYS, pp. 104–6.

55. Haas/AUFFÜHRUNGSPRAXIS, p. 267.

56. Dörffel/GEWANDHAUS, p. 177.

57. Scholes/MIRROR, I, p. 408.

58. Ellis/PITCH must be mentioned here as an indispensable source in this area. But Mendel/PITCH probably comes as close to being definitive as is currently possible in this difficult and tangled subject.

Bibliography

Abravanel/UTAH — Abravanel, Maurice. "The Utah Symphony Orchestra: An Orchestra in the Deep Interior," *The American Symphony Orchestra* ed. H. Swoboda. New York: Basic Books, 1967, pp. 43–56.

Adam/DERNIERS — Adam, Adolphe. *Derniers souvenirs d'un musicien.* Paris: Levy, 1859.

Adam/SOUVENIRS — _____. *Souvenirs d'un musicien.* Paris: Calmann-Lévy, 1857.

Aldrich/NEW YORK — Aldrich, Richard. *Concert Life in New York, 1902–1923.* New York: G. P. Putnam's Sons, 1941.

AMZ — *Allgemeine musikalische Zeitung.* Jahrgang 1–50, 1798–1848; neue Folge, Jahrgang 1–3, 1863–65; 3te Folge, Jahrgang 1–17, 1866–82. 70 vols. Leipzig: Breitkopf & Härtel, 1798–1882.

Antonicek/FESTSAAL — Antonicek, Theophil. *Musik im Festsaal der Österreichischen Akademie der Wissenschaften.* Wien: H. Böhlaus, 1972 (Veröffentlichungen der Kommission für Musikforschung, hrsg. E. Schenk, Heft 14).

Arnold/MUSIKDIREKTOR — Arnold, Ignaz Theodor Ferdinand Cajetan. [I. F. K. Arnold]. *Der angehende Musikdirektor; oder die Kunst ein Orchester zu bilden, in Ordnung zu erhalten, und überhaupt allen Forderungen eines guten Musikdirektors Genüge zu leisten.* Erfurt: Henning, 1806.

Aubert & Landowski/ORCHESTRE — Aubert, Louis and Marcel Landowski. *L'Orchestre.* Paris: Presses Universitaires de France, 1951.

Bach/DOKUMENTEN — Bach, Johann Sebastian. *Leben und Werk in Dokumenten,* hrsg. H.-J. Schulze. Kassel: Bärenreiter, 1975.

Bach/ESSAY — Bach, Carl Philipp Emanuel. *Essay on the True Art of Playing Keyboard Instruments,* trans. & ed. W. J. Mitchell. New York: Norton, 1949.

Bach/VERSUCH — Bach, Carl Philipp Emanuel. *Versuch über die wahre Art, das Clavier zu spielen.* Faksimile-Nachdruck der 1. Aufl., Berlin, 1753 & 1762, hrsg. L. Hoffmann-Erbrect, 2 vols, in 1. Leipzig: VEB Breitkopf & Härtel, 1969.

Bache/BROTHER — Bache, Constance. *Brother Musicians: Reminiscences of Edward and Walter Bache.* London: Methuen, 1901.

Baines/INSTRUMENTS — Baines, Anthony, ed. *Musical Instruments through the Ages.* Baltimore: Penquin, 1961.

Baines/WOODWIND — ———. *Woodwind Instruments and their History,* rev. ed. New York: Norton, 1963; 1st ed. 1957.

Bartók/MUSIC — Bartók, Béla. *Music for String Instruments, Percussion, and Celesta,* min. score. London: Boosey & Hawkes, 1939.

Bate/OBOE — Bate, Philip. *The Oboe, an Outline of its History, Development and Construction,* 3rd ed. London: E. Benn, 1975; 1st ed. 1956.

Bayreuth/GEBURTSTAG — Bayreuth. *Zum 150. Geburtstag Richard Wagners: Ein Leben für das Theater.* Bayreuth: Festspielleitung, 1963.

Becker/ORCHESTER — Becker, Heinz. "Das neuere Orchester." *Die Musik in Geschichte und Gegenwart.* Kassel: Bärenreiter, 1949–73, X, col. 172–94.

Becker/WEBER — Becker, Wolfgang. *Die deutsche Oper in Dresden unter die Leitung von Carl Maria von Weber, 1817–1826.* Berlin-Dahlem: Colloquium, 1962 (Theater und Drama, hrsg. H. Knudsen, Band 22).

Beethoven/BRIEFE 1 — Beethoven, Ludwig van. *Sämtliche Briefe,* hrsg. A. C. Kalischer, 5 vols. Berlin: Schuster & Loeffler, 1906–8.

Beethoven/BRIEFE 2 — ———. *Sämtlicher Briefe,* hrsg. E. Kastner, Neuausg. J. Kapp. Leipzig: Hesse & Becker, 1923.

Beethoven/LETTERS — ———. *The Letters of Ludwig van Beethoven,* coll., trans. & ed. E. Anderson, 3 vols. London: Macmillan, 1961.

Beethoven/NEW LETTERS — ———. *New Beethoven Letters,* trans. & annotated D. W. MacArdle & L. Mish. Norman: University of Oklahoma, 1957.

Beethoven/WELLINGTONS — ———. *Ouverturen und Wellingtons Sieg,* Score, hrsg. H.-W. Küthen. München: G. Henle, 1974 (Beethoven Werke, Abt. II, Bd. 1).

BEMERKUNGEN — *Bemerkungen eines Reisenden über die zu Berlin vom September 1787 bis Ende Januar 1788 gegebene öffentliche Musiken, Kirchenmusik, Oper, Concerte, und königliche Kammermusik betreffend.* Halle, 1788.

Bennett/FORTY — Bennett, Joseph. *Forty Years of Music, 1865–1905.* London: Methuen, 1908.

Beranek/ACOUSTICS — Beranek, Leo L. *Music, Acoustics & Architecture.* New York: J. Wiley, 1962.

Berlioz/CARNAVAL

Berlioz/CHANTS

Berlioz/CHEF

Berlioz/CONDUCTOR

Berlioz/ESSAYS

Berlioz/EVENINGS

Berlioz/FANTASTIC

Berlioz/HAROLD

Berlioz/MEMOIRES

Berlioz/MEMOIRS

Berlioz/NOUVELLES

Berlioz/REQUIEM

Berlioz/ROMEO

Berlioz/SOIREES

Berlioz/TE DEUM

Berlioz/TRAITE

Berlioz-Strauss/
   INSTRUMENTATION

Berlioz-Strauss/
INSTRUMENTATIONSLEHRE

Berlioz, Hector. *Le Carnaval romain, ouverture caractéristique à grand orchestre,* op. 9. Min. score. London: E. Eulenburg, 1929.

———. *A travers chants: Études musicales, adorations, boutades et critiques,* 2e éd, Paris: M. Lévy, 1872; 1st ed. 1862.

———. *Le chef d'orchestre; théorie de son art.* Paris: Schonenberger, 1856.

———. *The Orchestral Conductor: Theory of His Art.* New York: C. Fischer, 19—.

———. *Mozart, Weber and Wagner, with Various Essays on Musical Subjects,* trans. E. Evans. London: W. Reeves, 1969.

———. *Evenings with the Orchestra,* trans. & ed. J. Barzun. Chicago: University of Chicago, 1973.

———. *Fantastic Symphony; An Authoritative Score, Historical Background, Analysis, Views and Comments,* ed. E. T. Cone. New York: Norton, 1971.

———. *Harold en Italie,* score. New York: E. F. Kalmus 19— (Complete Works, vol II).

———. *Mémoires,* éd. P. Citron, 2 vols. Paris: Garnier-Flammarion, 1969, 1st ed. 1870.

———. *The Memoirs of Hector Berlioz, Member of the French Institute, including his travels in Italy, Germany, Russia and England.* 1803–65; trans. & ed. E. Cairns. New York: Norton, 1975.

———. *Nouvelles lettres de Berlioz, 1830–68,* trad, anglaise J. Barzun. New York: Columbia University, 1954.

———. *Requiem (Grand Death-Mass),* op. 5, min. score. New York: E. F. Kalmus, 19—.

———. *Roméo et Juliette,* score. New York: E. F. Kalmus, 19— (Complete Works, vol. III).

———. *Les soirées de l'orchestre,* ed. L. Guichard. Paris: Gründ, 1968; 1st ed. 1852.

———. *Te Deum,* score. New York: E. F. Kalmus, 19— (Complete Works, vol. VIII).

———. *Grand traité d'instrumentation et d'orchestration modernes,* nouvelle éd., suivie de *l'Art du chef d'orchestre.* Paris: H. Lemoine, 188-.

———. *Treatise on Instrumentation,* enlarged & rev. R. Strauss, including *Essay on Conducting,* trans. T. Front. New York: E. F. Kalmus, 1948; Strauss's Foreword 1904.

———. *Instrumentationslehre,* ergänzt & rev. R. Strauss, 2 vols. in 1. Leipzig: C. F. Peters, 1905.

Bernstein & Picker/
INTRODUCTION

Blaze/ACADEMIE

Blaze/CHAPELLE

Blaze/ITALIEN

Blaze/OPERA

Blitz/CHEF

Bobillier/CONCERTS

Borland/BALANCE

Borris/ORCHESTER

Boult/CONDUCTING

Boyden/VIOLIN

Bragard & De Hen/
INSTRUMENTS

Bülow/CORRESPONDENCE

Bülow/LETTERS

Bülow/NEUE

Bülow & Strauss/
CORRESPONDENCE

Bernstein, Martin and Martin Picker. *An Introduction to Music,* 4th ed. Englewood Cliffs, NJ: Prentice-Hall, 1972.

Blaze, François Henri Joseph [Castil-Blaze]. *L'Académie Impériale de Musique; histoire littéraire, musicale, choréographique, pittoresque, morale, critique, facétieuse, politique et galante de ce théâtre, de 1645 à1855,* 2 vols. Paris: Castil-Blaze, 1855 (Théâtres Lyriques de Paris).

———. *Chapelle-musique des rois de France.* Paris: Paulin, 1832.

———. *L'Opéra-italien de 1548 à 1856.* Paris: Castil-Blaze, 1856 (Théâtres Lyriques de Paris).

———. *De l'opéra en France,* 2 vols. Paris: Janet & Cotelle, 1820.

Blitz, Eduoard E. *Quelques considérations sur l'art du chef d'orchestre.* Leipzig: Breitkopf & Härtel, 1887.

Bobillier, Marie [Michel Brenet]. *Les Concerts en France sous l'ancien régime.* New York: Da Capo, 1970; 1st ed. 1900.

Borland, John E. "Orchestral and Choral Balance." *Proceedings of the Musical Association,* XXVIII (1901–2), pp. 1–24.

Borris, Siegfried. *Die grossen Orchester: eine Kulturgeschichte.* Hamburg: Claasen, 1969.

Boult, Adrian C. *Thoughts on Conducting,* London: Phoenix, 1963.

Boyden, David D. *The History of Violin Playing from its Origins to 1761 and its Relationship to the Violin and Violin Music.* London: Oxford University, 1965.

Bragard, Roger and Ferdinand J. De Hen. *Musical Instruments in Art and History;* trans. B. Hopkins. New York: Viking, 1968.

von Bülow, Hans. *The Early Correspondence;* ed. his Widow, trans. C. Bache. New York: D. Appleton, 1897.

———. *Letters to Richard Wagner, Cosima Wagner, His Daughter Daniela, Luise von Bülow, Karl Klindworth, Carl Bechstein,* ed. R. du Moulin Eckart, trans. H. Waller, translation ed. S. Goddard. New York: A. A. Knopf, 1931.

———. *Neue Briefe,* hrsg. R. Moulin Eckart. München: Drei Masken, 1927.

———and Richard Strauss. *Correspondence;* ed. W. Schuh & F. Trenner, trans. A. Gishford. London: Boosey & Hawkes, 1955.

Burney/FRANCE

Burney/GERMANY

Burney/HANDEL

Carse/BEETHOVEN

Carse/18TH

Carse/HISTORY

Carse/ORCHESTRA

Carse/WIND

Chorley/MUSIC

Chorley/RECOLLECTIONS

Coar/MASTERS

Corneloup/ORCHESTRE

Cramer/MAGAZIN

Creuzburg/GEWANDHAUS

Cucuel/ETUDES

Dart/INTERPRETATION

David & Mendel/BACH

Burney, Charles. *The Present State of Music in France and Italy: or, The Journal of a Tour through those Countries, undertaken to collect Materials for a General History of Music,* 2nd ed., corr. London: T. Becket, J. Robson, & C. Robinson, 1773.

————. *The Present State of Music in Germany, The Netherlands, and United Provinces, or, The Journal of a Tour through those Countries, Undertaken to Collect Materials for a General History of Music,* 2nd ed., corr. 2 vols. London: T. Becket, J. Robson, & C. Robinson, 1775.

————. *An Account of the Musical Performances in Westminster-Abbey and the Pantheon, May 26th, 27th, 29th; and June the 3d, and 5th, 1784. In Commemoration of Händel.* London: Musical Fund, 1785.

Carse, Adam. *The Orchestra from Beethoven to Berlioz.* New York: Broude Bro., 1949.

————. *The Orchestra in the XVIIIth Century.* New York: Broude Bro., 1969.

————. *The History of Orchestration.* New York: Dover, 1964; 1st ed. 1925.

————. *The Orchestra.* New York: Chanticleer, 1949.

————. *Musical Wind Instruments.* New York: Da Capo, 1965; 1st ed. 1939.

Chorley, Henry F. *Music and Manners in France and Germany: A Series of Travelling Sketches of Art and Society,* 3 vols. London: Longman, Brown, Green, & Longmans, 1844.

————. *Thirty Years' Musical Recollections,* ed. E. Newman. New York: A. A. Knopf, 1926.

Coar, Birchard. *The Masters of the Classical Period as Conductors.* De Kalb, Ill.: B. Coar, 1949.

Corneloup, Marcel. *L'Orchestre et ses instruments.* Paris: Presses d'Ile de France, 1955.

Cramer, Carl Friedrich, ed., *Magazin der Musik;* 2 vols. in 4. Hildesheim: G. Olms, 1971; 1st ed. 1783-6.

Creuzburg, Eberhard. *Die Gewandhaus-Konzerte zu Leipzig, 1871-1931.* Leipzig: Breitkopf & Härtel, 1931.

Cucuel, Georges. *Études sur un orchestre au XVIIIme siècle.* Paris: Fischbacher, 1913.

Dart, Thurston. *The Interpretation of Music.* New York: Harper, 1963; 1st ed. 1954.

David, Hans. T. and Arthur Mendel, eds. *The Bach Reader: A Life of Johann Sebastian Bach in Letters and Documents,* rev., with supplement. New York: Norton, 1966; 1st ed. 1945.

Davison/MENDELSSOHN

Davison, James William. *From Mendelssohn to Wagner, Being the Memoirs of J. W. Davison, Forty Years Music Critic of "The Times,"* comp. H. Davison. London: W. Reeves, 1912 (Music during the Victorian era).

Deldevez/CHEF

Deldevez, Edouard Marie Ernest. *L'Art du chef d'orchestre.* Paris: Firmin-Didot, 1878.

Devrient/MENDELSSOHN 1

Devrient, Eduard. *Meine Erinnerungen an Felix Mendelssohn-Bartholdy und Seine Briefe an mich.* Leipzig: J. J. Weber, 1869.

Devrient/MENDELSSOHN 2

_____. *My Recollections of Felix Mendelssohn-Bartholdy, and His Letters to Me,* trans. N. MacFarren. London: R. Bentley, 1869.

Dittersdorf/
AUTOBIOGRAPHY

von Dittersdorf, Karl Ditters. *The Autobiography of Karl von Dittersdorf Dictated to His Son,* trans. A. D. Coleridge. New York: Da Capo, 1970; 1st ed. 1896.

Dittersdorf/
LEBENSBESCHREIBUNG

_____. *Lebensbeschreibung, seinem Sohn in die Feder diktiert.* München: Mösel, 1967; 1st ed. 1800.

Dörffel/GEWANDHAUS

Dörffel, Alfred. *Geschichte der Gewandhausconcerte zu Leipzig vom 25. November 1781 bis 25. November 1881.* Leipzig: Concert-Direction, 1884 (Festschrift zur hundertjährigen Jubefeier der Einweihung des Concertsaales im Gewandhause zu Leipzig).

Dorn/LEBEN

Dorn, Heinrich. *Aus meinem Leben,* 3 vols. Berlin: B. Behr (E. Bock) & Hausfreund-Expedition (E. Graetz), 1870–72.

Elkin/LONDON

Elkin, Robert. *The Old Concert Rooms of London.* London: E. Arnold, 1955.

Elkin/ROYAL

_____. *Royal Philharmonic: The Annals of the Royal Philharmonic Society.* London: Rider, 1946.

Ellis/PITCH

Ellis, Alexander J. *The History of Musical Pitch.* London: W. Trounce, 1880.

Elwart/SOCIETE

Elwart, Antoine Aimable Elie. *Histoire de la Société des Concerts du Conservatoire Impérial de Musique,* 2e éd, Paris: Castel, 1864; 1st ed. 1860.

Fétis/CURIOSITES

Fétis, François Joseph. *Curiosités historiques de la musique, complément nécessaire de La Musique mise à la portée de tout le monde.* Paris: Janet & Cotelle, 1830.

Fétis/REVOLUTIONS

_____. "On the Revolutions of the Orchestra," *The Harmonicon,* VI (1828), pp. 194–97.

Forkel/ALMANACH

Forkel, Johann Nikolaus, ed. *Musikalischer Almanach für Deutschland auf das jahr 1782, 1783, 1784, 1789,* 4 vols. Leipzig: Schwickert, 1782–84, 1789.

Forkel/BEGRIFFE ———. "Genauere Bestimmung einiger musikalischer Begriffe," *Magazin der Musik*, ed. C. F. Cramer, I (1783), p. 1039–72.

Forsyth/ORCHESTRATION Forsyth, Cecil. *Orchestration;* 2nd ed. New York: Macmillan, 1949; 1st ed. 1914.

Fuld/OPERATIC Fuld, James J. "Nineteenth-Century Operatic Violin Conductors' Scores," *Music Library Association Notes* XXXI (1974); 278–80.

Fürstenau/DRESDEN Fürstenau, Moritz. *Zur Geschichte der Musik und der Theaters am Hofe zu Dresden;* 2 vols. Dresden: R. Kuntze, 1861–62.

Galeazzi/ELEMENTI Galeazzi, Francesco. *Elementi teorico-prattici di musica, con un saggio sopra l'arte di suonare il violino analizzato;* 2 vols. Roma: 1791 and 1796.

Galkin/CONDUCTING Galkin, Elliot W. *The Theory and Practice of Orchestral Conducting since 1752.* Ann Arbor: University Microfilms, 1960 (Ph.D. Dissertation, Cornell University, 1960).

Gassner/DIRIGENT Gassner, Ferdinand Simon. *Dirignet und Ripienist, für angehende Musikdirigenten, Musiker und Musikfreunde.* Karlsruhe: C. T. Groos, 1844.

Gassner/PARTITUR ———. *Partiturkenntniss, ein Leitfaden zum Selbstunterrichte für angehende Tonsetzer oder solche, welche Arrangiren, Partiturlesen lernen oder sich zu Dirigenten von Orchestern oder Militärmusiken bilden wollen;* 2te Ausg., 2 vols. Karlsruhe: C. T. Groos, 1842.

Geiringer/INSTRUMENTS Geiringer, Karl. *Musical Instruments, their History in Western Culture from the Stone Age to the Present*; trans. B. Miall. New York: Oxford University, 1945.

Geiringer/VINCI ———. "Eine Geburtstageskantate von Pietro Metastasio und Leonardo Vinci," *Zeitschrift für Musikwissenschaft* IX (1926/7): pp. 270–83.

Gerber/MUSIKFESTE Gerber, Ernst Ludwig. "Nachricht von einem in Thüringen seltenen Musikfeste," *Allgemeine musikalische Zeitung* XII (1809/10), col. 745–58.

Gerlach/HAYDNS Gerlach, Sonia. "Haydns Orchestermusiker von 1761 bis 1774," *Haydn-Studien* IV, no. 1 (1976): pp. 35–48.

Gregory/HORN Gregory, Robin. *The Horn, a Comprehensive Guide to the Modern Instrument & its Music.* New York: F. A. Prager, 1969; 1st ed. 1961.

Haas/AUFFÜHRUNGSPRAXIS Haas, Robert. *Aufführungspraxis der Musik.* Wildpark-Potsdam: Athenaion, 1931 (Handbuch der Musikwissenschart, hrsg. E. Büchen).

Haas/ORCHESTER ———. "Zur Frage der Orchesterbesetzungen in der zweiter Hälfte des 18. Jahrhunderts," *III. Kongress der Internationalen Musikgesellschaft, Wien, 25. bis 29. Mai 1909, Bericht.* Wien: Artaria, 1909, pp. 159–67.

Haller/PARTITUR — Haller, Klaus. *Partituranordnung und musikalischen Satz.* Tutzing: H. Schneider, 1970.

Hanslick/CONCERT — Hanslick, Eduard. *Aus dem Concert-Saal. Kritiken und Schilderungen aus 20 Jahren der Wiener Musiklebens 1840-1868. Nebst einem Anhang: Musikalische Reisebriefe aus England, Frankreich u. d. Schweiz;* 2te durchgesehene & verbesserte Aufl. Wien: W. Braumüller, 1897.

Hanslick/KRITIKEN — ———. *Concerte, Componisten und Virtuosen der letzten fünfzehn Jahre: 1870-1885.* Kritiken, 2te Auf. Berlin: Allgemeiner Verein für Deutsche Literatur, 1886.

Hanslick/STATIONEN — ———. *Musikalische Stationen.* Berlin: Allgemeine Verein für Deutsche Literatur, 1885 (Der "Moderner Oper," II. Theil).

Hanslick/VIENNA — ———. *Vienna's Golden Years of Music, 1850-1900,* trans. & ed. H. Pleasants III. Freeport, NY: Books for Libraries, 1969; 1st ed. 1950.

Hanson/EDUCATION — Hanson, Howard. "The Education of the Orchestra Musician," *The American Symphony Orchestra;* ed. H. Swoboda, pp. 99-107. New York: Basic Books, 1967.

HARMONICON — *The Harmonicon, A Journal of Music; 1823-33.* 11 vols. London: W. Pinnock *et al., 1823-33.*

Haydn/BRIEFE — Haydn, Joseph. *Gesammelte Briefe und Aufzeichnungen;* hrsg. D. Bartha. Kassel: Bärenreiter, 1965.

Haydn/CORRESPONDENCE — Landon, Howard Chandler Robbins. *The Collected Correspondence and London Notebooks of Joseph Haydn.* London: Barrie & Rockliff, 1959.

Hedler/DÜSSELDORFER — Hedler, Gottfried. *100 Jahre Düsseldorfer Symphoniker, 1864/1964.* Düsseldorfer: L. Schwann, 1964.

Henschel/BRAHMS — Henschel, George. *Personal Recollections of Johannes Brahms.* Boston: R. G. Badger, 1907.

Henschel/MUSINGS — ———. *Musings and Memories of a Musician.* New York: Macmillan, 1919.

Hensel/MENDELSSOHN 1 — Hensel, Sebastian. *Die Familie Mendelssohn, 1729-1847, nach Briefen und Tagebüchern;* 6te Aufl., 2 vols. Berlin: B. Behr (E. Bock), 1888.

Hensel/MENDELSSOHN 2 — ———. *The Mendelssohn Family (1729-1847), From Letters and Journals;* trans. C. Klingemann & an American Collaborator, 2d rev. ed., 2 vols. New York: Harper & Bros., 1882.

HF — *High Fidelity.* vol. 1- , 1951- . Great Barrington, Mass.: ABC Leisure Magazines, 1951- .

Hiller/MENDELSSOHN 1 — Hiller, Ferdinand. *Felix Mendelssohn-Bartholdy, Briefe und Erinnerungen;* 2te Aufl. Köln: M. DuMont-Schauberg, 1878.

Hiller/MENDELSSOHN 2 — ———. *Mendelssohn, Letters and Recollections;* trans. M. E. von Glehn, 2nd ed. London: Macmillan, 1874.

Hiller/NACHRICHT — Hiller, Johann Adam. *Nachricht von der Aufführung des Händelschen Messias, in der Domkirche zu Berlin, den 19. May 1786*. Berlin: C. S. Speyer, 1786.

Hoffman/RECOLLECTIONS — Hoffman, Richard. *Some Musical Recollections of Fifty Years*. New York: C. Scribner's Sons, 1910.

Hoffmann/ESECUZIONE — Hoffmann, Hans. "La prattica dell'esecuzione musicale," *L'Orchestra*, pp. 69–111. Firenze: G. Barbera, 1954.

Howe/BOSTON — Howe, Mark Antony De Wolfe. *The Boston Symphony Orchestra, an Historical Sketch*. Boston: Houghton Mifflin, 1914.

Howe & Burk/BOSTON — ———. *The Boston Symphony Orchestra, 1881–1931*; semicentennial ed., rev. & extended in collaboration with J. N. Burk. Boston: Houghton Mifflin, 1931.

Howes/FULL — Howes, Frank. *Full Orchestra*. London: Secker & Warburg, 1942.

Hurd/ORCHESTRA — Hurd, Michael. *The Orchestra*. New York: Facts on File, 1980.

Huschke/BEETHOVEN — Huschke, Konrad. *Beethoven als Pianist und Dirigent*. Berlin: Schuster & Loeffler [1919]

Huschke/BRAHMS — ———. *Johannes Brahms als Pianist, Dirigent und Lehrer*. Karlsruhe: F. G. Verlag [1935]

Inghelbrecht/CHEF — Inghelbrecht, Desiré Émile. *Le chef d'orchestre et son équipe*. Paris: R. Julliard, 1949.

Inghelbrecht/CONDUCTOR'S — ———. *The Conductor's World*; trans. G. Prerauer & S. M. Kirk. New York: Library Publishers, 1954.

Israël/FRANKFURTER — Israël, Carl. *Frankfurter Concert-Chronik von 1713–1780*. Frankfurt am Main: Kumpf & Ries, 1876. (Neujahre-Blatt des Vereins für Geschichte und Alterthumskunde zu Frankfurt am Main für das Jahr 1876).

Jerger/WIENER — Jerger, Wilhelm. *Die Wiener Philharmoniker: Erbe und Sendung*. Wien: Wiener Verlagsgesellschaft, 1942.

Johnson/HALLELUJAH — Johnson, Harold Earle. *Hallelujah, Amen! The Story of the Handel and Haydn Society of Boston*. Boston: B. Humphries, 1965.

Junker/ALMANACH — Junker, Carl Ludwig. *Musikalischer Almanach auf das Jahr 1782*. Alethinopel, 1782.

Junker/KAPELLMEISTERS 1 — ———. *Einige der vornehmsten Pflichten eines Kapellmeisters oder Musikdirektors*. Winterthur: H. Steiner, 1782.

Junker/KAPELLMEISTERS 2 — ———. "Einige der vornehmsten Pflichten eines Capellmesiters oder Musikdirectors," *Magazin der Musik*; ed. C. F. Cramer, II (1784/7): pp. 741–77.

Kennedy/HALLE — Kennedy, Michael. *The Hallé Tradition: A Century of Music*. Manchester: Manchester University, 1960.

Kerst/BEETHOVEN

Kerst, Friedrich, ed. *Die Erinnerungen an Beethoven*; 2 vols. Stuttgart: J. Hoffmann, 1913.

Klausner/COMMUNITY

Klausner, Tiberius. "The Orchestra Musician and the Community," *The American Symphony Orchestra*; ed. H. Swoboda, pp. 90–98. New York: Basic Books, 1967.

Kleefeld/HAMBURGER

Kleefeld, Wilhelm. "Das Orchester der Hamburger Oper 1678–1738," *Sammelbände der Internationalen Musik-Gesellschaft* I (1899–1900): pp. 219–89.

Kling/VOLLKOMMENE

Kling, Henri. *Der Vollkommene Musik-Dirigent*; verf. & hrsg. H. Kling. Hannover: L. Gertel, 1890.

Krips & Frankenstein/ SAN FRANCISCO

Krips, Josef and Alfred V. Frankenstein. "The San Francisco Symphony Orchestra: A Western Outpost," *The American Symphony Orchestra*; ed. H. Swoboda, pp. 28–42. New York: Basic Books, 1967.

Kufferath/DIRIGER

Kufferath, Maurice. *L'Art de Diriger. Richard Wagner et La "Neuvième Symphonie" de Beethoven. Hans Richter et La Symphonie en "ut" mineur. L'Idylle de Siegfried—Interpretation et Tradition*; 3e éd. Paris: Fischbacher, 1909.

Kupferberg/ PHILADELPHIANS

Kupferberg, Herbert. *Those Fabulous Philadelphians: The Life and Times of a Great Orchestra*. New York: C. Scribner's Sons, 1969.

Landon/CHRONICLE

Landon, Howard Chandler Robbins. *Haydn: Chronicle and Works*; 5 vols. Bloomington: Indiana University, 1976–78.

Landon/SYMPHONIES

————. *The Symphonies of Joseph Haydn*. New York: Macmillan, 1956.

Lang & Bettmann/ PICTORIAL

Lang, Paul Henry and Otto Bettmann. *A Pictorial History of Music*. New York: Norton, 1960.

Lavignac/BAYREUTH 1

Lavignac, Albert. *Voyage artistique à Bayreuth*; 2e éd. Paris: C. Delagrave, 1898.

Lavignac/BAYREUTH 2

————. *The Music Dramas of Richard Wagner and His Festival Theatre in Bayreuth*; trans. E. Singleton. New York: Dodd Mead, 1902.

Leitzmann/BEETHOVEN

Leitzmann, Albert, ed. *Beethovens Persönlichkeit*; 2 vols. Leipzig: Insel, 1914–27.

Löbmann/TAKTIERENS

Löbmann, Hugo. *Zur Geschichte des Taktierens und Dirigierens*. Düsseldorf: L. Schwann, 1913.

MacGillivray/WOODWIND

MacGillivray, James A. "The Woodwind," *Musical Instruments through the Ages*; ed. A. Baines, pp. 237–76. Baltimore: Penguin Books, 1961.

Machlis/ENJOYMENT

Machlis, Joseph. *The Enjoyment of Music*; 3d ed./shorter. New York: Norton, 1970.

Madeira/PHILADELPHIA Madeira, Louis C., comp. *Annals of Music in Philadelphia and History of the Musical Fund Society from its Organization in 1820 to the Year 1858*; ed. P. H. Goepp. Philadelphia: J. B. Lippincott, 1896.

Mahler/BRIEFE Mahler, Gustav. *Briefe, 1879–1911*; hrsg. A. M. Mahler. Berlin: P. Zsolnay, 1924.

Mahler/SYMPHONY 1 ———. *Symphony No. 1*; min. score. New York: E. F. Kalmus, 19— (Kalmus Miniature Orchestra Scores).

Mahling/MOZART Mahling, Christoph-Hellmut. "Mozart und die Orchesterpraxis seiner Zeit," *Mozart-Jahrbuch*, 1967, pp. 229–43.

Marpurg/BEYTRÄGE Marpurg, Friedrich Wilhelm. *Historisch-Kritische Beytraǧe zur Aufnahme der Musik*; 5 vols. Berlin: J. J. Schützens sel. Wittwe, 1754–62.

Mee/OLDEST Mee, John H. *The Oldest Music Room in Europe: A Record of Eighteenth-Century Enterprise at Oxford*. London: J. Lane, 1911.

Mendel/PITCH Mendel, Arthur. "Pitch in Western Music since 1500: A Re-examination," *Acta Musicologica*, L (1978), pp. 1–93.

Mendelssohn/BRIEFE Mendelssohn Bartholdy, Felix. *Briefe aus den Jahren 1830 bis 1847*; hrsg. P. & C. Mendelssohn Bartholdy, 2 vols. Leipzig: H. Mendelssohn, 1875 & 1882.

Mendelssohn/ITALY ———. *Letters of Felix Mendelssohn-Bartholdy from Italy and Switzerland*; trans. G. Wallace. New York: Leypoldt & Holt, 1866.

Mendelssohn/LETTERS ———. *Letters of Felix Mendelssohn-Bartholdy, from 1833 to 1847*; ed. P. & C. Mendelssohn Bartholdy, with catalogue of compositions comp. J. Rietz, trans. G. Wallace. Philadelphia: F. Leypoldt, 1864.

Menke/TRUMPET Menke, Werner. *History of the Trumpet of Bach and Händel*; trans. G. Abraham. London: W. Reeves [1934].

Mennicke/HASSE Mennicke, Carl. *Hasse und die Brüder Graun als Symphoniker*. Leipzig: Breitkopf & Härtel, 1906.

MGG *Die Musik in Geschichte und Gegenwart; allgemeine Enzyklopädie der Musik*; ed. F. Blume, 15 vols., including suppl. Kassel: Bärenreiter, 1949–73.

Monk/BRASS Monk, Christopher W. "The Older Brass Instruments: Cornett, Trombone, Trumpet," *Musical Instruments Through the Ages*; ed. A. Baines, pp. 277–94. Baltimore: Penguin Books, 1961.

Moscheles/LEBEN *Aus Moscheles' Leben, nach Briefen und Tagebüchern*; hrsg. seiner Frau, 2 vols. Leipzig: Duncker & Humbolt, 1872–73.

Moscheles/RECENT — Moscheles, Ignaz. *Recent Music and Musicians as Described in the Diaries and Correspondence*; ed. his wife, trans. A. D. Coleridge. New York: Da Capo, 1970; 1st ed. 1873.

Mozart/BRIEFE — Mozart, Wolfgang Amadeus. *Briefe und Aufzeichnungen, Gesamtausgabe*; hrsg. W. A. Bauer & O. E. Deutsch, 7 vols. Kassel: Bärenreiter, 1962–75.

Mozart/LETTERS — ———. *The Letters of Mozart and His Family*; trans. & ed. E. Anderson, 2nd ed. A. H. King & M. Carolan, 2 vols. New York: St Martin's Press, 1966.

Mozart/TREATISE — Mozart, Leopold. *A Treatise on the Fundamental Principles of Violin Playing*; trans. E. Knocker, 2d ed. London: Oxford University, 1951.

Mozart/VIOLINSCHULE — ———. *Gründliche Violinschule*; 2te vermehrte Aufl. Augsburg: J. J. Lotter, 1770.

Mueller/AMERICAN — Mueller, John H. *The American Symphony Orchestra: a Social History of Musical Taste.* Bloomington: Indiana University, 1951.

MUSICAL MAGAZINE — *The Musical Magazine; or Repository of Musical Science, Literature, and Intelligence*; 2 vols. (1839–40). Boston: Otis, Broaders, 1839 (I), G. P. Reed, 1840 (II).

MUSIKDIREKTOR — "Was soll man von dem Musikdirektor eines Operntheaters verlangen?" *Allgemeine musikalische Zeitung* VI (1803/4), col. 165–74, 181–87.

Nettel/ENGLAND — Nettel, Reginald. *The Orchestra in England: A Social History.* London: J. Cape, 1956.

Neumann/WAGNER 1 — Neumann, Angelo. *Erinnerungen an Richard Wagner*; 3te Aufl. Leipzig: L. Staackmann, 1907.

Neumann/WAGNER 2 — ———. *Personal Recollections of Wagner*; trans. E. Livermore. New York: H. Holt, 1908.

Newman/WAGNER — Newman, Ernest. *The Life of Richard Wagner*; 4 vols. New York: A. A. Knopf, 1966–69; 1st ed. 1937–46.

Norlind/DIRIGERINGS — Norlind, Tobias. *Dirigerings Konstens Historia.* Stockholm: Nordtska Musikförlaget, 1944.

Nösselt/GEWANDHAUS — Nösselt, Hans-Joachim. *Das Gewandhausorchester: Entstehung und Entwicklung eines Orchesters.* Leipzig: Koehler & Amelang, 1943.

NZFM — *Neue Zeitschrift für Musik*; 84 vols. (1834–88). Leipzig: 1834–88.

Otis/CHICAGO — Otis, Philo Adams. *The Chicago Symphony Orchestra: Its Organization, Growth, and Development, 1891–1924.* Chicago: C. F. Summy, 1924.

Paris Conservatory/ARCHIVES — Paris Conservatory Archives. Boston University Libraries, Special Collections.

Parke/MEMOIRS — Parke, William Thomas. *Musical Memoirs, Comprising an Account of the General State of Music in England from the First Commemoration of Händel in 1784 to the Year 1830*; 2 vols. London: H. Colburn & Bentley, 1830.

Pegge/HORN   Pegge, R. Morley. "The Horn, and the Later Brass," *Musical Instruments Through the Ages*; ed. A. Baines, pp. 295-317. Baltimore: Penguin Books, 1961.

Phillips/RECOLLECTIONS   Phillips, Henry. *Musical and Personal Recollections during Half a Century*; 2 vols. London: C. J. Skeet, 1864.

Pierre/CONCERT   Pierre, Constant. *Histoire du Concert Spirituel 1725-1790*. Paris: Société Française de Musicologie, Heugel, 1975 (Publications de la Société Française de Musicologie, 3e Sërie, T. III).

Pohl/HAYDN   Pohl, Carl Ferdinand. *Joseph Haydn*; 3 vols.; III completed H. Botstiber. Berlin: A. Sacco, 1875 (I); Leipzig: Breitkopf & Härtel, 1882 & 1927 (II & III).

Pohl/LONDON   _____. *Mozart und Haydn in London*; 2 vols. Wien: Carl Gerold's Sohn, 1867.

Polko/MENDELSSOHN   Polko, Elise. *Reminiscences of Felix Mendelssohn-Bartholdy: A Social and Artistic Biography*; trans. G. Wallace. New York: Leypoldt & Holt, 1869.

Praeger/WAGNER   Praeger, Ferdinand. *Wagner as I Knew Him*. New York: Longmans, Green, 1892.

Prawy/VIENNA   Prawy, Marcel. *The Vienna Opera*. New York: Praeger, 1970.

Previn/ORCHESTRA   Previn, André, ed. *Orchestra*. Garden City, NY: Doubleday, 1979.

Quantz/FLÖTE 1   Quantz, Johann Joachim. *Versuch einer Anweisung die Flöte traversiere zu spielen*. Faksimile-Nachdruck der 3. Aufl., Breslau 1789, hrsg. H. P. Schmitz/ Kassel: Bärenreiter, 1953.

Quantz/FLÖTE 2   _____. *Versuch einer Anweisung die Flöte traversiere zu spielen*. Kritisch rev. Neudruck nach dem Original Berlin 1752, ed. A. Schering. Leipzig: C. F. Kahnt, 1906.

Quantz/FLUTE   _____. *On Playing the Flute*; trans. E. R. Reilly. London: Faber & Faber, 1966.

Rackwitz & Steffens/
HÄNDEL   Rackwitz, Werner and Helmut Steffens. *Georg Friedrich Händel; Persönlichkeit, Umwelt, Vermächtnis*. Leipzig: VED Deutscher Verlag für Musik, 1962.

Raynor/ORCHESTRA   Raynor, Henry. *The Orchestra, a History*. New York: C. Scribner's Sons, 1978.

Rees/HALLE   Rees, Clifford Burwyn. *One Hundred Years of the Hallé*. Norwich: Macgibbon & Kee, 1957.

Ricks/RUSSIAN   Ricks, Robert. "Russian Horn Bands," *Musical Quarterly* LV (1969): pp. 364-71.

Rochlitz/BRUCHSTÜCKE   Rochlitz, Friedrich. "Bruchstücke aus Briefen an einen jungen Tonsetzer," *Allgemeine musikalische Zeitung* II (1799/1800), cols. 1-5, 17-22, 57-63, 161-70, 177-83.

Rockstro/HANDEL — Rockstro, William Smith. *The Life of George Frederick Handel.* London: Macmillan, 1883.

Rosen/CLASSICAL — Rosen, Charles. *The Classical Style: Haydn, Mozart, Beethoven.* New York: Norton, 1972.

Rousseau/DICTIONNAIRE — Rousseau, Jean Jacques. *Dictionnaire de Musique.* Paris: la Veuve Duchesne, 1768.

Russell/THOMAS — Russell, Charles Edward. *The American Symphony Orchestra and Theodore Thomas.* Garden City: Doubleday, Page, 1927.

Ryan/RECOLLECTIONS — Ryan, Thomas. *Recollections of an Old Musician.* New York: E. P. Dutton, 1899.

Schindler/BEETHOVEN 1 — Schlinder, Anton Felix. *Biographie von Ludwig van Beethoven.* 2 vols. in 1. Münster: Aschendorff, 1871.

Schlinder/BEETHOVEN 2 — _____. *Beethoven as I knew Him, a Biography*; ed. D. W. MacArdle, trans. C. S. Jolly. New York: Norton, 1972; 1st ed. 1960.

Schlindler/PARIS — _____. *Beethoven in Paris. Nebst anderen den unsterblichen Tondichter betreffenden Mittheilungen und einem Facsimile von Beethoven's Handschrift. Ein Nachtrag zur Biographie Beethoven's.* Münster: Aschendorff, 1842.

Schmidt/REISE-MOMENTE — Schmidt, August. *Musikalische Reise-Momente auf einer Wanderung durch Norddeutschland.* Hamburg: Schuberth, 1846.

Scholes/MIRROR — Scholes, Percy Alfred. *The Mirror of Music, 1844-1944: A Century of Musical Life in Britain as reflected in the pages of the Musical Times*; 2 vols. Freeport, NY: Books for Libraries, 1970; 1st ed. 1947.

Scholes/OXFORD — _____. *The Oxford Companion to Music*; 8th ed. London: Oxford University, 1950.

Scholz/DIRIGIERLEHRE — Scholz, Horst Günther. *Dirigierlehre.* Leipzig: N. Simrock, 1943.

Schonberg/CONDUCTORS — Schonberg, Harold C. *The Great Conductors.* New York: Simon & Schuster, 1967.

Schreiber/ORCHESTER — Schreiber, Ottmar. *Orchester und Orchesterpraxis in Deutschland zwischen 1780 und 1850.* Berlin: Triltsch & Huther, 1938.

Schroeder/HANDBOOK — Schroeder, Carl. *Handbook of Conducting*; trans. and ed. M. Matthews. London: Augner [1889].

Schroeder/KATECHISMUS — _____. *Katechismus der Dirigierens und Taktierens.* Leipzig? M. Hesse, 1889.

Schubert/KONTRAVIOLONS — Schubert. "Vorschläge zur Verbesserung des Kontraviolons," *Allgemeine musikalische Zeitung* VI (1803/4), col. 187-91.

Schubert/MUSIKDIREKTOR — Schubert, Franz Ludwig. *Der praktische Musikdirektor oder Wegweiser für Musik-Dirigenten*; 2te Auffl. Leipzig: C. Merseburger, 1873; 1st ed. 1864.

Schünemann/DIRIGIERENS — Schünemann, Georg. *Geschichte des Dirigierens.* Hildesheim: G. Olms, 1965; 1st ed. 1913.

Seiffert/HÄNDELS — Seiffert, Max, "Die Verzierung der Sologesänge in Händel's 'Messias'." *Sammelbände der Internationalen Musikgesellschaft* VIII (1906/7): pp. 581-615.

SERAPHIM GUIDE — *The Seraphim Guide to the Instruments of the Orchestra.* Sir Adrian Boult & Members of the London Philharmonic Orchestra. Stereo disc. Seraphim S-60234.

Sittard/HAMBURG — Sittard, Josef. *Geschichte des Musik- und Concertwesens in Hamburg vom 14. Jahrhundert bis auf die Gegenwart.* Altona: A. C. Reher, 1890.

Smart/JOURNALS — Smart, Sir George. *Leaves from the Journals of Sir George Smart,* by H. Bertram Cox & C. L. E. Cox. London: Longmans, Green, 1907.

Somfai/HAYDN — Somfai, László. *Joseph Haydn: His Life in Contemporary Pictures.* New York: Taplinger, 1969.

Sonneck/BEETHOVEN — Sonneck, Oscar George. *Beethoven: Impressions by his Contemporaries.* New York: Dover, 1967; 1st ed. 1926.

Spitta/BACH — Spitta, Philipp. *Johann Sebastian Bach: His Work and Influence on the Music of Germany, 1685-1750*; trans. C. Bell & J. A. Fuller-Maitland, 3 vols. New York: Dover, 1951.

Spohr/JOURNEYS — Spohr, Louis. *The Musical Journeys of Louis Spohr*; trans. & ed. H. Pleasants. Norman: University of Oklahoma, 1961.

Spohr/LEBENSERINNERUNGEN — _____. *Lebenserinnerungen*; hrsg. F. Göthel, 2 vols. in 1. Tutzing: H. Schneider, 1968; 1st ed. 1840.

Stokowski/INNOVATIONS — Stokowski, Leopold. "Innovations: Acoustics and Seating," *The American Symphony Orchestra*; ed. H. Swoboda, pp. 115-25. New York: Basic Books, 1967.

Strauss/HELDENLEBEN — Strauss, Richard. *Ein Heldenleben (A Hero's Life)*; op. 40, score. New York: E. F. Kalmus, 19—.

Strauss & Schuh/BRIEFWECHSEL — _____. *Briefwechsel mit Willi Schuh.* Zürich: Atlantis, 1969.

Taubman/MAESTRO — Taubman, Howard. *The Maestro: The Life of Arturo Toscanini.* New York: Simon & Schuster, 1951.

Tchaikovsky/DIARIES — Tchaikovsky, Peter I. *The Diaries of Tchaikovsky*; trans. W. Lakond. New York: Norton, 1945.

Tchaikovsky/SYMPHONY 6 — _____. *Symphony No. 6, B minor*; min. score. Wien: Wiener Philharmonischer, 19—.

Terry/BACH — Terry, Charles Sanford. *Bach, a Biography*; 2nd ed. London: Oxford University Press, 1950.

Terry/ORCHESTRA — _____. *Bach's Orchestra.* London: Oxford University Press, 1932.

Thayer-Forbes/BEETHOVEN

Thayer's Life of Beethoven; rev. and ed. E. Forbes, 2 vols. Princeton, NJ: Princeton University Press, 1967; 1st ed. 1921.

Thienemann/DIRIGIERENS

Thienemann, Alfred. *Die Kunst des Dirigierens: Selbst-Unterrichts-Briefe*; 3te Aufl. Potsdam: Bonness & Hachfeld, 19—.

Thomas/AUTOBIOGRAPHY

Thomas, Theodore. *A Musical Autobiography*; ed. G. P. Upton, 2 vols. Chicago: A. C. McClurg, 1905.

Thomas/MEMOIRS

Thomas, Rose Fay. *Memoirs of Theodore Thomas.* New York: Moffat, Yard, 1911.

Thomas-Stein/
    AUTOBIOGRAPHY

Thomas, Theodore. *A Musical Autobiography*; ed. G. P. Upton; new intro. L. Stein. New York: Da Capo, 1964; 1st ed. 1905.

Thompson/CYCLOPEDIA

Thompson, Oscar, ed. *The International Cyclopedia of Music and Musicians*; 7th ed., rev., ed. N. Slonimsky. New York: Dodd, Mead, 1956.

Travenol & Durey/
    OPERA

Travenol, Louis and Jacques Bernard Durey de Noinville. *Histoire du théâtre de l'opéra en France: Depuis l'établissement de l'Académie Royale de Musique jusqu'au présent*; 2 vols. Paris: J. Barbou, 1753.

Unold/STELLUNG

Unold, Georg von. *"Einige Bemerkungen über die Stellung de Orchester und Einrichtung der Musiksäle,"* Allgemeine musikalische Zeitung IV (1801/2), col. 782–84.

Volbach/HÄNDEL

Volbach, Fritz. *Die Praxis der Händel-Aufführung.* Charlottenburg: "Gutenberg," 1899.

Volbach/ORCHESTER

———. *Das moderne Orchester in seiner Entwicklung.* Leipzig: B. G. Teubner, 1910.

Wagner/BAYREUTH

Wagner, Richard. *The Story of Bayreuth as Told in the Bayreuth Letters of Richard Wagner*; trans. and ed. C. V. Kerr. New York: Vienna House, 1972.

Wagner/BAYREUTHER

———. *Bayreuther Briefe (1871–1883).* Berlin: Schuster & Loeffler, 1907.

Wagner/BEETHOVEN'S 1

———. "Zum Vortrag der neunten Symphonie Beethoven's," *Gesammelte Schriften und Dichtungen*; 2d Aufl., IX, pp. 231-57. Leipzig: C. W. Fritzsch, 1888.

Wagner/BEETHOVEN'S 2

———. "The Rendering of Beethoven's Ninth Symphony," *Richard Wagner's Prose Works*; trans. W. A. Ellis, V, pp. 229-53. New York: Broude Bros., 1966; 1st ed. 1898.

Wagner/CHORAL

———. "Beethoven's Choral Symphony at Dresden, 1846," *Richard Wagner's Prose Works*; trans. W. A. Ellis, VII, pp. 239-55. New York: Broude Bros., 1966; 1st ed. 1898.

Wagner/CONDUCTING

———. *On Conducting (Ueber das Dirigieren): A Treatise on Style in the Execution of Classical Music*; trans. E. Dannreuther, 3d ed. London: W. Reeves, 1919.

Wagner/DIRIGIREN

Wagner/LEBEN

Wagner/LIFE

Wagner/MEISTERSINGER

Wagner/NATIONAL 1

Wagner/NATIONAL 2

Wagner/NEUNTEN

Wagner & Liszt/
  BRIEFWECHSEL

Wagner & Liszt/
  CORRESPONDENCE

Walter/GESCHICHTE

Walter/MAHLER

Walther/LEXIKON

Weber/BEMERKUNGEN

Weber/WEBER 1

Weber/WEBER 2

Weingartner/BEETHOVEN

————. "Uber das Dirigiren," *Gesammelten Schriften und Dichtungen*. VIII, pp. 325–410. Leipzig: C. W. Fritzsch, 1873; 1st ed. 1869.

————. *Mein Leben*; 1ste authentische Veröffentlichung. München: List, 1963; 1st ed. 1865–80.

————. *My Life*; authorized trans., 2 vols. New York: Dodd, Mead, 1911.

————. *Die Meistersinger von Nürnberg*; min. score, 2 vols. London: E. Eulenburg, 19—.

————. "Entwurf zur Organization eines deutschen National-Theaters für das Königreich Sachsen (1849)," *Gesammelte Schriften und Dichtungen*; 2e Aufl, II, pp. 233–73. Leipzig: C. W. Fritzsch, 1887.

————. "Plan of Organization of a German National Theatre for the Kingdom of Saxony," *Richard Wagner's Prose Works*; trans. W. A. Ellis, VII, pp. 319–60. New York: Broude Bros., 1966; 1st ed. 1898.

————. "Bericht über die Aufführung der neunten Symphonie von Beethoven im Jahre 1846 in Dresden," *Gesammelte Schriften und Dichtungen*; 2e Aufl, II, pp. 50–64. Leipzig: C. W. Fritzsch, 1887.

Briefwechsel zwischen Wagner und Liszt; hrsg. E. Kloss, 3e Aufl., 2 vols. in 1. Leipzig: Breitkopf & Härtel, 1910.

Correspondence of Wagner and Liszt; trans. F. Hueffer, new rev. ed. W. A. Ellis, 2 vols. New York: Greenwood, 1969; 1st ed. 1897.

Walter, Friedrich. *Geschichte des Theaters und der Musik am kurpfälzischen Hofe*. Hildesheim; G. Olms, 1968; 1st ed. 1898 (Forschungen zur Geschichte Mannheims und der Pfalz, hrsg. Mannheimer Altertumsverein, I).

Walter, Bruno. *Gustav Mahler*; trans. supervised L. Walter Lindt. New York: Schocken, 1974.

Walther, Johann Gottfried. *Musicalisches Lexicon oder musicalische Bibliothec*; Faksimile-Nachdruck, hrsg. R. Schaal. Kassel; Bärenreiter, 1953; 1st ed. 1732.

Weber, G. "Praktische Bemerkungen," *Allgemeine musikalische Zeitung* IX (1806/7), col. 805–11, 821–24.

Weber, Max Maria von. *Carl Maria von Weber, Ein Lebensbild*; 3 vols. Leipzig: E. Keil, 1864–66.

————. *Carl Maria von Weber, the Life of an Artist*; trans. J. P. Simpson, 2 vols. New York: Greenwood, 1969; 1st ed. 1865.

Weingartner, Felix. *On the Performance of Beethoven's Symphonies*; trans. J. Crosland. New York: E. F. Kalmus [1906].

Weingartner/RATSCHLÄGE

————. *Ratschläge für Aufführungen klassischer Symphonien; I: Beethoven*; 3e Auf. Leipzig: Breitkopf & Härtel, 1928; 1st ed. 1906.

Werner/MENDELSSOHN

Werner, Eric. *Mendelssohn: A New Image of the Composer and His Age*; trans. D. Newlin. London: Free Press of Glencoe, 1963.

Westrup & Zaslaw/
  ORCHESTRA

Westrup, Jack (with Neal Zaslaw). "Orchestra," *The New Grove Dictionary of Music and Musicians*; ed. S. Sadie, vol. 13, pp. 679–91. London: Macmillan, 1980.

Westrup, Zaslaw &
  Selfridge-Field/ORCHESTRA

Westrup, Jack (with Neal Zaslaw and Eleanor Selfridge-Field). "Orchestra," *The New Grove Dictionary of Musical Instruments,* ed. S. Sadie; 3 vols. London: Macmillan, 1984, vol. 2, p. 823–37.

Widor/ORCHESTRA

Widor, Charles Marie. *The Technique of the Modern Orchestra; A Manual of Practical Instrumentation*; trans. E. Suddard, rev. ed. London: J. Williams, 1946; 1st ed. 1906.

Widor/ORCHESTRE

————. *Technique de l'Orchestre Moderne, faisant suite au Traité d'Instrumentation et d'Orchestration de H. Berlioz*; 2e éd. Paris: H. Lemoine, 1904.

Williamson/ORCHESTRA

Williamson, H. S. *Introducing the Orchestra.* London: Faber & Faber, 1964.

Wood/CONDUCTING

Wood, Sir Henry. *About Conducting.* London: Sylvan Press, 1945.

Wooldridge/CONDUCTOR'S

Wooldridge, David. *Conductor's World.* New York: Praeger, 1970.

Zaslaw/REVIVAL

Zaslaw, Neal. "Toward the Revival of the Classical Orchestra," *Proceedings of the Royal Musical Association* CIII (1976/7): 158–87.

Zlotnik/SCHUMANN

Zlotnik, Asher George. *Orchestration Revisions in the Symphomies of Robert Schumann*; 2 vols., Ann Arbor: University Microfilms, 1972 (Ph.D. Dissertation, Indiana University).

Zopff/DIRIGENT

Zopff, Hermann. *Der angehende Dirigent.* Leipzig: C. Merseburger, 1881.

ZUGE

"Züge von dem Bilde eines Musikdirektors, wie er nicht seyn soll," *Allgemeine musikalische Zeitung* XVI (1814), col. 391–94.

Name Index

Subject Index